THE GODS
OF
NORTHERN BUDDHISM

THE GODS

OF

NORTHERN BUDDHISM:

THEIR HISTORY, ICONOGRAPHY AND PROGRESSIVE EVOLUTION THROUGH THE NORTHERN BUDDHIST COUNTRIES

ALICE GETTY,

TRANSLATOR

J. DENIKER

GYAN

Published by

Gyan Publishing House
5, Ansari Road
Daryaganj, New Delhi-110002
Phone: 011-47034999, 9811692060
E-mail: books@gyanbooks.com

Distribution Network
gyanbooks.com
India, USA, Canada, UK, Australia

ISBN: 978-93-6433-651-2 (HB)

First Published, 1914

2nd Impression 2024

Printed at: Gyan Press, Delhi.

THE GODS OF NORTHERN BUDDHISM
Author: ALICE GETTY
Translator: J. DENIKER

THE GODS

OF

NORTHERN BUDDHISM

THE GODS
OF
NORTHERN BUDDHISM

THEIR HISTORY, ICONOGRAPHY AND PROGRESSIVE EVOLUTION THROUGH THE NORTHERN BUDDHIST COUNTRIES

BY

ALICE GETTY

WITH A GENERAL INTRODUCTION ON BUDDHISM

TRANSLATED FROM THE FRENCH OF

J. DENIKER

DOCTEUR ÈS SCIENCES

ILLUSTRATIONS FROM THE COLLECTION OF

HENRY H. GETTY

OXFORD

AT THE CLARENDON PRESS

1914

AUTHOR'S PREFACE

It is difficult for those who are unacquainted with the iconography of the gods of the Mahāyāna Pantheon to realize the degree of interest that may be attached to even a crude representation of a Northern Buddhist divinity.

To the uninitiated the images of these deities are only of value as works of art, or as grotesque curios, with their various heads and many arms ; but to the initiated, apart from their artistic merit, they furnish an almost inexhaustible fund for study and research.

The most accurate source of information in regard to the Northern Buddhist divinities has been found in the *sādhana*, or texts of invocations of the gods, in which they are described with much detail. Unfortunately, *sādhana* of all the gods of the Mahāyāna Pantheon have not as yet been discovered, and there remain a number of deities about whom very little is known. At any moment, however, a flood of light may be thrown on these obscure divinities, for, among others, Mr. Ekai Kawaguchi (a Japanese Buddhist priest who spent three years in Tibet disguised as a Chinese monk) is translating some valuable manuscripts which he succeeded in carrying out of Tibet.

The study of the iconography of the Northern Buddhist deities is therefore in its infancy. With the exception of a few erudite books, little has been written on the subject, and it is only by persistent research, and by a comparative study of the examples in the museums of Europe, India, and Japan, as well as in the temples of the Northern Buddhist countries, that one can arrive at a comprehensive knowledge of these gods and of their evolution during the process of transmission from India via Chinese Turkestan (and later, through Tibet) to China, Mongolia, and Japan.

The Tibetan and Mongolian lamas, from whom one would expect to get much valuable information, are, unfortunately, with few exceptions, more versed in the tenets of their religion than in the iconography of their gods: and as Tibet is still 'a forbidden land', intercourse with the Tibetan lamas in their own country is practically impossible. Among the Japanese Buddhist priests, however, there are some very learned men.

Through the kindness of the late Professor Arthur Lloyd, whose death has recently deprived Japan of one of its greatest authorities on Japanese Buddhism, I was put into communication with Mr. S. Tachibana, Buddhist priest and Sanskrit scholar, who has kindly made many researches for me. I have also to thank Śramaṇa Kawaguchi of Benares, Śramaṇa Jeshu Oda, Rector of the Chomoji Monastery at Nagoya, and Mr. Hanazono of Tokyo, for their help in making certain researches possible.

I owe special thanks to M. A. Foucher for his kindness in reading through my manuscript and, as I am not a Sanskrit scholar, in revising the marking of the letters in the Sanskrit words used in the text. I am also much indebted to him, as well as to Sir Aurel Stein, explorer in Central Asia, to Herr von Le Coq, explorer in Chinese Turkestan and attached to the Museum für Völkerkunde, Berlin, as well as to Mr. E. Denison Ross, officer in charge of the Records of the Government of India, and philological secretary of the Asiatic Society of Bengal, for their kindness in giving me opportunities of studying Buddhist temple paintings, frescoes, and miniatures which are not accessible to the general public.

My initiation into the intricacies of the Mahāyāna system I owe to M. J. Deniker, whose general study on the vast and complicated doctrine of Buddhism in its various ramifications will form a sufficient introduction to the subject for the general reader, and will enable him to approach with a fair measure of equipment the detailed discussion of the individual deities, their symbols and characteristics, found in the following pages.

I place my book under the protection of the goddess Sarasvatī. May she inspire her consort Mañjuśrī to draw his sword of Wisdom and 'cleave the clouds of Ignorance' so that in time the West may come to a clearer understanding of the East.

A. GETTY.

PARIS, *March* 1913.

CONTENTS

LIST OF ILLUSTRATIONS

Design on the cover: Buddhist wheel with the six syllables of the mantra of Avalokiteśvara *Ōm, maṇi, padme hūṃ.* In the centre is his vīja-mantra *Hri!* E. Schlagintweit, *Buddhism in Tibet*, Atlas, Plate XIV.

NOTE

The Tibetan names are written according to the method used in the Dictionary of Sarat Chandra Das with small modifications, and translated by J. Deniker.

For the Mongolian names, the Ramstedt method has been followed with the exception of the Greek *gamma,* which has been replaced by the letters *gh.* The translations are by J. Deniker.

The Chinese characters are by Kia Kien Tchou and the English transcriptions have been made by Professor Bullock.

The Japanese names are transcribed by S. Tachibana.

ADDENDA AND ERRATA

Pages 3 and 27, note 5. Although Amida, in Japan, is one of the five Dhyāni-Buddhas (Gochi Nyorai) the Amida sects do not worship the other four Dhyāni Buddhas.

Page 6. The apparent confusion in Japan in regard to the representations of Kongōsatta and Fugen may be explained by the fact that in the Secret Doctrine they are identified.

Page 23. Manla may hold in his left hand in dhyāna mudrā a bowl resembling a begging-bowl, in which case the medicinal fruit is usually held in the right hand in vara mudrā. In Japan, Yaku-shi also holds the medicine-bowl in the left hand which, however, is in vara mudrā while the right is lifted in abhaya mudrā. If the medicine-bowl is missing, Yaku-shi resembles the representations of Shaka.

Page 27. The Dhyāni Bodhisattva of Vajrasattva is Ghaṇṭāpāṇi.

Page 31. The dhyāna mudrā of Vairocana when in the centre of the Garbhadhātu maṇḍala differs from the usual mystic gesture in that the tips of the thumbs touch each other.

Page 33. *Myō-ken* and not Mio·ken.

Page 39. O-mi-to fō in China has also the usual dhyāna mudrā of the Indian representation.

Amaterasu is sun-*goddess*.

Page 40. Amida, when standing (he may also be seated) has the right hand in abhaya and the left in vara mudrā, and thus resembles Shaka with this difference that the tip of the thumb touches the tip of the index in both hands, forming the 'dogmatic' gesture. The three poses of the hands of Amida: dhyāna, dharmacakra, abhaya and vara, may have three variations, the tips of the thumbs touching the indexes, second or third fingers. The second finger is the most popular in Korea. The third is very rare.

Pages 46 and 99. The Buddha in the triad with Fugen and Monju, in Japan, is always *Shaka*, although he may resemble Amida when, in the abhaya and vara mudrās, the fingers are somewhat bent. If the second finger is slightly bent, it indicates the Shingon sect.

Page 150. The writer, in accordance with Satow and other authorities, has placed Kōmoku guardian of the South. In the *Himitsu-jirin* he is made guardian of the West, in which case, if correct, Zōchō would be guardian of the South.

Getty, Northern Buddhism. *Face p.* xvi.
July, 1914.

INTRODUCTION

GENERAL SURVEY OF BUDDHISM AND ITS EVOLUTION

'*Namo Buddhāya, namo Dharmāya, namo Saṅghāya*': 'I worship Buddha, I worship the Doctrine, I worship the Community'—such is the formula which represents the quintessence of the Buddhist religion. It is uttered and repeated several times a day by numberless Buddhist monks and priests as well as by those of the laity who are at all instructed in their faith. The others content themselves with murmuring ceaselessly the magic formula: '*Ōṃ, maṇi padme, hūṃ*' ('Oh, the jewel in the lotus!').

Now, to give a general idea of the great religion whose followers form a third part of the human species, it is sufficient to develop this formula of the three jewels (*Triratna*). First we shall examine the life of the sole and unique historical Buddha (enlightened one), Śākya-muni, founder of the faith; then we shall summarize briefly the doctrine preached by him, following its evolution across space and time, in order that we may see and understand the forms under which it has existed in the various countries to which it has penetrated; lastly we shall give a description of the constitution of the Buddhist clergy (especially the Lamaite), and sketch what may be called the material side of the religion.

I. Buddha

It is towards the end of the sixth century B.C.[1] that the majority of historians place the birth of Siddhārtha, future founder of Buddhism, the son of Prince Śuddhodana and of his wife Māyā. Prince Śuddhodana was one of the chiefs of the tribe of the Śākya in the kingdom of Magadha and belonged to the clan (*Gotra*) of Gautama. For this reason the name of Gautama Buddha is often, especially among the Southern Buddhists, applied to Siddhārtha, in the same way as among the Northern he is generally called Śākya-muni ('muni' having the significance simply of 'wise' or 'saint' in Sanskrit).

The Buddhist books give as the birth-place of Śākya-muni the garden of Lumbinī near Kapilavastu, the capital of the little principality of which Śuddhodana was chief. It is situated in the north of India at the foot of the Himalaya, near the present frontier of Nepal. In the literature of Buddhism there is no complete biography of Śākya-muni, and one is obliged to reconstruct it from fragments contained in various documents,[2] which have only a single common characteristic—

[1] For details see p. 15.

[2] The 'Jātaka' or 'Adventures of Buddha in previous Incarnations', with their introduction and commentaries in the Pāli language (a dialect intermediary between Sanskrit and Prakrit, the sacred language of the Southern Buddhists), carry

the surrounding of the actual facts by a haze of legends. The life of Śākya is divided by the Buddhist theologians into twelve 'acts',[1] which can be summarized according to Northern Buddhists as follows: (1) The Bodhisattva; Śākya-muni descends from the higher heaven (*Tushita*) to earth in the form of a young white elephant.

(2) He enters into the body of his mother, Māyā, by the right side without causing her any pain.

(3) Ten months later he reappears from his mother's body, but with human aspect. His birth, signalized by various prodigies, is honoured by Brahma, Indra, and the other Brahman divinities.

(4) Despite the supernatural powers shown by this child who, at the time of his birth, took seven paces in the four directions corresponding to the four miseries of life (see later), he receives the education reserved for the sons of princes. Losing his mother seven days after his birth, Prince Siddhārtha is brought up first of all by his aunt, Mahāprajāpatī, then taken to school. There, however, he astonishes all his masters by reciting to them everything they desire to teach him and much else besides. In like fashion he proves himself pre-eminent at sports. Nevertheless melancholy pervades his being, and he surrenders himself more and more to meditation.

(5) To dispel his sadness his parents conceive the idea of giving him a wife, and he marries a princess of the Koliya clan, to whom the Buddhist texts ascribe the name of Yaśodā or of Gopā. By her he becomes father of a son Rāhula. But not the joys of wedded life, nor the pleasures of the harem, nor his love for his son can overcome in the young prince preoccupations of a philosophical and moral kind. The evolution of his thought is well represented in the legend by the symbol of 'the four meetings'. Harassed by the question of the purpose of life, Siddhārtha leaves the city in his chariot and falls in with an old man whose decrepit air strikes him. 'We live then to grow old and decrepit!' he cries. In the course of similar wanderings he comes upon a sick man and a funeral procession. 'So this is life,' he meditates, 'suffering—then final annihilation!' Fortunately the fourth meeting dissipates his pessimism. Seeing a hermit perfectly calm in his retreat, perfectly happy in his contemplation, the prince divines that the true way of salvation lies in the renunciation of the joys of life, causes of three great evils, old age, sickness, and death,[2] and in the surrender of oneself to contemplation which frees one from the ties of earth.

(6) At the age of twenty-nine or thirty, having failed to obtain from his father leave to adopt the ascetic life, Siddhārtha secretly leaves the palace, and abandons

us only to the moment when Śākya-muni, after attaining perfect knowledge (*Bodhi*), begins his preaching. The Lalita Vistara (in Tibetan Rgya-cer-rol-pa) and the Mahāvastu of the Northern Buddhists supply us with only very few new elements. Some fragments touching on the end of the life of 'Bhagavat' (the Blessed One) are to be found in the Vināya (the most ancient portion of the Pāli canon), &c.

[1] Cf. Foucher—*Une liste indienne des Actes du Buddha*. Paris, 1908 (*École prat. des hautes études*).

[2] In certain Buddhist writings birth is added, thus making the evils of life four.

wife, children, kinsfolk, concubines, and all his possessions. The legend tells the story of his journey at some length. He sets out on his horse, Kanthaka, under whose shod hooves the gods place their hands lest the noise should waken the guard. At a certain distance from his native town he discards his princely attire for rough garments of orange colour, cuts his hair, and so forth. From this moment Prince Siddhārtha deserves the sacred name of Śākya-muni or Gautama. He goes forward on foot 'to seek salvation'; but where is salvation to be sought? At this period India did not lack various sects and schools, metaphysical, religious, and mystical. Among the most widely spread was the school of Sānkhya, which taught the doctrine of deliverance from the cycle of renewed births recognized by all the creeds of India. Not less known was the school of Yoga, which was derived from the above, and principally developed the ascetic side of its doctrine. To one of the initiated of this latter school, the monk Alāra (or Arāda)-Kālāma, Śākya-muni applies on reaching the town of Vaiśalī. Dissatisfied, however, with the monk's teaching, he continues his journey and comes to Rājagṛiha, the capital of the kingdom of Magadha, where, after refusing the offer made by King Bimbisāra of a share of the throne, he retires to the mountains and follows the teaching of a celebrated Yogist, the ascetic Udraka Rāmaputra. In its desire to emphasize the originality of the doctrine of Buddha, the legend describes him as equally little satisfied with the instructions of this philosopher, but we are forced to believe that as a matter of fact the young ascetic benefited by the teaching of several masters, for we find in Buddhism more than one fundamental feature of the doctrines of Sānkhya, of Yoga, and of other contemporary schools (see later).

(7) The legend shows us Śākya-muni, wearied at last of all these false teachers, seeking in the mortification of the body the solution of the problems which vex him. Leaving the country of Magadha, he retires with five disciples whom he has succeeded in gathering about him, to a desert place in the small district of Urubilvā near Gayā. There for six years he gives himself over to the most painful mortifications; he attains to the consumption of a single grain of rice in the day, and ends by reducing himself almost to the condition of a skeleton.

However, finding in asceticism no help towards the solution of the problems of metaphysics and moral philosophy, he changes his system and returns to ordinary life, a course which wins for him the contempt of his five pupils, who stigmatize him as glutton and voluptuary because he accepts a little milk and honey offered by two young village women, the sisters (according to certain versions) Nandā and Nandabalā.

(8) Unmoved by these reproaches, Śākya-muni goes forth to the town to-day called Bodh'-Gayā. There he seats himself at the foot of a tree and declares that, though his body may wither away in this position of meditation, he will not leave it until he has attained the 'Bodhi' or perfect knowledge.[1] And one night the miracle happens; Śākya-muni has attained the Bodhi; an inward illumination lays

[1] There is still shown at the present time in Bodh'-Gayā a fig-tree bearing the name of 'The Tree of Bodhi', under the shadow of which legend declares the founder of Buddhism to have sat.

all things open to his understanding. Successively he gains (1) the knowledge of previous existences; (2) the destruction of evil desires; (3) knowledge of the nexus (*incatenation*) of the twelve interrelated causes; and finally (4) complete knowledge in its three divisions (see later). In a word from his former state of being Bodhisattva he becomes Buddha.

(9) But at what price of superhuman effort has he won this supreme knowledge! To all the causes of difficulty inherent in his task has been added the malevolence of Māra, the Genius of Evil and his personal enemy. Alike during the ascetic life of Śākya at Urubilvā and during his sojourn under the Bodhi tree this maleficent being spares no effort, according to the legend, to prevent Śākya from becoming Buddha. At first he tries to turn him from the way of holiness by threats and by loosing against him all the elements of nature and the fury of the armies of evil spirits. Then he seeks to reach him by the attractions of three virgins and numberless beautiful women. But Śākya comes victorious from these trials. It will be recognized that these narratives are a parable, easily comprehensible by the multitude, of the inward strife waged in the soul of Śākya between natural attachment to the outer world and pleasures of life and the total renunciation of the ascetic. In the same way the refusal of Buddha when Māra offers to make him at once into the heavenly Buddha without his passing through the stage of Mānushi-Buddha (see p. 9), implies the desire of Śākya to propagate his teaching, to make known to men the true path of salvation, and thus to deliver them from the fated circle of renewed births.

(10) The possession of the Bodhi once attained, Śākya remains yet seven (or seven times seven) days at the foot of the tree in order fully to enjoy his beatitude. Afterwards he goes forth under other trees and walks by the side of rivers and streams where the nāgas (serpents) shield him from the rays of the sun with their heads miraculously multiplied and enlarged. This legend, which is of purely Hindu origin (Vishnu was shielded by serpents in exactly the same way), clearly reflects the period of early hesitations and experiments which preceded the actual propagation of the teaching. According to the texts of the Southern Buddhists, this propagation opened with the conversion of two merchants, Trapusa and Bhallika, who are considered by the theologians of Buddhism not as the first disciples, but as lay adherents to the faith (*Upāsaka* in Sanskrit). Just at first the preaching of the new gospel does not seem to have had much success. The environment, it would appear, was not very favourable, for Buddha decided to set out for Benares. On the road towards that city he met an aged 'monk', Upaka, to whom, for the first time, he declared his quality of *Arhat* (the Saint or 'Worthy') and of *Jina* (the victorious).

(11) The real propagation of the faith and the foundation of a school and of a community (*saṅgha*), after the fashion of the other 'churches' of contemporary India, only began with the arrival at Benares, where Buddha found once more his five original disciples. At first they receive him with contempt, but are quickly converted by the preaching known as *dharmacakrapravartana*, i.e. the preaching 'of the foundation of

the reign of the Law', or literally, 'the turning (or setting in motion) of the wheel of the Law'. For the first time in this discourse Buddha sets forth the foundation of his teaching on 'the four truths' (see later). Conversions become numerous after this success; there is the rich young man Yaśas, with his kinsfolk and dependants; then at Urubilvā we find the thousand Brahmans whose leaders, the brothers Kāśyapa, become the first apostles of the new faith; and many more besides. Lastly, Bimbisāra, king of Magadha, with the majority of his people, adopts the Buddhist doctrine, and presents to Buddha the 'Park of bamboos' (Veluvana) near Rājagriha, which becomes the head-quarters of the community. There are converted Śāriputra and Maudgalyāyana, the two chief followers of Buddha.

(12) The Buddhist documents are sparing of detail about the forty-five later years of Buddha's life, consecrated to the propagation of his teaching and to the organization of the monastic communities. They give, however, the description of his division of his day; narratives of the attacks directed against him by his cousin, the renegade Devadatta, who was eventually converted, and by the six jealous enemies designated collectively as Tīrthika; the story of his journey to the city of his birth, Kapilavastū, where he converts his father, and where all the inhabitants become monastics; the foundation of a community of nuns in this city by Gautami, aunt of Śākya; the conversion of Rāhula, the son of Buddha; the donation by the courtesan Āmrapālī; finally, the wars which brought ruin to the fatherland of Śākya. On the other hand, there are in the Buddhist works abundant details about the death of Śākya-muni. When over eighty years of age, Buddha sets out for the town of Kuśinagara, capital of the Malla tribe. Thence he goes to the village of Pāvā, where he eats a meal offered him by the blacksmith Cunda. Unable to digest the unhealthy food, Buddha falls ill, and, feeling death at hand, he lays him down on his right side, his head turned towards the north, and gives to his faithful disciple and lieutenant, Ānanda, his last instructions for the organization of the community. Warned by Ānanda, the people of the Malla tribe (and even the beasts, avers the legend) assemble around the dying master, who speaks a last word on the vanity of all things that are, and on the necessity of seeking salvation in meditation and the renunciation of worldly pleasures. After seven days of prayer, music, and ceremonies, in which all the living creatures share, the body of Buddha is burnt, and the ashes, distributed among several kings and peoples, are preserved in eight funerary monuments (see *Stūpa* in the Glossary).[1] One of these groups of relics has recently been discovered (in 1908) in its reliquary of silver, which was the work of a Greek artist, and bears inscriptions. The precious casket was buried under a *Stūpa*, raised by King Kanishka, near the city of Peshawar. The date of Buddha's death was probably 477 B.C.

[1] Certain Buddhist texts divide this last 'act' into two—the death and the distribution of the relics, while they make into a single 'act' those events here given under numbers 9 and 10. Our present division is the more orthodox for Northern Buddhists. It figures, for instance, in the catechism taught to Mongol children. Properly to emphasize all the details of the life of Buddha a division into sixty-four paragraphs should be made of the story, as was done by Foucher in the memoir cited above (p. xviii, n.).

II. The Teaching; its Propagation and Modifications

(*a*) ***Primitive Teaching.*** Śākya-muni left behind him no writings; his instruction was entirely oral. It is, accordingly, impossible to form an idea of his doctrine except from the most ancient sacred books which constitute the primitive 'canons'. The religion founded by Śākya-muni did not form a wholly new element in the Hindu world. Like all the creeds of India, it was based upon two fundamental 'verities': *transmigration*, or 'renewed birth' (*Sansāra* in Sanskrit), and *the remuneration*, or 'the consequences' or 'the fruits of the deeds' (*Karman*). According to the Brahmanists and the various sects which existed in India at the time of the appearance of Buddhism, all living beings die only to be reborn in the form of other beings, superior or inferior[1] according to the deeds committed in their previous lives. Man, therefore, may be reborn as god or as beast, as he has proved good or evil in his human existence. Primitive Buddhism accepted this conception without criticism as an axiom, and, indeed, no sect—Brahmanist, Buddhist, Sānkhya, or Jain—has ever sought to dispute or to deny what may be termed a national article of Hindu faith. But the discrepancy between Śākya-muni and the Brahmanists and other sectaries lies in the pre-eminently *moral* nature of his doctrine, a doctrine rather psychological than theological. While the Brahmanists teach that there exists a God creator of all things (*Īśvara*) and that the circle of transmigrations of the soul through material coverings must be terminated, by the virtue of offerings, sacrifices, and adoration of the gods, in the absorption of individual souls into the universal, primitive Buddhism, on the contrary, is an atheistic religion, or rather philosophy, recognizing neither creator nor organizer of the universe, neither personal soul nor universal, and admitting worship of deities as something secondary. The entire weight of its metaphysical edifice rests on a single basis—the idea of deliverance. But deliverance from what evil? From the interminable and fate-ordained circle of renewed births, which, with all its accompanying evils, seemed a thing of terror. But why and how must a man free himself from this circle of destiny in order that he may attain the condition of Buddha and may exist in another world, opposed to the Sansāra and named *Nirvāṇa*? The reply to this last question is the essential stuff of the whole Buddhist religion. Śākya-muni formulated it excellently in his renowned discourse at Benares (see p. 20) when he announced the four holy 'truths' (*Catvāri āryasatyāni*), namely: (1) the existence of pain (*Duha*); (2) the definition of the cause of pain (*Samudaya*); (3) the suppression of this cause (*Nirodha*); (4) the path which leads to this suppression, the so-called noble eightfold path (*ārya ashṭāngika mārga*).

It amounts to this, that all things existent are but passing; all that is born is condemned to death; all that is created is condemned to dissolution. In a word

[1] To-day Northern Buddhism confesses the existence of six classes of living beings: two living upon earth, men and beasts; two living beneath the earth, the *Preta* (in Sanskrit) or *Birit* (in Mongol), condemned to an eternal hunger and thirst by reason of their narrow throats, which shoot forth fire when they desire to drink, and the inhabitants of hell, divided into twenty-two classes according to their torments; lastly two living in heaven, the Asura—who struggle continually against the gods—and, highest of all, the various divinities themselves.

every pleasure is only the prelude to grief and pain; life brings on old age, the activity of our organs brings on disease, love brings on separation from the beloved, &c. (Truth 1). This pessimistic conception, born in the brain of Śākya-muni more than 2,000 years before Schopenhauer, caused him to reflect on the cause of suffering (Truth 2). This cause is the 'thirst for life', that impulse towards activity which we Western people, on the contrary, exalt. While man is under the domination of this 'joie de vivre', of this 'will to live', he is not liberated from the ties of rebirth (Truth 3). To be delivered from the sorrows of *Sansāra* man must therefore be delivered from the 'thirst for life' (Truth 4). To explain better these 'verities' as well as the meaning of life the first Buddhist theologians invented a 'causal nexus', or connexion of causes (*pratītyasamutpāda*), comprising twelve causes (*Nidāna*, literally, 'preliminary condition') which are formulated as follows:

(1) Ignorance (*avidyā*) produces the syntheses or concealed impressions or tendencies (*sanskāra*).

(2) The syntheses produce cognition or the substance of thought (*vijñāna*).

(3) Cognition produces name and form (*nāmarūpa*).

(4) Name and form produce 'the sixfold sphere' or six organs of senses (*shaḍāyatana*).

(5) 'The sixfold sphere' produces contact (*sparśa*).

(6) Contact produces feeling (*vedanā*).

(7) Feeling produces craving or 'thirst' (*tṛishṇā*).

(8) Craving produces grasping at, or attachment to existence (*upādāna*).

(9) Grasping produces renewed existence or origination (*bhava*).[1]

(10) Renewed existence produces birth (*jāti*).

(11) Birth (*jāti*) produces

(12) Old age and death, grief, lamentation, distress, &c., i. e. the real or actual life (*maraṇa*).[2]

This series of almost incomprehensible phrases forms the obscurest point in the Buddhist dogma, and one which the savants of the West have attempted to explain in various ways. However, the obscurity can be elucidated, if the formula be taken in reverse order, as Śākya-muni himself was accustomed to take it.[3] Read in this way, the twelve 'causes' constitute in sum a development of the third Truth. To be delivered from old age, death, and what follows, man must be delivered from birth; to be delivered from birth he must be delivered from rebirth (renewed existence), and so on in succession through all the Buddhist metaphysic which explains 'the quality of life', up to the very last phrase, which declares that to be delivered from the syntheses man must be delivered from ignorance. But what is the nature of this ignorance? The commentaries upon the Buddhist works inform us that it consists in lack of

[1] It is only a question here of existence in one of the worlds of desire (*kāmabhava*) or of *Sansāra*. Existences in one of the worlds of form (*rūpabhava*) or in one of the transcendent worlds (*arūpabhava*) is not considered by the causal nexus.

[2] Cf. Mrs. G. A. F. Rhys Davids, *A Buddhist Manual*, London, p. 348.

[3] This appears the more natural course from the psychological standpoint also.

knowledge of the Buddhist religion. Here then we grasp the first point—for deliverance acceptance of Buddhism is a necessity. In like fashion one may go on to explain the other 'causes'. The second 'cause', *Sanskāra,* is a psychological conception; it signifies a sort of impress left by our actions upon our conscience, and capable, under certain circumstances and after a certain time, of manifesting itself in the form of new actions. This interpretation, as also that of the third 'cause', the primitive Buddhists were obliged to borrow from the school of Sānkhya, which teaches that the 'concealed impressions' act upon a mental substance (*Buddhi*), which is the basal matter of a fine covering or ethereal body, forming the centre of the soul-life and called *lingaśarīra.*[1] These concealed impressions may be envisaged as the actions of a man, which, coming slowly to maturity, have the property of manifesting themselves in the course of his reincarnations. Thus with the Buddhists this *Sanskāra* takes the place of 'the soul' of the Brahmanists.[2] By 'causes' four and five it is signified that the individuality (name and form) manifests itself by the aid of the six organs of sense (the sixfold sphere), and that these put it in connexion with the exterior world (contact). Hence arise feeling, thirst, and the like, which lead to all the evils. But let us return to the third Truth. Summed up briefly, it is but a presentment of *Nirvāṇa,* that is to say, of a kind of existence not subject to rebirths. But what is its nature? The Buddhist works do not anywhere explain this clearly. All that one can extract from them is that it is a condition of perfect blessedness, a state of sanctity or bliss. For our European logic it is existence outside all sensation, all desire, all will, all function—an existence, in fact, without life, which our mentality refuses to grasp. The fourth Truth speaks of the way of salvation, of the path which leads to deliverance and ends in *Nirvāṇa.* This way is made up of eight parts as follows: right belief or views, right resolve or aims, right words, right behaviour, right occupation or mode of livelihood, right effort or exertion, right contemplation or mindfulness, and right concentration or meditation and tranquillity.[3] For the conduct of such a life it is clearly necessary to renounce the ordinary life for that of a monk, if not of an ascetic. The laity labours, so to speak, under a disability for 'deliverance'. Accordingly, more than one opponent of Śākya-muni has objected that if every one followed his precepts there would be no more men upon the earth; the result would be that 'gradual suicide' spoken of by the German poet Heine as implied in Christian asceticism. The theologians of Buddhism, however, came to a workable arrangement by formulating, parallel with this 'way of salvation', ten 'commandments', of which the first five are obligatory upon the laity for the attainment

[1] This *lingaśarīra* is often spoken of in the writings of modern European theosophists.

[2] The term *vijñāna* used by the Buddhists corresponds sometimes to the *lingaśarīra,* sometimes to the *Buddhi* of the school of Sāṅkhya. Elsewhere it signifies 'reason', intelligence, ideas, and forms one of the six elements of the universe (the other five being earth, water, fire, air, and ether), as well as one of the five aggregates (*Skandha*) which, combined, constitute every living man or animal, the four others being body, sensations, perceptions, and consciousness.

[3] This translation of the original Pāli terms is from Mr. Warren's *Buddhism in Translation.* Cambridge, Mass., 1900, 2nd edition. According to the Sanskrit-Tibetan texts one should read: 'the "perfection": of faith, judgement, speech, action, life, application, reflection or meditation, and extasy or contemplation.'

of salvation, while the whole must be strictly observed by monastics. These 'commandments' are:

(1) Not to take life.

(2) Not to steal.

(3) To refrain from unlawful sexual intercourse (for the monks, from *all* sexual intercourse).

(4) Not to tell lies.

(5) Not to drink intoxicating liquors.

(6) Only to take food at certain specified times.

(7) Not to take part in dancing, music, performances, and similar pleasures.

(8) Not to adorn the body with flowers, nor to use perfumes and unguents.

(9) Not to sleep on any high or wide bed.

(10) Not to possess gold or silver.[1]

It must be borne in mind that the Buddhist understands each of these prohibitions in a very wide sense. Thus, for instance, according to the first commandment, it is forbidden to kill and in general to harm not merely men, but any living creature of whatever kind, even parasitic insects, for the injured creature may haply be the rebirth of a kinsman. According to the second 'commandment' man must respect the property of his neighbour to the point of appropriating no single article without the consent of its owner, even though it have no value of any kind.

(*b*) *Subsequent Development of Primitive Buddhism.* At the moment of his death Śākya-muni, who had organized the little religious community under his own direction, did not appoint a successor. One of his oldest disciples, Kāśyapa, proposed to summon an assembly of five hundred *Arhats* (sages), whose business it should be to work out a 'canon' and to edit a rule for the common life of the monastics. This first council, held at Rājagṛiha, edited, according to tradition, the first two books of the canon, *Vinaya*, i.e. the statutes and rules of the community (its discipline), and the *Sūtras*, or collection of Śākya-muni's Exposition of the Doctrine. It is probable, however, that nothing at all was written at this council, but that its proceedings, as in the case of other half-civilized races, consisted of chanting and reciting by heart the words of the wisest among the wise men. It is, moreover, certain that the works cited above were written at a later period. Much later still the *Abhidharma*, a metaphysical treatise based on the *Sūtras*, was added, and thus was formed the entirety of the Buddhist sacred code which is in full force to-day and is known as the *Tripiṭaka* ('the three Baskets', i. e. Collections). This code was drawn up in the Māgadhī dialect of the Prakrit language, the speech of Śākya-muni's country. The absence of discipline and authority, and a too wide tolerance of ideas, which prevailed in the first communities, caused numerous disputes. Moreover, among certain of the Buddhist monastics there arose a slackness of morality which compelled the assembling of a second Council to prevent the ruin of

[1] In the canon of the Northern Buddhists there exists in addition the prohibition against committing ten sins which are grouped together as follows: three sins of the body, murder, theft, adultery; four sins of speech, lying, calumny, insult, idle talk; three sins of thought, hatred, covetousness, dogmatic error.

the Doctrine. This Council, held at Vaiśalī a century later than the first, was composed, we are informed, of seven hundred *Arhats.* It attempted, but unsuccessfully, to introduce a certain unity among the different parties and to re-establish the ancient discipline. The cleavages became more marked; the sects multiplied till there were already eighteen in the third century B.C. One of these, the *Vibhjavādis,* finished by gaining the ascendancy and caused to be drawn up in Pāli a canon termed 'the orthodox', the most ancient now extant in written form which it assumed in Ceylon in 45 B.C. The canons of the other sects, which were reformers, were drawn up in Sanskrit and Prakrit and are known to us only through Tibetan and Chinese translations. Some fragments in the original language have been discovered, however, in Nepal, and quite recently in Chinese Turkestan. Towards the middle of the third century B.C. the learned among the sect of the *Vibhjavādis* succeeded in converting Aśoka Piyadasi (Aśoka the pious), king of North-east India, who in 242 B.C. ordered the assembling of the third Council in his capital, Pāṭaliputra. The thousand *Arhats* who came together drew up a final canon and resolved to send missionaries into the various countries to propagate 'the excellent law'. The propaganda met with its greatest success in Ceylon. The convent founded there by Mahendra (in Pāli Mahinda) became the centre of Buddhism as codified by the Council of Pāṭaliputra. Thence the creed spread into other regions. The Buddhists of India, however, continued their internal dissensions, and the fourth Council, convoked by Kanishka, the king of the Yue-Chi (*Indoscythians*), towards the year A. D. 100 at Jalandhara in Kashmir, ended in schism between the Buddhists of the south (Ceylon) and those of the north (India). The former refused to recognize its decisions, and held fast to the ancient doctrine which received the name of *Hīnayāna* (the little vehicle), while the representatives of the eighteen other sects accepted the new canon, drafted at the fourth Council, but not formulated definitely until a great deal later, which bears the title of *Mahāyāna* (the great vehicle). This canon was taken as the foundation of his teaching by the real founder of *Mahāyāna,* the monk Nāgārjuna, who lived towards the end of the second century A.D. The canon of the south (*Hīnayāna*) represents better than that of the north a state of Buddhism which, if not quite primitive, is at least the oldest known to us. It gives the rule of life of the monastics and a moral code much akin to that of the Brahmans and Jains. The canon of the north (*Mahāyāna*), on the other hand, which includes the canon of the south almost in its entirety, and is known to us only through translations (the Tibetan *Kanjur* and the Chinese *Tripiṭaka,* with an additional volume), is contaminated with metaphysical and, especially, with magical dissertations, formulas, incantations, and so forth (Tantra), borrowed from the Sivaites of India.

The difference of dogma between the two 'vehicles' is quite considerable. While the *Hīnayāna* preserves almost intact the 'primitive Buddhism' as we have sketched it above, the *Mahāyāna* adds thereto several innovations which completely change the meaning of the old faith. Of these innovations the following are the chief:—(1) The recognition of a supreme God (Ādi-Buddha, see p. 2) and the worship of the divinities. These two articles were borrowed from the Brahmans, and were unknown to primitive

Buddhism, in which the gods, belonging to the *Sansāra*, or circle of rebirth, and consequently always liable to return to one of the lower states, were far below the Buddhas who were free of the *Sansāra* and living in a very much higher world, that of *Nirvāṇa*. The Mahāyānists, on the other hand, relegated the Buddhas to the background, or rather made of them a sort of special divinity. (2) The Mahāyānists introduced the conception of the *Bodhisattvas*, predestined Buddhas-designate so to speak, who are accomplishing the last stages of their avatars before attaining to the dignity of Buddha (see p. 42). (3) Again, the Mahāyāna recognizes the *Mānushi Buddhas*, inhabitants of earth, and incarnations in flesh and bone of the *Dhyāni-Buddhas* or Buddhas of contemplation who dwell in heaven. It is the same also with the *Bodhisattvas*. (4) The adoption of magical formulas and 'tantric' practices of mages and sorcerers, formally forbidden to the monastics by the canon of the South. (5) Finally, the adoption of the theory of 'the void'. In the *Prajñā pāramitā* (ideal knowledge), the gospel of the Mahāyāna, attributed to Nāgārjuna, the theory of 'the void' is developed at great length, as well as that of the adoration of the gods (the *Bhakti* of the Brahmans), and the whole is curiously interspersed with metaphysical discourses and magic. Since then there have been schisms among the Mahāyānists themselves.[1] In the sixth century Asaṅga founded the sect of the Yogācārya, which developed the magical side of Buddhism to its highest power. The adherents of the ancient teaching then took the name of followers of *Madhyamika* (the *via media*).

III. The Expansion of Buddhism

The Southern Buddhism flourished in *Ceylon*, where the famous Buddhaghosha wrote in the fifth century some commentaries on the canon of the little vehicle. Then, spreading to *Burma*, it replaced there, about the sixth century and again in the fifteenth, the meagre remains of the mahāyānist propaganda of the time of Aśoka and Kanishka. The *Mahāyāna*, however, had a great triumph in other countries. In *India* itself the *Mahāyāna* and the *Hīnayāna* existed side by side for some long time, but both eventually were forced to give way, first by Brahmanism and then by the creed of Islam. The fall of Buddhism began with the eighth century. By the thirteenth it was no longer a living force in Central India, but it continued at the foot of the Himalayas and in the east of the peninsula. In the fifteenth century it disappeared from Bengal, and it is to be met with to-day, disfigured under the form of Lamaism, only in Nepal, Sikkim, Bhutan, and Ladak, and in some communities settled about its historic seats, such as Benares or Bodh'-Gayā. To-day attempts are being made to re-establish Buddhism in India. Unfortunate in its own country, the faith has succeeded better in less civilized districts or in those whose inhabitants were less enervated than the Hindus by religious musings and magical practices. From India primitive Buddhism and, subsequently, the *Mahāyāna* spread first to the neighbouring countries, to *Eastern Bactria* and *Gandhāra*,

[1] A detailed exposition of the doctrine of Mahāyāna has been made by Aśvaghosha, a poet attached to the court of Kanishka and author of 'The Life of Buddha'. It has been translated by S. Beal, Cowell, and Teitaro Suzaki (see Bibliography).

which to-day are included in the Punjab, Kashmir, and Kafiristan. Thence both forms of the creed penetrated into the lands of Khotan, Turfan, Kuchar, &c., in *Chinese Turkestan.* Flourishing there exceedingly from the second to the seventh century, mahāyānist Buddhism persisted till the ninth, the age of the Mohammedan conquests. Numerous expeditions of recent times (those of Sir Aurel Stein, Grünwedel, von Le Coq, Pelliot, Klementz, Beresowski, Yamagushi, and others) have brought to light artistic and literary traces of the Buddhism of Turkestan. Such was the expansion of Buddhism in the regions to the north of India. As for its propagation towards the east, mahāyānistic Hindu Buddhism penetrated into *Burma, Siam,* and *Cambodia,* where its presence is attested by numerous ruins (e.g. those of Angkor-Vat in Cambodia); but it proved unable to maintain itself there. Later it was replaced by the hīnayānist form of the faith. Southwards the Mahāyāna spread to the *Malay Archipelago.* In the island of Java, where it was probably introduced in the fifth century and had reached its highest power towards the eighth (as is proved by the famous ruins of Boro-Budur, see later under Buddhist Art), it most likely lived on side by side with Brahmanism, but was destroyed by the Mohammedans. It was from Java that the *Mahāyāna* reached the island of Bali, where degenerate remains of it exist even to-day. There remain evidences of the existence of Buddhism in the east and south of Sumatra from the eighth to the twelfth centuries.[1]

The introduction of Buddhism into *China* dates from the first century A. D., although Chinese writers make vague mention of certain attempts, probably by scattered individuals, which would date back to the second century B. C. The positive and historical fact is that in A.D. 65 the Emperor Ming-Ti, of the Han dynasty, sent into Khotan a deputation of eighteen persons, who, accompanied by the Indian theologians Mātanga and Gobharana, brought back in the year 67 a collection of Buddhist works. From among these some (notably 'the Sūtra in forty-two paragraphs', a kind of selection of thoughts made from the whole canon) were at once translated in the first Buddhist temple at Lo-yang (now Ho-nan-fu). Up to the fourth century the activity of the Buddhist missionaries in China (mostly foreigners) was limited to the translation of the sacred books; but from the reign of Yao-Shing (379–415) Buddhism was recognized as the state religion and the Chinese began to study it for themselves. Several pilgrims betook themselves to India and Ceylon to gain some idea of the faith in its own country. Among the most famous must be cited the monks Fa-Hien, who travelled from 399 to 413, and Yüan-Chuang or Hiuen-T'sang, whose journey is dated between 629 and 645. Others, as, for instance, the layman Sung-Yün (in 518–521), visited more especially the land of Gandhāra, and others. We owe to them valuable information on India, and the state of Buddhism in general, from the fifth to the seventh centuries. On the other hand, there were during this period several embassies from India and Ceylon to the Emperor of China. The envoys of the Hindu princes congratulated the ruler of China on the success won by the New Law in 'the Middle Kingdom'. One of the great Hindu priests, Bodhidharma,

[1] Verbeek, *Oudheden van Java,* S'Gravenhag, 1891. —Groeneveldt, Notes on the Malay Archipelago; in *Verhandelingen van het Bataviaasch Genootschap van Kunsten en Wetenschappen,* Batavia, t. 39, 1877.

succeeded (in 526) in converting to Buddhism the Emperor Wu-Ti of the Lyang dynasty, which then reigned in Southern China. For a time the Emperor became a monk, and Bodhidharma was made head of all the Buddhist monastics in China, and took up his residence in a famous convent near the present Kiu-Kiang on the Yang-Tze. In spite of these triumphs the Buddhists had to sustain a struggle against their enemies, the faithful of the Taoist creed and the disciples of Confucius. To a certain degree they were able to amalgamate with the former, but the latter aroused against them persecutions which were particularly bitter at the beginning of the eighth century and down to the tenth. Thousands of convents were destroyed by violence, and hundreds of thousands of monks compelled to return to secular life. Since that date, the doctrine of ***Mahāyāna***, slightly modified by borrowings from Taoism, has endured till the present time. Its followers, divided into ten sects, live peaceably in their convents, often quite close to Taoist monastics or Buddhist-Lamaites (see later). The latter, however, are not very numerous in China.

From China Buddhism passed into *Korea*. It was brought by a Chinese monk named Sun-Do, who carried 372 sacred images and books with him. The new faith grew very rapidly and attained its apogee from the tenth to the fourteenth century. In 1447 a Buddhist monk invented the present Korean alphabet called Un-mwn which is derived from the Sanskrit (M. Courant). At the end of the fourteenth century, with the fall of the dynasty which had protected it, Buddhism began to decline in Korea, and to-day only a few degraded remains of it are to be discovered there.

From Korea the spark of the Buddhistic faith passed to *Japan*, where the starting-point of the Buddhist propaganda was the introduction of an image of Buddha into the court of the Emperor by a monk sent by the king of Hyakusai, one of the states into which Korea was at this time (552) divided. At the end of the sixth century (*c.* 588) the new religion found a firm footing in the country despite the opposition of the Shintoists, who, after a vigorous struggle, ended by fusing themselves with the Buddhists, as the Taoists have done in China. An excellent example of this fusion is to be found in the sect of the ***Ryobu***, which was founded in the ninth century and is a veritable mixture of both creeds. At this period the centre of Japanese Buddhism was at the court of the Emperor. Certain princes, Shōtoku Daishi (canonized in 621), for instance, even distinguished themselves as ardent propagandists of the new faith. As in Korea, Buddhism caused the invention of a national system of writing, the ***Kana*** (*Katakana* and ***Hiragana***), and introduced into the country the fine arts, the taste for letters, and the like. Several of the sacred books in Sanskrit were brought thither, and there have since been discovered in Japan portions of the Buddhist canons in that tongue which elsewhere are unknown. It is a curious fact, however, that until quite lately the Buddhistic works in Chinese or Sanskrit have never been translated into Japanese (Chamberlain). At the time of its introduction into Japan, Sino-Korean Buddhism already comprised several divisions, which in the Land of the Rising Sun developed into six sects, the chief being: *Tendai*; *Shingon* (True-Word); *Jōdo* (Pure-Land) and *Zen*. To these must be added six others, of local origin, of which the most important are: the *Ryobu* already mentioned; the *Shin* (true), called also *Monto* or *Ikko*; and the *Nichiren* or *Hokke*. Of these sects the last, founded in 1222, is considered the most fanatical. The *Shin* (a 'protestant' sect, so to speak) allows the marriage of priests; the sect of the *Jōdo* introduces the idea of 'the western paradise'; that of the *Zen* shows artistic and literary tendencies. The establishment of Chinese Confucianism in the seventeenth century, and then, to some extent, the first steps taken to introduce Christianity, dealt Buddhism a blow. The more cultivated minds became disinclined for it, and the revolution of 1867–8 brought about its almost complete downfall by declaring Shintoism the state religion. A series of measures taken by the government from 1871 to 1874 left Buddhism wholly disestablished and disendowed. Lately there has been a revival of Buddhistic studies in Japan, but it is rather towards scientific and evolutionary ideas or theosophical speculations that the neo-Buddhists turn their attention.

From China Buddhism penetrated into *Annam*, where it was considerably modified by the introduction of indigenous animistic elements and magical practices. This mutilated Buddhism numbers, however, only a few devotees. There is no ecclesiastical organization nor clergy. The 'bonzes', living apart or in small bodies in the convents, are also sorcerers, faith-healers and the like.

In *Tibet* and later in *Mongolia* the doctrine of the Mahāyāna developed into a new religion—Lamaism—of which we shall give a short account. The introduction of Buddhism into Tibet dates from the year 632, when the King Srongtsan-sgam-po (Sroṅ-btsan sgam-po), influenced by his two wives, one a Chinese princess, the other from Nepal, but both ardent Buddhists, ordered from India images, sacred books, and (most important of all) theologians. These last invented the Tibetan alphabet (derived from the Sanskrit), undertook the translation of the canonical writings, and applied themselves to a very active propaganda of the new Law. In the eighth century, the King Ti-sron De-tsan summoned to his court Hindu theologians whose names have remained famous, for instance Śānta-Rakśita (venerated to-day as Acārya-Bodhisattva) and Padmasambhava (in Tibetan Guru Rin-po-c'e, 'Precious Teacher'), a native of Udyāna, now Dardistan in the north-west of Kashmir. The latter, a keen disciple of the school of Yogācārya, came to Tibet in 747, and succeeded in firmly implanting his doctrine, owing, it is true, to a compromise with the native religion of *Bon-pa*, whose demons he admitted to his pantheon. Two years later he laid the first stone of Tibet's first Buddhist monastery, that of Sam-yas (Bsam-yas). To him is due the introduction into the mahāyānist doctrine of the division of men into two categories, *Nan-pa* ('insiders' or Buddhists) and *Ci-pa* ('outsiders' or non-Buddhists), as well as many other modifications which transformed the 'Mahāyāna' into the Church or sect known under the name of *Rñiṅ-ma-pa* which adores Samantabhadra as the supreme divinity. Under the King Ral-pa-can (*c.* 899) was finished the translation of the sacred books, which were brought together into two collections, forming to this day the foundation of the Lamaist religion—the *Kanjur* (*Bkah-hgyur*) and the *Tanjur* (*Bstan-hgyur*) [see later]. But a terrible reaction was produced by the accession to the throne of the brother of Ral-pa-can, by name Langdarma (Glaṅ-dharma). This monarch, the Julian the Apostate of Buddhism, won over by those who practised the religion of *Bon-pa*, inaugurated an era of persecution, burned monasteries, and slew or banished thousands of monks. The banished monks retired to the mountains in the east of the country, but avenged themselves at the end of three years by bringing about Langdarma's death. After this, the Buddhists again dared to raise their heads and the propaganda was recommenced. A century later the country was covered with convents and full of monks. The arrival of the great Hindu priest Atīśa in 1040 marked an epoch in the history of Tibetan Buddhism—the conclusion of the *Nga-dar*, or period of primitive Buddhism, and the beginning of the *C'yi-dar*, or period of Lamaism. Atīśa founded the sect of *Ka-dam-pa*, less ascetic and more ritualistic than that of *Rñiṅ-ma-pa*, and this sect became later (in 1417) the chief 'church' of the Lamaist creed, under the name of *Ge-lug-pa* (*dge-lugs-pa*, the 'sect of the righteous', or of 'the yellow caps'). The founder of the sect, the real reformer of Lamaism, was the famous Tsoṅ-k'a-pa (1356–1418), born in the country where stands to-day the convent of Kum-bum (Kham province in the north-east of Tibet). He had made it his chief object to re-establish discipline in the convents, where it was so slack that several monks were either married or openly kept mistresses. Moreover, he also introduced new dogmas of which the most important is the recognition of 'living Buddhas' or reborn lamas (*Qubilghan* in Mongolian), i.e. priests and monks in whose very flesh and bones are incarnated the famous saints and even the different deities. This dogma gave an enormous power to the Lamaist clergy and found its expression towards the end of the fifteenth century in the creation of a Grand-Lama, and later in 1640 of a sole temporal and spiritual chief of all Tibet, bearing the title of the Dalai-Lama. Indeed the fifth Grand-Lama (the incarnation of Avalokiteśvara), called Nag-wan Lo-zang (Ṅag-dbaṅ blo-bzaṅ), was honoured by the Mongol prince Gushi Khan with the title of King of Tibet, and was confirmed in this dignity by the Emperor of China in 1650. The institution of the Dalai-lama has lasted in Tibet up to the present time in spite of the wanderings undergone by the present bearer of the title after the Anglo-Tibetan war. Tsoṅ-k'a-pa founded the monastery of Galdan or Gah-dan, which became the centre for the reformed Buddhists (*Ge-luk-pa*) who assumed the yellow cap (*Sha-ser* in Tibetan), while the orthodox (*Rñiṅ-ma-pa*) adhered to the red cap (in Tibetan *Sha-mar*). The former spread all over Tibet, among the Mongols, and in China (where they exist side by side with the mahāyānist Buddhism); the latter are numerous in Nepal, in Sikkim, in Bhutan, and on the frontiers of China and Tibet. Alongside of these two principal 'churches' exist some twelve Lamaist sects, but their importance is insignificant in comparison with that of 'the red caps' and 'the yellow'. Several among them are attached by origin to the orthodox 'reds'. Such is the sect of *Sakya-pa*, with its subordinate bodies, whose faithful adore principally the Bodhisattva Mañjuśrī. Others, e.g. the *Orgyen-pa*, are descended from the Ñiṅ-ma-pa before the reformation. Finally, a certain number sprang from the sect founded in the twelfth century by Mar-pa and spread afterwards by the poet-monk Mi-la ras-pa (the cotton-clad) (1038–1122). The faithful of the *Kargya-pa* revere above all others Ādi-Buddha. In essentials there is not any great difference of doctrine between all these sects of Lamaists. To-day they are distinguished only by their recognition or repudiation of certain saints, their veneration of certain divinities, the character of their practices, and the number of miracles wrought by their magicians.

At the time of the conquest of Tibet by the Mongols, a monk of the country, Saskya-Pandita, was summoned to Mongolia by the Khan Godan, or Qutan, the second son of Chinghis-khan. He arrived in 1246 in order to propagate Lamaism, and made the first attempt to invent a script for the Mongolian language, drawing his inspiration from the *Uigur* alphabet. He failed, however, in his experiment, and his nephew, the monk Matidhvaja ('the standard of wisdom'), better known under the name of P'ags-pa ('the famous,' 'the saint') [in Mongol. *qutuqtu*], invented 'the square script' (*dürbeljin üsük* in Mongol.) which was derived from the Tibetan alphabet. This, despite its phonetic value, had only a small success. It was replaced by the present Mongol script, which is only a modified form of the *Uigur* script proposed several years before by Saskya-Pandita. It was perfected by the Lama Čojqu oǰer (in Mongolian, Ch̲os-kyi-h̲od-zer in Tibetan) in the reign of Kuluk-khan (1308–11). P'ags-pa converted to Buddhism the famous Khubilai-khan (Qubilai-qaghan) (1260–91), who became one of its most ardent propagators. But, notwithstanding the protection of the emperors, Buddhism did not make any great progress in either China or Mongolia, and even suffered a temporary eclipse after the fall of the Mongolian dynasty of the Yuen (1368). In Mongolia the people returned to their beloved Shamanist beliefs, and the monks fell very far away from the rules of the discipline. Buddhism was, so to speak, re-introduced in Mongolia two centuries later, in 1577, under the form of the sect of Ge-luk-pa (*see* above), by the saint (*Qutuqtu*) Sodnam-jamju (Bsod-nams-rgya-mtsh̲o), who, having been proclaimed Dalai-Lama by Altan-khan, chief of the Tumet Mongols and king of Tibet, came to Mongolia, where he laid down the rules for monastics, did away with the sacrifice of animals at funerals, and performed such services for Buddhism, that by the Mongols he is considered their first national saint. Towards the end of the sixteenth century the Mongol princes had as much influence with the Dalai-Lamas as had the emperors of China, and from 1602 we find one of the descendants of Altan holding the throne of the Grand-Lama under the name of Dalai-Erden. He it was who in 1604 settled the *qutuqtu* Maydari in the convent of Urga on the banks of the river Tola. The successors of this personage, who are held to be *qubilghan* (reincarnations) of one of the pupils of Śākya-muni, are among the most powerful members of the Lamaist clergy. It was the last of these incarnations, the Bogdo-Gegen ('shining excellence') or Je-btsun dam-pa ('holy chief'), who lately (in 1912) proclaimed himself at Urga king of an independent Mongolia.

Towards 1625 Lamaism was introduced among the *Kalmuks* by Boibeghus-baghatur, chief of the Khoshot (*qośot*) tribe. Later it spread among the other princes, nobles, and landholders. Finally, towards the end of the eighteenth century all the Kalmuk race, or Ölöt, from Lake Kuku-Nor to the banks of the Volga and the Don, had become Buddhist. As to the third branch of the Mongols, the *Buriats,* they were not affected by Buddhism before the middle of the eighteenth century, and a part of them remains Shamanist even at the present time.

IV. The Religious Community (*Saṅgha*)

(*a*) *Clergy.* The first Buddhist community was founded by Śākya-muni himself, and the rules of its organization served as a base for the compilation of the *Vinaya*, that part of the canon (*Tripiṭaka*) which is devoted to 'the discipline'. These rules, however, which resembled those of many other religious communities of ancient India, did not acknowledge the existence of a chief, and up to the present the southern Buddhists, like those of Ceylon, have never had one, or, at most, have had leaders appointed by the temporal power, as in Siam. As we shall shortly see, the case is different in the north. The primitive Buddhist community admitted to itself every man without distinction of caste, and was thereby differentiated from the other contemporary communities of India. It is even maintained by some authors that to this principle of equality and democracy Buddhism owes its success. On the other hand, it must be pointed out that Śākya-muni himself established, as a set-off to the privileges enjoyed at his time by every religious community in India (exemption from taxes, right of asylum, &c.), certain prohibitions: thus slaves, criminals, soldiers, persons afflicted with infirmities or contagious diseases, were all inadmissible. In the same way persons of less than twenty years and above eight were admitted only as pupils or novices (*Śrāmaṇera* in S.,[1] *Bandi* in M.), and that with the consent of their parents. As to women, though all, even those living in concubinage, could become Buddhists, their constitution in communities was permitted by Śākya-muni only very reluctantly, at the instance of his aunt who reared him. He maintained, even, that the time of his apostolate on earth as *Mānushi-buddha*, and therefore the total benefit which he could confer upon humanity, had been reduced one-half by this concession.

In the primitive community the admission to two grades (*Pravrajyā* 'departure', and the great admission *Upasampadā*) were accompanied by several ceremonies, the cutting of hair, the clothing in monastic habit, and the taking of an oath to observe the four fundamental commandments—not to kill, not to thieve, to abstain from sexual connexion, and not to boast the possession of supernatural qualities. Monks were bound to live by alms, to sleep under trees, to be clad in rags, &c. Usually their life was passed in walking from one town to another, with no more baggage than an earthen bowl (*Pātra* S., *Batir* M.) holding food, a razor, and a sieve to strain from their drinking-water the living creatures which might be therein and run the risk of being swallowed. A pilgrim's staff was allowed.[2] They slept in the open air, and only

[1] The words Sanskrit, Tibetan, and Mongolian are here represented by the letters S., T., and M.

[2] Some of these rules are in practice to-day. Thus the monks of Ceylon go bareheaded and barefooted, and the monk of Tibet always has his *pātra*. Others have disappeared (e. g. the fourth commandment), or at least have changed. For instance, in Ceylon the umbrella has replaced the staff, and among the Mongolian Buddhists the future monk, during the ceremony of admission, is given, instead of a sieve, a sort of fan made of dry herbs, with which he must drive away the insects which might fall into his drinking-water.

in the rainy season assembled in houses (*Vihāra*) built for them by the faithful. These *Vihāra* later became monasteries. The day of the primitive monk began with household toil and was afterwards divided between meditation, collection of alms, and worship paid to the relics of Buddha or to the Bodhi tree. It ended with reading or copying the sacred books. Strictly speaking there were no prayers, for to whom could they be addressed? The primitive faith did not allow a personal deity, and Buddha is in Nirvāṇa, outside the universe in whose midst living beings are compelled to exist until their deliverance (*Sansāra*). Meetings for any common rite were rare: there were a public confession every eight days and a great mutual confession at the end of the rainy season. Such a cult might satisfy a few ecstatic monks, but made no appeal to the common people; and it is no matter for surprise if the new religion immediately after Śākya-muni's death made concessions to the latter. They began with the public adoration of the relics of Gautama himself and then of other Buddhas. Afterwards came pilgrimages to spots which recalled his life and his works, and where commemorative monuments (*Stūpa* S., *Thūpa* in Pāli, *mC'od-rten* T., *Suburga* M.) had been erected.[1]

The simple organization of the primitive *Saṅgha* has undergone, like any other institution, its processes of evolution. Among the southern Buddhists it has resulted in the foundation of convents, each containing but a few monks (*bhikshu*), while among those of the north it has been transformed into a regular church, which, in some countries, as for instance in Tibet, has ended by absorbing the entire life of the people.

With the northern Buddhists the clergy is composed of monks of various grades, some of whom follow a special course of teaching, and, after examination, receive an ordination which endows them with power to perform the sacred rites. The number of these monks is considerable. More than half the population in Mongolia, more than a third in Tibet, consists of 'Lamas'.[2] But it must not be supposed that all Lamas are true monks living in convents. Those who have attained to the first two grades of the hierarchy live, for the most part, outside such institutions and attend to their businesses like ordinary Mongols and Tibetans. Moreover, to mention only the most important class, there are laymen of all ages who, desirous of proving their devotion, undergo a sort of affiliation to the monastic life, and acquire the title of *Ubasi* (M.) or *Upāsaka* (S.). In their case ordination takes place in the tent of the postulant or his parents at the hands of a priest (*Gelüng*, see later), who demands of the candidate obedience to the first five commandments (see p. xxv). The *Ubasi* afterwards follows the life of the other nomads, and is not, strictly speaking, a monk.

The real hierarchy begins with the grade of *Genyen* (*dge bsñen* T., *Śrāmaṇera* S., *Bandi* M.). The usual age for candidates for this grade is from infancy up to seven or eight years, and the rank is attained after two or three years of study under the

[1] Till quite lately 'the real tooth' of Buddha was shown at Kandi in Ceylon, and 'the real Bodhi tree' existed as late as 1876 near the ancient town of Urubilvā in India.

[2] This is the European term for Buddhist monks, but the word in Tibetan signifies 'superior' or 'revered master', and is applied only to high dignitaries, who gain a right to it only after the completion of higher studies.

direction of a teacher appointed by the superior of the convent. Ordination is accompanied by a certain amount of ceremonial. The head of the new *Genyen* is shaven; flowers are thrown over him, after he has been made to submit to a kind of confession in order that his freedom from infectious disease may be assured, as also his sex, and the fact of his not having taken life, and so on. The *Bandi* is compelled to observe the ten commandments (see p. xxv). He is given the monastic habit of red and yellow, the *pātra*, and a bundle of dry herbs for driving away insects (see p. xxxiii, n.). The next rank, that of novice or *Getsül* (*dge-ts'ul* T., *Geǰül* M., *Śramaṇa* S.), can be tried for only after fifteen years of age. The ordination resembles that of the *Bandi*, but with more ceremonial and a harder examination. To become a perfect monk or *Gelüng* (M.) ('a virtuous mendicant'—*dge-sloṅ* T.) the candidate must be between twenty and twenty-five years old, must pass an examination which lasts for three days, and must maintain in debate various theses in theology. Those who are successful in this examination, remain at the convent, those who fail are obliged to leave it and to become sorcerer-Lamas (in Tibet), or (in Mongolia) to adopt nomadic life, always preserving their religious character and title of *getsül*.

The *Gelüng* are qualified to officiate in all the ceremonies of the religion, and can even become the superiors of smaller convents.

At this rank the monastic hierarchy (strictly speaking) reaches its term. All other distinctions depend upon the functions fulfilled by the various *Gelüng* or upon academic degrees. As a matter of fact, the more ambitious and intelligent among the *Gelüng* continue their studies in the universities of the great convents where is taught the *tsanit* (*bjanit* M.) or *Mts'an-ñid* (T.), i.e. the distinctive signs of 'the things of the quintessence', or (to put it more accurately) the commentaries to the *Kanjur* and the *Tanjur* (see p. xxx), accompanied by special studies in astrology, medicine, and the occult sciences. After studies, more or less long, and severe examinations, the students obtain successively the degrees of Bachelor (*Dkah-bcu* T., *Arkan bergedeï* M.), of Licentiate (*Rabs-hbyams-pa* T., *Masi-Kedüreksen* M.), of Master (*Sṅas-rams-pa* T.), and of Doctor (*Hla-rams-pa* T.).

As to the offices of the monks in the convents, they are more than twenty in number. The highest is that of *Qambo-Lama* (M.), *Upādhyāya* (S.), *Mkhan-po* (T.), or Superior of one of the greater convents. The *Qambo* are nominated by the incarnated Lamas (see below) and confirmed in their office by the civil power (up to lately by the Emperor of China). A *Qambo* has supreme direction of the entire life of the convent, while the management of convent affairs lies in the hands of a functionary of the rank immediately below, who is called *Čorgi-Lama* (M.) or *Tsos-rje* (T.). Then follow in order the *siretu* (M.), who presides at all ceremonies of the religion; the *Dge-bskos* (T.) or *Gebgüi* (M.), a kind of overseer or beadle with extensive authority, always armed with his staff, which he plies on the columns of the temple to stop the noise of talking, and also, after a summary cross-examination, on the backs of such monks as may disturb the order of the services. Finally comes the *Umčat* (M.) or *Dbu-mtsat* (T.) who organizes all the religious services and has the special function of leading the intoning of the hymns and chants.

Besides the assistants of the three officers just named, we have to reckon a crowd of underlings; the *Takilči* (M.) or *Mtsod-pa* (T.) who arranges the offerings; the *Ja-ma* (T.) who prepares them and looks after everything concerning the feeding of the monks; the musicians, the monks who, by ringing a gong or blowing into a shell, give the signal to the rest to assemble in the temple or elsewhere.

There are also monks especially employed in instruction, who, like the higher officers, are chosen from among those possessed of academic degrees. Such are the *C'os-skyoṅ* (T.) or professors of the occult sciences, who interpret difficult passages of the sacred books and are also busied in averting or attracting rain, in indicating the places where are reborn the souls of the departed, and so forth. These must be distinguished from the magicians (*Čoijin-Sanghasak* M.) who do not live in monasteries, and who, although they receive investiture from the Dalai-Lama himself, do not follow the monastic rules. Usually they are married and devote themselves to rites akin to Shamanism. Some are renowned as oracles. Along with the *C'os-skyoṅ* must be classed the doctor-Lamas (*Emči* M., *Sman-pa* T.) and the astrologers (*Jiruqaici* M., *Gaṅaka* S., *Rtsis-ṇan* T.).

In spite of the number of grades and functions all monks, at least in Mongolia (Pozdnieev), believe in their mutual equality, and act upon this principle. In this respect the traditions of the ancient brotherhood of the Saṅgha have been preserved up to our day.

Beside the 'regular' clergy (so to speak) exists a special class of ecclesiastical dignitaries—the 'incarnations' (*Qubilghan* M., *Sprul-ba* T.) or living Buddhas who are at the summit of the lamaist hierarchy and who, in right of their very origin, differ from the rest. A Qubilghan is, in fact, the representative, in flesh and blood, of some Buddha, Bodhisattva, god or saint, whose spirit is incarnated in him at the moment of his birth, and will pass, at his death, into the body of the child destined to become his successor in the functions fulfilled by him. The incarnation is thus less a matter of person than of function. The system is a useful one; for by exploiting the belief in transmigration or rebirth and the veneration for famous ancestors it creates positions which are to some extent hereditary and precludes the competition and party-strife which an election might occasion. Besides the Dalai-Lama (supreme head of the Lamaist church of the 'yellow caps', and at the same time incarnation of the Bodhisattva Avalokiteśvara) who lives at Lhassa, and the Pan-c'en Rimpoce (supreme head of the 'church' of the 'red caps', and also incarnation of Buddha Amitābha) who lives at Tashi-Lumpo, there are in Tibet, as in Mongolia and China, a certain number of 'saints' (*Qutuqtu* M.) and 'Qubilghan', incarnations of numerous saints and deities. Every greater convent has its own Qubilghan whose authority is purely local. As to the Qutuqtu there are only very few of them. Such for example is the Qutuqtu of the convent of Urga in Mongolia, called Bogdo-Gegen (see p. xxxii), incarnation of one of the pupils of Śākyamuni. There are also the Grand-Lama of Pekin, head of the Lamaist clergy in China, and the Depa-raja, spiritual and temporal sovereign of Bhutan.

When one of the incarnate Lamas dies, his 'spiritual being' or, as we should say, his soul, goes first to a celestial abode, then, at the end of a period varying from forty-six days to four years, is reborn in the body of a child, who from his birth gives signs of his supernatural character. When public report or the inquiries of the Lamas have pointed out the locality where the child in question is to be found, the chapter of the monastery, or (if it is a matter of the Dalai-Lama) the sacred college of the *Qambo* (counsellors) holds an inquiry into the authenticity of the facts alleged, and goes to the spot to subject the child to a series of tests, the chief of which consists in making him recognize among several similar objects (cups, books, rosaries, &c.) those which the dead Qubilghan or Dalai-Lama habitually used. After due trial, the child is proclaimed a rebirth and is brought to the convent or the palace of Po-ta-la, if it is a question of succession to the Dalai-Lama. There up to the age of eighteen he receives the necessary education. Afterwards he may exercise his authority.

The day of a Tibetan monk is passed very much in the following manner. Rising about five, he makes his ablutions, recites the prayers in honour of his tutelar divinity or patron (*Yi-dam*), then, summoned by the trumpet or the shell, joins the procession of other monks who are going to the temple. There, after prayer, is made the first distribution of tea to the monks. This rite over, he retires to his cell and does not return to worship till nine o'clock; then at midday come service and tea. After this he is free and takes a rest, only returning to the temple towards three to take part in theological controversies and receive tea again. About seven he goes back to his cell, after having revised the tasks to be done by his pupils, if there is occasion. Apart from the hours devoted to worship, the Lamas are occupied with various matters according to their particular capacities. Some give instruction; others copy the saced books; others, again, design and carve images of the deities or perform some manual labour. Some travel about among the encampments to aid the laity with their counsel; others, to complete their education, travel from one convent to another.

The costume of the Mongolian monks consists of a skirt of blue linen or red cloth (*Pancali* S., *S̲ham-t'abs* T., *Banǰal* M.), a sort of shirt of white linen (*janǰa* M.), and a long full robe of cloth or of silk (*Debel* M.) ornamented with fur for the winter, and of a colour varying in accordance with the wearer's grade: brown for the Bandi, red for the Getsül, and yellow for the Gelüng. In Tibet trousers also are worn, and a long red shawl (*Bla-gos* T.) thrown over the left shoulder and leaving free the right arm as among the primitive Buddhists. In Mongolia the same shawl (*Kimǰi* M.) is donned only for the religious service. The headgear varies with the circumstances and rank of the monks and Lamas. The conical hat, red or yellow according to sect, with large turned-up brim, is common to all. Another, shaped like a biretta and trimmed with a yellow or red fringe, is worn only by monks resident at the convent. For the services is worn a sort of helmet with a crest (*Śaser* M., *Rtse-swa* T.), while the Lamas of high rank wear different kinds of tiaras (*Obbotai* M.). For some of the divine services is assumed the *titim* (M.) (or *chodpan*, see Glossary) or another head-dress, shaped like an inverted barber's dish and topped by a *vajra*. The conical cap, with long appendages in the form of ribbons falling on the shoulders and the temples, is only adopted by the 'reincarnations'.

An indispensable accessory of the costume of the Gelüng is the water-bottle wallet (*C'ab-lug* T., *ǰabori* or *ǰavrun* M.), a little flagon sewn up in a bag and containing holy water with which the monk washes his mouth after meals. There are also rosaries (*Akshamālā* S., *P'ren-ba* T., *Erike* M.) of 108 beads of the same size, made of bone, wood, coral, metal, seeds, and the like. These are divided into nine series by larger beads. In addition, the Lamas carry with them a drinking-cup, reliquaries, a little book wrapped in cloth with which they give the blessing, and sometimes a bag containing small necessaries, tobacco, pipe, tinder-box, writing-materials, and the like.

Besides the monks there are Lamaist-Buddhist nuns (*Bhikshuṇī* S.). Formerly numerous, they are met with to-day only in the south and east of Tibet. They wear the same costume as the monks and shave the head completely. Their principal order has its seat at the monastery of Samding (*Bsam-lding* T.), on Lake Palte or Yamdok, the abbess of which is an incarnation of Vajravārāhī (*Rdo-rje p'ag-mo*) (see p. 117). In Dzungaria and western Mongolia are found also some female 'Qubilghan'.

(*b*) *Religious Ceremonies.* Presence at the daily offices in the temple of the convent is obligatory only on the Bandi, the Getsül, and some Gelüng specially charged with the performance of the services. The remaining Gelüng and the Lamas of the higher grades assist only at the high services (*ǰke qural* M.). These take place usually on the 15th of each lunar month, with an extra service (*Qanghal* M.) towards the end of the month; but there are others which last several days, usually from the 1st to the 15th of the month or from the 8th to the 15th.

Besides the daily services there are solemn religious ceremonies at certain appointed seasons: first on the 15th of each lunar month, then on the days of certain feasts. Among these feasts the most important are the new year or 'white moon' (*Zal-ba Daṅ-po* T., *Čaghan-sara* M.), which lasts from the 1st to the 16th of the first 'moon' of the year (according to the Chinese cycle, i.e. between the middle of January and the beginning of February). It corresponds to the sixteen days during which Śākya-muni sustained his struggle with the adversaries of his doctrine (see p. xx), and coincides with the civil feasts of a sort of carnival which lasts, at Lhassa for instance, for more than six weeks. Another feast commemorating the first preaching of the four ruths by Śākya-muni (see pp. xx–xxi), is kept by a high service from the 8th to the 15th of the third 'moon' of the summer (towards the end of July), and is followed by a special ceremony on the 16th of the same month, the day of Śākya-muni's conception. Afterwards begins the 'Lent', imposing hard and painful service and repentance, and called *Jara* (M.) or *Dpyar-gnas* (T.), i.e. 'the solitary summer fasting' of the monks. This lasts for forty-five days, during which the monks may not leave the convent and must remain all day seated in the temple. The 25th day of the first month of the winter, 'the feast of Lanterns', gives opportunity for one of the most impressive ceremonies, accompanied by a sudden illumination of all the buildings of the convent with thousands of lanterns, and by other features. This has been rendered popular in Europe by the picturesque narrative of the Abbé Huc. Lastly, in the third 'moon' of the winter (end of January or beginning of

February) occur the three high services. On the 15th is the secret congress (*Nighuǰa qurianghui* M.); from the 27th to the 28th the feast called *Sor*, when offerings of butter are burnt, and on the 29th the service of sacrifices (*balin* M.). Besides these festal days there are high services from the 8th to the 15th of the first month of summer in commemoration of the entry of Buddha into Nirvāṇa, and on the 15th day of the third month of autumn in honour of Man-la (see p. 23), and a few others.

We must add that the laity assist at the daily services in Tibet only on rare occasions, and never in Mongolia. It is only on feast days that they throng as if on pilgrimage to the vicinity of the convents. In Tibet they enter the temples, but in Mongolia they are content to make genuflexions and salutations, prostrating themselves upon the earth outside the temple. Moreover in Tibet, as also in Mongolia, they make 'the circumambulation' of the temple, either walking or prostrating themselves continually so as to measure with the length of their bodies the circuit of the shrine. The more fervent act in the same manner all the way from their encampment to the convent; it is even said that the most ecstatic use the same fashion of progression during the whole journey from the frontier of Tibet up to Lhassa.

The usual daily service (*Jis* T.) includes the same cycle of prayers and repetitions which are intoned by the *Unčat* (see p. xxxv), and taken up in chorus by the rest of the monks. According to the 'Sumbrum' or 'breviaries' in vogue in Mongolia the offices are composed of three parts: (1) the 'rapsal' (*rab-gsal* T.), 'the most luminous collection of hymns in honour of Buddha, which include the 'credo', the 'praises', the 'prayers', and the 'wishes and benedictions'; (2) the litanies addressed to the *dokshit* or defenders of the Faith (see p. 130), which vary according to the divinity to whom they are addressed; (3) *ündüsün* (M.) or *Tantra* (S.), esoteric invocations to the Yi-dam (see p. 123) grouped under four heads. In the larger convents these magic *Tantra* are read in special chapels called *Jud* (T.).

The three kinds of 'sung prelections' of the liturgy are the same for the low and the high services, which only differ in the number of chapters read. Thus at the low service are read only four or five 'rapsal' and a single 'dokshit' in honour of the deity who protects the convent, while at the high service the entire series of 'rapsals' is exhausted, and six or eight litanies are sung to the 'dokshits'. To these daily services, at which the monks are present in their ordinary dress, seated, and without making any gestures or imitative actions, others are from time to time added. First there is a 'dokshit' service, specially composed for invoking the protective deities and the 'defenders of the faith'. This service is invested with more splendour than usual. The presiding Gelüng assumes a special dress; the *banǰal* (see p. xxxvii) is worn above the robe and not below; his shoulders are draped with a sort of tippet (*do-dik* T.); lastly, the head is crowned by the *chodpan* (see the Glossary). The principal celebrant stands upright and makes a certain number of gestures. The office is accompanied by music and includes offerings and sacrifices to the divinities. The objects indispensable for this service are (1) the gong and *vajra* (see Glossary), which the celebrant generally holds; (2) the *kapāla* (see Glossary) on a tripod, filled, according to the deity to whom sacrifice is made, with tea, wine, or blood; (3) the *bum-pa*, vessel of holy water with a peacock's feather for sprinkling it; (4) a little plate with grains of corn or rice to be thrown in the air as a sacrifice to the spirits.

Moreover special offerings are prepared (*balin* M.), a kind of pyramid made of paste mixed with sugar and currants and covered with ornaments made of coloured butter which represent the sun and moon, the jewel (*cintāmaṇi* S.), flowers, and so forth. The preparation of these *balin* demands the greatest care. Since the breath of the maker must not touch them, he puts over his mouth a hair-net (*galgabči* M.). The priest's gestures have relation to the seven special offerings, the flower, lamp, scented wands, and the rest (see p. xlviii). The assistants mark these gestures by clapping their hands in a special 'tempo' or cadence. The prayers recited are taken from the *Sādhana* (see Glossary).

Another service, known by the Mongolian name of *Tüiürgükji*, has for object the preparation of the lustral water (*rasāyana* S.). It includes prayer, the absolution of sins, a recital of all the ablutions made by Śākya-muni, and finally the thanksgiving. Between the first and second part of the rite is performed the preparation of the holy water. One of the priest's assistants raises a mirror so that it reflects one of the statues of the divinities; another takes the vessel (*Kuǰe* M.) filled with water and pours it upon the mirror. The water which flows off and is believed to have caught the image of the divinity, is collected in a special dish (*K'ris-gc'os* T.) held by a third acolyte, while a fourth wipes the mirror with a silken napkin (*qadaq* M.). Fifteen libations are made in this way, and at the end of the ceremony the lustral water is poured off into a *bum-pa* and set on the sacrificial altar. Thereafter it is used for the aspersion of offerings, and for washing the mouths of the Lamas, while among the laity it serves the same purposes as does holy water among Catholics.

The service called *so-jin* (*gso-sbyon* T.) is worthy of special treatment. It is held on the fifteenth and thirtieth of each month, and is really the ancient *upoṣadha* or collective confession of the monks; being of a very intimate character, it involves the wearing of special habits. The monks are called to it not by the sound of bells or trumpets, but by that of a great block of wood (*gaṇḍī* S.) struck by a small staff. In reality it is no longer the primitive confession, but a sort of renewal of vows; for to all the questions (253 at least) put by the presiding official, the monks make invariably the same replies. For the sake of record we may mention the special annual ceremonies. These are the tour made by Maitreya, when the statue of this divinity is drawn about on an enormous wooden horse; and the *tsam*, a kind of mystery with masked figures representing the Citipati, the god Vajrapāṇi, the Jamsaran or earth-spirit under the form of an old man, several monsters with heads of oxen, stags, and the like.

V. Short Survey of Buddhist Art

After this description of the organization and life of the Buddhist clergy as well as of the ritual, there remains the task of saying a few words on the buildings and cult-objects amid which a great number of Lamas pass their existence; that is to say, the convents and temples and also the images they contain must be described. Since, however, these images are the subject of the volume to which this is but the Introduction, we shall limit ourselves to giving some general idea of the architecture of the convents and temples and of the sculptures and pictures representing the deities.

Notwithstanding numerous works, among which must be mentioned as of first rank those of Foucher, Grünwedel, von Le Coq, and S. Oldenburg, the study of Buddhist art still presents considerable lacunae and numerous uncertainties.

This art must have first appeared soon after the institution of the first *saṅgha*, probably towards the middle of the fifth century B. C., but the most ancient monuments known to us do not date back beyond the third. From that period down to the present day can be distinguished four stages of development (1) the art of the ancient Indian school, (2) the so-called art of Gandhāra, (3) the mediaeval art varying according to locality, (4) and lastly the art of modern times.

(1) *The ancient art* is almost purely Hindu in character. At most, we can recognize in it a few Greek and Iranian influences. It is known to us by a small number of architectural monuments; sculpture is represented by architectural ornament only, and painting up to the present has not been discovered. Apart from the hypogea which have served as temples, and the huge monolithic pillars set up by King Aśoka (*c.* 250), of which one was found at Benares in 1905, crowned by a superb capital supporting the wheel of the Law, the monuments are principally *Vihāras* and *Stūpas*. The former are houses once inhabited by monks, or chapels of a kind, once occupied by images of the divinities. A collection of these constitutes a monastery (*Saṅghārāma*). Very few have been preserved to our day (examples are found in the monasteries of Swat or at Takht-i-Boghas). These consist of a kind of tower with cupola or pitched roof, and trapezoidal door. As to the *Stūpas*, they were originally commemorative tumuli faced with stones and surrounded by a balustrade. Each of these monuments is composed of three essential elements whose legendary origin is as follows. When Śākya-muni was desirous of showing his disciples the right way to construct the *Stūpas* and decorate them symbolically, he took off his three monastic garments, folded each into a square, and laid them one upon another; then he set on top his beggar's bowl (*pātra*), and arranged above all his staff of pilgrimage. Thenceforth the *Stūpa* was composed of a square base of several steps; of a mass recalling a cupola or dome; and of a pinnacle or finial formed of an upright, garnished with several discs (five to twelve) one above another, which represent as many parasols, ensigns of authority. In the subsequent development of these buildings the highest and lowest portions (the base and the pinnacle) tended to increase more and more at the expense of the middle (the cupola). The primitive tumulus must have been surrounded by a wooden palisade. The stone *Stūpas*, the only ones that remain to us, were surrounded by a round or quadrangular balustrade also of stone, but imitating a wooden structure. This balustrade was furnished with several doors and covered with bas-reliefs. Surviving from the ancient period of Buddhist art are several *Stūpas* known to us: that of Barhut, whose bas-reliefs are preserved in the Calcutta Museum; that of Sanchi, whose four doors have been restored; and lastly that

of Bodh'-Gayā which is in a fair state of preservation. All date from the second century B. C. and are situated in Central India.

The sculptural ornaments of these *Stūpas* have this much in common that they combine in a single whole various consecutive scenes of the life of Buddha or of his previous rebirths (*jātaka*), scenes which in the later periods are reproduced separately. The style is conventional with a leaning to realism. But what chiefly characterizes this art is the absence of representation of the Master, or Buddha, in human form. His throne, surrounded by worshippers, is often seen, but it is empty; empty also is the place beneath the tree where Buddha was seated when he attained Bodhi. At most, some symbols (a wheel, for instance) replace his figure. According to Foucher this abstention from representations of the form of Buddha is due to the fact that at the outset of Buddhism the ex-votos and smaller objects which must have been brought back from pilgrimages represented only the symbols of the places of pilgrimage (e. g. a wheel where Buddha held his first discourse, and so forth). Respect for tradition and the principle of survival have probably caused this method of representing Buddha to be adopted in the first manifestations of Buddhist art.

(2) *Graeco-Buddhist* art is so called because it adopted classical forms to express Buddhist motives; but it is also called the art of *Gandhāra* after the north-west district of India (now Peshawar) where it originated towards the end of the first century A. D. It lasted up to the end of the fifth century, remaining purely Hellenistic except for some debts to Iranian forms and style. It treated, however, only Buddhist subjects, which sometimes demanded modifications even of form if they were to be in accord with the rules of the religion. Unlike what is to be seen in ancient Indian art, the art of Gandhāra introduces the representation of Buddha in human shape, his prototype being Apollo and the sole addition being a nimbus. As for the state of Bodhisattva, it is represented by the figure of an Indian prince in all the splendour of his ornaments. It is also in the bas-reliefs of Gandhāra, that the figures of Buddha and the saints appear seated on a reversed lotus-bloom, the base of whose bell-shaped calix serves for a throne. The favourite subjects, unlike those of the older Indian art, are rarely scenes from the *jātakas*, but principally from the life of Buddha, and are of an edifying character. They are disposed in separate panels which run in order from right to left, a system which (in *Stūpas*, for example) is connected with the custom of circumambulation in the direction of the sun's course; that is to say, the building around which the circuit is made is kept on the right hand. The bas-reliefs of this period are remarkable in point of execution for their very high relief approaching treatment in the round: also for their correctness of proportion, for the absence of stiffness in their draperies, and for delicacy of features.

But if the ornamentation of the buildings shows a considerable advance on the older art, their architecture did not greatly vary. At the same time, thanks to modification in the organization of the Saṅghas, which had grown larger, the cells (*Vihāra*) where the monks lived had come to be built one on to another and to form a sort of quadrangular cloister, surrounding a court in the middle of which were placed the *Stūpas*. These accumulated *Vihāras* formed a monastery (*Saṅghārāma*). Moreover, such *Vihāras* as contained images of the gods had been joined likewise. These had lost their partition-walls, which were now replaced by columns; and thus they became temples.

Finally these buildings were combined: a quadrangle of cells was constructed round the temple, and the *Stūpa* was moved outside. Such a combination is still exemplified in our own day in the construction of the Lamaist convents (see p. xlvi).

The best specimens of the art of Gandhāra are in the museums of Calcutta, Lahore, and Peshawar, and also in the British Museum, and the Museum für Völkerkunde at Berlin. We know nothing of the painting of this period, but to judge from later works of a derivative art which have been observed in the caves of Ajanta and in Chinese Turkestan (see later), it must have attained a high degree of perfection in fresco.

(3) The art of Gandhāra forms the base of several *mediaeval schools of art*. In Central India it persists almost pure in the school of *Mathurā* with its beautiful bas-reliefs of Bacchic subjects; while the school of *Magadha* which developed the Indian elements (i.e. the Brahman Pantheon) invented new forms. To it are due those well-known figures with long thin legs, salient hips, flexible as reeds—those figures overloaded with jewels, gesticulating extravagantly upon bosky backgrounds of stylized plants, that one sees on so many Buddhist buildings in India, Java, and Cambodia.

In Bengal an art analogous to that of Magadha lasted till the eleventh century in miniature-paintings on palm-leaves, whose technique passed presently to Nepal and Tibet.

In the south-east of India the remains of the magnificent *Stūpa* of Amāravatī, not far from the mouth of the river Kistna, which are preserved to-day in the Museum at Madras and in the British Museum, exemplify a very happy combination of Hellenistic with Indian art, indicating the existence of a local school during the first three centuries of our era.

On the other hand, in the famous grottoes of Ajanta, east of Bombay (West India), are found sculptures and, in particular, frescoes in bright colours of an individual style. They date from the first to the seventh centuries and represent scenes in the life of Buddha (the temptation contrived by Māra, &c.) as well as the Jātaka. This style is characterized by realism in the treatment of human figures and, still more, of animals. The ornamentation is rich, abundant, and varied.

(4) With the disappearance of Buddhism the art inspired by this religion died out in India towards the twelfth century. Let us consider its development in other regions, in some of which it has continued to the present day.

In *Ceylon* Graeco-Buddhist art had penetrated along with the religion in the second and third centuries, but only a few monuments survive. Then came the Indian mediaeval art which struck root, and is still found in our day, but in full decadence. In *Java*, on the other hand, this mediaeval art was grafted upon a native stock, and the temple of Boro-budur, built in the ninth century, and still in admirable preservation (out of 2,000 bas-reliefs only about 600 are missing), is one of its most striking manifestations.

In *Indo-China* the same art has undergone Brahman influences, as the ruins of Angkor in Cambodia prove. In Siam and Burma the modern art which has been evolved from it is distinguished, on the architectural side, chiefly by bell-shaped *Stūpas*, by the pointed towers of the temples, and by the affected and distorted forms of the figures of divinities and genii. The surfaces are overloaded with gold and with encrustations of tinsel which tire the eye.

But the most unexpected influence of Graeco-Buddhist art, and one which was only discovered a very few years ago, is that which it exercised on Central Asia, and, probably through that region, on China and Japan.

Excavations, carried out in recent years by learned expeditions from England, France, Germany, Russia, and Japan, have thrown a vivid light upon Buddhism and its art in *Eastern* or *Chinese Turkestan* and the territories immediately adjacent to the Chinese province of Kan-su. In the south of this country the oasis of Khotan was an important centre of the Buddhist faith. The art of Gandhāra, and subsequently that of mediaeval India, were transported there, to be modified only by the exigencies of the plastic medium, namely, clay, which the artists were obliged to employ; for quarry-stone does not exist in Eastern Turkestan. The wooden statues, which are excellently preserved, thanks to the dry climate of the country, are profusely painted and gilded. Imposed on an art which is fundamentally Indian or Hellenistic are to be noted some Persian influences and, to a slight degree, the influence of Chinese art. The miniatures found at Khotan show a quite original style.

From Khotan Buddhist art penetrated farther to the north-west towards the oasis of Kashgar and beyond to Tamchuk (to the north-east of Maralbashi), where have been discovered sculptures of the pure Indian type. More to the north, near the town of Kucha, numerous frescoes have been found in underground buildings, the subjects and the execution of which are Indian with traces of Iranian and Chinese influences. To the east of Kucha, in the marshy regions of Lake Lob-Nor, other frescoes have been noted by the learned traveller Sir Aurel Stein—very remarkable and close akin in style to the works of Hellenistic art. In the north of Chinese Turkestan, near Karashar, monuments have been met with in which the most diverse styles are associated, while at Turfan the frescoes show us a new art, that of the Uigurs, a Turkish people. This is an art formed of a native element with a mixture of Chinese elements and later of Tibetan, not to mention an influence of Iranian art exercised through the Manichaean monks in whose ranks Uigurs were found in considerable numbers.

Finally, outside Turkestan, but quite near to its frontier at Tun-huang (Kan-su province), the grotto 'of the thousand Buddhas', visited by Sir Aurel Stein and by Pelliot, has supplied us with several specimens of Buddhist art dating from the sixth to the tenth centuries, which present a very remarkable mixture of Indian, Chinese, Persian, and Tibetan styles.

The existence of this art of Gandhāra in a state of greater or less degeneration in Eastern Turkestan explains the presence of certain features in the Buddhist sculptures and paintings of *China* and *Japan* (in this matter we know almost nothing about Korea).

In purely national motives appear certain details, which are of Hellenistic style, e. g. the nimbus, the arrangement of the folds of the robes of Śākya-muni and the other Buddhas, and the costume of certain Bodhisattvas. Finally, it explains the very composition of certain pictures or bas-reliefs, as for example those treating of the scene of Śākya-muni's death or of his passage into Nirvāṇa.

But apart from these remnants of Hellenistic influence the style of the mediaeval sculptures and paintings of China and Japan is dependent upon tendencies identical with those which manifest themselves generally in the national art of these two countries. For *Korea* we lack documents, as we have already said, but we may suppose that Buddhist art there differs but little from that of China.

In *Nepal* the old Indian art is now represented by the five *Stūpas* raised, according to tradition, by King Aśoka; while the mediaeval art of India is reflected there in the *Stūpa* of Svayambhū-Nātha, near Katmandu. This monument, which has been repaired several times, is covered now with paintings and gilded plaques in the Lamaite fashion (see later). But it is in the making of large wooden statues and the casting of bronze statuettes of Lamaite divinities that the Nepalese, clever carvers and founders, excel. Miniature painting, introduced into the country about the eleventh century, has prospered continuously. A number of Persian and Tibetan motives make their appearance in what is, fundamentally, an Indian art (Sylvain Lévi).

The art of *Tibet* which dominates all aesthetic expressions of the Lamaites in general, whether Tibetan, Mongolian, or Chinese, has a distinctively individual character. In architecture especially, the Tibetans have developed a special type, remotely reminiscent of the Egyptian style, but of still unknown origin. Its characteristic feature is the predominance of straight lines and geometrical forms, and ornament is confined to uniform coloration of large spaces. The result is that the Tibetan buildings look like fortresses. The most remarkable monuments of the purely geometrical type are the 'gilded temple' of Gyantse and the gate near the temple of Marbo-ri at Lhassa. As an example of the uniform colouring may be cited the palace of the Dalai-Lama (*Po-ta-la*). In sculpture, the Tibetans borrowed the style of the statues at first (from the twelfth to the fourteenth centuries) from Nepal; but their national genius has so far transformed them that to-day it is Tibetan art which dominates Nepalese artists in their production of statues and statuettes. It is a curious fact that bas-reliefs, so widely known in all other Buddhist countries, are almost completely lacking in Tibet except on very ancient monuments, probably the work of Indian artists (S. Oldenburg). They are replaced everywhere by single statues and statuettes. Temple figures are often grotesquely muffled in costumes of rich stuffs like certain Madonnas or saints in Spain, Italy, and, above all, Latin America. As regards painting, Tibet lived at the outset upon its borrowings from Nepal or Northern India; but very few monuments of this period remain to us. The most important have been discovered recently (1911) in the ancient convents of Quara-qoto (M.) in the country of the Tangutes (province of Kuku-nor) by the Russian traveller Kozlof. These remnants of the ancient Tibetan-Indian art, which evidently had been imported into the country where they have been found, are mingled with products of the art which may be called *Tangut.* This displays Uigur, Chinese, and even Persian influences imposed on a fundamentally Indo-Tibetan art (S. Oldenburg). In its later development Tibetan painting transformed its Indian models at will, without experiencing any foreign influence, except perhaps, to a very slight degree, that of China, so far at least as concerns fineness of brush-work and perfect sureness of line. True, that this last characteristic is partly owed to the established and theoretically immutable rules, in accordance with which Lamaite pictures must be executed. Nevertheless, a certain freedom of fancy is permitted and one sees sometimes non-canonical attitudes and accessories which produce the best possible artistic effect. Certain painters add bits of landscape to the likenesses of gods and of saints with very happy result. Others try to give portraits in place of conventional figures. One of the characteristic features of Tibetan paintings is the extreme brightness of their coloration, which is, perhaps, the best means which could be used to make them visible in the half-darkness of Lamaite temples.

The only manner of painting among Tibetan and Mongolian artists is that of the miniaturist, and it is applied even to surfaces which attain the dimensions of several yards, as, for example, banners in certain processions or pictures exposed during the great feasts at Lhassa and other centres of pilgrimage. This manner is governed by the desire to omit no detail, and it is really astonishing to see in the imagery on one of the *Ts'ogs-šin* (see later), ten inches in height and eight in width, for instance, more than one hundred figures, each scarcely one inch high, but represented with all details which make them readily recognizable, though these are often indicated by no more than a single but characteristic stroke.

VI. Convents, Temples, and Sacred Images

(*a*) *The Convents.* The modern Buddhist Lamaite convents (*Dgon-pa* T., *Küren* M.) are ordinarily situated in remote places, often difficult of access, and if possible on a mountain and not far from a lake. They are planned on the lines of the ancient *Saṅghārāma.*[1] A quadrilateral space of ground is usually surrounded by a wall surmounted by numerous *dorjaq* (M.), streamers of ribbon on the end of a stick which are imprinted with the sacred formulas. These ribbons are held to have the power of keeping evil spirits away from the convent. We have here a relic of ancient animism. The principal entrance is on the south and it is surmounted by a kind of pavilion, in which are seen the statues of the four guardians of the temple (*Lokapāla*, see p. 139). Before this gateway at a distance of sixty yards are two columns, upon which on feast days are placed a vessel of incense and a lighted lantern. At the same distance and all round the enclosing wall of the convent are placed large cylinders (*Kürde* M.) covered with inscriptions and containing rolls of paper printed with prayers or *maṇi.* The pilgrims who have whirled these cylinders are considered to have pronounced the sacred formula *Ōm, maṇi padme, hūṃ* as many times as the cylinder has revolved. There are also little *Kürde*, which are carried by hand and

[1] This Sanskrit term is applied to-day only to the convent libraries.

turned for the same purpose. Nearer to the entrance are erected the *Stūpas* (see Glossary).

Inside, the convent is divided into three courts by walls either at a right angle or parallel to the south side. In the first case the principal temple is situated in the central court, with the cells of the monks on the right and left; in the second it is in the third court, the two previous ones being occupied by the monks' cells. In both cases, however, the main way, which leads from the principal door to the temple, traverses the entire length of the convent from south to north, for the temple is always placed under the north wall. In the middle of this way is placed an altar with incense-vessels, and at each side of it (or on the right and left of the principal temple) are smaller temples or chapels. The cells, which are replaced in Mongolia by felt tents, are of various sizes and are placed in accordance with the rank of the monk who is lodged there. Their importance diminishes from left to right, or from north to south. The dwellings of the superiors of the convent and of the 'Qubilghans' are close to the principal temple.

(*b*) *The Temples.* There are hardly any temples outside convents with the exception of some buildings at Lhassa and other great towns. The principal temple of a convent, whether of Tibetan, Chinese, or mixed architecture, invariably has its entrance towards the south. This entrance is often preceded by a vestibule, usually containing the images of the 'four guardians' and a prayer-wheel. The wall looking towards the north (the abiding-place of Buddha) is the only one which must have no windows, and against this wall are placed on its inner side the statues of the divinities, before which stands the principal altar of sacrifice. The roof is sometimes gilded, but must be always surmounted by one or two *Ghanǰir* (M.), a kind of gilded vessel filled with rolls of paper containing the prayers (*maṇi*). Moreover, in Mongolia, on the four corners of the roof there are gilded cylinders containing, besides the *maṇi*, a copy of the book of Atīśa (the 'sacred' organizer of Lamaite Buddhism) called *Lam-sgron* (T.) or *Bodhipatha pradīpa* (S.), i. e. the way of attaining the *Bodhi*. In Tibet the cylinder is covered with black yak-hair striped cross-wise with white. It bears the name of *J̌alǰan* (M.) or *Rgyal-mts'an* (T.) or *Dhvaja* (S.). Above the principal entrance, near the roof, is a gilded wheel with two gazelles regardant on either hand, to commemorate the preaching of the wheel of the law or of the four truths in the park of the gazelles.

Inside, the end of the temple towards the north wall is occupied by the altar of the divinities, frequently separated by a rank of columns from the main body of the building. This latter is divided by other ranks of columns into four or five parts. Thus are formed a central nave, and on each side one or two lateral naves where the seats of the monks are placed. These seats differ in shape according to the rank of the monk: arm-chairs with backs for the superior and the head of the choir, stools for the Gelüng, plain benches for the ordinary monks. The number of flat cushions (*qolboq* M.) made of felt and covered with yellow stuff, which are placed upon these seats, varies from one to nine in accordance with the rank of the Lama. Rank also accounts for the position in which the seats are placed. As in the cells, the left hand is more honourable than the right, and the importance of a seat diminishes from the altar on the north to the entrance of the temple on the south. The *Gebgüi* (see p. xxxv) are seated on each side of the door. The Superior of the Convent and the principal celebrant have in front of their seats small low tables upon which they place their *Vajra*, gong, bowl of holy water, rosary, and other things. The *Qubilghan* have seats apart, placed in the nave in front of the altar opposite the door, so that these 'living gods' partly mask the images of the divinities placed against the north wall.

The columns of the temple are painted red and draped with stuffs, or covered with frescoes like the walls; moreover, along the colonnades and also from the crown of the ceiling hang long ribbons of every colour of the rainbow. This mass of bright-coloured stuffs, which stirs at the least breath, combines with the absolutely unique odour and the half-darkness which broods in the building (the doors and windows are always covered with thick curtains), to impart a curious sensation, and to give a wholly singular aspect to a Lamaite temple.

(*c*) *The Altar and Objects of Ritual.* In front of the statues of the divinities grouped along the north wall rises the Altar, a kind of table covered with rich stuff, and of length varying with the size of the temple. Upon it are placed the following objects: (1) the eight 'glorious emblems' (*Ashṭa maṅgala* S., *Uljeitü naiman temdek* M., *Bkra-śis-rtags-brgyad* T.), i.e. the white parasol (*Chattra* S., *Gdugs-dan* T., *Sikür* M.) which keeps away the 'heat of evil desires'; the 'two gilded fishes' (*Matsya* S., *Gser-ña* T., *J̌ighasun* M.), 'symbol of happiness and utility'; the sea-shell (*Śankha* S., *Duṅ-dkar* T., *Labai* M.), symbol of the 'blessedness of turning to the right'; the lotus-flower (*Padma* S. and T., *Badma* M.), 'pledge of salvation or Nirvāṇa'; the sacred bowl (*Kalaśa* S., *Bum-pa* T., *Bumba* M.), 'the treasury of all the desires'; the mystic diagram (*Śrīvatsa* S., *Dpal-be'u* T., *Balbu* M.), 'the thread which guides to happiness'; the standard (*Dhvaja* S., *Rgyal-mts'an* T., *Doǰa* M.), 'erected on the summit of the palace of salvation'; and, finally, the wheel (*Cakra* S., *Kor-lo* T., *Kürde* M.), 'which leads to perfection'. All these objects, whose dimensions vary according as they are made in wood or in gilded metal, are supported on stands more or less decorated.

(2) Beside or behind this group is set a similarly arranged tableau of the 'seven jewels': the wheel, the '*Cintāmaṇi*', the woman, the official, the elephant, the horse, the military leader (see *Ratna* in the Glossary).

(3) In front of these two groups are arranged seven cups of brass or silver containing the seven offerings; the first two are filled with water; the third holds a flower and the fourth the scented wands (*Küǰi* M.); the fifth (filled with oil and furnished with a wick) represents a lamp, the sixth is full of water, and the seventh of viands. This is a symbolic survival of the objects offered in ancient India to every recipient of hospitality; water to wash the feet, water to wash the face, flowers and perfumes for the charm of their appearance and odour, and finally everything necessary to provide light, drink, and food.

(4) Among these seven cups is placed another vessel with incense (*Bdug-spas* T., *Jeke Küǰi* M.), and a large lamp (*Mar-me* T., *Jeke ǰula* M.), which must stay alight and shine with even brilliance by night and day without flickering. In summer this is

replaced by a lantern, lest the insects attracted by the light should scorch themselves and die of their burns.

(5) During certain of the services, for instance that of the Man-la (see p. 23), there are put also upon the altar the 'eight glorious offerings', or 'eight blessed substances' (or 'things') (*Bkra-śis-rdsas-brgyad* T., *Ü ljeitü naiman ed* M.), namely: the mirror (*Ādarsa* S., *Me-lon* T., *Toli* M.); the bezoar (*Ge-ham* or *Chi-dam* T.), i.e. concretions which form themselves in the stomachs of certain animals, and, as is said, also at the back of the elephant's neck; the curdled milk (*Sho* T., *Taraq* M.); the herb '*durvā*' (*Dur-bas* T., *Öbösün* M.); the fruit '*bilva*' (*Bil-ba* T., *Modonoi-temesün* M.); the shell (*Duṅ* T., *Labai* M.); finally the red lead, a piece of lead ore (minium) or mercury (cinnabar) (*Li-gti* T., *Singghu* M.). All these offerings recall the objects which were presented by a particular spirit or person to Śākya-muni himself.

(6) Sometimes are set also upon the altar the sacrifices of the five senses; a mirror (sight), a shell (hearing), a cup filled with nutmegs (smell), a bowl filled with fruit or sugar (taste), and a morsel of yellow silk stuff (touch).

(7) Finally a *pātra* and a gong (*K'ar-gsil* T., *Duldui* M.) with some decorative vases and flowers complete the furniture of the altar. The ritual objects employed during the service are also placed upon the altar for the time being. These are, in addition to the *vajra* and little bell which the celebrants generally hold in their hands, the following objects: the *Mandal* M. (*Maṇḍala* S., *Dkyil-k'or* T.), i.e. a dish of bronze, silver, or gold upon which are set representations of Mount 'Meru' in the same metal and of the four great and eight little divisions of the world (*Dvīpa* S., *Tib* M.). In the spaces between these representations, which suggest the toys of children, the offerings are set: little piles of rice, coins, shells, and the like. The *mandal* is placed at the right corner of the altar; beside it is the 'Kapāla' or *Tod-ma* T. (see Glossary), filled with blood or wine during the service of 'dokshit'. Balancing these two objects there stand on the left side of the altar, upon a pedestal, a mirror and the Bum-pa filled with lustral water for the same 'dokshit' (cf. above, p. xxxix).

For the sake of ornament there are also placed upon the altar, as has been already said, vases and pots of flowers, and the whole is surmounted by a kind of baldachino (*Bla-bri* T., *Labari* M.). Behind the altar and consequently immediately in front of the images of the divinities hang from the ceiling quantities of ribbons of five colours (*Ba-dang* T. and M.), cylinders (*J̌alčan* M.), and globes (*Čima-purma* M.) made of pieces of stuff in five colours sewn together and filled with scented hay, like our balls; further parasols, lanterns, scarves of silk (*Qadaq* M., *K'a-bdags* T.), and the like. All this forms a veritable forest in front of the images and obstructs almost completely the view of the divinities. We will, however, pull aside the tremulous curtain and penetrate to the images of the gods themselves.

(*d*) *The Images of the Divinities.* The Buddhist Pantheon includes, as we know, at least 500 deities. Each has a counterfeit presentation sculptural or pictorial. The statues, whose dimensions vary from the length of half an inch to several feet in height, are made of wood, papier-maché, ivory, stone, copper, iron, silver, gold, and especially bronze. They are covered with painting, with lacquer, and with gilding.

It is compulsory that there should be made in the lower part of each statue a kind of cavity in which are placed with certain ceremonies rolls of paper with inscribed or printed prayers (*maṇi*). These cavities are closed with a plate of bronze, sometimes bearing the image of the double *vajra*. Before being filled with this 'spiritual body' the statue is treated like any other object, but afterwards it can be treated only as a sacred object though it merely represents 'the image of the divinity'; it is not an 'idol', but a mere 'sacred image' such as are possessed by certain Christian churches. The best statues are made in Nepal, Lhassa, and at the convent of Dolon-Nor in Eastern Mongolia. Usually they represent but a single divinity, sometimes, however, accompanied by his attendants; but often groups of three, five, or eight statues are made, all having the same character and the same dimensions so that they compose groups (for instance, the Buddha triad or Ts'oṅ-k'a-pa with their two favourite pupils; the eight *Bodhisattvas*, the eight '*Drag-ched*' or 'the terrible ones', and others).

Pictorial art on the contrary represents a great number of divinities or persons symmetrically grouped. Most often the picture will portray on a large scale a divinity or personage as principal figure, and around him, on a smaller scale, scenes from his life, or divinities and accessory persons. Besides these there exist paintings representing maṇḍala or 'the domain of the saint' (Pl. XVI), as well as views of certain celebrated monasteries, and the like. The pictures are painted on a sized canvas prepared with chalk. This is stretched on a frame with zig-zag lacing as we should stretch a piece of tapestry. The colours are diluted with oil or water.

Among the pictures should be noted particularly the *wheel of life* or of the *sansāra* (*Sansarjin kürde* M.), which sums up pictorially certain principal parts of the Buddhist doctrine. A huge dragon holds a disc formed of three concentric circles. The central and smallest of these encloses the likeness of three animals—the snake, the pig, and the chicken, symbolizing the sins of anger, ignorance, and voluptuousness. The surrounding and much larger circle is divided into six segments representing the life of the six categories of living beings (cf. p. xxii, n.). Therein are to be seen men busy at their affairs, animals real or imaginary, the *preta* tormented by thirst, the twenty-two compartments of Hell grouped around its divinity (*Erlik-qaghan* M.), who presides over the last judgement and computes good and bad actions with the help of white or black counters which his attendants throw down before him. Finally the last two segments represent the war of *Asura* (see Glossary) against the gods, and the dwelling of the latter, a kind of Paradise. The third circle contains twelve images which represent, more or less vaguely, the nexus of the twelve causes (cf. p. xxiii).

Another class of paintings is formed by what is called *Tsok-shin* or *Ts'ogs-šin* (T.). These have not yet been studied in any of the works written on Buddhist iconography.[1] I shall proceed to give a brief sketch of them based on my own researches.

We know that all the Buddhist-Lamaite divinities are divided into six large

[1] With the exception of ten lines concerning them in Grünwedel's *Obzor sobranya*, &c. (Review of the collection of the objects of lamaite cult, belonging to Prince Ukhtomsky, *Bibliotheca buddhica*, VI, St. Petersburg, 1905, text, p. 54.)

groups: (1) the Buddhas, (2) the Bodhisattvas, (3) the Feminine deities, (4) the 'protectors' or tutelary gods (*Yi-dam*), (5) the Defenders of the Faith (*C'os-skyon* T.) and the 'eight terrible ones' (*Drag-ched* or *Drag-gsed* T.); finally (6) 'the minor divinities', genii, guardians of the four cardinal points, &c.

In the native albums of images of gods, e. g. that of the 300 divinities reproduced by Pander or by S. Oldenburg (see Bibliography), these divinities, to which are joined the saints and the *Arhats*, are classed as follows: the Saints (to the number of 51), the Protectors (42), the Buddhas (48), the Bodhisattvas (12), the Goddesses (9), the Defenders (27), the *Arhats* (18), the *Drag-ched* or *Drag-gsed* (12), the *Dākinī* and the *Devī* (*Gon-po*) (15), lastly the Yama, Lamo, Guardians of the cardinal points, genii, &c. (45). But what is the relative importance of each of these classes, and how are the divinities arranged in the Temple? No work on Buddhism answers this question in a precise and detailed manner. The pictures of the *Ts'ogs-śin* alone give some guidance in the subject to the student who has learned how to decipher and interpret them. Of the five pictures which I have been able to study, the largest comes from Nepal and dates from the beginning of the nineteenth century (collection of Mr. H. Getty); two others, of moderate size, come from Eastern Tibet (collection of M. Bacot in Paris) and seem to date from the middle of the last century; finally the two smallest come from Pekin and are still more recent (Getty and Deniker collections). In spite of their different sources, ages, and sizes, all these pictures are painted on the same scheme which I attempt to state in the lines which follow. (For the orientation see the frontispiece with the tracing of it and p. 160.)

At the top are three medallions surrounded with a border often of the colours of the rainbow, inside which are crowded numerous Buddhas (Frontispiece: A, B, C). Below is seen the image of the principal divinity (Śākya-muni in the *Ts'ogs-śin* of Nepal, Ts'oṅ-k'a-pa in the four others), surrounded by smaller images of his different attendants grouped to right and left (D). Lower still, and occupying the largest part of the picture, is what we may call the principal pyramid of the divinities (G). This is a tree which supports the images of a great number of the divinities, arranged in a certain order which I shall give later. On both sides of this tree-pyramid are seen, in the upper field, two spaces (E, F) filled by groups of monks or genii on clouds, while below can be distinguished the row of guardians of the four cardinal points, and on each side of the trunk of the tree two sirens or *Nāgas*. Besides these are displayed on the right of the trunk the images of the seven jewels and eight emblems (see p. xlviii), while upon the left there is invariably a personage who presents upon a plate the offering to all these deities, an offering which consists of a kind of pyramidal cake.

In the explanation of the frontispiece (p. 160) will be found the names of most of the divinities which I have been able to identify in the *Ts'ogs-śin* of Nepal. Here I shall give only their arrangement in groups. It is in a way concentric, and the rank of every one of the divinities is determined by the distance at which it is put from the centre; the principal divinities are the nearest to the central point of the pyramid which is occupied by Avalokiteśvara (No. 49 of the frontispiece). Above the chief divinity are three ranks of Bodhisattvas (Nos. 18–22, 27–31, 37–41) as his attendants;

on his right are three Buddhas (Akshobhya, Ratnasambhava, &c.) (46–48), and on his left three others (but of this I am not sure) (50–52). This central group, then, includes the principal divinities. It is surrounded on right and left by the goddesses (Nos. 17, 26, 36, 45, 23, 32).

Above the principal group is the double rank of the 'Protectors' (Nos. 2–6, 10–14), flanked on right and left by feminine divinities of the second order (*Kurukullā*, &c., 1, 7–9).

Below Avalokiteśvara stands the rank of Tathāgata or Buddhas which overflows on to the sides of the pyramid above and below (15–16, 24, 25, 33–35, 42–44, 53–68, 77–82, 91–93). In the rank below reappear different Bodhisattvas (69–76) and below them the *Man-la* (No. 101) with his twelve acolytes (83–90, 94–95, 107–108). In the same rank as he on right and on left and encroaching also at each end on the rank immediately below, whose centre is occupied by the *Dākinī* (113–119), are placed the eighteen *Arhats* (96–100, 102–106, 109–112, 120–123). Finally the very lowest rank is occupied by the 'Defenders' and the *Drag-ched* (124–138).

As for the *Ts'ogs-šin* which come from Pekin and Eastern Tibet, in No. 1, the large figure of Śākya-muni is replaced by that of Ts'oṅ-k'a-pa carrying upon his breast in a nimbus a little figure of Śākya-muni which itself encloses a tiny image of a Buddha of a bluish-grey colour. From this small image radiate rainbow-coloured ribbons or golden threads towards the groups of monks at the sides (E, F) and towards the 'pyramid of divinities'. The number of Bodhisattvas and of Dhyani-Buddhas is considerably reduced in the imagery of Eastern Tibet and of Pekin. On the other hand new personages appear in the most recent of the *Ts'ogs-šin* (e. g. that from Pekin in H. Getty's collection). Padmasambhava is seen there to occupy a place of honour, namely, that of the Buddhas, and to be surrounded by a multitude of feminine divinities. Among these figure Kwan-yin, unknown in the other *Ts'ogs-šin*. Several other Chinese saints are also to be seen in them.

However, if I attempted to treat this subject I should invade the domain of the author of the book to which I do but supply an introduction. Indeed everything that has been written above is to be regarded only as a means to facilitate the use and study of A. Getty's work by the reader. Thanks to the orientation which this introduction gives the latter, he will be able readily to understand the details involved in the history and representation of each of the divinities of the Buddhist Pantheon. It is not my business to estimate the value of A. Getty's work, but perhaps I may plead that in this book for the first time the problems of Buddhist iconography in general and in detail are to be found collected and systematically treated. Moreover the treatment is based on the author's own researches in Europe and in the Far East, and on information drawn from specialist works which the public finds difficult of access. These words should be enough to show the very great interest and utility of the book for general Buddhist studies.

J. Deniker.

PLATE I

GAUTAMA BUDDHA

ĀDI-BUDDHA

Table I

Ādi-Buddha	I. Vajradhara.
	II. Vajrasattva (J.) Kongōsatta.

ĀDI-BUDDHA

(T.) *mc'og-gi dan-poḫi saṅs-rgyas* (lit. most excellent first Buddha); or *dus-kyi ḫkor-loḫi mts'an* (lit. the saint of (the religion of the) wheel of Time).

(M.) *anghan burhan* (the beginning deity).

In the Guṇa Kāraṇḍa Vyūha it is written: 'When nothing else was, Śambhū was: that is the Self-Existent (*svayambhū*): and as he was before all, he is also called Ādi-Buddha.'[1]

The first system of Ādi-Buddha was set up in Nepal[2] by a theistic school called Aiśvarika, but was never generally adopted in Nepal or Tibet, and had practically no followers in China and Japan.[3]

The Nepalese school supposed an Ādi-Buddha infinite, omniscient, self-existing, without beginning and without end, the source and originator of all things, who by virtue of five sorts of wisdom (*jñāna*) and by the exercise of five meditations (*dhyāna*) evolved five Dhyāni-Buddhas or Celestial Jinas called Anupapādaka, or 'without parents'.

When all was perfect void (*mahā-śūnyatā*)[4] the mystic syllable *aum*[5] became manifest, from which at his own will the Ādi-Buddha was produced. At the creation of the world he revealed himself in the form of a flame which issued from a lotus-flower, and in Nepal the Ādi-Buddha is always represented by this symbol.[6]

All things, according to Hodgson, were thought to be types of the Ādi-Buddha, and yet he had no type. In other words, he was believed to be in the form of all things and yet to be formless, to be the 'one eternally existing essence from which all things are mere emanations' (Monier Williams).

According to the system, Ādi-Buddha was supposed to dwell in the Agnishṭha Bhuvana (the highest of the thirteen[7] Bhuvana, or celestial mansions), quiescent and removed from all direct communication with the world which he had caused to be created by the Dhyāni-Bodhisattva, through the medium of the Dhyāni-Buddha.

[1] Ādi (first), Buddha (wise one).

[2] According to Grünwedel, in the eleventh century A.D. Other authorities give earlier dates, but also posterior to the system of five Dhyāni-Buddhas.

[3] Although the system of Ādi-Buddha was not adopted in Japan, the Amitābha sects look upon Amida as the One Original Buddha (Ichi-butsu), while the Hossō, Tendai, Kegon, and Shin-gon sects call Vairocana (Dai-nichi Nyorai) 'the Supreme Buddha'.

[4] v. Glossary.

[5] The mystic syllable *aum* signifies the Tri-ratna (Three Jewels): Buddha (*a*), Dharma (*u*), Saṅgha (*m*), or Buddha, the Law, the Community. In the mantra, it is written *ōm*. v. *Tri-ratna* and *ōm*.

[6] The flame symbol is also represented in the centre of a moon crescent. v. Pl. XIX, fig. *d*.

[7] In Nepal, 13; in India, 10 Bhuvana.

PLATE II

a. Dai-nichi-nyorai

(b.) Vajradhara

(c.) Akshobhya

(d) Akshobhya

PLATE III

a. Amitāyus

b. Gautama Buddha

c. Vajradhara

d. Mañjuśri

It was believed that neither the Ādi-Buddha nor the Dhyāni-Buddha ever descended to earth, but left the creation and direction of the world's affairs to the active author of creation, the Dhyāni-Bodhisattva, and that as they were absorbed in perpetual contemplation, prayers were not to be addressed to them.

Other sects in Nepal, besides the Aiśvarika, set up an Ādi-Buddha, the most important being the Svābhāvika, which afterwards became the most popular Buddhist sect in China.

Svayambhū, or Ādi-Buddha, was called Iśvara by the Aiśvarika, and Svabhāva by the Svābhāvika ; but he was also given such special names as Vairocana, Vajrapāṇi, Vajradhara, and Vajrasattva. In the *Nāmasaṅgīti* (compiled before the tenth century A. D.) Mañjuśrī, god of Transcendent Wisdom, is referred to as Ādi-Buddha.

The Ādi-Buddha is always represented as a 'crowned' Buddha, that is to say, that although he is a Buddha, he wears the five-leaved crown as well as the other traditional ornaments of a Dhyāni-Bodhisattva, and is dressed in princely garments. His consort is Ādi-Dharma (Ādi-Prajñā).

In Japan, although the term 'Ādi-Buddha' is not known, the Dhyāni-Buddhas, Amitābha and Vairocana, are both looked upon as Supreme. They are not believed, however, to have evolved the five Dhyāni-Buddhas. The Amida sects claim that Vairocana and the other three Dhyāni-Buddhas are manifestations of Amitābha, while the Shin-gon sect claims that Amida and the other three Dhyāni-Buddhas are manifestations of Vairocana. They are never worshipped in company with their *śakti*,[1] while in Nepal and Tibet the Ādi-Buddha is frequently represented with his female energy, in which case he is called Yogambara,[2] and the *śakti*, Jñāneśvarī.

VAJRADHARA (Ādi-Buddha)

(Thunderbolt-bearer).

(T.) *rdo-rje-ḥc'aṅ* (He who holds a thunderbolt).
(M.) *Očirdara* (corruption of Vajradhara), or *Vačir bariqči* (He who holds a thunderbolt).
Symbols : *vajra* (thunderbolt).
ghaṇṭā (bell).

Mudrā : *vajra-hūṃ-kāra*.[3]
Colour : blue.
Śakti : Prajñāpāramitā.
Other names : Karmavajra, Dharmavajra.

Vajradhara is the supreme, primordial Buddha without beginning or end, lord of all mysteries, master of all secrets. It is to him the subdued and conquered evil spirits swear allegiance and vow that they will no longer prevent or hinder the propagation of the Buddhist faith. He is thought to be too 'great a god and

[1] Female energy.

[2] Ādi-Buddha as Yogambara, or the esoteric form (Pl. IV, fig. *d*), is represented nude with the legs closely locked. He wears no jewels and has the *ūrṇā* and *ushṇīsha* (v. Glossary). Hodgson, *Sketch of Buddhism derived from the Bauddha Scriptures of Nepal*, pub. Royal Asiatic Society, vol. ii, 1830, Pl. I, fig. *a*.

[3] Mystic gesture ; v. Glossary.

too much lost in divine quietude to favour man's undertakings and works with his assistance, and that he acts through the god Vajrasattva, and would be to him in the relation of a Dhyāni-Buddhi to his human Buddha '.[1]

Vajradhara is looked upon as Ādi-Buddha by the two greatest sects of the Mahāyāna school: the dKar-hGya-pa (Red Bonnets) and the dGe-lugs-pa (Yellow Bonnets).[2]

He is always represented seated, with his legs locked and the soles of his feet apparent, and wears the Bodhisattva crown as well as the dress and ornaments of an Indian prince. He has the *ūrṇā* and *ushṇīsha.*[3] His arms are crossed on his breast in the *vajra-hūṃ-kāra mudrā* holding the *vajra* and *ghaṇṭā*. These two symbols may, however, be supported by flowering branches on either side, the stems being held in the crossed hands, which is his special mystic gesture (v. Pl. II, fig. *b*, and Pl. III, fig. *c*).

As 'Karmavajra' (*Dorje las*) his left hand holds a lotus and his right hand is in *vitarka* (argument) *mudrā*: arm bent, hand raised, palm turned outward, all fingers extended upward except the index and thumb which touch at the tips, called 'triangular pose' (v. *vitarka*).

As 'Dharmavajra' (*Dorje c'os*) his right hand balances a double *vajra* at his breast, and the left holds the bell on the hip.

When Vajradhara holds his *śakti* in *yab-yum* [4] attitude, his arms are crossed at her back, holding his usual symbols. The *yum* holds a *vajra* and *kapāla* (skull-cup).

VAJRASATTVA [5] (Ādi-Buddha)

(Whose essence is the Thunderbolt).

Buddha of Supreme Intelligence.

(T.) *rdo-rje sems-dpaḫ* (soul of the thunderbolt).
(C.) *Süan-tzŭ-lo-sa-tsui* (斡資羅薩埵).
(J.) *Kongōsatta* (essence of a diamond).
Symbols: *vajra* (thunderbolt).
ghaṇṭā (bell).

Colour: white.
Bodhisattva of Akshobhya (Dhyāni-Buddha) and chief (Tsovo) or president of the five Dhyāni-Buddhas.

The position of Vajrasattva in the Mahāyāna pantheon is difficult to determine. He is looked upon as the spiritual son of Akshobhya, and is at the same time Tsovo or chief of the five Dhyāni-Buddhas. M. de la Vallée Poussin identifies him with Vajradhara. Eitel calls him the sixth Dhyāni-Buddha of the Yogāchārya school.[6]

[1] Schlagintweit, *Buddhism in Tibet*, p. 51.

[2] Prof. S. Chandra Vidyābhūshaṇa, 'On certain Tibetan scrolls and images', *Memoirs of the Asiatic Society of Bengal*, vol. i, No. 1.

[3] v. Glossary.

[4] The *yum* (*śakti*) in the embrace of the god (*yab*).

[5] *Vajra* (thunderbolt or diamond), *sattva* (essence).

[6] v. *The Dhyāni-Buddhas.*

The Svābhāvika sect in Nepal identified Svabhāva[1] (Ādi-Buddha) with Vajrasattva, who, according to the Nepalese Buddhist writings, manifested himself on Mount Sumeru in the following manner. A lotus-flower of precious jewels appeared on the summit of the mountain which is the centre of the universe, and above it arose a moon-crescent upon which, 'supremely exalted', was seated Vajrasattva.

It is not probable that the *image* of the Ādi-Buddha Vajrasattva is here meant, but rather the *symbol* which designates the Ādi-Buddha, a liṅga-shaped flame. If the moon-crescent, which arose above the lotus-flower, is represented with the flame symbol in the centre, instead of the 'image of Vajrasattva', it *forms a trident*.[2] The special emblem of the Svābhāvika sect was a trident rising from a lotus-flower, which, if we accept the above hypothesis, symbolized the manifestation of Vajrasattva as Ādi-Buddha on Mount Sumeru.

In the Musée Guimet there is an example of a Bodhisattva (or 'crowned' Buddha), *with four heads*,[3] seated, with the legs locked, and balancing a *vajra* on his hands in *dhyāna mudrā*. As the Ādi-Buddhas are always represented with the Bodhisattva ornaments, it may be a representation of Vajrasattva as Ādi-Buddha; and since Brahmā, chief of all the Brahman gods, has four heads, the idea of representing Vajrasattva in the same manner may have been borrowed from Brahmanism to distinguish Vajrasattva as Ādi-Buddha, chief of all the gods of the Mahāyāna system, from his manifestations which occupy a less exalted position in the Northern Buddhist pantheon.

As sixth Dhyāni-Buddha, Vajrasattva presides over the Yidam,[4] and has the same relation to the Ādi-Buddha that the Mānushi (human) Buddha has to his ethereal counterpart or Dhyāni-Buddha. The sixth sense is believed to have emanated from him, as well as the last of the six elements of which man is composed—the *manas*, or mind (v. *The Dhyāni-Buddhas*).

Vajrasattva is always represented seated, wearing the five-leaved crown and the dress and ornaments of a Dhyāni-Bodhisattva. He generally holds the *vajra* against his breast with the right hand, but the *vajra* may be held in the hand or balanced on its point in the palm of the hand. With the left, he holds the *ghaṇṭā* on his hip (Pl. IV, fig. *c*).

When seated on a white lotus, he is looked upon by certain sects as Guardian of the East.[5]

Unlike the other Dhyāni-Buddhas, he is always crowned with or without his *śakti*, whom he presses against his breast in the *yab-yum*[6] attitude, with the right hand holding the *vajra*, while the left holds the *ghaṇṭā* on his hip. The *yum* holds the *kapāla* (skull-cup) and *vajra*.

[1] *Sva* (own), *bhāva* (nature). Hodgson, *The Languages, Literature, and Religion of Nepal and Tibet*, p. 73.

[2] v. illustration, G. d'Alviella, *The Migration of Symbols*, fig. 159. Also see *Stūpa*.

[3] Collection Bacot, No. 28. It is catalogued as 'Brahmā' (Ts'aṅgs-pa), but Ts'aṅgs-pa does not carry the *vajra*. In the Pantheon des *Tschangtscha Hutuktu*, there is the representation of a Bodhisattva *with four heads* balancing a wheel, which seems to indicate Vairocana (v. *Vairocana*).

[4] Protectors of Buddhism.

[5] v. *Lokapāla*.

[6] v. Glossary.

In Nepal, according to Hodgson, he is seldom represented in statuary form, but is more often met with in paintings, and especially in miniatures. In Tibet, however, bronzes of Vajrasattva are not infrequently found, while in paintings, especially in *maṇḍala*,[1] he is often met with. In Japan he is found in statues as well as in paintings, and is called 'Kongōsatta'. The Japanese look upon Trailokya-vijaya Bodhisattva as a form of Vajrasattva.

KONGŌSATTA [2]

(Japanese form of Vajrasattva).

Symbols: *vajra* (thunderbolt).
ghaṇṭā (bell).

Colour: pinkish white.
Vāhana [3]: elephant (white).

There is a divergence of opinion in Japan in regard to the divinity whose representations seem to correspond with that of Vajrasattva in Tibet. He is seated with the legs locked, dressed like the usual Japanese Bodhisattva. The right hand holds the *vajra* at the breast, like Vajrasattva. The left hand rests the *ghaṇṭā* on the left knee instead of holding it on the hip like Vajrasattva. He may have from two to six or more arms, and has both a 'mild' and 'ferocious' form.

The 'mild' form has usually two arms, and is seated on a lotus-throne which is often supported by an elephant,[4] for which reason he is sometimes mistaken for Fugen (Samantabhadra), especially as the elephant frequently has three heads [5] and is always white (Pl. IV, fig. *b*, and Pl. V, fig. *c*). The *vajra* and *ghaṇṭā*, however, are not Fugen's symbols (v. *Fugen*), and the elephant may have four heads. If this form has four or six arms, the original arms hold the same symbols as the above, and in the same manner, while two of the accessory arms always brandish the bow and arrow (v. *Trailokya-vijaya*). If there are six arms, the symbols held by the fifth and sixth may vary.

Kongōsatta may also be supported by four elephants, on each of which is one of the Lokapāla or guardians of the Four Cardinal Points (Pl. IV, fig. *a*). He holds the *vajra* and *ghaṇṭā*; but instead of the bell, he may hold a lotus, which is the symbol of Samantabhadra, and this seems to be a form of Kongōsatta and Fugen merged into one. One often finds him in Japanese as well as in Tibetan *maṇḍala* (magic circles) in the centre, surrounded by the four Lokapāla. He is always represented seated, holding the *vajra* against the breast with the right hand, and the *ghaṇṭā* in the left which lies on his lap.

[1] Magic circles; v. Glossary.

[2] *Kongō* (diamond), *satta* (*sattva*—element or essence).

[3] v. Glossary.

[4] The elephant is the mount of the spiritual father of Vajrasattva, the Dhyāni-Buddha Akshobhya.

[5] Fugen is, however, usually supported by a white elephant with one head and six tusks, but it may also have only two tusks.

a. Kongōsatta

b. Kongōsatta

(c) Vajrasattva

(d) Esoteric Buddha

PLATE V

a. Saṃvara (?)

b. Aizen-myō-ō

The 'ferocious' form has six arms, a third eye, and a ferocious expression. Above the forehead is a skull, and a *vajra* issues from the *ushṇīsha*. The *vajra* and *ghaṇṭā* are carried in the same position as the above form, and he holds the bow and arrow and other Tantra symbols. His colour is red. The author has never seen the 'ferocious' form supported by an elephant. He is worshipped by the Tendai and Shingon sects, and is called 'Aizen-myō-ō (Pl. v, fig. *b*, and Pl. xxxix, fig. *a*). He is found in a triad with Kwan-non and Fudō and, in spite of his ferocious appearance, is looked upon by the common people as god of Love. As both the 'mild' and 'ferocious' forms hold the same symbols, *in the same manner*, may not Aizen-myō-ō be termed the 'ferocious' form of Kongōsatta?

THE BUDDHAS

Table II

The Buddhas	I. Dīpaṅkara Buddha.
	II. Kāśyapa.
	III. Gautama Buddha.
	IV. Maitreya[1] (The Coming Buddha).
	V. Manla (Buddha of Medicine).

[1] v. *The Dhyāni-Bodhisattva.*

PLATE VI

a. Gautama Buddha

b. Gautama Buddha

c. Dīpaṅkara Buddha

d. Gautama Buddha speaking his first words

THE BUDDHAS (NIRMĀṆA-KĀYA)[1]

'THE Buddhas who have been, are, and will be, are more numerous than the grains of sand on the banks of the Ganges' (*Aparimita-Dhāraṇī*).

The early Northern Buddhist school in Nepal adopted the system of 1,000 fictitious Buddhas, which so closely correspond to the 1,000 Zarathustras of the Zoroastrians that the system is believed to have originated in Persia. In this list appears for the first time the name of Amitābha, who became the fourth Dhyāni-Buddha.

Hodgson gives a list of fifty-six Buddhas taken from the *Lalita Vistara*, in which the last seven Tathāgata, called the 'Saptamānushi-Buddhas' (the seven human Buddhas), are: Vipaśyi, Sikhī, and Viśvabhu of the preceding *kalpa*,[2] and Krakucchanda, Kanakamuni, Kāśyapa, and Śākya-muni of the present cycle. Sometimes the Dīpaṅkara Buddha and Ratnagarbha were added, making a group of nine Buddhas.

Later on, there appeared a group of twenty-four mythical Buddhas, of whom the Dīpaṅkara Buddha (the first of the twenty-four) is the best known, and Gautama Buddha is added to this group, making twenty-five in all. Sometimes the last seven of the group (including Gautama Buddha) are reckoned as the seven Principal Buddhas, who, with the coming Buddha Maitreya, form a group of eight, and eight has remained a popular number among Buddhists for grouping the gods (the eight Bodhisattva, the 'eight Terrible Ones', &c.).

The group of the five Mānushi-Buddhas,[3] corresponding with the five Dhyāni-Buddhas and five Dhyāni-Bodhisattva, became, however, the most popular in Nepal; and was adopted not only in Tibet, but in China and Japan, and has lasted up to the present day.

A Mānushi-Buddha, according to the system of Ādi-Buddha, is one who has acquired such enlightenment (*bodhi-jñāna*) by his previous incarnations as Bodhisattva, that he is capable of receiving Bodhi, or Supreme Wisdom, a particle of the essence of Ādi-Buddha. He has become a Tathāgata[4] and can have no more rebirths, but at his death will attain Nirvāṇa-pada, or absorption into the Ādi-Buddha.

Those of the Northern Buddhist sects that did not adopt the system of Ādi-Buddha, looked upon the Mānushi-Buddha as a manifestation of, or an emanation from, the Dhyāni-Buddha; or, according to the system of the Tri-kāya, as a distinct nature or body (*kāya*) representing the embodiment of intellectual essence.

The system of the Tri-kāya[5] supposed each Buddha to have three *kāya* or

[1] Body of Transformation.

[2] v. Glossary.

[3] Krakucchanda, Kanakamuni, Kāśyapa, Śākya-muni, Maitreya. For the twenty-four mythical Buddhas, see R. S. Hardy, *A Manual of Buddhism*, p. 94.

[4] v. Glossary.

[5] v. Schmidt, *Mémoires de l'Académie des Sciences de Saint-Pétersbourg*; Schlagintweit, *Buddhism in Tibet*; and de la Vallée Poussin, 'The Three Bodies of a Buddha', *Journal of the Royal Asiatic Society of Great Britain and Ireland*, Oct. 1906.

bodies—that is to say, three distinct natures, which might be said to be living in three spheres at the same time.

1. On earth, as Mānushi-Buddha—mortal and ascetic, having passed through innumerable transformations on earth and arrived at the Nirmāṇa-kāya state of practical Bodhi (knowledge).

2. In Nirvāṇa, as Dhyāni-Buddha—abstract body of absolute purity, in the Dharma-kāya state of essential Bodhi.

3. In reflex in the Rūpadhātu heavens as Dhyāni-Bodhisattva, body of supreme happiness, in the Sambhoga-kāya state of reflected Bodhi.[1]

The *kāya* of a Mānushi-Buddha is material, visible, and perishable. Being of human form, the Mānushi-Buddha is born into the world and released from it by death. He did not, however, enter the world as a Buddha but as a Bodhisattva, nor did he reach the stage of Buddhahood until the moment when he attained Supreme Enlightenment, such as Śākya-muni under the Bodhi-tree. 'After the Enlightenment', according to M. de la Vallée Poussin,[2] 'nothing earthly, human, heavenly, or mundane remains of a Tathāgata. Therefore his visible appearance is but a contrived or magical body . . . the unsubstantial body which remains of a Bodhisattva after he has reached Buddhahood.'

It was believed by the Mahāyānists that when the Bodhisattva arrived at the stage of Bodhi, he would have acquired the thirty-two superior and eighty inferior outward marks[3] of a Buddha. In the *Mahāvastu* it is written that the future Buddha would have all the outward 'signs' at his last rebirth;[4] but the representations of Śākya-muni as a child do not show the protuberance on the skull[5] (*ushṇīsha*) which is the most important and probably the last acquired of the thirty-two outward signs. Nor as an ascetic is he represented with the full-sized *ushṇīsha*.[6] It is only after his attainment of Supreme Wisdom that the representations of the Buddha show the fully-developed protuberance on the skull—the receptacle, presumably, of the divine mind (*manas*), which was thought too great to be held in a normal-sized skull.

Although the different Mahāyāna sects disagreed as to the source of the divine intelligence, they were all of accord in believing that after the attainment of Bodhi the 'body' of the Tathāgata was animated by a divine force. This 'body of Transformation' (Nirmāṇa-kāya) of the Mānushi-Buddha has been variously explained. M. de la Vallée Poussin is of the opinion that it is a 'magical' body, in other words, an illusion; while Mr. G. R. S. Mead calls it the 'outer shell of the inner body of

[1] Eitel, *Handbook of Chinese Buddhism*. Sometimes a fourth body is given, the *Svabhāva-kāya*. According to Hodgson, *The Languages, Literature, and Religions of Nepal and Tibet*, p. 92, there are five bodies, the last two being Mahāsukha-kāya and Jñāna-kāya.

[2] 'The Three Bodies of a Buddha', *The Journal of the Royal Asiatic Society of Great Britain and Ireland*, Oct. 1906.

[3] *lakshaṇa*; v. Glossary.

[4] According to M. de la Vallée Poussin, the Bodhisattva would possess the marks in 'germ state' and 'ripen' them in course of his different reincarnations.

[5] v. Pl. VI, fig. *d*, and Pl. VII as well as illustration, A. Foucher, *L'Art gréco-bouddhique*, fig. 155.

[6] v. Pl. X.

PLATE VII

GAUTAMA BUDDHA (FIRST BATH GIVEN BY THE NAGAS)

PLATE VIII

a. Gautama Buddha

b. Gautama Buddha

c. Gautama Buddha

d. Gautama Buddha

Transformation'. Might it not also mean the transformation of the 'body' of the Bodhisattva as he approaches Buddhahood—the acquiring (or developing) one by one, in his different rebirths, of the thirty-two superior and eighty inferior marks which are outward proofs of his inner progress toward Bodhi?

Certain Northern Buddhist sects designated the Tri-kāya by the triad 'Buddha, Dharma, and Saṅgha'. 'Buddha' symbolized the generative power, 'Dharma' (or Prajñā) the productive power, and their union produced 'Saṅgha' (Dhyāni-Bodhisattva), the active author of creation.

The Mānushi-Buddha is always represented in monastic garments without ornaments, and with the right shoulder and breast, or only the breast, bare, and with the *ūrṇā*,[1] *ushṇīsha*, and long-lobed ears. He is usually seated with closely locked legs, but may also be standing.

Suzuki, in his *Outlines of Mahāyāna Buddhism*, writes: 'If we draw a parallel between the Buddhist and the Christian Trinity, the Body of Transformation (Nirmāṇa-kāya) may be considered to correspond to Christ in the flesh, the Body of Bliss (Sambhoga-kāya) either to Christ in glory or to the Holy Ghost, and Dharma-kāya to the Godhead.'

DĪPAṄKARA BUDDHA

(Buddha of Fixed Light).[2]

(T.) *mar-me-mdsad* (the illuminator or enlightener).
(M.) *ǰula ǰoqiaqči* (the maker of light).
(C.) *Ting-kuang-fo* (定光佛).[3]

Mudrā: *abhaya* ('blessing of Fearlessness').
vara (charity).
Colour: yellow.
Bodhi-tree: pulila.

In one of the innumerable past *kalpas* there lived a king called Arcishṭra in the royal city of Dīpavatī. During the same *kalpa*, Dīpaṅkara was a Bodhisattva in the Tushita heaven, and, as the time had arrived for him to manifest himself as a Buddha, he descended to earth, and, finding the king Arcishṭra[4] a suitable father, entered into the womb of his virtuous spouse Suśīlā.

The *Mahāvastu Avadāna* goes on to relate that 'when in the throes of childbirth, she requested the king to send her to a lotus tank. When she arrived at the side of the tank, lo! an island (*dvīpa*) sprang up in the midst of it. The Bodhisattva was born on the island. At the moment of his birth there was a miraculous manifestation of a large number of bright lamps (*dīpa*), hence his name Dīpaṅkara. On the second

[1] v. Glossary.

[2] Eitel. According to E. Denison Ross, 'that makes a lamp or light'.

[3] Beal. According to Edkins, 'Jan-teng'.

[4] In the *Mahāvastu* his father is called Arcismat and his mother Sudīpa.

day of his birth Dīpaṅkara commenced his philanthropic tour round the earth, equally useful to gods and men. . . . Megha offered five lotus-flowers [1] to Dīpaṅkara and asked that he might become, in one of his future existences, equal to Dīpaṅkara in power and knowledge and in every good quality. His request was granted. It was foretold on this occasion that Megha would become Buddha Śākya-muni of Kapilavastu.' [2]

The above legend has several variations. According to the *Bodhisattvāvadāna-Kalpalatā*, a Brahman, Sumati [3] by name, was present at the sacrifice of the King of Benares. The king's daughter, Sundarī, saw the Brahman and became enamoured of him ; but when he sternly rejected her suit, she became a Bhikshuṇī (Buddhist nun). Sumati then had a strange dream and repaired to Dvīpavati, where dwelt the Buddha Dvīpaṅkara,[4] to ask for its interpretation. There he met the Bhikshuṇī, Sundarī, who was carrying seven lotus-flowers of Utpala.

Now, the king had commanded that all the flowers in the surrounding country should be brought to the palace, for the Buddha Dvīpaṅkara was to pass through the city and the flowers were to be strewn in his path. Thus had Sumati hunted in vain for flowers to offer before the Buddha, and seeing that Sundarī carried seven lotus-flowers, be begged them of her. She willingly gave them to him, at the same time praying that, in their next existence, he might be her husband. Sumati promised that such would be the case, and telling her he would offer two of the flowers in her name, prostrated himself before the Dvīpaṅkara Buddha. He then offered the flowers, which, according to some accounts, arose in the air and formed a *baldachin* over the Buddha's head. Sumati then unbound his long hair and spread it on the ground before the Dvīpaṅkara Buddha, who, treading upon it, exclaimed, 'You shall become a great Buddha, Śākya-muni by name !' [5] This incident, as well as that of the flowers, is a favourite one in Buddhist art.

According to Grünwedel, the Dīpaṅkara Buddha is the twenty-fourth teacher of Buddhist law before Śākya-muni, and the last four alone (with Maitreya added to them) belong to the present period. The Southern school accepts the list of twenty-four Tathāgata, while the Northern Buddhists reckon the Dīpaṅkara Buddha as the fifty-second predecessor of Śākya-muni. Hodgson places him as the first Tathāgata of the actual universe, and the ninth predecessor of Gautama Buddha. The most popular system, however, is the list of twenty-four Tathāgata, with the Dīpaṅkara Buddha as the first and Gautama Buddha added as the twenty-fifth.

The Dīpaṅkara Buddha is believed to have lived 100,000 years on earth. According to Beal, he was 3,000 years on earth before finding any one worthy of hearing the divine truth. He then decided to convert the world and caused 'the appearance of a great city to proceed from his lamp and fix itself in space'.

[1] These flowers are generally represented as growing on one stalk or stem (Beal).

[2] R. Mitra, *Nepalese Buddhist Literature.*

[3] Or Sumedha, or Megha, one of the incarnations of Gautama Buddha.

[4] Called Dīpaṅkara in the *Mahāvastu.*

[5] Herr von Le Coq discovered a fresco representing this scene in a temple at Turfan, Chinese Turkestan. It is now in the Museum für Völkerkunde in Berlin.

While the people of Jambudvīpa (India) were gazing upon this miracle, fierce flames were emitted from the four walls. Fear filled their hearts and they looked for a Buddha to save them. Then Dīpaṅkara came forth from the burning city, descended to Jambudvīpa, seated himself on the Lion Throne,[1] and began to teach the Law. Legend claims that he remained another *kalpa* on earth 'turning the Wheel of the Law'.

In the *Mahāvastu* the Tathāgata is called 'Dīpaṅkara' (from *dīpa*, meaning 'lamp'),[2] while in the *Bodhisattvāvadāna-Kalpalatā* he is called 'Dvīpaṅkara' (from *dvīpa* or island'). Either name applies to him, for he was born on an island and miraculous lamps burned at his birth. One can, therefore, understand his popularity on the islands of Java and Ceylon and at all Buddhist festivals celebrated by illuminations.

According to M. Foucher[3] many of the merchants who carried on commerce with China and the Southern islands were Buddhists. As it was their custom to put their cargo and equipage under the protection of a Buddha, he thinks it not unlikely that the Dīpaṅkara Buddha was looked upon as 'Protector of Mariners'. In the *Saddharmapuṇḍarīka*[4] there is the description of a Buddha walking on the waves while his disciples remain in the boat, and in the caves of Ajaṇṭā there is a fresco depicting this scene.[5]

The Dīpaṅkara Buddha is represented in Java and Ceylon with the right hand in *abhaya mudrā*—gesture of protection, called 'blessing of Fearlessness'. He is always standing, with the monastic garment draped over the left shoulder, the folds being held by the left hand either at the shoulder or at his hip. The right shoulder is uncovered, which, according to M. Foucher, indicates an occasion of ceremony. One finds in India the statues of a Buddha much resembling those of the Dīpaṅkara Buddha in Ceylon and Java, but the right shoulder is generally covered and the folds of the garment are held below the hip. Like all Buddhas, Dīpaṅkara has the short, curly hair, the *ushṇīsha*, *ūrṇā*, and long-lobed ears.

In Siam, the Dīpaṅkara Buddha has either both hands in *abhaya mudrā* or the right only, while the left hangs against the folds of the monastic garment. (Pl. vi. fig. *c*.)

The triad in Java is:

Mañjuśrī—Dīpaṅkara Buddha—Vajrapāṇi.

In Ceylon:

Avalokiteśvara—Dīpaṅkara Buddha—Vajrapāṇi.

In Nepal and Tibet:

Śākya-muni—Dīpaṅkara Buddha—Maitreya, called the 'Three White Buddhas'.

[1] *Siṃhāsana*; v. Glossary.

[2] His name is also translated in this sense in the Tibetan and Mongolian sacred books.

[3] *Iconographie bouddhique*, vol. i, p. 80.

[4] Lotus of the Good Law.

[5] See miniature in the MS. Add. 1643 of the University Library, Cambridge.

The earliest images of Buddha in Japan resemble the Dīpaṅkara Buddha, with the exception that while the right hand is in *abhaya*[1] *mudrā*, the left is in *vara mudrā*, gesture of charity. The right shoulder is almost invariably covered.

In China, the Dīpaṅkara Buddha has always been popular, and is still worshipped there. In the cave temples of Yunkang[2] near Ta-t'ong-fou there are many examples, but only a few standing; the rest are all sitting with legs locked—with both the shoulders covered but with the breast bare. The right hand is in *abhaya mudrā*, while the left generally holds the folds of the monastic garment either at the shoulder or on the left knee. In the Long-men temple caves there are also many examples much resembling those at Yun-kang.

KĀŚYAPA[3] (THIRD MĀNUSHI-BUDDHA)

(The Keeper of Light).

(T.) *hod-sruṅ* (luminous protector).
(M.) *ghasiba* (from the Sanskrit) or *gerel-sakiqči* (luminous protector).
Mudrā : *vara* (charity).
Vāhana : lion.

Colour : yellow.
Bodhi-tree : banyan.
Dhyāni-Bodhisattva : Ratnapāṇi.
Dhyāni-Buddha : Ratnasambhava.
Mānushi-Buddha : Kāśyapa.

Kāśyapa was Mānushi-Buddha in the *kalpa* preceding that of Śākya-muni who had been his disciple in a former *kalpa*, and whose eventual Buddhahood he had predicted. He lived on earth 20,000 years and converted 20,000 people.

It is believed that he is buried under Mount Kukkuṭapada, in Northern India, near Bodh-Gayā, and that when Maitreya comes upon earth as a Mānushi-Buddha, he will go first to the mountain which will open miraculously. Kāśyapa will then come forth and give to Maitreya the garments of a Buddha, after which his body will be consumed by holy fire[4] and he will enter Nirvāṇa.

According to the Mahāyāna system, Kāśyapa is the third Mānushi-Buddha of the group of five, and the sixth of the group of seven ancient Buddhas.

Kāśyapa is sometimes represented seated on a Lion Throne, and is always clothed like a Buddha. His right hand is in 'charity' *mudrā*, and his left holds a fold of his monastic garment. The two folds held in the hand look like the ears of an animal.

[1] v. Glossary.

[2] v. plates of Chavannes, *Mission archéologique dans la Chine septentrionale.*

[3] Kāśyapa, lit. '(one who) swallowed light'. In other words, 'the sun and moon which caused his body to shine like gold Eitel).

[4] See R. S. Hardy, *A Manual of Buddhism*, p. 97.

PLATE IX

Gautama Buddha

GAUTAMA ŚĀKYA-MUNI[1] (FOURTH MĀNUSHI-BUDDHA)

Siddhārtha of Kapilavastu.

The Supremely Happy One (Bhagavān or Bhagavat).

(T.) *śha-kya thub-pa* (the sage Śākya).
(M.) *Sigemuni* or *Burqan* (Buddha Śākya-muni).
(C.) *Kiao-ta-mo* (喬答麿) and *Ju-lai*.
(J.) *Shakamuni*.
Mudrā: *vitarka* (argument).
dharmacakra (turning the wheel of the law).
bhūmisparśa (witness).
or *dhyāna* (meditation).

Symbol: *pātra* (begging-bowl).
Colour: golden.
Support: red lotus.
Bodhi-tree: *Ficus religiosa*.
Fourth Dhyāni-Buddha: Amitābha.
Dhyāni-Bodhisattva: Avalokiteśvara.
Mānushi-Buddha: Śākya-muni.

According to Buddhist tradition, Śākya-muni, after passing through 550 existences[2] as animal, man, and god, was born in the Tushita heaven as Bodhisattva in the *kalpa* preceding the present era. When the time came for him to manifest himself on earth and receive Buddhahood, it is believed that he descended to earth in the form of a white elephant with six tusks. Certain Buddhist sects, however, claim that Śākya-muni descended from the Tushita heaven on a ladder brought to him by Indra, and that the white elephant was only the dream of his mother, Māyā.

The conception of Māyā is variously treated by Buddhist writers. According to Satow, the Japanese Buddhists believe that 'Māyā saw a golden pagoda on a cloud. The doors opened and she saw a golden Buddha within. A white elephant with a red head[3] and six tusks appeared, carrying on its head a white lotus, on which Buddha took his seat. From the white spot[4] on his forehead shone a brilliant light which illuminated the whole universe, and alighting from the white elephant, he passed into her bosom like a shadow.'

Māyā's conception does not seem to have inspired the Indian sculptors to the same extent as the incidents of the birth of the Buddha;[5] of his first bath at which assisted the Nāga gods;[6] or of his first steps, when lotus-flowers sprang from the earth under each foot as he walked; or of his flight into the wilderness and meditation under the Bodhi-tree,[7] his temptation by Māra, and of his Parinirvāṇa or death. (Pl. XII, fig. *a*, and Pl. XIII, fig. *d*.)

[1] Śākya, the mighty (the Śākya Sage).

[2] Eitel gives '5,000 existences'.

[3] In one of the miniatures in the MS. Add. 1643 in the University Library, Cambridge, the Buddha is represented surrounded by four elephants with red heads.

[4] *ūrṇā*; v. Glossary.

[5] Every Buddha is born from the right side of his mother; v. miniature in the MS. Add. 1643 in the University Library, Cambridge.

[6] v. the *Nāgas* and Pl. VII.

[7] Each Buddha had his sacred tree under which he attained Buddhahood.

Up to the first century of our era, the sculptors in India were still so strongly under the influence of the Buddha's teachings that they had made no image of him. In fact, according to M. Foucher, they succeeded in 'representing the life of Buddha without Buddha'.[1] In the panels of the famous *stūpa* at Amarāvatī (North-west India), his birth and his presentation to the sage Aśita are represented by the imprints of his feet. On the Sānchi *stūpa* his departure from the palace is depicted by a horse with its saddle empty. At the temple of Bodh-Gayā, his first meditation is symbolized by a vacant seat. At Barhut, according to M. Foucher, an inscription on the *stūpa* explains that the personages depicted kneeling before a vacant throne are rendering homage to the very 'Happy One'.

As he was called a 'wheel king',[2] the Tathāgata was sometimes represented by a wheel with eight spokes. If the sermon in the deer park at Benares was meant, the wheel was flanked on either side by a gazelle.[3] A 'bodhi' tree, as well as a column topped by a trident,[4] symbolized his teachings. A ladder with footprints on the top and bottom rungs denoted his descent from the Tushita heaven, and a white elephant with six tusks his last incarnation.

According to Hiuen-tsang, the first image of the Buddha was made at the command of King Udayana, while the Tathagāta was in the Trayastriṃśa heaven, where he had gone to convert his mother to Buddhism. Upon his return to earth, after ninety days, the statue was completed. It was five feet high and was made from a precious sandal-wood called *gośīrsha*. When the Buddha appeared before the statue it lifted itself in mid-air and saluted him, whereupon the Tathāgata prophesied that Buddhism would spread to China one thousand years after his Parinirvāṇa.[5] The Chinese Buddhists claim that the sandal-wood statue was taken to China by Kāśyapa Mataṅga when he joined the Emperor Mingti's mission in the first century A. D., and that it was presented to the emperor.

According to other accounts[6] it was King Prasenajit who was the originator of Buddhist idolatry. He caused an image of Gautama to be made in 'purple' gold. It was five feet high. The Japanese Buddhists believe that this statue was made by the Buddha himself from gold brought from Mount Sumeru. Chinese history records a golden image of Buddha taken in a warlike expedition 122 B. C. in the Hieou-thou, a country beyond Yarkand, and sent to the Chinese Emperor.

At Lhassa, in the temple of the Dalai Lama, there is a gilt statue of the Buddha said to have been brought from China in the seventh century A. D. by the Chinese wife of the Tibetan king, Srong-tsan-gam-po, who was the daughter of the Chinese emperor.

The first image of Buddha in Japan was brought by a Chinese priest A. D. 534, and eighteen years later the Korean king sent to the Emperor of Japan a golden

[1] *Débuts de l'art bouddhique*, p. 8.

[2] 'A king who rules the world and causes the wheel of doctrine everywhere to revolve'—Edkins. (v. *Cakra.*)

[3] Symbol which is represented over the door of the entrance of every Buddhist temple in Tibet and Mongolia.

[4] *triśūla* ; v. Glossary.

[5] The Chinese, in order to fulfil this prophecy date back the birth of Buddha one thousand years.

[6] Fah-hian.

a. Gautama Buddha, ascetic

b. Gautama Buddha, ascetic

c. Gautama Buddha, ascetic

d. Gautama Buddha, ascetic

image of the Buddha, which is believed to be the statue now in the Zenkoji temple at Nagano.

The Indian images of the Buddha represent him with short locks, for, according to Buddhist tradition, Gautama, after his flight from the palace, drew forth his sword and cut off his long hair. In the *Mahāvastu* it is written that the hair was caught by the gods and carried to the Trayastriṃśa heavens, where it was worshipped as a sacred relic. According to some accounts, they carried away his turban as well.[1] The Gandhāra school never portrayed the Buddha, however, with short locks, but depicted the event by his taking off his turban and ear-rings. The short locks, following tradition, should curl from left to right [2] and were represented by the Indian artists in the shape of sea-shells. In China and Japan they sometimes took the form of round beads or sharp spikes.

He always has the *ushṇīsha* or protuberance on the skull, which is presumably the seat of the *manas*, or divine mind (soul) of the Buddha. It may be terminated by a round ornament [3] (the flaming pearl), or have, as in Nepal, a single flame issuing from it. In Ceylon, the flame is three or five-forked (v. Pl. VI, fig. *b*), and in Siam it may be seven-forked. The Buddhas, however, in Siam, as well as in Burma, often have the *ushṇīsha* covered by an ornate head-dress which is tapering in shape and somewhat resembles a *stūpa* (v. Pl. VIII).

There is usually the auspicious mark (*ūrṇā*) on the forehead of the Indian Buddha, and the lobes of the ears are long. The monastic garment is almost invariably draped over the left shoulder, leaving the right arm and shoulder bare, which fact indicates a ceremony of importance. In the early Indian images of the Buddha, the right hand is generally raised, the fingers extending upward, the palm turned outward,[4] while the left hand lies on the lap, with the palm turned upward. If seated, the legs are closely locked in the 'adamantine' pose; both feet apparent, the soles turned upward, sometimes marked by a wheel, or a button resembling the *ūrṇā* on the forehead. There may be, in Tibet, a *svastika* (but rarely) marked on the breast, or lying on the throne before the Buddha (Pl. II, fig. *c*).

When the sculptor wished to indicate the sermon in the deer park at Benares, a wheel was apparent somewhere on the statue, but in later images the fact was indicated by a pose of the hands called *dharmacakra* [5] *mudrā* (turning the Wheel of the Law).

Another early *mudrā* or mystic pose of the hands of the Buddha was the *dhyāna mudrā*, representing his meditation (*samādhi*) under the Bodhi-tree. In this pose both hands lie on the lap, the right on top of the left, with the palms turned upwards,[6] and the figure, with the legs closely locked, formed a *perfect triangle* v. (*Trikoṇa*).

[1] A. Foucher, *L'Art gréco-bouddhique*, p. 363.

[2] One of the thirty-two superior marks of a Buddha, v. *Lakshana*. The priests of the Ge-lugs-pa sect always turn their prayer-wheels from left to right.

[3] *Cintāmaṇi*, v. Glossary.

[4] The *abhaya mudrā* (v. Glossary) gesture of the Buddha in the episode of the mad elephant. v. miniature in the MS. Add. 1404 in the University Library, Cambridge.

[5] *Dharmacakra mudrā*, v. Glossary.

[6] Also *mudrā* of Amitābha.

As Buddha, 'Liberator of the Nāgas'[1] (*kLu-dban-rgyal-po*), he may have either the *dhyāna mudrā* or a special pose[2] of the hands, held at the breast with all fingers locked except the indexes, which are raised and touch at the tips. Gautama Buddha may be represented either seated on the coils of a serpent with its hood of five or seven heads spread over him, or seated on a lotus throne with only the serpent's hood protecting his head. (v. Pl. VI, fig. *a*, and Pl. XI, figs. *a* and *b*.) According to Buddhist scriptures, the Buddha once sat near a lake absorbed in meditation. The tutelary deity of the lake was the Nāga king, Mucalinda, who 'wishing to preserve him (Buddha) from the sun and rain, wrapped his body seven times around him and spread his hood over his head, and there Buddha remained seven days in thought'.[3]

Buddha, invoking the earth to witness his resistance of the temptations of the spirit of evil, Māra, is represented by the *bhūmisparśa mudrā*. The right arm is stretched downwards, all the fingers are extended, the tips touching the earth, the palm turned underneath (v. Glossary and Pls. I and VIII).

Buddha of the Vajrāsana (diamond throne)[4] has also the *bhūmisparśa mudrā*. He is awakening to the consciousness of Buddhahood from the state of Bodhisattva. He is seated under the Bodhi-tree on the 'diamond' throne, 'supposed to be the centre of the universe and the only spot capable of supporting the weight of a Buddha and his thoughts'.[5] The 'diamond' throne is sometimes indicated by a *vajra* lying in front of Buddha on the lotus throne.[6] The most beautiful example of Buddha of the Vajrāsana is in the temple of Mahābodhi at Bodh-Gayā, where he is not only worshipped by the Buddhists, but also by the Brahmans, as one of the *avatārs* of Vishṇu, and there is a Vishṇu mark on his forehead.

The Buddhas of the Gandhāra sculptures show strong Hellenic influence. The features are Grecian. The hair, long and wavy, is caught up in a knot in place of the protuberance of the skull of the Indian images. (v. Pl. XI, fig. *c*.) The *ūrṇā* is sometimes omitted, and the lobes of the ears are somewhat elongated by the weight of the ear-rings which he wore during his youth, but not to the abnormal extent characteristic of the Indian school. In the early images there is no moustache, but later statues have a slight moustache which one also sees in Japan and in China. In fact the Gandhāra images of the Buddha may have both a moustache and, when in the ascetic form of Gautama, a beard. The right arm and shoulder are never bare, but are covered by the monastic garment draped in the Grecian fashion over the left shoulder.

It is this form of the Buddha that found its way from India into China and Japan, presumably via Khotan (Chinese Turkestan), where there was an art-loving court in the seventh century A. D. The celebrated painter, Wei-chï-I-song, of Khotan, lived at that time and was much at the Chinese court. It is believed

[1] *Nāgas*, serpent gods.

[2] v. Glossary *renge-no-in*.

[3] Oldenberg, *Life of Buddha*, p. 23.

[4] *Vajra* is here translated 'diamond' in the sense of 'indestructible'.

[5] A. Foucher, *Iconographie bouddhique*, p. 91.

[6] Pl. II, fig. *c*.

PLATE XI

a. BUDDHA

b. GAUTAMA BUDDHA

c. HEAD OF GAUTAMA BUDDHA, GANDHARA SCHOOL I.

to have been through his influence that the Gandhāra school was introduced into China, where, however, the influence lasted but a few centuries, and into Japan, where it made a deep impression which has lasted till the present day.

Some of the statues of Buddha in China and Japan have a curious wavy line in the folds of the monastic garment, and Grünwedel explains that when the Buddha posed for the statue ordered by Udayana, the artist was so blinded by his glory that Buddha caused himself to be mirrored in the water so that the statue might be finished. 'The artist produced this reflection and thus the wavy lines of the robe are accounted for.'

Gautama Buddha is believed to have had thirty-two superior and eighty inferior marks of beauty.[1] The thirtieth of the thirty-two superior marks is: 'Webbed fingers and toes.' In the Völkerkunde Museum, Berlin, there is a fresco, discovered by Herr von Le Coq at Turfan, Chinese Turkestan, which represents the Buddha with webbed fingers, the webbed part being painted bright red. In the collection of Buddhist divinities owned by Mr. Okura, of Tokyo, there is a life-sized statue of the Buddha, with wavy lines in the folds of the monastic garment draped in Grecian fashion and with the fingers and toes webbed. But although the draperies of the Japanese representations of the Buddha often indicate the influence of the Gandhāra school, the features are never Grecian; and (with the exception of the eyes) closely resemble the Indian Buddhas with the long-lobed ears. The Buddha is never represented in Japan with Mongolian features and rarely with the right shoulder and arm bare, but the breast is sometimes uncovered and may be marked with a *svastika*. (v. Pl. XVIII, fig. *a*.)

Other examples of the historic Buddha found in China and Japan, and but rarely in Tibet, are:

1. Buddha as a child, standing with the right arm pointing upward while the left points towards the earth. It represents Buddha immediately after his birth speaking his first words: 'Now for the last time am I incarnate.' (Pl. VI, fig. *d*.)

2. Buddha as an ascetic, sometimes standing, but generally seated with his right knee raised. He is represented very emaciated and often with moustache and beard (Pl. X, fig. *c*.)

3. Buddha as entering into Nirvāṇa. He is represented lying on the right side with his right hand under his head. He is often accompanied by his two favourite disciples, Śāriputra and Maudgalyāyana. (Pl. XII, fig. *a*.)

The Buddhist formula is 'Buddha, Dharma, Saṅgha' (Buddha—the Law—the Assembly). In China, Dharma and Saṅgha are personified and form a popular triad with the Buddha. They symbolize the generative power (Buddha), the productive power (Dharma), and the active power of creation (Saṅgha).

'Dharma' is represented with four arms. The normal ones are in *namaḥkara* (prayer) *mudrā*—the other two hands hold respectively a rosary and a book.

'Saṅgha' is represented with two arms—one resting on the knee and the other holding a lotus-flower.

[1] *Lakshaṇa*, v. Glossary.

When the Buddha is in the centre with Dharma at the right and Saṅgha at the left, the triad is called the Upāyikā, or Theistic Triad. When Dharma is in the centre with the Buddha at the right and Saṅgha at the left, it is called the Prajñikā or Atheistic Triad.

The statue representing Dharma seems to combine Avalokiteśvara, god of Mercy, and Mañjuśrī, god of Wisdom, by its *mudrā* and symbols, for the *namaḥkara mudrā* and rosary belong to the former, and the book, the Prajñāpāramitā, to the latter.

One also finds the Buddha in a triad with Maitreya and Avalokiteśvara, as well as surrounded by the 'eight Bodhisattva'.

MAITREYA (the future fifth Mānushi Buddha)

(The Compassionate One).

(T.) *byams-pa* (pro. *cam-pa*) (kind, loving).
(M.) *maijdari* (from the Sanskrit).
(C.) *Mi-lo-fo* (彌 勒 佛).
(J.) *Miroku*.

Mudrā: *dharmacakra* (turning the Wheel of the Law), or
vara (charity), and
vitarka (argument).

Symbols: *kalaśa* (vase).
cakra (wheel).

Colour: yellow.
Emblem: *campa* (*nāga pushpa*)[1] (white flower with yellow centre).
Distinctive marks: *stūpa* in head-dress.
scarf around the waist tied at left side.
Dhyāni-Buddha: Amoghasiddha.
Dhyāni-Bodhisattva: Viśvapāṇi.
Mānushi-Buddha: Maitreya.
The Dhyāni-Bodhisattva form of Maitreya belongs to the group of eight Dhyāni-Bodhisattva.

Buddhist tradition divides the period between the death of Buddha and the manifestation of Maitreya in the actual universe into three divisions of time[2]: I. Period of 500 years, 'the turning of the Wheel of the first Law'. II. Period of 1,000 years, 'the law of images' (*Saddharma pratirūpaka*). III. Period of 3,000 years, 'the turning of the Wheel of the second Law', after which Maitreya will leave the Tushita heaven and come upon earth to 'establish the lost truths in all their purity'.

Śākya-muni is supposed to have visited Maitreya in the Tushita heaven when he appointed him to be his successor, and many Buddhist sages (*arhats*) are believed to have had communion with him, transporting themselves by supernatural means to the Tushita heaven to seek enlightenment on various religious points. The great Asaṅga, one thousand years after the birth of Buddha, ascended to the Tushita heaven, where

[1] Foucher, *Iconographie bouddhique*, p. 113.

[2] Grünwedel, *Buddhist Art*, p. 181. Usual length of time given 5,000 years, in China 3,000.

he was initiated, by Maitreya, into the mystic doctrine of the Tantra, which he grafted on to the Mahāyāna school in the beginning of the sixth century. Maitreya is therefore looked upon, by certain sects, as the founder of the Tantra school.

He is the only Bodhisattva who figures in Southern Buddhism, and statues of him are found in Ceylon, Burma, and Siam, generally in company with Gautama Buddha. His worship was at its height in India, according to the accounts of the Chinese pilgrims, in the fifth century, and there are many statues of him in the Gandhāra sculptures of that period. He is represented either seated as a Buddha with his long hair drawn up in a knot on the top of his head forming the *ushṇīsha*, his legs closely locked, and his hands in *dharmacakra* (teaching) *mudrā*; or as a Bodhisattva, in which case he is standing, with his long hair hanging over his shoulders, while a part of it is caught up in a knot on his head. His hands form 'argument' and 'charity' *mudrā*.

In the Indian sculptures, as Bodhisattva, he is standing. His hair is arranged mitre-shaped. His hands form the usual *mudrā*, and in the left is a vase which is round, while in the sculptures of the Gandhāra school the vase is oval or pointed in shape.

The early Mongolian images of Maitreya are also generally standing and hold in their hands, forming 'argument' and 'charity' *mudrā*, the stems of flowers called 'campa', which, however, in the bronzes often resembles the lotus-flower. If painted, the campa is white with a yellow centre.

In Tibet, Maitreya is also represented both as Buddha and Bodhisattva. As Buddha, he has short curly hair, the *ushṇīsha*, *ūrṇā*, and long-lobed ears. He wears the monastic garment, with the right shoulder bare, and the hands are in *dharmacakra mudrā*. He is seated, but the legs, instead of being locked, are both pendent, and the feet may be unsupported. He is the only divinity in the Northern Buddhist pantheon represented seated in European fashion. (Pl. xv, fig. *b*.)

As Bodhisattva, he may be also seated with the legs closely locked, which, according to M. Foucher,[1] was possibly his attitude in the Tushita heaven when teaching the Arhats; but as Bodhisattva he is usually seated in European fashion with each foot resting on a small lotus-flower *āsana*. (v. Pl. xv, fig. *a*.) He is represented as an Indian prince with all the Bodhisattva ornaments, and in the crown is generally a *stūpa*-shaped ornament which is his distinctive mark, but he may be without a crown and have the *stūpa* in his hair. His hands are in *dharmacakra mudrā* and may be holding the stems of flowers supporting his two symbols, the vase and the wheel, on a level with his shoulders. (Pl. xv, fig. *c*.) He may be seated on a throne supported by lions and have five Dhyāni Buddhas in the nimbus. (Pl. xiv.)

He may have an antelope skin over his left shoulder, in which case he is generally standing. His hands are in *vitarka* and *vara mudrā*, and he either carries the vase, or the two symbols—vase and wheel—are supported by lotus-flowers on a

[1] *Iconographie bouddhique*, p. 113. (v. Pl. iii, fig. *d*.)

level with each shoulder. It is in this latter attitude that he is represented in the group of 'eight Bodhisattva'. He never carries the wheel, which is always supported by a lotus-flower.

When the *stūpa* is not well defined in the crown and he is standing with the hands in 'argument' and 'charity' *mudrā* holding the vase, with the antelope skin over the left shoulder, he resembles a form of Padmapāṇi [1] and is extremely difficult to determine. Padmapāṇi's distinctive mark is a small image of Amitābha in his crown, but it may be missing.

Maitreya's two distinctive marks are a *stūpa* in the crown and a scarf wound around the waist and tied on the left side with the ends falling to the feet; but these may be missing. According to Grünwedel, if all the distinctive marks are missing, one may call this form 'Maitreya', as he is a more popular deity than Padmapāṇi.

The *stūpa* in the crown of Maitreya is thought to refer to the belief that a *stūpa* on Mount Kukkuṭapada near Bodh-Gayā covers a spot where Kāśyapa Buddha is lying. When Maitreya leaves the Tushita heaven, he will go to the mountain, which will open by magic, and Kāśyapa will give him the garments of a Buddha.[2]

In the Gandhāra sculptures, Maitreya was represented much larger than his assistants. According to Hiuen-tsang, there is a statue of Maitreya at Dardu, north of the Punjab, in wood, which is one hundred feet high. It is believed to have been made by an artist whom the Lohan Madhyāntika caused, by magic, to mount three times to the Tushita heaven to contemplate the form of Maitreya before carving the statue.[3]

The Chinese claim that Maitreya was thirty feet high. According to Edkins, in the province of Che-kiang there is a stone image of Maitreya forty feet high, and still another seventy feet high. At Peking in the Yung-ho-kung, there is a wooden image still higher.

The bronze and stone images of Mi-lo-fo (Maitreya) of the sixth century A.D. are usually standing, with the right hand in *abhaya mudrā*, and the left in *vara mudrā*. In the cave temples of Yun-kang and Long-men there are many examples of Maitreya seated European fashion, but the feet are crossed.

In Japan, he is seated with legs locked, his hands in *dhyāna mudrā* holding a vase, and in this form he somewhat resembles the Tibetan Amitāyus.

Maitreya is found in a triad with Gautama Buddha and Avalokiteśvara, and also with the goddesses, Kurukulā and Bhṛikutī.

[1] v. *Padmapāṇi*.

[2] v. *Kāśyapa*.

[3] Beal, *Buddhist Records of the Western World*, vol. i, p. 134.

a. The Parinirvāṇa of the Buddha

b. Mañjuśrī

c. Juntei Kwan-non

MANLA (rank of Buddha)

(The Supreme Physician).

(S.) *Bhayśajaguru* or *Pindolā*.
(T.) *sman-bla* (pro. *Manla*) (supreme medicine).
(M.) *otoči* (prince of medicine) or *binduria* (beryl).
(C.) *Yaō-shih-fo* (藥 師 佛).
(J.) *Yaku-shi* and *Binzura sama*.

Mudrā: *vara* (charity).
dhyāna (meditation).
Symbols: *pātra* (begging-bowl).
myrobalans (T. A-ru-ra, a golden fruit).[1]
Colour: blue.

Manla, the Buddhist Aesculapius, is not only venerated in Tibet and Manchuria, but in China and Japan, where he is a most popular divinity. He is called the 'Healing Buddha', and is said to dispense spiritual medicine when properly worshipped. It is even believed in all these countries that an efficacious cure may be accomplished by merely touching the image.

In China he is worshipped under the name of 'Yaō-shih-fo' (Bhayśajaguru), or Healing Teacher and Medical King. He is the ruler of the Eastern world and has two attendants, the Bodhisattva, Ji-kwang-pien-chau and Yue-kwang-pien-chau, who are believed to assist him in removing all suffering.

In Japan, as Yaku-shi, he is sometimes counted among the five Dhyāni-Buddhas, taking the place of either Vairocana or Akshobhya. He is also one of the thirteen Buddhas of the Shingon sect, and is believed to look after the soul on the seventh week after death (v. *Fudō*). Yaku-shi is always placed inside the temple, and may be found in a triad with Amitābha and Gautama Buddha.

There is a popular form of Yaku-shi in Japan called 'Binzura Sama', which is worshipped by the common people as a veritable fetish. His head is usually covered by a hood, his hands with mittens, and there are often so many bibs around his neck, one on top of the other, that his face is scarcely visible. He is looked upon as Piṇḍola, one of the sixteen Japanese Rakhan (Arhats), and is always placed outside of the temple or principal shrine, for the following reason: 'According to popular Japanese tradition he was expelled from the Sixteen for having violated the vow of chastity by remarking upon the beauty of a woman, and hence his usual situation outside the temple.' (Satow.) It is also believed that, at Manla's request, the power of curing all ills was conferred on him by Gautama Buddha.

As a Buddha, he is represented with the *ūrṇā*, *ushṇīsha*, and short, curly hair. He wears the monastic robe, and is seated with the legs crossed. His left hand, lying in his lap in 'meditation' *mudrā*, holds either a branch with the fruit, or the fruit alone, of the myrobalans, a medicinal plant found in India and other tropical countries. The fruit resembles a lemon and is five-sided. (v. Pl. LX, fig. *c*.)

In Tibet, as Bodhisattva, he wears the five-leaved crown as well as all the usual

[1] *Terminalia* of botanists.

ornaments, and is represented in paintings rather than in bronzes. In China and Japan, on the contrary, he is more usually found in bronzes; and while he wears the five-leaved crown, he is dressed like a Buddha and wears few ornaments. His symbols and *mudrā* are the same as his form as Buddha. If painted, he is blue.

There is a group of eight medical Tathāgata who are believed to have created the medicinal plants, and Manla is the most popular of this group.[1] They figure in Pander's *Pantheon des Tschangtscha Hutuktu*, and Manla is represented (No. 142) as a Buddha holding a branch of the myrobalans on which is the fruit. If painted, three of the gods are red, and four yellow, while Manla is blue.

[1] v. plate of *tsok-shin* (frontispiece), where all the eight Tathāgata are represented with the alarm staff (*khakkhara*).

PLATE XIII

a. Stūpa containing prayers

b. Gautama Buddha

PLATE XIV

Maitreya on a Lion Throne

THE DHYĀNI-BUDDHAS

TABLE III

Dhyāni-Buddhas	I. Vairocana.	
	II. Akshobhya.	
	III. Ratnasambhava.	
	IV. Amitābha . .	I. Amitāyus. II. Amito-fō. III. Amida.
	V. Amoghasiddha.	

THE DHYĀNI-BUDDHAS (DHARMA-KĀYA)

(Buddhas of Meditation).

The Dhyāni-Buddha is the first *kāya* or 'body' in the Buddhist Trinity (Tri-kāya), and dwells quiescent in the Arupadhātu heaven in abstract form of perfect unity. He is the 'body of Dharma' (Dharma-kāya), or the *inner enlightened* body of a Buddha. According to the Yoga doctrine, the law preached by the Nirmāṇa-kāya (Mānushi-Buddha) is exoteric. When he preaches the *esoteric* doctrine he is inspired by the Dharma-kāya—his Dhyāni-Buddha. The 'body of Dharma' is identified by certain Buddhist sects with Dharma, in the Triad, 'Buddha, Dharma, Saṅgha', or the *Tri-ratna* (Three Jewels). Dharma is looked upon by them as the material essence, which, united with the intellectual essence (Buddha), produced Saṅgha, or the Dhyāni-Bodhisattva, the active power of creation.

According to the system of Ādi-Buddha, the group of five Dhyāni-Buddhas (Vairocana, Akshobhya, Ratnasambhava, Amitābha, and Amoghasiddha) was evolved by the Ādi-Buddha. Each of the Dhyāni-Buddhas received, 'together with his existence, the virtues of that *jñāna* (wisdom) and *dhyāna* (meditation), to the exertion of which, by Ādi-Buddha, he owed his existence: and by similar exertion of both he produced a Dhyāni-Bodhisattva.'[1]

Besides the five Dhyāni-Buddhas who evolved the five Dhyāni-Bodhisattvas, there is a sixth,[2] Vajrasattva, who is looked upon as 'president' of the group of five, and was adopted by certain sects as Ādi-Buddha. It is believed that the sixth sense of man emanated from him, while the other five organs of sense (sight, sound, smell, taste, and touch) proceeded from the five Dhyāni-Buddhas.

Likewise the five colours, white, blue, yellow, red, and green, are believed to emanate from the five Dhyāni-Buddhas as well as five of the six elements of which man is composed: earth, water, fire, air, and ether. The sixth element, variously called wisdom, the soul, or the mind (*manas*), is claimed to be a particle of the essence of Ādi-Buddha.

The five Dhyāni-Buddhas, with the direction where they are located, their corresponding elements, senses, colours, *bīja*, and Dhyāni-Bodhisattva, are:

[1] Hodgson, *The Languages, Literature, and Religion of Nepal and Tibet*, p. 28.

[2] The group of five is the exoteric group. The sixth belongs to the esoteric system.

	Location.	*Element.*	*Sense.*[1]	*Colour.*	*Bīja.*[2]	*Dhyāni-Bodhisattva.*
Vairocana	central	ether	sound	white	A	Samantabhadra.
Akshobhya	east	air	touch	blue	Y	Vajrapāṇi.
Ratnasambhava	south	fire	sight	yellow	R	Ratnapāṇi.
Amitābha	west	water	taste	red	V or (B)	Avalokiteśvara.
Amoghasiddha	north	earth	smell	green	L	Viśvapāṇi.

The sixth Dhyāni-Buddha, with the corresponding direction where located, element, sense, and colour, is :

Vajrasattva—location, above the central point ; element, the divine mind (*manas*) ; sense, intuition ; colour, white.

In Japan Vajrasattva is sometimes represented with a rainbow aura, which possibly signifies the 'rainbow' body, or the accomplishment of Perfection. According to M. de la Vallée Poussin, Vajrasattva may be looked upon as 'a combination of the five elements'. As his colour is 'white', which potentially contains all the five colours, the 'rainbow' aura may be the esoteric sign of Vajrasattva as the sixth Dhyāni-Buddha.

According to Lloyd,[3] the Chinese and Japanese Buddhists invoke the Dhyāni-Buddhas by a six-syllabled *mantra* composed of six Chinese characters, the sounds of which are : A-ba-ra-ka-ki, and the sixth is *un*, which they claim signifies *hūṃ*. Might it not be inferred from this that the *bīja-mantra* of the sixth Dhyāni-Buddha is *hūṃ* ?

The Dhyāni-Buddhas are generally seated in 'adamantine' pose of deepest meditation, the legs firmly locked with the soles of the feet turned upward ; and they wear the monastic garments with the right shoulder usually bare, and no ornaments. They have the sign of fore-knowledge (*ūrṇā*) on the forehead and the lobes of the ears are long. The hair may be drawn up on the head, in a knot,[4] forming the traditional *ushṇīsha*, or be represented in short curls resembling sea-shells or beads. In the latter case, the skull has always a protuberance (also called *ushṇīsha*) from which, in the southern images of Buddha, usually issues a flame, three or five-forked.

In Japan the Dhyāni-Buddhas are also represented in monastic garments, with the *ūrṇā* and long-lobed ears, but instead of the protuberance on the skull like the Tibetan Dhyāni-Buddhas, they may have the hair arranged in a high *ushṇīsha*. (v. Pl. II, fig. *a*.) In Japanese Buddhism there is no such term as *Dhyāni*-Buddha (nor *Dhyāni*-Bodhisattva). The four Celestial Buddhas, Akshobhya, Ratnasambhava, Amitābha, and Amoghasiddha, are believed by the Shingon sect to be merely manifestations of Vairocana,[5] who, as Bodhisattva, was known as *Prajñā*, while the other four were : Vajrasattva, Ākāśagarbha, Avalokiteśvara, and Vajrapāṇi. The list of

[1] According to Hodgson, the Nepalese school claimed that from Vairocana proceeded the sense of sight ; from Akshobhya, sound ; from Ratnasambhava, smell ; from Amoghasiddha, touch.

[2] Germ or seed ; v. Glossary.

[3] *The Creed of Half Japan*, p. 240.

[4] Gandhāra school.

[5] The Amida sects claim that Vairocana and the other three Dhyāni-Buddhas were emanations or manifestations of Amitābha.

Celestial Buddhas in Japan also varies. One often finds: I, Yakushi (Bhaishajya-guru); II, Taho (Prabhūtaratna); III, Vairocana; IV, Akshobhya; and V, Amoghasiddha or Śākya-muni. Yakushi is sometimes placed second and Jizō third.

Each Dhyāni-Buddha possesses a *śakti* (female energy), who, if painted, takes his special colour but in a paler tonality. When represented with his *śakti*, the Dhyāni-Buddha is seated in the *yab-yum* attitude and is dressed like an Indian prince with the thirteen Bodhisattva ornaments. The Dhyāni-Buddhas are always crowned when holding the *śakti*, and hence are called by the Tibetans the 'crowned Buddhas'. Vajrasattva alone is always crowned, with or without his female energy. Schlagintweit, however, in his Atlas, gives the reproduction of a temple drawing where Vajrasattva is represented as a Buddha, uncrowned and holding his *śakti*, but this is practically unique.

The heads of the Dhyāni-Buddhas are often encircled by a nimbus, which, in the most ancient form, was round; but later examples, especially in Japan, were often pointed at the top in the shape of the leaf of the Bodhi-tree under which the Buddha attained Supreme Knowledge. The five Dhyāni-Buddhas are represented in India in the aura of a Dhyāni-Bodhisattva when preaching the Law.[1] In the *Mahāvastu* it is written that when a Bodhisattva is about to preach the Law '*five thrones appear*'. In Tibet the five Dhyāni-Buddhas surrounding the Dhyāni-Bodhisattva are more often found in paintings than in statues, but in Japan they are frequently found in both. (Pl. XIV.) In China there may be only three Dhyāni-Buddhas in the aura of a Bodhisattva. (v. Pl. XXI, fig. *b*.)

In Nepal the Dhyāni-Buddhas are represented in niches around the base of the *caitya*.[2] Amoghasiddha is enshrined in the North; Ratnasambhava in the South; Akshobhya in the East; Amitābha in the West. Vairocana is believed to be in the interior, but if he is represented outside, his statue, according to Hodgson, is at the right of Akshobhya. The sixth Dhyāni-Buddha, Vajrasattva, is never represented in statue form on the *caitya*.

Each Dhyāni-Buddha has his own colour, mount (*vāhana*), *śakti*, and mystic pose of the hands, taken from the *mudrā* invented by the Gandhāra and Indian schools to symbolize certain events in the life of Gautama Buddha, whose ethereal form is Amitābha.

Of the various groups of Dhyāni-Buddhas, the five Celestial Jinas are alone of interest to the student of iconography, being the Buddhas of the actual universe—the fourth world.

[1] v. illustration of Siṃhanāda-Lokeśvara, A. Foucher, *Iconographie bouddhique*, Partie II, p. 33.

[2] v. Glossary.

VAIROCANA[1] (First Dhyāni-Buddha)

(Buddha Supreme and Eternal).'

(T.) *rnam-par-snaṅ-mdsad* or *rnam-snaṅ* (maker of brilliant light).
(M.) *masi geigülün ǰoqiaqči* (maker of perfect light).
(C.) *Pi-lo-chê-na* (毗盧遮那).
(J.) *Dai-nichi Nyorai* (Great Sun).

As Ādi-Buddha.

Mystic mudrā of the Six Elements[2] (earth, water, fire, air, ether, and wisdom).

As Dhyāni-Buddha.

Mudrā : *dharmacakra* (teaching).

Symbol : *cakra* (wheel).
Colour : white.
Vāhana : lion.
Śakti : Vajradhātvīśvarī (white).
Support : blue lotus.
Element : ether.

Dhyāni-Buddha : Vairocana.
Dhyāni-Bodhisattva : Samantabhadra.
Mānushi-Buddha : Krakucchanda.

When the system of Ādi-Buddha appeared in Nepal, certain Northern Buddhist sects set up Vairocana as Ādi-Buddha ; but, prior to this, he was worshipped as the first of the five Dhyāni-Buddhas of the actual universe, and is best known under that form.

The Tibetan Northern Buddhists do not associate Vairocana[3] with the founding of the Yoga system, but the Chinese and Japanese Buddhists of the Yogācārya[4] school claim that he transmitted the doctrine directly to the Hindu sage Vajrasattva, who, it is believed, lived in an Iron Tower in Southern India. They further claim that Nāgārjuna visited Vajrasattva in his Iron Tower[5] and learned from him the mystic doctrine of the Maṇḍala of the Two Parts[6] (Vajradhātu and Garbhadhātu), which he transmitted to Nāgabodhi, his disciple. Nāgabodhi, in his turn, taught the doctrine to Vajrabodhi, who transmitted it to Amoghavajra.

In the year A. D. 720, Vajrabodhi, accompanied by his disciple, Amoghavajra, introduced the Yoga system into China. After his death, Amoghavajra continued the propagation of the Yoga doctrine by transmitting it to the Chinese scholar Kei-kwa, who spread it to all the provinces of China.

Toward the end of the eighth century, the Japanese sage Kukai (Kōbō Daishi) went to China to study the doctrine of the Yogācārya school with Kei-kwa (Jap. Hiu-kio), and after being initiated into the most secret mysteries of the system, carried it into Japan and founded the Shingon sect.

In India the Yogācārya school was grafted on to the Mahāyāna in the middle of

[1] Lit., the Illuminator. Pro. Vairochana.

[2] I use this term as I have been unable to find a Sanskrit or other name for this *mudrā*.

[3] They look upon Samantabhadra as the founder of the Yoga doctrine.

[4] In Japan the Hossō, Tendai, Kegon, and Shingon sects were founded on the Yoga doctrine.

[5] v. *Nāgārjuna*.

[6] The secret doctrine of the *Two Parts* forms the body and substance of the Yoga system (v. *Vajradhātu*).

the sixth century by Asaṅga,[1] who claimed to be inspired by Maitreya from the Tushita heaven. The doctrine was purely esoteric, and 'taught that by means of mystic formularies (*tantra*) or litanies (*dhāraṇī*) or spells (*mantra*), the reciting of which should be accompanied by music and certain distortions of the fingers (*mudrā*), a state of mental fixity might be reached, characterized by their being neither thought, nor annihilation of thoughts, and consisting of sixfold bodily and mental happiness (*yogi*), from which would result endowment with supernatural miracle-working power.' (Eitel.)

The fundamental principle of the Yoga[2] system is the ecstatic union of the individual with the Universal Spirit, and in Japan Vairocana is looked upon as the highest vehicle of the mystic Union, which is called by the Japanese the 'action of the Dainichi Nyorai'. The *mudrā* of Vairocana indicate the mystic Union. As Dhyāni-Buddha he has the *dharmacakra mudrā* (v. Glossary), which the Tibetans call *Thabdong-shesrab*, or the Union of Wisdom with Matter. As Ādi-Buddha he has the *mudrā* of the Six Elements, which also indicates the same principle, and, although rare in Tibet,[3] is often found in Japan. The index finger of the left hand is clasped by the five fingers of the right. The six fingers represent the Six Elements which, when united, produce the 'sixfold bodily and mental happiness'. The five fingers of the right hand represent the five material elements of which man is composed: earth (little finger), water (ring finger), fire (middle finger), air (index), and ether (thumb). The index finger of the left hand represents the flame-symbol of Ādi-Buddha, for the sixth element, the mind (*manas*), is a particle of his essence.

The two hands, thus representing the union of the Spiritual with the Material, correspond with the Vajradhātu and Garbhadhātu of the Maṇḍala[4] of the Two Parts. The Vajradhātu, represented by the index finger, is the 'diamond' element corresponding to the spiritual world (v. *Vajradhātu*). The Garbhadhātu, indicated by the five fingers, is the matrix element, corresponding to the material world.

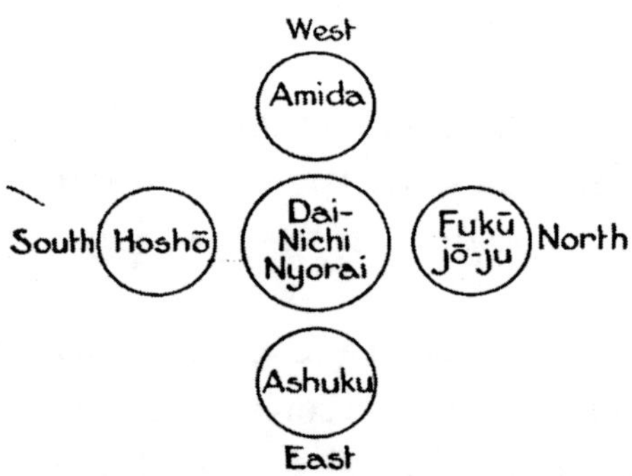

The Shingon sect represents the 'Two Parts' of the Yoga Maṇḍala by two diagrams. In the Vajradhātu diagram, Vairocana is the sun—the centre of a planetary system around which revolve his manifestations, the four Dhyāni-Buddhas, as planets.[5] It is believed that 'in him as in a mighty sun all things visible and invisible have their consummation and absorption'. He is in fact the 'one Truth surrounded by the four constituent elements'. (Lloyd.)

Vairocana is represented in the centre of the diagram. He is seated, dressed

[1] Lloyd places Asaṅga about A.D. 300. Prof. Takakusu A.D. 445, and Grünwedel A.D. 550, which is the usual date given.

[2] Derived from the Sanskrit root *yuj*, or 'union'.

[3] v. Tibetan statuette, Bacot collection, Musée Guimet, Paris, No. 23. Japanese examples, v. Pl. II, fig. *a*, and Pl. LXII. fig. *d*.

[4] Mystic circle. v. Pl. XVI and Bunyiu Nanjio, *A Short History of the Twelve Buddhist Sects*; A. Lloyd, *Developments of Japanese Buddhism*.

[5] Dai-nichi Nyorai (Vairocana), Ashuku (Akshobhya), Hoshō (Ratnasambhava), Amida (Amitābha), Fukū-jō-ju (Amoghasiddha).

PLATE XV

a. MAITREYA

b. MAITREYA

like a Bodhisattva, with a crown and the traditional ornaments, and his hands are in the *mudrā* of the Six Elements (see above). It is believed that from him proceeded the element ether (*ākāśa*),the organ of sight and all colours. The colour of Vairocana is white.

In the centre of the diagram of the Garbhadhātu [1] is an eight-leaved lotus-flower which represents the 'heart' (*hridaya*) of beings. It is the solar matrix, 'the mysterious sanctuary to which the sun returns each night to be re-born' (v. *Vajradhātu*). Vairocana is represented in the centre, and is looked upon as the source of all organic life—the 'heart' of the lotus. (According to Hodgson,[2] his symbol, the wheel, may be represented by the round top of the seed-vessel of the lotus, in the centre of which is the Nepalese *yin-yang* [3] around which are eight seed-cells.) The eight petals around the 'heart' of the lotus represent the four Dhyāni-Bodhisattva who have created the four worlds (the fifth being yet to come), and their respective four Dhyāni-Buddhas, or spiritual fathers. Around the eight-leaved lotus enclosure are twelve other enclosures. In the centre of the Sarvajña enclosure, immediately above the eight-leaved lotus enclosure, is a triangle resting on its base, which is the symbol of Ādi-Dharma, or Matter (v. *trikoṇa*, *tri-ratna*, and v. Pl. XVI).

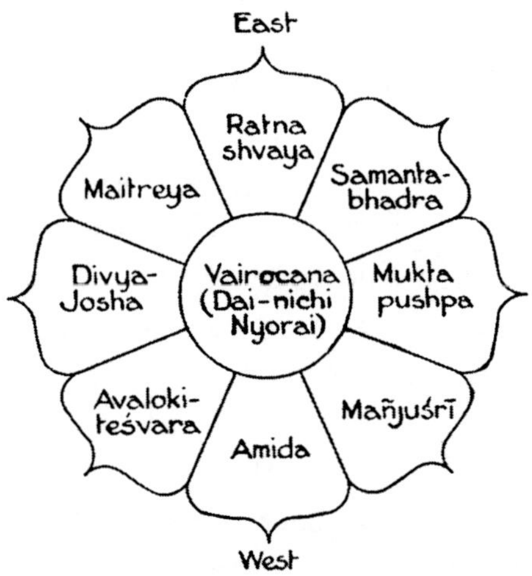

Vairocana, seated in the heart of the lotus of the Garbhadhātu, is represented like a Bodhisattva, with a crown and many ornaments. He is not, in the Maṇḍala, a simple Dhyāni-Buddha, but the president of the Dhyāni-Buddhas—almost an Ādi-Buddha (in which case he would also be represented like a Bodhisattva). His hands are in his lap in *dhyāna mudrā*, balancing his special symbol, the eight-spoked wheel.

The fundamental principle of the Yoga doctrine, the Union of the Spiritual with the Material, is represented in Nepal and Tibet by the divinity and his *śakti* (female energy) in the attitude called '*yab-yum*'. The *yab* is the divinity representing the Vajradhātu, while the *yum* (the *śakti*) represents the Garbhadhātu. But this crude representation of the union of Spirit and Matter, while it found favour in Mongolia, highly displeased the more refined sense of the Chinese and Japanese, and was never adopted in either country.[4] They considered the mystic *mudrā* of the Six Elements as sufficiently representing the principle on which the Yoga school was founded, and one finds many beautiful examples of Dai-nichi Nyorai in Japan, expressing this principle with great dignity and much religious feeling.

The Shingon sect associates Vairocana with its funeral ceremonies. Lloyd says

[1] v. Pl. XVI.

[2] Notice on Buddhist symbols, *Journal of the Royal Asiatic Society of Great Britain and Ireland*, vol. xviii, Part II.

[3] v. Glossary.

[4] One finds examples in the Lamaist temple in Peking, but carefully covered.

in his *Shinran* : 'When, prior to its removal to the Temple, the corpse has been placed before a temporary altar in the house, on which stand the thirteen Buddhas [1] whom the Shingon reverence, the priest commences the service with lustrations. . . .' Then comes an invocation of the Being who represents to the Shingon the 'sum total of the Universe', who manifests himself to man through his five personified attributes : earth, fire, water, air, and ether.

The five Dhyāni-Buddhas are next invoked : Vairocana, Akshobhya, Ratnasambhava, Amitābha, and Amoghasiddha, after which, Amitābha, as 'conductor of souls', accompanied by Kwannon and Seishi (Mahāsthāna-prāpta) is invoked 'to come and meet the soul in its passage from this world to the next'. Then follows an invocation of Jizō (Kshitigarbha), also 'conductor of souls', and of Fudō (Acala), 'champion of the righteous'. When all these gods have been invoked, 'the celebrant at last raises his heart to the invocation of Vairocana, *the great Buddha*'.

This ceremony shows that the Shingon sect worships Vairocana in his three forms : as Buddha Supreme,[2] Dhyāni-Buddha, and in his manifestation of Fudō, the form which he takes to combat Evil, the flames about him symbolizing the destruction of Evil.

The 'thirteen Buddhas' invoked in the ceremony are Vairocana, his eleven disciples, and his manifestation, *Fudō*, who are looked upon as 'Guardians of the spirits of the dead'. The Kegon sect worships a triad of Vairocana with Fugen and Monju (Samantabhadra and Mañjuśrī). (v. *Fudō*.)

In Nepal and Tibet the statues of Vairocana, either as Ādi-Buddha or Dhyāni-Buddha, are extremely rare, but in Japan he is frequently found in statues and paintings. As Ādi-Buddha he is always represented in Tibet as a Bodhisattva and is seated with his legs locked, his hands forming the mystic *mudrā* of the Six Elements ; or he may be represented holding his special symbol, the wheel, balanced in his hands in *dhyāna mudrā*.

In Pander's *Pantheon*, illustration No. 76, there is the representation of a deity with *four heads*, wearing a Bodhisattva crown, but called by Pander a 'Dhyāni-Buddha'. He is seated, with his hands in *dhyāna-mudrā*, *balancing a wheel* surrounded by flames. He is called *kun-rigs*, which means 'omniscient', one of the qualities of Vairocana, and may possibly be his Tibetan form as Ādi-Buddha.

As Dhyāni-Buddha he is represented in Tibet with the monastic garments and short, curly hair, the *ushṇīsha*, *ūrṇā*, and long-lobed ears. His hands are in *dharmacakra mudrā*, and his legs are closely locked. He is sometimes in company with his *śakti*, in which case he is dressed like a Bodhisattva and holds a wheel and a bell. The *śakti* encircles his body with her legs, and holds a skull cup and a knife or a wheel. If painted, Vairocana is white, and when with his *śakti* is seated on a blue lotus.

The goddess Ushṇīshavijayā holds in the hands, lying in her lap in *dhyāna mudrā*,

[1] Illustration, Pl. XVII.

[2] The Nepalese system of Ādi-Buddha was not adopted in Japan. There is no Japanese term for 'Ādi-Buddha', but Vairocana is nevertheless looked upon as the 'origin of all, even of the universe'.

PLATE XVI

MAṆḌALA (GARBHADHĀTU)

a vase which is believed to contain a particle of the essence of Vairocana—thus symbolizing the Spiritual, enveloped by the Material—or the 'Two Parts', Vajradhātu and Garbhadhātu.

The goddess Mārīcī has a small image of Vairocana in her head-dress.

In Japan, Vairocana (Dai-nichi Nyorai) is represented with the high head-dress of the Japanese Bodhisattva, but is, however, dressed in the monastic garments of the Japanese Buddhas, with the right shoulder bare and wears no ornaments. His hands form the mystic *mudrā* of the Six Elements (Pl. II, fig. *a*, and Pl. LXII, fig. *d*).

Mio-ken (Polar Star)[1] is worshipped in Japan under the form of Dai-nichi Nyorai, who balances a wheel in his hands lying in *dhyāna mudrā* on his lap.

FUDŌ-MYŌ-Ō

Form of Dai-nichi Nyorai (Vairocana).

Symbols: *khadga* (sword).
pāśa (lasso).

Colour: black.
Distinctive mark: glory of flames.

Fudō, champion of the Righteous, is chief of the five Devas called *myō-ō* (*mahā deva*), and is believed in Japan to be a manifestation of the Dhyāni-Buddha Vairocana, for the purpose of combating Evil. This form, however, so closely resembles one of the Dharmapāla forms of Vajrapāṇi,[2] that one cannot but believe with Satow, that it is the Japanese manifestation of Acala rather than of Dai-nichi Nyorai.

His appearance is fierce and angry. He holds the sword in his right hand to smite the guilty, and the lasso in his left to catch and bind the wicked. He may, however, have four arms and be standing on a dragon. Behind him is a glory of flames, symbolizing the destruction of Evil (v. Pl. LIII, fig. *d*).

Fudō figures in the group of thirteen Buddhas (illustration, Pl. XVII) used in the funereal ceremonies of the Shingon sect, and is believed to take charge of the soul after death. The central Buddha at the top of the group is Dai-nichi Nyorai (Vairocana), while the figure surrounded by flames at the left of the lowest row is Fudō, who is believed to meet the soul and look after it for the first week.

Śākya-muni for the 2nd week,
Monju (Mañjuśrī) ,, ,, 3rd ,,

[1] 'The Polar Star was a type of the Eternal because apparently it never changed with time. It was the earliest type of Supreme Intelligence . . . which was unerring, just and true . . . a point *within the circle* from which you could not err.' Churchward, *Signs and Symbols of Primordial Man*. It was called the 'Eye upon the mountain', the radiating centre of light surmounting the triangle. (v. *trikoṇa*.)

[2] v. *Vajrapāṇi*.

Fugen (Samantabhadra) for the 4th week,
Jizō (Kshitigarbha) ,, ,, 5th ,,
Miroku (Maitreya) ,, ,, 6th ,,
Yakushi (Bhaishajyaguru)[1] ,, ,, 7th ,,
Kwannon (Avalokiteśvara) for 100 days,
Seishi (Mahāsthānaprāpta) ,, 1 year,
Amida (Amitābha) ,, 3 years,
Ashaku (Akshobhya) ,, 7 years.
Kokuzo (Ākāśagarbha) and Vairocana remain its guardians for ever.[2]

AKSHOBHYA (second Dhyāni-Buddha)

(The Immovable).[3]

(T.) *mi-bskyod-pa* (pro. *mijod-pa*) or *mi-hkhrugs-pa* (pro. *mintug-pa*) (unagitated).
(M.) *ülü küdelükči* (without movement).
(C.) *Pu-tung-fo* (不動佛).
(J.) *Ashuku.*
Mudrā: *bhūmisparśa* (witness).
Symbol: *vajra* (thunderbolt).

Colour: blue.
Vāhana: elephant.
Śakti: Locanā (blue).
Element: air.
Dhyāni-Buddha: Akshobhya.
Dhyāni-Bodhisattva: Vajrapāṇi.
Mānushi-Buddha: Kanaka-muni.

Akshobhya is supposed to reside in a realm called Abhirati, the Eastern Paradise, which, however, has never been so popular as the Western Paradise of Amitābha.

It has been claimed by certain Buddhist sects that the Bodhisattva of Akshobhya is Vajrasattva, while others look upon Vajradhara as his spiritual son; but, according to the system of five Dhyāni-Buddhas, his Dhyāni-Bodhisattva is Vajrapāṇi.

His worship extended to China and Japan, but Akshobhya was never popular to the same extent as Vairocana or Amitābha. He is represented less frequently in statues than in religious paintings and *maṇḍala,* where he is found in company with the other Dhyāni-Buddhas.

Akshobhya is represented seated, like all the Dhyāni-Buddhas, with the legs locked and both feet apparent. There are often wheels marked on the soles of his feet, or a protuberance like a button, resembling the *ūrṇā* on the forehead. His left hand lies on his lap in 'meditation' *mudrā.* His right touches the earth with the tips of the outstretched fingers, the palm turned inward. This is called the *bhūmisparśa* or 'witness' *mudrā,* and is the same pose of the hands that the Gandhāra school gave to Gautama Buddha, when representing his invoking the Earth

[1] v. *Manla* (Chin. Yo-shi Fo), *or the Healing Buddha,* and Edkins, *Chinese Buddhism,* p. 235.

[2] Lloyd, *Creed of Half Japan,* p. 65.

[3] Or 'the undisturbed'.

PLATE XVII

THE THIRTEEN SHINGON BUDDHAS

to bear witness that he had resisted the temptation of the God of Evil, Māra (v. Pl. I).

The Hīnayāna Buddhists in Ceylon, Java, Burma, and Siam worship Gautama Buddha under this form, while those of the Mahāyāna school look upon it as Akshobhya; for, with but rare exceptions, the historic Buddha is only appealed to by the Northern Buddhists in his ethereal form of Amitābha.

Akshobhya may also take in Tibet another form of Gautama Buddha called 'Vajrāsana' (diamond throne).[1] The attitude is the same as the above, but before him on the lotus throne lies a *vajra*, or it may be balanced in the palm of the left hand lying in 'meditation' *mudrā* on his lap.

In St. Petersburg, according to Oldenburg, there is a unique representation of Akshobhya with the *vajra* in the hand which holds the folds of his monastic garment on the left shoulder.

A small image of Akshobhya is often in the head-dress of Mañjuśrī, Yamāntaka, Tārā, and Prajñāpāramitā.

In his *yab-yum* form he is crowned and presses his *śakti* to his breast, with arms crossed at her back, holding the *vajra* and bell. She holds the *kapāla* (skull-cup) and *vajra*.

RATNASAMBHAVA[2] (Third Dhyāni-Buddha)

(Buddha of Precious Birth).

(T.) *rin-byuṅ* (source of the treasure).
(M.) *erdeni-in oron* (the place of the jewel).
(C.) *Pao-shêng-fo* (寶生佛).
(J.) *Hōshō*.
Mudrā: *vara* (charity).
Symbol: *cintāmaṇi* (magic jewel).
Colour: yellow.

Vāhana: horse.
Śakti: Mamakī.
Support: yellow lotus.
Element: fire.
Dhyāni-Buddha: Ratnasambhava.
Dhyāni-Bodhisattva: Ratnapāṇi.
Mānushi-Buddha: Kāśyapa.

Ratnasambhava, the third Dhyāni-Buddha, seems to have been the least popular of all the five Dhyāni-Buddhas. His statues are extremely rare, but one may come across him in paintings.

He is represented seated, with his legs closely locked. His left hand, lying on his lap, holds the *cintāmaṇi* (magic jewel), and his right is in *vara* (charity) *mudrā*—the arm is stretched downwards, the hand having all the fingers extended, and the palm is turned outwards. He has the *ushṇīsha*, *ūrṇā*, and long-lobed ears.

There may be a small image of Ratnasambhava in the head-dress of Jambala.

[1] v. *Gautama Buddha* and Pl. II, fig. *d*.

[2] Ratna-sambhava, 'the source of precious (or holy) things'.

AMITĀBHA (Fourth Dhyāni-Buddha)

(Buddha of Infinite Light).

(T.) *ḥod-dpag-med* (infinite light).
(M.) *čaghlasi ügei gereltü* (he who is eternally brilliant).
(C.) *O-mi-t'o-fo* (阿弥陀佛).
(J.) *Amida*.
Mudrā: *dhyāna* (meditation).
Symbol: *pātra* (begging-bowl).
Vāhana: peacock.
Colour: red.
Śakti: Pāndarā (rose).
Element: water.
Dhyāni-Buddha: Amitābha.
Dhyāni-Bodhisattva: Avalokiteśvara.
Mānushi-Buddha: Śākya-muni.
'Crowned' form of Amitābha, without *śakti*—Amitāyus.

Amitābha is the fourth Dhyāni-Buddha and the ethereal form of Śākya-muni. It is claimed by the Northern Buddhists that Gautama Buddha, before entering into Nirvāṇa, transmitted to Śāriputra (one of his favourite disciples) the dogma of the Western Paradise (Sukhāvatī) over which presides Amitābha, Buddha of Boundless Light, immortal, and bestowing immortality on the people of his paradise.

Amitābha is only known in Northern Buddhism. His name does not appear in the canons of the Hīnayāna school, and his worship is unknown in Ceylon, Burma, and Siam. Neither Fa-hian in the account of his travels in India (399–414) nor Hiuen-tsang (629–45) mentions him, although both refer to Avalokiteśvara and Mañjuśrī.

The name of Amitābha first appears in a list of one thousand fictitious Buddhas introduced by the Nepalese Mahāyāna school. The list so closely coincides with the thousand Zarathustras of the Zoroastrians that Amitābha (in reality a sun-god) and his Western Paradise are thought to have been evolved in Nepal, or Kashmir, from Persian sources. His worship reached China at the same time as the Mahāyāna doctrine of Dhyāni-Buddhas and Bodhisattva, by the northern route, and it is therefore believed that the birthplace of the worship of Amitābha was probably north of the Himālayas.

The description of Sukhāvatī,[1] the Western Paradise of Amitābha, varies according to the imagination of the author. In the *Saddharma puṇḍarīka* (Lotus of the Good Law) it is written that women are debarred from Amitābha's paradise, but by acts of merit may attain masculinity in the next world, and thus be eligible to the joys of Sukhāvatī. The thirty-fifth vow of Amitābha, according to the *Aparimitāyus-sūtra*, is as follows: 'If I become Buddha, all women in innumerable other Buddhist countries shall hear my name and be filled with joy and gladness and dislike their womanhood, desiring enlightenment. If they again resume the feminine form after death and

[1] v. Glossary.

remain unsaved. I will not receive Buddhahood.' One finds, however, in other Buddhist writings, reference to the inmates of the Western Paradise as sexless.

Amitābha is represented seated with his legs closely locked. His hands lie on his lap, in *dhyāna* (meditation) *mudrā*, and hold the *pātra* (begging-bowl). He has the *ushṇīsha* and *ūrṇā* and long-lobed ears (v. Pl. XVIII, fig. *a*).

He is sometimes represented with his *śakti* held in the *yab-yum* attitude, but his manifestations in China and Japan are never with the female energy. In this form he wears a crown and is dressed like a Bodhisattva. His arms are crossed behind her back and hold the *vajra* and *ghaṇṭā*, while the *śakti* holds the skull and either the *grigug* (chopper) or wheel.

A small image of Amitābha is in the head-dress of Avalokiteśvara, or may be held above the ten heads by two of his arms. He may also be in the head-dress of the goddess Kurukullā.

Besides being Buddha of Boundless Light, Amitābha is Buddha of Boundless Life,[1] in his form of Amitāyus, and of Boundless Compassion in his Bodhisattva form of Avalokiteśvara.

AMITĀYUS (APARIMITĀYUS)

(Buddha of Eternal Life).

(T.) *ts'e-dpag-med* (eternal life).
(M.) *ajusi* or *čaghlasi ügei nasutu* (having eternal life).
(C.) *Ch'ang shêng-fo* (長生佛).

Mudrā: *dhyāna* (meditation).
Symbol: *tsé-bum* (ambrosia vase).
Colour: bright red.

Amitāyus (Dispenser of Long Life) is the name given to Amitābha in his character of bestower of longevity, and the Tibetans, unlike the Chinese and Japanese, never confuse the two forms.

The Lamaist ceremony for 'Obtaining Long Life' is a curious mixture of Buddhism and demon-worship, and takes place in Tibet at stated intervals with much pomp. According to Waddell, 'in the preliminary worship, the pills are made from buttered dough and the ambrosia (*amṛita*) is brewed from spirit or beer and offered in a skull-bowl to the great image of Amitāyus'. The Lama then places a *vajra* on the ambrosia vase, which the image of Amitāyus holds in its lap, and applies a cord, which is attached to the *vajra*, to his own heart. 'Thus, through the string, as by a telegraph wire, passes the divine spirit, and the Lama must mentally conceive that his heart is in actual communion with that of the god Amitāyus.'[2]

The wine in the *tsé-bum*, or ambrosia vase, is then consecrated, and the people partake of it, as well as of the sacred pills, with the firm conviction that their

[1] v. Pl. XV, fig. *d*.

[2] Waddell, *Lamaism*, p. 445.

lives will be prolonged through their faith in Amitāyus. He is, therefore, a very popular divinity, and one sees many of his images and paintings in Tibet.

Amitāyus may be termed either a 'crowned Buddha', or a Bodhisattva, and is therefore richly clad and wears the thirteen ornaments. His hair is painted blue and falls on either side to his elbows, or may be curiously coiled. He is seated [1] like a Buddha, and his hands lie on his lap in *dhyāna* (meditation) *mudrā*, holding the ambrosia vase, his special emblem. The vase is richly decorated, and from the cover fall four strings of beads, which represent the sacred pills quoted above; and from this cover often sprouts a tiny *aśoka*-tree (tree of Consolation, v. *Vajradhātu*). (v. Pl. III, fig. *a*; Pl. XV, fig. *d*; Pl. XVIII, figs. *c* and *d*; Pl. XIX, fig. *b*.)

Amitāyus never holds a *śakti*, or female energy, nor has he a consort.

He is often found in a triad between Mañjuśrī and Vajrapāṇi. The presence of Vajrapāṇi in company with Amitāyus might be accounted for by the fact that the Buddhas put him in charge of the Water of Life, which they had procured by churning the ocean with the mountain Sumeru.[2]

In China and Japan Amitāyus is worshipped under the usual form of Amitābha.

O-MI-TO FŌ

(Chinese Buddha of Boundless Light).

The first Amitābha *sūtra* is supposed to have been brought from Nepal or Kashmir into China by a Buddhist priest, about A.D. 147; but the doctrine of Amitābha made no headway until the fourth century A.D., when an exoteric sect called the 'Lotus School' (Lien Tsung), more commonly called the 'Pure Land School', was founded. In the next century an Amitābha *sūtra* was translated into Chinese by Kumārajīva; and Amidaïsm then began to spread so rapidly that the Confucianists took alarm—the result of which was a heated controversy between the *literati* of both sides as to the relative merits of Buddhism and Confucianism.

The Chinese had never been able to understand the Indian conception of Nirvāṇa. Ancestor worship was a universal custom in China. It found its way even into the Buddhist monasteries,[3] where ancestral tablets were set up dedicated to members of the community who had died in sanctity.

The great teachers, philosophers, moralists, were themselves ancestor worshippers, and while they would not accept the Indian doctrine of complete annihilation after death, they as greatly disapproved of the doctrine of immortality in Amitābha's paradise. They avoided as much as possible discussing the problem of life after

[1] Statues of Amitāyus standing are very rare.

[2] v. *Vajrapāṇi*.

[3] Edkins, *Chinese Buddhism*.

PLATE XVIII

a. Amida

b. Amida

c. Amitāyus T

turquoise ornaments

d. Amitāyus T

death, preferring to teach men how to live. They claimed that an act of merit with hope of ultimate recompense was no real act of merit. The Northern Buddhist reply was that no man would till his field without ultimate hope of harvest.

The common people understood nothing of the controversy. They were Taoïsts, and Taoïsm, indigenous to China, promised life hereafter in glowing colours. The step from Taoïsm to Amidaïsm was easy enough, with its promise of paradise, and faith in O-mi-to Fō was not difficult, when he was flanked by the popular god (or goddess) Kwan-yin on the left (place of honour in China) and Ta-shi-chi on the right.[1] Thus Amitābha became the object of much veneration in China.

The Chinese representations of Amitābha resemble the Southern Buddhist images of Buddha, with short, curly hair, long-lobed ears, the *ushṇīsha*, the *ūrṇā*, and the half-closed eyes indicating deep meditation (the eyes and features are always Indian, not Mongolian). He is seated with closely locked legs, and his hands are against his breast with the tips of the index fingers touching and pointing upwards, while the other fingers are locked. This *mudrā* in India indicates Buddha as 'Liberator of the Nāgas', and in Japan is the mystic gesture of the Ba-to Kwannon. It is said to be emblematical of the lotus-flower.

There is another form of O-mi-to Fō sometimes seen in China. He is standing, his arms abnormally long, and is called Chien-yin Fō, or the 'Buddha who guides into Paradise'.

AMIDA NYORAI

(Japanese Buddha of Infinite Light).

Amitābha was pronounced incarnate in the great Sun god Amaterasu[2] by Kōbō Daishi in the ninth century A.D., but the actual worship of Amida in Japan does not date further back than the twelfth century.

The Jōdo-shū (Pure Land Sect) was founded by Gen-kou A.D. 1175 on the doctrines of the Amitāyurdhyāna *sūtra*. Towards the thirteenth century another Amida sect, the Shin-shū, was founded by the great Shin-ran, and Amidaïsm, with its dogma of the Western Paradise and salvation through faith in Amida, became so popular that these two sects alone constituted more than half the Buddhist population of Japan.

Amida is looked upon as the One Original Buddha (Ichi-butsu), without beginning and without end, besides whom there is none other. He is the 'Father of the World', and all the Buddhas and Bodhisattvas are temporary manifestations of him, but is he the creator? Here the Amida sects disagree. They call him the 'Supreme

[1] Avalokiteśvara and Mahāsthānaprāpta.

[2] According to A. Lloyd, *Creed of Half Japan*, p. 201, *goddess* identified with *Vairocana*.

Buddha', although the doctrine of Ādi-Buddha, as evolved in Nepal, does not appear to have been adopted by the Japanese Mahāyānists.

The Amida sects claim, however, that Amida revealed himself in Nepal as Ādi-Buddha, and that when Nāgārjuna [1] went there to worship the Ādi-Buddha, he became acquainted with the Bodhisattva Mahānāga, who taught him the doctrine of faith in Amida. When Nāgārjuna was sufficiently enlightened, Mahānāga conducted him to the Dragon Palace under the sea, where he received further instruction, and was then given the treatise on which the Amida doctrine is founded.

According to Mr. A. Lloyd, the Amida sects claim that Amida 'revealed himself many times in a long list of Tathāgata, of which Śākya-muni was the last manifestation'. He is believed to have two special qualities, Mercy and Wisdom, which are personified by Kwan-non (Avalokita), god of Mercy, and Dai-sei-shi (Mahāsthāna-prāpta), who is the spiritual manifestation of the wisdom of Amida, and these two, with Amida, form a trinity. According to Lloyd, they 'are at once distinct in Person and one in Essence, and bear a striking resemblance to the unity of Three Persons in our Christian Trinity'.

Amida is represented like the Amitābha of Northern Buddhism with the exception that, while he wears the usual monastic garments, both shoulders are covered, the breast partly bare. If sitting, the legs are closely locked, the soles of the feet turned upward. The hands may be forming the *dharmacakra mudrā*, but are usually both lying in the lap in *dhyāna mudrā*, differing, however, from the Indian pose. The palms are held upward with all the fingers locked underneath, except the indexes, which touch the tips of the thumbs with their tips (the second joints of the indexes against each other), thus forming two 'triangular' poses.[2]

The eyes are almost closed in deep meditation, and the features with the long-lobed ears are Indian.

[1] v. *Nāgārjuna*.

[2] v. Glossary for *vitarka* and *dhyāna-mudrā*. Illus. Pl. XVIII, fig. *b*. and Pl. LVII.

PLATE XIX

a. Nāga lamp

b. Amitāyus

c. Mañjuśrī (or Avalokita?)

d. Buddhist emblematic vase

AMOGHASIDDHA (Fifth Dhyāni-Buddha)

(Buddha of Infallible Magic).

(T.) *don-grub.*
(J.) *Fukū jō-ju.*
Mudrā : *abhaya* (protecting).
Symbol : *viśva-vajra* (double thunderbolt).
Colour : green.

Vāhana : *shen-shang* (dwarf).
Śakti : Tārā.
Support : blue-green lotus.
Element : earth.

Amoghasiddha, the fifth Dhyāni-Buddha, is believed to be 'unfailingly successful' and to have the power of infallible magic. He is seated in 'adamantine' pose (legs closely locked, with the soles of the feet apparent). The left hand lies in his lap, with the palm upwards, and may balance the double thunderbolt, or hold a sword. The right hand is lifted in *abhaya mudrā* ('blessing of Fearlessness'), a pose of the hands indicating protection. All the fingers are extended upwards, palm outwards.

At Touen-houang (or, more exactly, in the Chinese province of Kantsu) a statue of Amoghasiddha [1] was discovered by the Pelliot mission, with the right hand in *abhaya* and the left in *vara* (charity) *mudrā.* The right shoulder is bare, and he is seated in European fashion like his Mānushi-Buddha, Maitreya.

[1] Amoghasiddha, lit. unfailingly successful, according to E. Denison Ross, *Memoirs of the Asiatic Society of Bengal.*

THE DHYĀNI-BODHISATTVA

Table IV

- Dhyāni-Bodhisattva.
  - Group of Five.
    - Samantabhadra.
    - Vajrapāṇi.
    - Ratnapāṇi.
    - Avalokiteśvara . .
      - I. Kwan-shï-yin.
      - II. Kwan-non.
      - III. Legend of Miao-Chen.
      - IV. Hāritī.
    - Viśvapāṇi.
  - Group of Eight.
    - Avalokiteśvara.
    - Ākāśagarbha.
    - Vajrapāṇi.
    - Kshitigarbha . .
      - I. Ti-tsang.
      - II. Jizō.
    - Sarva-nīvaraṇa-vishkambhin.
    - Maitreya.[1]
    - Samantabhadra.
    - Mañjuśrī.
  - Mahāsthānaprāpta.
  - Trailokyavijaya.

[1] v. *The Buddhas.*

THE DHYĀNI-BODHISATTVA[1] (SAMBHOGA-KAYA)

(He whose essence is Perfect Knowledge).

According to the Northern Buddhist school, there are both mortal and celestial Bodhisattva.

A mortal Bodhisattva is one who has manifested himself on earth in human (*mānushi*) form, in a series of incarnations, until such a time as he has acquired sufficient merit and enlightenment (*bodhi-jñāna*) to receive Buddha-hood.

Like Gautama Buddha in his incarnation of the *arhat* Sumedha,[2] the Bodhisattva may have been, in a former re-birth, an *arhat*[3] bent on his own salvation who, becoming inspired with the desire for Bodhi in order to save mankind, renounced his *arhat*-ship.

It is unusual, however, according to M. de la Vallée Poussin,[4] for the future Bodhisattva to have been an *arhat*. In the first stage, he usually becomes a candidate for Bodhisattva-hood by the practice of the six Pāramitās, or Transcendent Virtues through which he is to accumulate merit.

The second stage of the Bodhisattva is reached when he becomes *conscious* of the desire for Buddha-hood. This illumination is called 'Bodhi-chitta'.[5] The aspirant, now aware of his wish for Bodhi, must make the vow that he will re-enter, or continue to remain in, the world of suffering for the sole purpose of saving mankind.

This, the Great Vow of the Bodhisattva, however, does not make the aspirant a Bodhisattva. It is only when he enters on the Path of Bodhi that he reaches the third stage, at which he becomes a Bodhisattva.

But in order to reach the ultimate goal of Buddha-hood, it is necessary for the Bodhisattva, in one of his incarnations, to meet the reigning Buddha of that *kalpa*, or epoch, and acquaint him with his desire for Buddha-hood. The Tathāgata will then look forward through the future re-births of the Bodhisattva and announce his eventual triumph.

The Bodhisattva, now aware of his future Buddha-hood, enters on a stage 'from which there is no return'. He must practise the ten Pāramitās which make a Buddha, and continue to accumulate merit in his different re-births, always bearing in mind that his sole aim in becoming a Tathāgata is to save all creatures from suffering.

When the future Buddha has reached the last stage of Bodhisattva-hood, and resides in the Tushita heaven, he is free to decide whether he will pass through the

[1] *Bodhi* (knowledge), *sattva* (essence)

[2] v. *The Dīpaṅkara Buddha.*

[3] v. *Arhat.*

[4] Hastings's *Encyclopedia of Religion and Ethics*, 'The Bodhisattva', vol. ii.

[5] *Bodhi* (knowledge), *chitta* (thought or aspiration).

intermediary stages of the thirteen Bodhisattva heavens [1] to reach Nirvāṇa, or will descend to earth and become a mortal Buddha, after which he will enter directly into Nirvāṇa.

The only Mānushi-Bodhisattva that is met with in Buddhist art is Maitreya, who has two representations : as Bodhisattva, his present form in the Tushita heaven, and as Buddha, the form he will take when he descends to earth as Mānushi-Buddha. (Pl. xv, figs. *a* and *b*.) All the other Bodhisattva representations are of Dhyāni-Bodhisattva.

The Dhyāni-Bodhisattva is celestial and is the second 'body' (*kāya*) in the Tri-kāya or Northern Buddhist Trinity.[2] He is believed to dwell in the Rūpadhātu heaven in the body of absolute completeness (Sambhoga-kāya), in a state of 'reflected spirituality', that is to say, that it is in this form that the Dharma-kāya (Dhyāni-Buddha) reveals himself to the Bodhisattva or future Buddhas in the Tushita heaven. Although, according to the Buddhist writings, the name is legion, there are comparatively few Dhyāni-Bodhisattva represented in Buddhist art, and these may be divided into two groups—of five and of eight.

The five Dhyāni-Bodhisattva correspond with the five Dhyāni-Buddhas and differ in many respects from the other celestial Bodhisattva. They are : Samantabhadra, Vajrapāṇi, Ratnapāṇi, Avalokiteśvara, and Viśvapāṇi.

Those belonging to the group of eight are found in Northern Buddhist temples on either side of an important divinity. The gods on the right are : Avalokiteśvara, Ākāśagarbha, Vajrapāṇi, and Kshitigarbha, while on the left are : Sarva-nīvaraṇa-vishkambhin, Maitreya, Samantabhadra, and Mañjuśrī.

Each Dhyāni-Bodhisattva in the group of five is evolved, according to the system, by his Dhyāni-Buddha. He is a reflex, an emanation from him ; in other words, his spiritual son. Certain Northern Buddhist sects that interlink the dogmas of the Tri-kāya and the Tri-ratna [3] look upon the Dhyāni-Bodhisattva as the active creator, Saṅgha, product of the union of Buddha (mind) and Dharma (matter). According to the system of Ādi-Buddha, the Dhyāni-Bodhisattva receives the active power of creation from Ādi-Buddha through the medium of his spiritual father, the Dhyāni-Buddha.

The Dhyāni-Bodhisattva of this group of five have a definite place in the Mahāyāna system and for a special purpose, that is, to evolve, *each in his turn*, from his own essence, a material and perishable world over which he is to preside until the advent of the Mānushi-Buddha *of his cycle*. At the death of his mortal Buddha, he must continue the work of the propagation of Buddhism until his successor creates a new world.

Three of the Dhyāni-Bodhisattva have created worlds, and are now engrossed in worshipping Ādi-Buddha, or, according to some, have been absorbed into Nirvāṇa. The present world is the fourth, and there is the fifth yet to come.

[1] In India, ten *bhuvana*.

[2] Dharma-kāya, Sambhoga-kāya, Nirmāṇa-kāya (Dhyāni-Buddha, Dhyāni-Bodhisattva, Mānushi-Buddha).

[3] Or 'Three Jewels', Buddha, Dharma, Saṅgha. v. *Tri-ratna*.

The first world was created by Samantabhadra (Dhyāni-Bodhisattva). His spiritual father Vairocana (Dhyāni-Buddha) manifested himself on earth in the form of Mānushi-Buddha, Krakucchanda. In the same way we have:

The second world.	The third world.
Dhyāni-Bodhisattva: Vajrapāṇi.	Dhyāni-Bodhisattva: Ratnapāṇi.
Dhyāni-Buddha: Akshobhya.	Dhyāni-Buddha: Ratnasambhava.
Mānushi-Buddha: Kanaka-Muni.	Mānushi-Buddha: Kāśyapa.

The fourth world is the present one, created by Avalokiteśvara (Dhyāni-Bodhisattva). His spiritual father, Amitābha (Dhyāni-Buddha), manifested himself on earth in the form of Gautama-Buddha, Śākya-muni. The Northern Buddhists believe that Avalokiteśvara continues the work that Gautama Buddha began, and, in order to do so, incarnates himself in each successive Dalai-Lama of Lhassa.

Five thousand years after the death of Gautama Buddha, Maitreya will appear as Mānushi-Buddha in the fifth world, which will be created by Viśvapāṇi (fifth Dhyāni-Bodhisattva), who dwells in the Rūpadhātu heaven waiting for the fifth cycle, when he will receive active power of creation and evolve the fifth world.

The Dhyāni-Bodhisattva is represented dressed in princely garments and wearing the thirteen precious ornaments, which are: a five-leaved crown, an ear-ring, a closely-fitting necklace, an armlet, a wristlet, a bracelet, an anklet, a shawl for the lower limbs and one for the upper; a garland reaching to the thigh and another to the navel; a girdle, and a sash. In the central leaf of the five-leaved crown is usually a small image of his Dhyāni-Buddha or spiritual father. The hair is drawn up in mitre shape, forming the *ushṇīsha*, and may be decorated with jewels. He generally has the *ūrṇā* on the forehead.

If the Dhyāni-Bodhisattva is in a sanctuary with his Dhyāni-Buddha he is always standing, but is represented seated when in his own chapel.

The first Dhyāni-Bodhisattva mentioned in the Buddhist scriptures is Mañjuśrī, personification of Wisdom. The second is Avalokiteśvara, personifying Mercy, while the third is Vajrapāṇi, bearer of the thunderbolt (*vajra*), personifying Power. These three form a very popular triad—the first triad in Northern Buddhism.

The Dhyāni-Bodhisattva may be in company with their *śakti* in *yab-yum* attitude, as well as the Dhyāni-Buddhas, who, in that case, are represented like the Bodhisattva and are called 'crowned Buddhas'.

The Chinese claim four Dhyāni-Bodhisattva: Ti-tsang (Kshitigarbha), who presides over the earth; Kwan-yin (Avalokiteśvara), who presides over water and symbolizes Mercy; Pu'hien (Samantabhadra), who presides over fire and symbolizes Happiness; Wen-shu (Mañjuśrī), who presides over ether and symbolizes Wisdom.

These are also practically the only Bodhisattva popular in Japan. The Bodhisattva in both China and Japan may be either dressed like a Buddha with only the high and complicated *ushṇīsha*, indicating his rank, or richly dressed and wearing many ornaments, which, however, do not correspond to the traditional thirteen ornaments quoted above. (v. *Kwan-yin* and *Kwan-non.*)

SAMANTABHADRA (First Dhyāni-Bodhisattva)

(Universal Kindness).

(T.) *kun-tu bzaṅ-po* (kind to all).
(M.) *qamugha sain* (all goodness).
(C.) *P'u hien* (普 賢).
(J.) *Fu-gen.*
Mudrā : *vitarka* (argument).
vara (charity).

Symbol : *cintāmaṇi* (magic jewel).
Colour : green.
Emblem : *utpala* (blue lotus).
Vāhana : elephant.
Dhyāni-Bodhisattva of the first Dhyāni-Buddha, Vairocana.

Samantabhadra was looked upon, among the ancient Northern Buddhist sects, as Highest Intelligence, a primordial Buddha ; but his popularity diminished when the two great sects, the Kar-gya-pa (Red Bonnets) and Ge-lug-pa (Yellow Bonnets), set up Vajradhara as Ādi-Buddha.

Certain of the Yogācārya sects claim that Samantabhadra, instead of Vairocana (his Dhyāni-Buddha), was the founder of the Yoga system, and look upon him as divinity of Religious Ecstasy. He is the special divine patron of those who practise Hokkésammai (ecstatic meditation).

Samantabhadra is the first Dhyāni-Bodhisattva corresponding with the five celestial Jinas, or Dhyāni-Buddhas, and is one of the group of eight Dhyāni-Bodhisattva found in Northern Buddhist temples. He is represented with the five-leaved crown, the ornaments and princely garments of the Bodhisattva, and holds his symbol, the *cintāmaṇi*, in his left hand, or it may be supported by a blue lotus at his left shoulder. The right hand makes *vitarka mudrā* : the hand raised—the thumb and index touching at the tips forming the 'triangular pose'. He may be either seated or standing ; and is sometimes with his *śakti* in the *yab-yum* attitude.

When in the group of eight Bodhisattva, he is standing with his hands in 'argument' and 'charity' *mudrā*, holding the stems of lotus-flowers which support his special symbol, the *cintāmaṇi*, at the right, and an accessory symbol, the *vajra*, at the left.

In Japan one finds Samantabhadra (Fu-gen) at the right of Amitābha in a triad with Mañjuśrī, seated on an elephant and holding a lotus-flower. The elephant may be crouching, but is more usually standing, and may have three heads or one head with six tusks (the more usual form). As Kongōsatta is sometimes represented supported by an elephant with three heads, he is often confused with Fu-gen (v. *Kongōsatta*).

In China the triad of Pu-hien (Samantabhadra) with Amitābha and Mañjuśrī is also popular. He is practically never represented alone, and is always on an elephant and usually holds a scroll (v. Pl. XXXIV, fig. *a*). The place of pilgrimage of Pu'hien is on Mount Omi (Wo-mei shan) in the province of Si-ch'wen, where, in one of the monasteries, there is a very fine bronze statue of the god, seated on an elephant.

PLATE XX

Dogmatic form of Avalokiteśvara

FORMS OF VAJRAPĀṆI

Table V

A. Human form:

I. Symbol:	*vajra* (thunderbolt) . . .	Dhyāni-Bodhisattva.
II. Symbols:	*vajra*, sometimes third eye. *ghaṇṭā* (bell). *pāśa* (lasso).	Ācārya-Vajrapāṇi (Dharmapāla).[1]

B. Other forms:

I. One head, four arms.	Symbols: *vajra*. Treads on personage lying on snakes.	Nīlāmbara-Vajrapāṇi (Yi-dam).[2]
II. Three heads, six arms.	Symbols: *vajra*. Holds snakes. Treads on Brahmā and Siva Form: *yab-yum*.	Mahācakra-Vajrapāṇi (Yi-dam).
III. Four heads, four arms, four legs.	Symbols: *khaḍga* (sword) *pāśa* (lasso) *vajra* (thunderbolt) Treads on demons.	Acala-Vajrapāṇi.
IV.	Form with head, wings, and claws like Garuḍa.	

[1] v. *Dharmapāla*.

[2] v. *Yi-dam*.

VAJRAPĀṆI (Second Dhyāni-Bodhisattva)

(Thunderbolt-bearer).

God of Rain.

(T.) *p'yag-na rdo-rje* (pro. *tchagdor*) (holding the thunderbolt).
(M.) *vačirbani* (corruption of *Vajrapāṇi*) or *modur taghan vačirtu* (with a thunderbolt in his hand).
(C.) *Ssŭ-kin-kang* (四金剛).
(J.) *Kongō.*[1]
Symbol: *vajra* (thunderbolt).
Colour: blue (dark).
Emblem: *utpala* (blue lotus).
Śakti: Sujata.
Mantra: *Ōm, Vajrapāṇi, hūm!*
Corresponds with the Brahmanical god Indra.

Dhyāni-Bodhisattva of the second Dhyāni-Buddha Akshobhya.
Dharmapāla (Drag-ched) forms.
Symbols: *vajra.*
khadga (sword).
pāśa (lasso).
ghaṇṭā (bell).
Distinctive marks: serpent.
small garuḍa (mythical bird).
One of both groups of five and eight Dhyāni-Bodhisattva.

VAJRAPĀṆI is both the ferocious emanation of Vajradhara and the spiritual reflex, the Dhyāni-Bodhisattva, of Akshobhya;[2] but in the early Buddhist legends, when mentioned as accompanying Gautama Buddha, he is referred to as a minor deity. In fact, according to certain accounts, he lived in the Trayastriṃśa heaven as king of the devas.

Grünwedel identifies Vajrapāṇi with Śakra or Indra, the Indian god of Rain. In the Buddhist records, Śakra is mentioned as being present at the birth of the Tathāgata[3] and as assisting at his flight from the palace. In the incident of the return of Śākya-muni from Kapilavastu, however, Vajrapāṇi is referred to as multiplying himself into eight devas to escort him, while the 'divine Śakra, with a multitude of devas belonging to Kāmaloka, took their place on the left hand'.

Hiuen-tsang mentions Vajrapāṇi as being with the Tathāgata when he subdued the gigantic snake in Udyāna. It is also related that when the Nāgas (serpent gods) appeared before the Buddha to listen to his teachings, Vajrapāṇi was charged by the Tathāgata to guard them from the attacks of their mortal enemies, the *garuḍas,*[4] and that, in order to deceive and combat the *garuḍas,* Vajrapāṇi assumed a form with head, wings, and claws like the *garuḍas* themselves. At the Parinirvāṇa of the Buddha it is recorded that 'letting fall his diamond sceptre[5] in despair, he rolled himself in the dust'.

[1] v. *Ni-ō.*

[2] Hodgson, however, calls him the 'aeon of Vajrasattva *Buddha*'.

[3] Grünwedel, *Buddhistische Kunst* (English translation), p. 90.

[4] A mythical bird of gigantic size.

[5] *vajra.*

PLATE XXI

a. AVALOKITEŚVARA

b. AVALOKITEŚVARA

c. AVALOKITEŚVARA

d. AVALOKITEŚVARA

The Nāgas are believed to control the rain-clouds, hence Vajrapāṇi, as their protector, is looked upon as the Rain God, and it is to him the Northern Buddhists appeal when rain is needed, or is too abundant.

Vajrapāṇi is rarely seen in statues alone, but often in a triad with Amitāyus (or Mañjuśrī) and Padmapāṇi. One finds him in religious paintings and in the miniatures of Nepalese books, where he is either at the left of the Dīpaṅkara Buddha or at the right of Tārā. He is represented holding the *vajra* and standing with his legs crossed.[1] This detail is of especial interest in identifying the personage in the Gandhāra sculptures who often accompanies Gautama Buddha, holding an object in his right hand which may be the primitive form of the *vajra*,[2] and whose legs are sometimes crossed. This same personage, holding the primitive *vajra*, was also found in the frescoes [3] discovered by Herr von Le Coq in Chinese Turkestan, as well as a Vajrapāṇi carrying a most ornate thunderbolt.

The non-Tantra Bodhisattva form of Vajrapāṇi is very rare. In Pander's *Pantheon* he is represented seated with the legs locked, balancing the *vajra* on his hands lying in 'meditation' *mudrā* on his lap, but he may be also making 'witness' (*bhūmisparśa*) *mudrā*, the *vajra* being balanced in the palm of his left hand on his lap.[4] In the collection of Mr. Gustave Schlumberger there is a Vajrapāṇi brandishing the *vajra* in his right hand while his left is in *vitarka mudrā.*

Besides being the protector of the Nāgas against the Garuḍas, Vajrapāṇi is the implacable enemy of the demons, the reason for which is explained in the following Buddhist legend.[5] Once upon a time the Buddhas all met together on the top of Mount Meru (Sumeru) to deliberate upon the best means of procuring the Water of Life (*amṛita*) which lies concealed at the bottom of the ocean.

The evil demons were in possession of the powerful poison, Halā-hala, and using it to bring destruction on mankind. In order to procure the antidote, they decided to churn the ocean with the Mount Meru. When the *amṛita* had risen to the surface of the water, they put it in the keeping of Vajrapāṇi, until they should decide on the best means of using it ; but Vajrapāṇi left the Elixir of Life a moment unguarded and the monster, Rāhu, stole it. Then followed a fearful struggle for the possession of the *amṛita*. Rāhu was conquered in the end, but the Water of Life had been defiled ; and the Buddhas, to punish Vajrapāṇi, forced him to drink it, whereupon he became dark blue from the poison mixed with the *amṛita.*

This legend seems to explain the presence of Vajrapāṇi as guardian of the Elixir of Life in a triad with Amitāyus, who holds the ambrosia vase, and Padmapāṇi, who carries a *kalaśa* (ewer of *amṛita*).

Vajrapāṇi is the second Dhyāni-Bodhisattva corresponding to the five Celestial Jinas. He is also one of the group of eight Dhyāni-Bodhisattva found in the

[1] Foucher, *Iconographie bouddhique*, p. 121.

[2] v. *Vajra.*

[3] Now in the Museum für Völkerkunde, Berlin.

[4] In one of the miniatures in the MS. Add. 1643 in the University Library, Cambridge, Vajrapāṇi is represented balancing the *vajra* in his left hand lying in his lap. He is painted white instead of blue.

[5] Schlagintweit, *Buddhism in Tibet.*

Northern Buddhist temples, in which case he is represented standing, with the *vajra* and *ghaṇṭā* supported by lotus-flowers, the stems of which he holds in his hands in 'charity' and 'argument' *mudrā*.

He has several ferocious (Dharmapāla) forms, assumed to combat the various demons. The most important of these forms are :

Vajrapāṇi-Ācārya (*Dharmapāla*).

He is represented in human form, with his dishevelled hair standing on end and wearing a skull crown. His expression is angry, and he has the third eye. Around his neck is a serpent necklace, and at his waist a belt of heads, underneath which is a tiger skin. He steps to the right, and in his uplifted hand is a *vajra*. If painted, he is dark blue, and is generally surrounded by flames in which are small Garuḍas.

Nīlāmbara-Vajrapāṇi (*Yi-dam*).

He has one head, a third eye, a skull crown, with sometimes a *vajra*, and snake in his dishevelled hair, and has four or six arms. Two hands are held at his breast in a mystic *mudrā*, and the second right arm is uplifted holding the *vajra*. He steps to the right on a crowned personage [1] lying on a bed of serpents.

Acala-Vajrapāṇi (*Dharmapāla*).

He has four heads, four arms as well as four legs, and his symbols are *vajra*, sword, lasso, and skull-cup (*kapāla*). He treads on demons.

Mahācakra-Vajrapāṇi (*Yi-dam*).

He has three heads with the third eye, six arms, and two legs. He is painted blue—the head at the right is white, at the left red. His symbols are the *vajra* and a long serpent, and he holds his *yum* with the two original arms. The *śakti* holds a *kapāla* (skull-cup) and *grigug* (chopper). He steps to the right on Brahmā and his left foot treads on Śiva.

Garuḍa form.

He is usually standing and has the wings and claws of a Garuḍa (Pl. LIX, fig. *c*). He may have a human head with a beak, or a head like a Garuḍa. He sometimes carries a sword and a gourd-shaped bottle, or his two hands may be in 'prayer *mudrā*.[2]

[1] Grünwedel suggests that it is Śiva, *Mythologie du Bouddhisme*, p. 164.

[2] Museum für Völkerkunde, Berlin.

PLATE XXII

Avalokiteśvara with twelve emanations

RATNAPĀṆI (Third Dhyāni-Boddhisattva)

(Jewel-bearer).

Symbol: *cintāmaṇi* (magic jewel).

Dhyāni-Bodhisattva of the third Dhyāni-Buddha Ratnasambhava.

Ratnapāṇi belongs to the group of five Dhyāni-Bodhisattva, but is not included in the group of eight.

The statues of Ratnapāṇi are very rare, and he is also seldom represented in paintings. He wears the usual five-leaved crown and ornaments of a Celestial Bodhisattva; and is seated with the right hand in 'charity' *mudrā*, sometimes holding the stem of a lotus-flower, while the left, balancing the *cintāmaṇi* (magic jewel) lies in his lap.[1]

There is a Chinese example in bronze, with three *cintāmaṇi* in the Bodhisattva crown. The flaming pearls are arranged with one above the other two, thus forming a triangle. In the left hand is a *cintāmaṇi*, also in the form of a pearl, from the top of which issues a three-forked flame. The right hand is in 'charity' *mudrā*.

The Japanese representations of Ratnapāṇi may hold the caitya (*stūpa*) instead of the magic jewel.

[1] v. Pander's *Pantheon*, Illus. LXXIX.

THE PRINCIPAL FORMS OF AVALOKITEŚVARA

Table VI

- **One head.**
  - **I. Human form.**
    - I. Avalokiteśvara. Mudrā : *namaḥkāra* (devotional).
      Symbol : rosary and pink lotus.
    - II. Padmapāṇi. Mudrā : *vara* (charity).
      Symbols : vase and lotus.
      Distinctive mark : Amitābha in crown.
    - III. Avalokita as Buddha.[1]
    - IV. Avalokiteśvara. Siṃhanāda (on roaring lion).
      Distinctive mark : crescent in hair.
    - V. Nīlakaṇṭhāryāvalokiteśvara.
    - VI. Trailokyavaśamkara-Lokeśvara.
    - VII. Harihariharivāhanodbhava.
  - **II. Human form with emanations.**
    - I. Avalokiteśvara with emanations of twelve 'crowned' Buddhas.
      Symbol : lotus.
    - II. Siṃhanāda-Lokeśvara with emanations of five Buddhas.
  - **III. Four arms.**
    - I. Form incarnate in the Dalai Lama.
      Mudrā : *namaḥkāra.*
      Symbols : lotus, vase, rosary or *mudrās.*
    - II. Upper hands : *mudrā namaḥkāra.*
      Lower hands : *mudrā dhyāna* (meditation) holding *pātra* (begging-bowl).
    - III. Mudrā : *dharmacakra* (turning the wheel of the law).
    - IV. Rakta-Lokeśvara.
  - **IV. Ten to eighteen arms.**
    - I. Ten arms—*añjali mudrā*—holding *Tārā.*
    - II. Padmanarteśvara.
  - **V.** Dogmatic form of Avalokiteśvara—twelve arms.
  - **VI.** Six to twenty arms. Amoghapāśa. Mudrā : *namaḥkāra* or *dharmacakra.*
    Special emblem : *pāśa* (lasso).
    Symbols : rosary, lotus, bow, &c.

[1] A. Foucher, *Iconographie bouddhique*, p. 94.

Three heads.

I. Third eye, four arms. Mudrā : *vara*.
Symbols : rosary, padma, bow and arrow.

II. Hālāhala-Lokeśvara.

Five heads.

I. Māyājālakramāryāvalokiteśvara.
Third eye—twelve arms.

II. Third eye, twenty-four arms. Mudrā : *añjali* (salutation).
namaḥkāra.
dhyāna.

Eleven heads.

I. Six to eight arms. Mudrā : *namaḥkāra*.
One pair of arms raised in *añjali mudrā*, holding Amitābha image.

I. 1,000 armed (if eyes in palms '1,000 eyes').
Symbols : rosary, lotus, *kalaśa*, &c.
Mudrā : *dharmacakra* or *namaḥkāra*.

II. 1,000 armed—two upper hands hold sword and shield—steps to right on serpent.[1]

III. '22,000' arms radiating from entire body.

Chinese form Kwan-shï-yin.

Japanese form Kwan-non.

[1] Difficult to determine (Illus. Pl. XXIII, fig. *b*).

AVALOKITEŚVARA (Fourth Dhyāni-Bodhisattva)

Lit. *avalokita* (looking on), *iśvara* (lord).

[The lord that looks down from on high.] [1]

(T.) *spyan-ras-gzigs* (pro. *tchen-re-si*) (with a pitying look).
(M.) *nidüberuǰükči* (lit 'he who looks with the eyes') or *qonksim-bodhisattva* (the smiling Bodhisattva).
(C.) *Kwan-shi-yin* (觀 音).
J.) *Kwan-non.*
Mudrā: *namaḥkāra* (prayer).

Symbols: *mālā* (rosary).
padma (pink lotus).
Colour: white [in Nepal, red [2]].
Consort: Tārā.
Mantra: *Ōm, maṇi padme, hūṃ!*
Vīja mantra: *Hri!*
Fourth Dhyāni-Buddha: Amitābha.
Dhyāni-Bodhisattva: Avalokiteśvara.
Mānushi-Buddha: Śākya-Muni.

IN the *Mani Kambum* [3] it is related that 'once upon a time, Amitābha, after giving himself up to earnest meditation, caused a white ray of light to issue from his right eye, which brought Padmapāṇi (Avalokita) Bodhisattva into existence'. It goes on to say that Amitābha blessed him, whereupon the Bodhisattva brought forth the prayer: '*Ōm, maṇi padme, hūṃ!*' 'Oh! the jewel (of creation) is in the lotus!' [4] (Beal).

Avalokiteśvara is thus the reflex or spiritual son of Amitābha, and, as the personification of Power, the All-pitying One, he is the most popular divinity in the Mahāyāna or Northern Buddhist Pantheon, and is the object of much veneration in Nepal and Tibet. In fact, his worship still extends northward to Lake Baikal and from the Caucasus eastward to Japan.

It is not known how early the worship of Avalokita existed in India. His name is mentioned in the *Suvarṇaprabhā-sūtra,* which dates before the Christian era, and Kāśyapa Mātaṅga [5] discoursed on this *sūtra* in India before introducing Buddhism into China, in the first century A. D. In Northern India his worship became popular toward the third century, and reached its climax in the seventh century. Fa-hian and

[1] According to the Tibetans, 'the lord who looks', but European scholars give 'the lord of what we see', 'the revealed lord', 'the lord whom we see', or 'the lord with compassionate glances'.

[2] Avalokiteśvara usually takes the colour of his spiritual father Amitābha (red) in Nepal. A. Foucher, *Iconographie bouddhique*, p. 99.

[3] A Tibetan historical work attributed to the Tibetan king Srong-tsan-gam-po.

[4] According to Hodgson the correct translation is: 'the mystic triform is in him of the jewel and lotus!' v. *Ōm.*

[5] Kāśyapa Mātaṅga is sometimes confounded with Kāśyapa Buddha. He returned with the Emperor Mingti's mission to China A. D. 67, and is believed to have been one of the first disciples of Gautama Buddha in a previous incarnation.

Hiuen-tsang speak of him with much reverence in the accounts of their travels in India.

Toward the eighth century the Mahāyāna school began to lose ground in India, and by the twelfth had practically disappeared, with the result that the very name of Avalokiteśvara is at present almost unknown south of the Himālayas.

His worship was introduced into Tibet in the middle of the seventh century, when he was proclaimed by the Buddhist priests incarnate in the king Srong-tsan-gam-po. He soon became the most popular of all the Northern Buddhist gods, being looked upon as a representative of Buddha, and guardian of the Buddhist faith until Maitreya should appear on earth as Mānushi Buddha.

Another reason for his popularity is that he is believed to have created the fourth world, which is the actual universe, and he is therefore our creator.

The worship of Avalokiteśvara was introduced into China toward the end of the first century A. D., where he was called Kwan-yin ; and penetrated into Japan in the beginning of the seventh century, where he was worshipped as Kwan-non.

Avalokita, who plays an important part in some of the *sūtras*, was endowed by the Northern Buddhists with innumerable virtues. Śākya-muni himself, according to the *Mahāyāna-sūtra*, acquainted the Bodhisattva Maitreya and Sarva-nīvaraṇa-vishkambhin with the perfections of Avalokita, and with the miracles he accomplished when he descended into hell to convert the wicked, deliver them and transport them to Sukhāvatī—paradise of Amitābha. Among other miracles, he relates how he himself was saved by the Bodhisattva, and recounts the legend of Siṃhala,[1] of his shipwreck off Tamradvīpa, of the beautiful women who were in reality Rākshasas,[2] who tempted him, and of the miraculous horse that appeared on the sea-shore and carried him away in safety. He ends by saying that he, Buddha, was Siṃhala, and that the miraculous horse was Avalokita.[3]

The figure of Avalokita was generally placed on a hill-top (which may account for his being called 'the lord that looks down from on high'), and, according to Beal, is probably a relic or revival of the old worship of the hill-gods. Hiuen-tsang speaks of him as manifesting himself on Mount Potala in Southern India. Eitel claims that he was first heard of at Potala,[4] at the mouth of the Indus, the reputed home of the ancestors of Śākya-muni ; but his chief sanctuary is on Mount Potala at Lhassa, 'on the top of which towers the residence of the Dalai-Lama, in whom and whose successors Avalokita is supposed to be incarnate.' (Eitel.)

Avalokiteśvara is in reality a kind of pope 'existing eternally in the heavens as a vicar of one of the Buddhas of the present age, but delegating his functions to a succession of earthly popes in whom he is perpetually incarnated and reincarnated, while at the same time preserving his personality in his own heaven'.

Buddhist legend claims that he manifested himself 333 times on earth for the purpose of saving mankind, and that all the manifestations were human, with

[1] v. Burnouf, *Introduction*, p. 199.

[2] Demons who devour men.

[3] According to Beal, Avalokita is often spoken of as a white horse.

[4] Eitel, *Three Lectures on Buddhism*.

the exception of the miraculous horse Keśi, and masculine, with the exception of the female forms of Kwan-yin in China and Kwan-non in Japan. He is supposed to have been incarnate in the Tibetan king Srong-tsan-gam-po, as well as in every successive Dalai-Lama, and is the principal tutelary deity of Tibet. He is worshipped in a triad with Mañjuśrī, God of Wisdom, and Vajrapāṇi, God of Power, on either side.

Although his first representations in India resembled Brahmā, with the hands in the Brahmāñjali *mudrā* (devotional attitude), his functions were those of Vishṇu—Preserver and Defender. But he also has much in common with Śiva, for the colour of both is white, and Avalokita may carry the trident with a serpent coiled about it—Śiva's symbol.

Avalokiteśvara is sometimes represented with five heads (v. Pl. XXIII, fig. *d*), in which case he resembles Śiva as Mahādeva with five heads;[1] but his form with more than one head has usually double that number, with the head of Amitābha on top, making eleven heads in all. He is often represented in *yab-yum* attitude with his *śakti*, but there are examples where he holds the *yum* on his knee in archaic manner, as Śiva holds Pārvatī.

In his earliest form he is represented with one head and two arms, and either sitting or standing. His hands may be in 'prayer' *mudrā*, or the right in 'charity' and the left in 'argument' *mudrā*. His most popular non-Tantra form is Padmapāṇi.

In the earliest representations of Avalokita, the hair is drawn up in a high *ushṇīsha*, but in later images he wears the five-leaved crown, in the centre leaf of which is usually a small image of his spiritual father Amitābha. In the paintings, however, according to M. Foucher, the image is usually omitted, and, if standing, the left hand is almost invariably in *vara* (charity) *mudrā*.[2]

Although Avalokiteśvara is more popular than Mañjuśrī, he is the second Bodhisattva mentioned in the Buddhist Scriptures, while Mañjuśrī is the first.

[1] v. Moor, *The Hindu Pantheon*, Pl. XV.

[2] A. Foucher, *Iconographie bouddhique*, p. 98.

PLATE XXIII

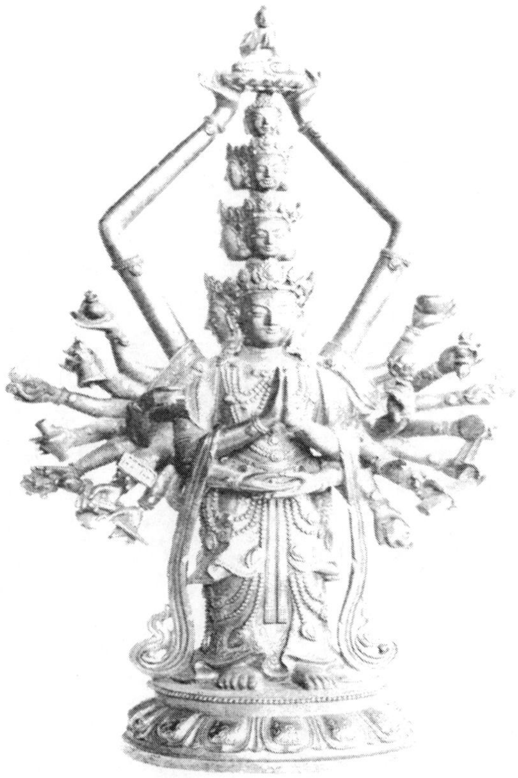

a. Avalokiteśvara

b. Avalokiteśvara (?)

c. Avalokiteśvara (Amoghapāśa)

d. Avalokiteśvara

SIṂHANĀDA-AVALOKITEŚVARA (or Siṃhanāda-Lokeśvara)

(The Lord with the voice of a lion).

Symbols : *padma* (lotus).
khaḍga (sword).
kapāla (skull-cup).
triśūla (trident).
Colour : white.

Siṃhanāda-Lokeśvara is a non-Tantra form of Avalokiteśvara invoked to cure leprosy. Northern Buddhists claim that the first success of Lamaism among the Mongols was due to the cure of a leprous king by means of the Siṃhanāda-sādhana.[1]

The title 'Siṃhanāda' means 'with the voice of a lion', and was also applied to Śākya-muni and Mañjuśrī. Grünwedel believes that it may have reference to an ancient legend in which the roaring of a lion awakened still-born babes to life.[2]

In this form, Avalokiteśvara is seated sideways on a roaring lion that is generally crouching, with the head always turned upward toward the god. According to the *sādhana*, the god should be seated on a lotus which is supported by a lion, but he is often seated on a cushion instead of on the lotus-throne.

In this Siṃhanāda form, Avalokita is represented in his manifestation of Padmapāṇi with one head and two arms. He wears all the Bodhisattva ornaments with a small image of Amitābha in the five-leaved crown. But the crown may be omitted, in which case his hair is drawn up into a mitre-shaped *ushṇīsha* elaborately decorated with jewels, and on the left side of the head-dress is usually a half moon. Over the left shoulder there may be an antelope skin. (v. Pl. XXXV, fig. *d.*) The right leg is either pendent (in which case the right hand is in 'charity' *mudrā*) or is in the attitude called 'royal ease', with the right knee raised and the right arm hanging loosely over the knee, the hand sometimes holding a rosary. In the latter attitude the left hand leans, behind the left knee, on the cushion (or lotus-throne), and holds the stem of a lotus-flower, which either supports a *kapāla* (skull-cup) out of which rises a sword, or the sword rises directly from the lotus-flower.[3] In the latter case, the *kapāla* filled with flowers is at his left side, but is often missing. Behind the right arm may rise a trident, around which is coiled a cobra,[4] but this also may be missing. In the bas-relief examples in Northern India there are usually emanations of the five Dhyāni-Buddhas.[5]

[1] v. *Sādhana*.

[2] *Mythologie bouddhique*, p. 130. According to Theobaldus in his *Physiologus*, when a lion is born it lies for three days as if dead and is then awakened to life by the roarings of its sire, the lion.

[3] v. Waddell, *Journal of the Royal Asiatic Society*, Jan. 1894, Pl. I.

[4] A. Foucher, *Iconographie bouddhique*, Partie II, illust., p. 33.

[5] v. *The Dhyāni-Buddhas*, and Pl. XIV.

The Siṃhanāda-Lokeśvara seems to unite the form of Avalokita and Mañjuśrī—the idea evidently borrowed from an ancient Brahman custom, but although the sword, the pose, and the support indicate Mañjuśrī, the god is undoubtedly Padmapāṇi, according to all the authorities.

Avalokiteśvara is represented as Siṃhanāda in a simpler form, but is always a Lokeśvara (or Lokanātha), a prince wearing rich garments and many jewels. In this form he is seated on the lion support with his hands at his breast in *namaḥkāra mudrā* (devotional attitude). His hair is drawn up on his head in a high *ushṇīsha*, mitre-shaped. His symbol, the rosary, is supported by a lotus-flower on a level with his right shoulder.

PADMAPANI (Dhyāni-Bodhisattva)

(Lotus-bearer)

(*Non-Tantra form of Avalokiteśvara*).

(J.) *Shō Kwan-non.*
Mudrā: *vitarka* (argument) and *vara* (charity).
Special symbols: *padma* (lotus).
kalaśa (vase).

Colour: white [in Nepal, red].
Distinctive mark: small image of his Dhyāni-Buddha, Amitābha, in his crown.

Padmapāṇi is a non-Tantra form of Avalokiteśvara, and is supposed to create all animate things by command of his Dhyāni-Buddha, Amitābha. According to the system of Ādi-Buddha, he received from the Ādi-Buddha, through the medium of his spiritual father, Amitābha, the active power of creation, of which the lotus he holds in his hand is the symbol.[1]

He is supposed to have created the actual world, which is the fourth, and according to Hodgson, to have produced 'Brahmā, for creating; Vishṇu, for preserving; Maheśa (Śiva), for destroying'.[2]

After the death of Gautama Buddha, Padmapāṇi is believed to have undertaken the work of propagation of Buddhism, until the creation of the fifth world by Viśvapāṇi, and it is probably for this reason that he is extremely popular in Tibet, and especially so in Japan, under the name of Shō Kwan-non.[3] He is also said to be the favourite deity of the Nāgas (serpent gods).

Padmapāṇi is represented as a slight, graceful youth, and, being a Dhyāni-Bodhisattva, is dressed like an Indian prince with many ornaments. His hair is drawn up in a mitre-shaped *ushṇīsha* behind the five-leaved crown, in which is a small image of Amitābha (his distinctive mark), but the crown may be missing, especially in the paintings.

In his earliest form he held the lotus-flower (his special symbol) indicated by his

[1] v. *Padma*. [2] v. *Padmapāṇi*, with twelve emanations. [3] v. *Kwan-non*.

PLATE XXIV

Avalokiteśvara '22,000 arms'

name; but in later representations the vase was added. The lotus-flower, however, was seldom represented in the vase, as in China and Japan.

According to his mantra, '*Ōm, maṇi padme, hūṃ!*', he should carry a jewel; but such examples are very rare in Tibet, while in both China and Japan the *cintāmaṇi* often figures as an accessory symbol carried by the Tantra forms of Avalokiteśvara, and the jewel and lotus are held as principal symbols by the Nyo-i-rin Kwan-non (when with six arms).

Padmapāṇi is generally represented standing, with his hands in 'argument' and 'charity' *mudrā*. The left hand in '*vara*' *mudrā* holds either the stem of a lotus-flower or the vase. When in the group of eight Bodhisattva, Padmapāṇi holds the stems of two lotus-flowers which support the vase and a rosary (symbol of Avalokiteśvara). When the vase is supported it usually has a spout like the libation *kalaśa* used in the Buddhist ceremonies. When carried in the hand it is held at the neck, and is round in shape if Indian, and oval or pointed if of the Gandhāra school.[1]

Padmapāṇi may have an antelope skin over his left shoulder, and in this form, if the small image of Amitābha is missing from his crown and he holds the vase, he resembles a form of Maitreya, whose symbol is also the *kalaśa*. (v. *Maitreya*.)

In Ceylon small bronze figures of Padmapāṇi have been found, considered to be between the sixth and ninth centuries, where he is represented seated in the attitude called 'royal ease' (*rājalīlā*) with the right or left foot pendent. The right hand may be in *vitarka*, *abhaya*, or *vara mudrā*, while the left, behind the left knee, rests on the throne, and usually holds the stem of a full-blown lotus-flower at the left shoulder (Pl. XXI, fig. *d*). This form is also found in China (Pl. XXI, fig. *b*), and closely resembles the Mahārājalīla-Mañjuśrī, the difference being that he carries the full-blown rose lotus (*padma*) instead of the blue lotus with the petals closed (*utpal*), and has a small image of his Dhyāni-Buddha in his head-dress, which is unusual in the images of Mañjuśrī.[2]

He sometimes accompanies the Dīpaṅkara Buddha, but he may himself have assistants to the number of four. In the latter case, the green Tārā is always at his right, and he is accompanied by Prajñāpāramitā (or Mārīcī) and the yellow Tārā, as well as by the god Hayagrīva. Padmapāṇi is also sometimes found in a triad with Mañjuśrī and Vajrapāṇī.

In the Lamaist temple pictures he is white, while in the Nepalese paintings, according to M. Foucher, he is red, and the small image of Amitābha in his crown is generally omitted.

Another form of Padmapāṇi, seldom seen except in temple paintings, is called 'Defender of the Eight Dreads'.[3] He is without the lotus and is painted white. In the museum at Colombo there is an image of Padmapāṇi, with a *kalaśa* above the forehead, in front of the *ushṇīsha*.

[1] v. *Kalaśa*.

[2] Illustration, A. Foucher, *Iconographie bouddhique*, Partie II, p. 43, and A. Coomaraswamy, 'Mahāyāna Buddhist Images from Ceylon', *Journal of the Royal Asiatic Society of Great Britain and Ireland*, April, 1909.

[3] This form may be the origin of the Pa-nan or 'Kwan-yin of the Eight Sufferings'.

PADMAPĀṆI

with emanations of twelve Bodhisattva (or 'crowned' Buddhas ?).

The bronze statue with emanations of twelve Bodhisattva (Pl. XXII) is, as far as the author knows, unique. It was purchased at Darjeeling, where, however, it was impossible to find any one who could give a satisfactory interpretation of its significance.

The difficulty in determining the signification of the Bodhisattva (or are they 'crowned' Buddhas ?) that emanate from the *ushṇīsha*, *urṇā*, ears, mouth, heart, navel, hands, and feet of the Padmapāṇi form of Avalokiteśvara is that there are no symbols or distinguishing *mudrā*. There are, however, several hypotheses which seem to explain, to a certain extent, the bronze.

1. Does it correspond with the eleven-headed form of Avalokiteśvara ?

The two emanations from the feet might be identified as Vishṇu and Śiva, for it was often the custom of the Northern Buddhists to represent Brahmā, Vishṇu, and Śiva at the feet of their gods. (Pl. XXIV.)

The ten Bodhisattva thus left are most difficult to identify, but may possibly correspond with the ten heads of Āryāvalokiteśvara, whose normal head is counted as the eleventh.

If we accept the hypothesis that the form of Padmapāṇi with the ten emanations corresponds with the Ārya Pāla form of Avalokiteśvara, the upper 'crowned' Buddha emanating from the *ushṇīsha* would be his Dhyāni-Buddha, and the one underneath issuing from the *ūrṇā* the Mānushi-Buddha. There still remain eight Bodhisattva to identify.

The lower emanation on the left, issuing from the heart, has every appearance of being his consort, the white Tārā. The second, from the top to the left, with a musical instrument, resembles Sarasvatī ; and the third, with the left leg pendent, is possibly the green Tārā. The rest seem impossible to identify. We know from the *sādhana*[1] that there was a form of Padmapāṇi called 'Padmanarteśvara', seated on an eight-petalled lotus, on each petal of which was a goddess, Tārā, Bhṛikutī, &c. Are then these eight emanations goddesses ?

2. Does it represent the 'vital breaths' ?

Ten of the twelve emanations might represent 'the ten vital breaths' (the five organs of sense and the five material elements, earth, water, fire, air, and ether, of which man is composed). The eleventh emanation would then be the sixth sense which proceeded from the Dhyāni-Buddha, and is indicated in the bronze by the divinity above the forehead. The twelfth emanation would be the sixth element, the mind (*manas*), which is believed to be a particle of the essence of Ādi-Buddha, and

[1] A. Foucher, *Iconographie bouddhique*, Partie II, p. 37.

would be represented by the divinity emanating from the *ushṇīsha* and placed above the Dhyāni-Buddha.

3. Does it represent the creation of the fourth world by Padmapāṇi?

In the *Kāraṇḍa-Vyūha* it is written that Padmapāṇi, at the command of Ādi-Buddha, produced, by the virtue of three *guṇas* (active principles), Brahmā, creator of *devas* and human beings; Vishṇu, preserver; and Mahā Devā (Śiva), destroyer. From the Bodhisattva also emanated Vayū, the air; Prithivī, the earth; Varuṇa, the water on which the earth was believed to rest; Indra, who brought rain; Sūrya, the sun; and Candra, the moon, whose rays fructified the earth. Added to these was Sarasvatī, goddess of music and poetry, and Lakshmī, goddess of beauty. Yama was also among the *devas*, to punish sin; for although from Brahmā emanated virtue, from Śiva proceeded evil.

In a passage in the *Kāraṇḍa-Vyūha* these deities are made to *proceed from the body of Padmapāṇi*, and they are twelve in number.

In the *Guṇa-Kāraṇḍa Vyūha* is the following passage: 'From between his (Padmapāṇi's) shoulders sprang Brahmā; from his two eyes, the sun and the moon; from his mouth, the air; from his teeth, Sarasvatī; from his belly, Varuṇa; from his knees, Lakshmī; from his feet, the earth; from his navel, water; from the roots of his hair, the Indras and devatās.' [1]

In the bronze the emanation from the shoulders has three heads; but the fourth, not showing behind the heads, may possibly have been omitted by the artist, in which case one could identify the Bodhisattva with Brahmā.

The *deva* emanating from the right foot and holding a mountain over the head may be easily identified with Pṛithivī, the earth, and the emanation from the teeth with Sarasvatī holding her lute. The *deva* with the serpent over the head, proceeding from the left foot, is evidently Varuṇa, water, but in the text Varuṇa proceeds from the navel.

None of the other emanations have anything to identify them either by way of a symbol or a *mudrā*, so that if we accept the hypothesis that the bronze represents the passage quoted above, we must look upon the emanation from the *ushṇīsha* as Indra; from the forehead, as Śiva; from the eyes, Sūrya and Candra; from the mouth (to the right), Vāyu; from the left knee, Lakshmī; and from the emanation between Sarasvatī and Lakshmī (which may possibly proceed from the navel, although the bronze does not clearly indicate it), Yama.

Among the Nepalese paintings from the collection of B. H. Hodgson in the Library of the Institut de France, there is a temple painting representing Padmapāṇi (red) with *eleven* emanations, which closely follows the above text with the exception that in his crown is a small image of Amitābha, in place of the twelfth emanation from the *ushṇīsha* in the bronze. The painting is divided into three *loka*: celestial, terrestrial, and the underworld. From each finger of the right hand of Padmapāṇi is an emanation (?) that is located in the third *loka* and is, according to M. Foucher,

[1] Hodgson, *The Languages, Literature, and Religions of Nepal and Tibet*, p. 88.

a *prēta.*[1] These five personages, which are also represented in the pedestal of the bronze, resemble Germanic gnomes.

None of the hypotheses apply absolutely to the bronze, possibly because the artist did not follow tradition in every detail, and also, very probably, because the correct interpretation has not yet been found.

AVALOKITEŚVARA

Tantra form.

The first Tantra form of Avalokita appeared in Northern India after the founding of the Tantra school by Asaṅga about the middle of the sixth century A. D., and differs from the non-Tantra form in that there are four arms instead of two. The god is represented dressed in princely garments, with many ornaments. The hair is drawn up on the head, mitre-shaped, like the non-Tantra form, and the *ushṇīsha* is often surmounted by a flaming pearl. There is generally a small image of his spiritual father, Amitābha, in his head-dress, especially when, later, the five-leaved Bodhisattva crown was added. The god is represented seated with the legs closely locked, and with the two original hands either against his breast in *namaḥkāra* (prayer) *mudrā*, resembling the attitude of Brahmā, when repeating the Vedas, or in *dharma-cakra mudrā* (Pl. XXI, fig. *c*). The hands, however, may clasp a jewel, symbolical of the *maṇi* (jewel) in his mantra: '*Ōm, maṇi padme, hūṃ!*'[2] or hold a conch-shell, but these forms are very rare. The other two hands hold the rosary, and either the lotus or book. It is this form that is supposed to be incarnate in the Dalai-Lama at Lhassa.

There is another form with one head and four arms, but standing. The upper arms are against the breast in *namaḥkāra mudrā*, the lower are in *dhyāna mudrā* and hold the *pātra* (begging-bowl) (v. Pl. XXI, fig. *a*).

In the Bacot Collection at the Musée Guimet there is a small copper-gilt statue of Avalokiteśvara with one head and ten arms. The upper arms are raised, the hands in *añjali* (salutation) *mudrā*, over the head, and hold a small image which should be his Dhyāni-Buddha, but in this case resembles his *śakti*, Tārā. It cannot be Amitābha, as catalogued, for a part of the hair is drawn up into a mitre-shaped *ushṇīsha*, while the rest hangs down the back, indicating a Bodhisattva. The right hand is in 'argument', the left in 'charity' *mudrā*. Against the right shoulder is a flowering branch. The left is pendent, indicating the green Tārā.

[1] *Catalogue des Peintures népalaises et tibétaines de la collection B. H. Hodgson à la Bibliothèque de l'Institut de France*, p. 26. According to M. Foucher, the *prētas* are receiving ambrosia from the finger-tips of Padmapāṇi, and there are three illustrations of this in the Nepalese MS. Add. 1643 in the University Library, Cambridge, where the ambrosia flows directly from his finger-tips into the mouths of personages or animals. v. Pl. IV, no. 28, Foucher, *Iconographie bouddhique*.

[2] v. Bacot Collection, Musée Guimet, Paris.

Avalokiteśvara may have four heads and twenty-four arms. There is a head on either side of the central head, and above them is a head of Buddha, which may be his Manushi-Buddha, Śākya-muni, for he holds his Dhyani-Buddha, Amitābha, over his heads by his upper arms, in *añjali mudrā* (Pl. XXIII, fig. *d*).

There are many variations of these different Tantra forms of Avalokiteśvara, and one of them, called *Amoghapāśa*, holds a special emblem, the *pāśa* (lasso). He has one head and from six to eight arms, and besides his special symbol, the lasso, he holds the rosary, trident, ewer, &c., and may wear a tiger-skin. He is sometimes accompanied by the green Tārā, Sudhana-Kumāra, Hayagrīva, and Bhṛikuṭī.

There is another form of Amoghapāśa, with one head and twenty arms, which is seated (Pl. XXIII, fig. *c*). The normal arms are against his breast, in *namaḥkāra mudrā*; the arms underneath lie on the lap, the right hand holding the lasso, the left the rosary. The two upper hands are close to the head and hold cymbals, the next pair holds lotus-buds, the next *vajra* and *ghaṇṭā*, and all the rest hold various symbols belonging to Avalokiteśvara.

The Dogmatic Form of Avalokiteśvara (Pl. XX).

In this form he has one head, twelve arms, and is seated with the legs firmly locked. He wears all the Bodhisattva ornaments, and his *ushṇīsha*, behind the five-leaved crown, is surmounted by a half *vajra*, above which the hands of the uppermost pair of arms make the 'lotus' *mudrā*. The author has been unable to find the Sanksrit name of this gesture, and will designate it as the *padma mudrā*,[1] which is made in the following manner: the middle and index fingers are stretched upward and touch at the tips; the ring and little fingers are locked (finger-tips underneath); the thumbs are upright and pressed against each other.

The hands of the next two pairs of arms hang over the shoulders, in *vitarka mudrā*, and, from their position, evidently held symbols—presumably the rosary and lotus-flower. The hands of the original arms are in *abhaya mudrā*.

The hands of the arms directly underneath are in 'lotus' *mudrā*, with, however, a slight variation, which is, that the indexes do not touch at the tips but are slightly bent, and the tips press against the middle fingers.[2] The position of the hands is reversed, that is to say, that the indexes and middle fingers are stretched downward instead of upward, and the tips of the latter descend into the vase held by the hands underneath, in *dhyāna mudrā*. This position is most unusual and represents the dominant principle of the Yogāchārya school: the Mystic Union. The hands, in 'lotus' *mudrā*, symbolize the *Vajradhātu*, and the vase the *Garbhadhātu*—the union of the Spiritual and the Material or the Two Parts (v. Glossary—*Vajra*, *Vajradhātu*, *Garbhadhātu*).

[1] Called by the Japanese *renge-no-in* (v. Glossary) or the '*mudrā* of the lotus'. v. Pl. LXIV.

[2] The middle fingers symbolize the element *fire*, and in this position represent the flame which is the symbol of Ādi-Buddha. This *mudrā* (with the fingers upright) is used by the Japanese priests in Buddhist ceremonies, and is called by them '*nirvāṇa*' *mudrā*.

ĀRYĀVALOKITEŚVARA (Ārya-Pāla)

(Eleven-headed).

(T.) *ḫp'ags-pa spyan-ras-gzigs* (the sublime (divinity of) penetrating (and) charming vision).
(M.) *ariabalo* (corruption of the Sanskrit).
(J.) *Ju-ichi-men* (eleven-headed) *Kwan-non.*

Mudrā: *namaḥkara* (prayer).
Colour: white (but may be yellow).
Distinctive mark: eleven heads.

Avalokiteśvara, in his manifestation with eleven heads, is *samantamukha* or the 'all-sided one'—the god who looks in every direction to save all creatures.

There are several versions of the legend explaining his eleven heads, but they all resolve themselves into the following: Avalokiteśvara, the All-Pitying One, descended into hell, converted the wicked, liberated them, and conducted them to Sukhāvatī, the paradise of his spiritual father, Amitābha.

He discovered, however, to his dismay, that for every culprit converted and liberated, another instantly took his place, and legend claims that his head split into ten pieces from grief and despair on discovering the extent of wickedness in the world, and the utter hopelessness of saving all mankind. Amitābha caused each piece to become a head and placed the heads on the body of his spiritual son, Avalokiteśvara, in three tiers of three, with the tenth head on top and his own image above them all. Thus, the 'On-looking Lord' was endowed with twenty-two eyes instead of two, to see all suffering, and eleven brains instead of one, to concentrate on the best means of saving mankind.

Monier Williams claims that the three tiers of heads indicate that Avalokiteśvara looks down on the three worlds: world of desire, world of true form, and world of no form. According to Eitel, the three groups of heads represent the triad Avalokita, Mañjuśrī, and Vajrapāṇi, for in this form of Ārya-Pāla he always carries a book and a thunderbolt, symbols of Mañjuśrī and Vajrapāṇi. Statues were found in the Magadha which combine these three gods,[1] and there are descriptions of this form in the Nepalese *sādhana*, where the Siṃhanādalokeśvara is mentioned as being seated on a lion with the sword (Mañjuśrī's symbol) on a lotus at his left, and a *vajra*-shaped trident, around which is coiled a snake, at his right, indicating Vajrapāṇi. The form is, however, looked upon as Avalokiteśvara. Griffis claims that these three gods were originally one divinity, and that the qualities attributed to this deity of Mercy, Wisdom, and Force were personified later in the forms of Avalokiteśvara, Mañjuśrī, and Vajrapāṇi.

But the signification of the eleven heads may go back further than the Buddhist legend. We have seen that Avalokita has much in common with Śiva, who is a development of the Vedic god Rudra.

In the Bṛihadāraṇyaka *Upanishad* there is reference to a group of eleven Rudras

[1] Foucher, *Iconographie bouddhique*, vol. ii, illustr., p. 33.

PLATE XXV

a. Padmapāṇi

b. Kwan-non

c. Padmapāṇi

d. Padmapāṇi

which represent the 'ten vital breaths with the heart as the eleventh' (Dawson). This seems to correspond with the ten heads of Ārya-Pāla, with his spiritual father, Amitābha, as the eleventh.

In the *Vishṇu Purāṇa* there is also a description which applies closely to the Ārya-Pāla form: Rudra is born from a wrinkle in the forehead of Brahmā, separates into male and female, and multiplies into eleven persons, 'some of which are white and gentle and others black and furious'.[1] These are evidently the eleven Rudras quoted above, and correspond with the painted forms of Ārya-Pāla, for the first row of heads of Āryāvalokiteśvara are white and of a sweet expression, the second row are yellow and smiling, while the third row are dark blue and of angry expression. The tenth head and the head of Amitābha are calm in expression, but there are examples of the Bodhisattva in which only the tenth head shows anger.

Āryāvalokiteśvara may have from six to '22,000' arms approximately. The original ones, in most of the examples, are against the breast, the hands usually making the devotional *mudrā*, but they may also be in *dharmacakra mudrā* (turning the Wheel of the Law), and below them are hands in *dhyāna mudrā*, sometimes holding an ambrosia vase. The other hands hold the rosary, wheel, &c. The upper arms may be raised above the head, in *añjali* (salutation) *mudrā*, holding the image of Amitābha over the ten heads. This form has usually twenty-two arms (Pl. XXIII, fig. *a*).

Avalokiteśvara with eleven heads is sometimes represented with thousands of arms, which radiate around him, forming an aura; but the original pair is always at his breast, in 'prayer' or 'teaching' *mudrā*, and several of the hands hold his special symbols. If there is an eye on the palm of each hand, he is called 'of '22,000 eyes', which means that the eyes of Avalokita are ever on the outlook for those in distress and carry with them a succouring hand. The various symbols he may carry are: book, vase, jewel, *vajra*, begging-bowl, wheel, &c., and one of the hands is usually making *vara* (charity) *mudrā*. Brahmā, Vishṇu, and Śiva are sometimes represented at the feet of the Bodhisattva (Pl. XXIV).

An image of Āryāvalokiteśvara, belonging to M. Deniker, has many arms radiating, even from the legs.

Forms of Avalokiteśvara from Sādhana.[2]

I. Avalokita as a Buddha is seated, legs closely locked, hands in *dhyāna-mudrā*. He is white, has the *ūrṇā*, but not the *ushṇīsha*, and his monastic garment is red.[3] According to the *sādhana*, it is his Chinese manifestation, Kwan-yin.

II. Siṃhanāda-Lokeśvara. He is white, and has one head and three eyes. He is seated in the attitude called 'royal ease', with the right knee raised, on a roaring lion, and has a tiger-skin covering. In his crown is a small image of Amitābha. Five

[1] Dawson, *Classical Dictionary of Hindu Mythology*.

[2] A. Foucher, *Iconographie bouddhique*. v. *Sādhana*.

[3] The *śramaṇa* of the White Horse Temple, at Loh-yang, China, wore red robes during the Han dynasty. Parker, *Studies in Chinese Religion*.

Buddhas emanate from him. He has two arms. The left hand, resting on the throne, holds the stem of a lotus, from which rises a sword (Mañjuśrī's emblem). The right arm rests on his right knee, and behind it is a trident around which is coiled a snake.

III. Nīlakaṇṭhāryāvalokiteśvara. Human form seated on an antelope-skin on a red lotus. In his head-dress is a small image of Amitābha. His hands are in *dhyāna-mudrā*, holding a skull of jewels. He wears the Brahmanical chord, and his covering is a tiger-skin. He has no jewels. His colour is yellow and his throat is blue.[1]

IV. Trailokyavaśaṅkara-Lokeśvara. Human form with third eye. Is seated on a red lotus, *à l'indienne*, and holds the lasso with a half *vajra* at each end and an elephant goad. His colour is red.

V. Harihariharivāhanobdhava-Lokeśvara-Avalokita is seated on Vishṇu, who is seated on Garuḍa, who is supported by a lion.[2]

VI. Rakta-Lokeśvara. He has one head and four arms, and is represented seated under an *aśoka*-tree. His symbols are: lasso, elephant, goad, bow, arrow. His colour is red.

VII. Padmanarteśvara. He may be human, or have eighteen arms. His normal ones embrace his *śakti*. He is seated on a lotus with eight petals, with a divinity on each petal—Tārā, Bhṛikuṭī, &c. If he has eighteen arms, he has only four assistants, among which are Hayagrīva.

VIII. Māyājālakramāryāvalokiteśvara, or 'he that passes through the net of illusion'. He has five heads, each with a third eye. The two on the right are white and red, the two on the left are yellow and green. He is black, as well as the central head. His twelve hands hold: a *kapāla*, lasso, *vajra*, *ratna*, lotus, &c., and his normal ones hold the bow and arrow.

IX. Hālāhala[3]-Lokeśvara. He has three heads, each with a third eye. The one to the right is blue, to the left red, and the centre one is white. In his chignon is an image of Amitābha and a crescent. He has many ornaments, and has a tiger-skin for covering. He has six arms, and his symbols are: rosary, lotus, bow and arrow, &c. He is seated on a red lotus, and holds his *śakti* on his left knee, the right being stretched out. There is a trident, round which is circled a serpent to the right, and a lotus supporting a skull filled with flowers to the left. His colour is white.

[1] Śiva's throat became blue after drinking the poison *Hālā-hala* to save mankind.

[2] This form is found in India with Vishṇu seated on Garuḍa, who stands on a turtle, with a dwarf, one of the *avatārs* of Vishṇu, between his legs.

[3] The *Hālā-hala* is the poison which was churned from the ocean by the gods.

PLATE XXVI

Kwan-yin (Sung-tsê)

FORMS OF KWAN-SHĬ-YIN

Table VII

Kwan-shĭ-yin.	I. Two arms.	I. Holds child. With or without acolytes. With or without dragon.	Sung-tsë (feminine).
		II. On lotus holding willow branch or *kalaśa*. Or rolls of prayers. Or hands making *dhyāna mudrā*.	Kwan-yin (feminine).
		III. *a*. Represented on the sea. *b*. Represented on a cloud.	Kwo-hai (feminine).
		IV. Seated on a lion.	Kwan-yin Siṃhanāda (feminine).
		V. Group of eight Kwan-yin (masculine or feminine).	Pa-nan.
		VI. Group of thirty-two Kwan-yin (masculine).	San-shĭ-rĭ-siang.
		VII. Kwan-yin with crown of eight heads called 'eight-faced' (masculine).	
	II. More than two arms.	I. Kwan-yin with ten arms (feminine).	
		II. Kwan-yin with eighteen arms (masculine).	
		III. 1,000 armed Kwan-yin (masculine or feminine).	
	III.	Japanese form : Kwan-non.	
	IV.	Legend of Miao Chen.	
	V.	Legend of Hāritī.	

KWAN-SHÏ-YIN

(S.) *Avalokiteśvara.* (J.) *Kwan-non.*

KWAN-SHÏ-YIN, god (or goddess) of Mercy, is confounded, in some of the Chinese texts, with Maitreya, whose title is 'family of Mercy', and with Pūrṇa Maitrāyaṇīputra (disciple of Śākya-muni), whose title is 'son of full Mercy'; but European, as well as most Chinese scholars, look upon the god as a manifestation of Avalokiteśvara, although they do not agree as to the meaning of the name itself, *Kwan-shï-yin.*

The word was used for the first time by Kumārajīva, who, in the fifth century A. D., translated a chapter of the *Saddharmapuṇḍarīka*[1] into Chinese. There is a divergence of opinion in regard to his use of the word 'Kwan-shï-yin' in his translation of the title of this chapter, which is: 'Avalokiteśvara Bodhisattva samantamukha'. Some claim that 'Kwan-shï-yin' is a Chinese version of 'Avalokiteśvara', while others are of the opinion that it is a translation of *samantamukha*, his title, which may mean 'universally manifested voices'.[2] According to Edkins[3] the literal translation may be thus interpreted: *kwan* (looks on), *shï* ('the region' of sufferers), *yin* (whose 'voices' of many tones, all acknowledging misery and asking salvation, touch the heart of the pitiful Bodhisattva).

The worship of Avalokiteśvara was introduced into China during the Han dynasty[4] towards the end of the first century A.D., and by the sixth century the god of Mercy was worshipped in all the Buddhist temples. In the seventh century he was still popular, for Hiuen-tsang speaks of him with enthusiasm; and by the twelfth he was practically forgotten, except in monasteries and temples where precedence demanded his presence.

But in spite of his popularity in China during several centuries, the Indian Buddhist priests were unable to impose the Sanskrit name of their god on the Chinese, and Avalokiteśvara was exclusively worshipped as 'Kwin-yin', god of Mercy.

The quality of 'mercy', however, seems to have appealed to the Chinese as feminine rather than masculine, for a goddess of Mercy, believed to be the feminine manifestation of Avalokiteśvara, made her appearance and drew many worshippers.

When later, the title 'Giver of Sons (Sung-tsë) was added to that of 'mercy' the goddess Kwan-yin acquired a popularity that defied all Indian Buddhist influence and has lasted up to the present day, in China as well as in Japan.

There are no records by which one can determine the earliest appearance of the female form of Kwan-yin in China, and hence much divergence of opinion in regard to her origin.

[1] Lotus of the Good Law.

[2] M. de la Vallée Poussin gives as translation 'The All-sided One'.

[3] *Chinese Buddhism*, p. 382.

[4] Ibid.

It is admitted by Eitel [1] that the goddess of Mercy may have been a divinity worshipped in China long before the introduction of Buddhism.[2] She may even have been a Taoist goddess, for Hackmann writes that deities peculiar to Taoism have been 'found under another guise in Buddhism'. Edkins confirms the above quotation when he says that Taoist idols were often employed in Buddhist temples. He also refers to a *sūtra* found by a Japanese priest, Tan-wu, in India in the fourteenth century, the subject of which was the 'admission of Kwan-shï-yin to a Buddhist life'.[3]

Lillie,[4] in referring to the goddess Kwan-yin, quotes from the Abbé Provèze and says: 'The Abbé Provèze is aware, however, that the Kwan-yin is much earlier historically than the Virgin Mary,[5] for he starts a second theory that the idea was plagiarized from an Old Testament in a synagogue that the Jews had in China two hundred years before Christ.'

If we accept the hypothesis that a goddess of Mercy was worshipped in China earlier than Avalokiteśvara, the divinity could have been none other than the Chinese princess and saint, Miao-Chen,[6] who, according to Chinese legend, lived 2587 B.C. Chinese historical accounts, however, identify her father with King Chanwang of the Chow dynasty 696 B.C., which date is probably more nearly correct.

According to her legend, Miao-Chen became a goddess and retired to an island in the Chusan Archipelago called P'u-to. The name *P'u-to* is believed to be a corruption of 'Potala', home of Avalokiteśvara, and probably only dates from the tenth century, when the Buddhist priests took possession of the island.

It is not known whether or not the Buddhist priests found the worship of a goddess already established on the island when they took possession of it; but such would seem the case since, although the island was dedicated to Padmapāṇi, it became the most popular shrine of the goddess Kwan-yin.

In one of the temples on the island there is a seated figure of the goddess of Mercy, while behind her, standing, is a figure of Padmapāṇi, and around the walls, also standing, is the group of thirty-two masculine Kwan-yin. This fact alone shows that the feminine form took precedence.

Unfortunately, no documents have been found to prove that the goddess Kwan-yin was a development of the saint Miao-Chen, or that Miao-Chen was worshipped as goddess of Mercy before the introduction of Buddhism into China. Only by inference and deduction, and by comparing the different manifestations of the goddess Kwan-yin,

[1] *Handbook of Chinese Buddhism.*

[2] Edkins says in his *Chinese Buddhism*, p. 415: 'Eitel, in his account of Kwan-yin, goes too far when he supposes there was a Chinese divinity of this name (goddess of Mercy) before the introduction of the Mahāyāna into China.'

[3] *Chinese Buddhism*, p. 247. On one of the *Tsok-chin*, Kwan-yin (feminine form) is represented with Avalokiteśvara in the place usually occupied by a feminine divinity.

[4] *Buddhism in Christianity*, p. 205.

[5] Dumoutier in his *Cultes annamites* speaks of a goddess in Annam called 'Quanam', who is represented seated on a rock, draped in a gown of many pleats, holding a child in her arms. When the 'troupiers' first saw this image they called it the *Virgin Mary*.

[6] v. *Legend of the Miao-Chen.*

can one piece together a hypothetical story of the development of her various forms.

The first idols were brought from India by King Mingti's mission when they returned to China in the first century A.D. Up to that time, the Chinese had not 'imaged' their gods.

It was not until the fourth century that the Chinese were admitted to the Buddhist priesthood, and, as the making of the idols had been entirely in the hands of the Indian Buddhist priests, the character of the representations of the gods remained Indian, with the long-lobed ears and Indian features. The Chinese Buddhists seem never to have entirely freed themselves from the Indian influence.

The Mahāyāna school of Buddhism was introduced into China in the fifth century A.D. If at that time the Northern Buddhist priests found a goddess of Mercy already popular in China, it is not improbable that, in order to make converts, they claimed her as a feminine manifestation of their god of Mercy. It was done a few centuries later by Padmasambhava in Tibet and by Kōbō Daishi in Japan.

Edkins, however, claims that the feminine form did not appear in China until the twelfth century.[1] If such is the case, one cannot explain the presence of certain female forms of Avalokiteśvara in the temples and museums of Japan which date back several centuries before that time.[2] As the feminine form came into Japan from China, it must then have existed in China long before the twelfth century.

There were two distinct manifestations of the goddess Kwan-yin in China. One shows Northern Buddhist influence, while the other can be traced back through Chinese Turkestan and Kashmir into India, and originates in the Indian goddess Hāritī.[3]

This latter form might easily have been brought into China by the celebrated Buddhist pilgrims, Fa-hian in the fifth century, Hiuen-tsang in the beginning, and Yi-tsing towards the end of the seventh century, when they returned from India.

Both Hiuen-tsang and Yi-tsing, in the accounts of their travels, mention seeing in India the representation of a goddess holding a child, called 'Giver of Children' (觀音與童子). They must also have come upon this form of the goddess on their return through Central Asia, for both Sir Marc-Aurel Stein and Herr von Le Coq, in their excavations in Chinese Turkestan, found representations of the 'Giver of Children' in Buddhist temples, placed opposite Kuvera.

A small painting[4] of the goddess with a head drapery, holding the child (the form adopted by the Chinese to represent the Kwan-yin, 'Giver of Sons' or Sung-tsë), which was discovered by Herr von Le Coq at Turfan, dates from the fifth century. It is therefore possible that Fa-hian was also acquainted with this form; and it seems more probable that this important representation of Kwan-yin should have been brought into China by one of these celebrated Buddhist travellers rather than by an obscure Buddhist pilgrim.

The most ancient form of the female Kwan-yin is probably the feminine

[1] *Chinese Buddhism*, p. 382.

[2] v. *Kwan-non*.

[3] v. *Hāritī*.

[4] Now in the Museum für Völkerkunde, Berlin; v. also illus., *La Madone bouddhique*, A. Foucher.

a. Kwan-yin (Sung-tsë)

b. Kwan-yin

c. Kwan-yin

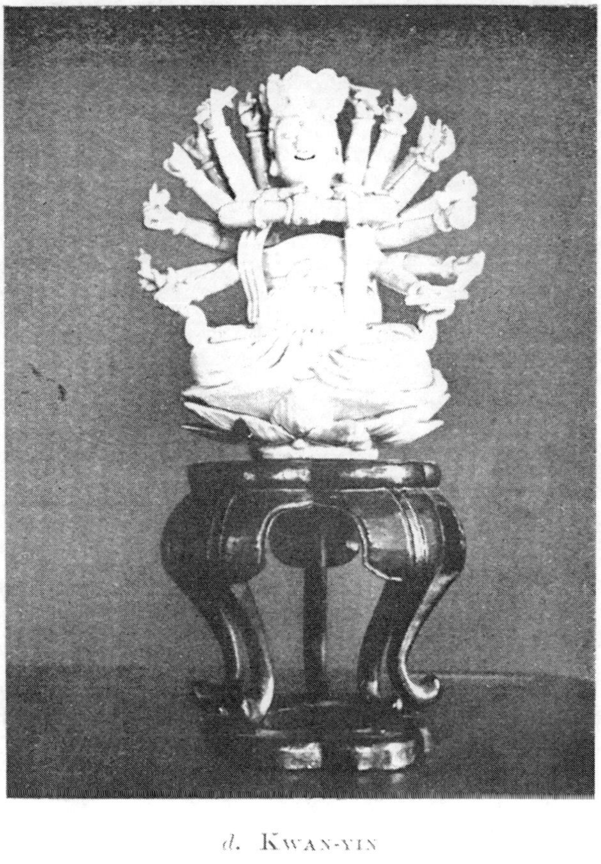

d. Kwan-yin

manifestation of Padmapāṇi, non-Tantra form of Avalokiteśvara (that is to say, with only two arms), which was his earliest representation in China.

The goddess is represented as a Bodhisattva, wearing many ornaments and the five-leaved crown in which is usually the image of the Dhyāni-Buddha, Amitābha. She is either seated with the legs locked, or is sitting sideways on a lion (*siṃhanāda*) with the right or left leg pendent (Pl. XXXIV, fig. *d*). One of her hands is in *vara* (charity) *mudrā*, while the other is in the 'dogmatic' pose (*vitarka*). Her hands may also be in *dhyāna* (meditation) *mudrā*, but in that case she is holding the luminous pearl (or is it the pomegranate?). On a lotus-flower at her right shoulder is the symbol of Padmapāṇi, a vase (*kalaśa*). At her left shoulder, also supported by a lotus, is a symbol which is purely Chinese, and her special emblem, a dove, symbol of fecundity (Pl. XXVII, fig. *d*). This form of Kwan-yin seldom holds the child (Pl. XXVII, fig. *c*).

The form of the goddess which entered China from Chinese Turkestan is represented with a child on her knee and is called 'Sung-tsë' (giver of sons). In China the group does not represent the mother and child. The child [1] is purely a symbol and is stiffly held by the goddess (v. Pl. XXVI and Pl. XXIX, fig. *c*). In this form she is represented with flowing garments, and usually a drapery falling from her high head-dress over her shoulders (v. Pl. XXVII, fig. *a*, and Pl. XXIX, fig. *b*). Later, the Sung-tsë Kwan-yin adopted the two symbols of the Northern Buddhist form, the vase and the dove, thus merging the two manifestations into one.

The form of the goddess, which is inexplicable if one does not accept the legend of Miao-Chen as its origin, is represented seated, her hands in 'meditation' *mudrā* holding the flaming pearl or with the hands in 'prayer' *mudrā*. She is accompanied by two acolytes, which are surely Chen Tsai and Loung Nu. Underneath her lotus-throne is the dragon (v. Legend of Miao-Chen ; v. Pl. XXVII, fig. *c*).

In this group she may have three different representations :

1. She takes the form of Padmapāṇi, non-Tantra form of Avalokiteśvara (two arms), and holds the flaming pearl.
2. She is represented in the Tantra form of Avalokiteśvara with many arms.[2] Her normal hands are in 'prayer' *mudrā*, while two hands may be lying on her lap in 'meditation' *mudrā*. In this form she is always seated, while the masculine form of Kwan-yin with a thousand arms is always standing. All the other arms are outstretched, holding various Buddhist symbols, and she is either represented with the head drapery or wearing the five-leaved crown (Pl. XXVII, figs. *b* and *d*).

[1] According to certain accounts, the child is Chen Tsai, the first disciple of Miao-Chen.

[2] In the legend of Miao-Chen, there is an incident which seems to explain the thousand arms of the female Kwan-yin. The father of Miao-Chen falling ill, 'she cut the flesh off her arms and made it into medicine which saved his life. To show his gratitude, he ordered a statue to be erected in her honour, saying "with completely formed (*ts'en*) arms and eyes"; but the sculptor mistook the order for "with a thousand (*ts'ien*) arms and eyes", whence it happened that a statue with a thousand arms and a thousand eyes perpetuated her memory' (Eitel). Pl. LXIV.

3. She is represented in flowing garments with the drapery over her high head-dress, against which may be a small image of her Dhyāni-Buddha, Amitābha, or she may wear a crown. She holds the flaming pearl in her hands, lying on her lap in 'meditation' *mudrā* (v. Pl. XXVII, fig. *b*).

   In this group she may hold the child instead of the flaming pearl, in which case her disciple, Loung Nu, holds the pearl, while Chen Tsai stands on the opposite side in attitude of prayer (Pl. XXVII, fig. *a*).

She is sometimes represented either holding a roll of prayers or a willow branch,[1] with which she is believed to sprinkle around her the divine nectar (San. *amṛita*), called by the Chinese 'sweet dew'. On her right is the ambrosia vase, and on her left the dove, symbol of fecundity (Pl. XXIX, fig. *d*). She is sometimes accompanied by the two acolytes, Loung Nu and Chen Tsai.

Other forms represent her in deep meditation, sitting or standing on a cloud [2] or a lotus-flower, or on the sea (called Kwo-Hai).

In the temples she is sometimes represented as a goddess of the sea, with rocks and crudely carved waves about her.

All these different representations seem to indicate the legend of Miao-Chen.

Monier Williams claims that the Chinese looked upon the goddess of Mercy as the Tibetans look upon the *śakti*, or female energy of their gods. This is surely erroneous, although there is a Chinese temple picture in the British Museum which seems to support this theory. The goddess Kwan-yin is seated in the pose of the *śakti* of Avalokiteśvara, the green Tārā, and is accompanied by two acolytes, Loung Nu and Chen Tsai.

It is evident, at all events, that the Tibetans did not understand the female manifestation of Avalokiteśvara in China from the following fact: The Mongolian Emperor Kang-hsi, in the fourteenth century, sent to Tibet for images of the goddess Kwan-yin, which he presented to the monasteries on the island of Pu-to. They represent the goddess seated with locked legs, the upper part of the body bare, but with a skirt of leaves [3] and with many jewels; and the Buddhist Chinese priests were evidently shocked by this representation of the goddess, for they covered all these statues with yellow mantles.[4]

In China, as well as in Japan, there seems to have been a confusion in regard to the sex of Kwan-yin, for there is a Chinese temple painting [5] representing the god dressed like the female Kwan-yin, seated in the attitude called 'royal ease' (knee raised). The left hand holds a vase in which is a willow branch, the special emblem of the goddess, but the head outlined against a white glory is that of a man with

[1] The first of the thirty-three Kwan-non in the Butsuzo Zui (Japanese Pantheon) is called 'Yorin' or 'willow', from the branch she holds in her hand, as does also the eleventh. The seventeenth has a willow branch in her vase.

[2] The second of the thirty-three Kwan-non is seated on a cloud and a dragon. The fifth is seated on a cloud. The twenty-fourth standing on a cloud. The thirtieth is sitting on a lotus on a cloud.

[3] In the Butsuzo Zui, the twenty-second of the thirty-three Kwan-non is called 'Haye', or 'clothed in leaves'.

[4] Edkins, *Chinese Buddhism*, p. 261.

[5] Belonging to Madame Langweil.

a moustache and beard. There is only one acolyte, Loung Nu, carrying the pearl. This painting is claimed to be Taoist, dating between the fourteenth and fifteenth centuries.

The first masculine form of Avalokiteśvara in China was the Padmapāṇi type, standing, dressed in princely garments and wearing many ornaments. His face is Indian in aspect, with long-lobed ears. In his left hand is a lotus—generally a bud, while the Tibetan Padmapāṇi holds a full-blown lotus-flower ; but he may also hold a vase (Pl. XXV, figs. *a*, *c*, *d*).

Kwan-yin, in his Padmapāṇi form, may wear a crown of heads, generally eight in number, which are disposed in two tiers of four, which possibly indicates the group of eight Bodhisattva called the Pa-nan Kwan-yin. The Chinese seldom adopted the Tantra form of Avalokiteśvara with eleven heads disposed in the Tibetan manner ; but there is an example of a Chinese bronze with *four* tiers of three heads—the thirteenth is missing.

He has a Tantra form called 'thousand-armed', which is very popular in China, and resembles the thousand-armed Avalokiteśvara in Tibet. In this form he is always standing.

There are two groups of the masculine Kwan-yin. One is composed of thirty-two metamorphoses[1] called the 'Kwan-yin san-shi-rï-siang'. They are all modelled on the Padmapāṇi form and differ little from each other.

The other group is called the 'Pa-nan' or 'Kwan-yin of the eight sufferings'. It is composed of eight metamorphoses which he (or she) assumes for the purpose of saving mankind from the eight kinds of sufferings.

The Legend of Miao-Chen.[2]

'In the eleventh year of the Epoch of the Heaven of Gold, 2587 B.C., lived a king called Miao Tohoang.' . . . He had three daughters and no sons and when they were old enough to marry, he found them suitable husbands so that he might have an heir to the throne. But Miao-Chen, the youngest, refused to marry, saying that she preferred to pass her life in seclusion in order to perfect herself by meditation and contemplation, and thus arrive at the state of Buddha.[3] She retired to the monastery of the White Sparrows[4] in order to live in perfect seclusion.

The king made every attempt to persuade her to return, and when every kindly tentative failed he resorted to cruelty, each trial being more horrible than the last,

[1] The group corresponds to the thirty-three Kwan-non in Japan.

[2] Extracts taken from the legend of Miao-Chen in the *Annales du Musée Guimet*.

[3] It is not surprising to find Buddhist influence in some of the versions of the legend of Miao-Chen. There are records of Buddhist missionaries in China as early as 225 B.C. and again 217 B.C., according to Max Müller in his *Buddhism and Buddhist Pilgrims*, p. 24. The fact, however, is not accepted by more recent writers.

[4] One of the Chinese titles of Kwan-yin is the 'White-Robed Great Scholar' (Eitel). In the *Butsuzo Zui*, the Japanese manual of the Buddhist Pantheon, the fourth of the group of thirty-three Kwan-non is 'Byaku-ye-no' (clothed in white).

but she came out unscathed from them all. Then he ordered her to be decapitated. During the execution there sprung up suddenly a great wind storm, the heavens were obscured, and light breaking forth, surrounded Miao-Chen.[1] Then the tutelary god of the place, having taken the form of a tiger, bounded out of the forest and carried her inanimate form into the mountains.

She visited Yama in Hell and by her magic power liberated the damned souls. Upon her return, Buddha appeared to her on a cloud, and counselled her to retire to the island of P'u-to some three thousand miles away, and give herself up to meditation. He gave her a peach[2] from the garden of Heaven to preserve her for a year from hunger and thirst, and to assure her eternal life. A local god of the island took the form of a tiger and carried her there with the rapidity of the wind.[3] For nine years she remained on the island practising meditation and performing acts of merit, after which she was raised to the rank of Buddha and took her first acolyte, Hoan Chen Tsai (he who prays in order that he may have virtue and talent).

Later, she acquired another acolyte in the following manner : The third son of a Dragon King of the Sea was wandering one day upon the waves in the form of a fish, when he found himself entangled in a fisherman's net and was offered for sale in the market.[4] Miao-Chen, whose eyes see all things, discovered the danger and sent Chen-Tsai in human form to buy the fish and set it at liberty. The Dragon King was much touched by her kindness and sent her, by his granddaughter, Loung Nu, a pearl that gave light in the dark, so that she might read the sacred books during the night. Loung Nu was so entranced with Miao-Chen that she conceived the idea of herself acquiring the state of Buddha, and asked to be permitted to remain with her and become her acolyte, to which Miao-Chen readily consented.

Miao-Chen converted her parents and became a 'Saviour of Men', and was able to remove all obstacles to their attaining Amitābha's paradise. She herself refused to enter it as long as any human being was excluded.

[1] The fifth of the thirty-three Kwan-non is called 'Yen-kwo' (sitting in bright rays).

[2] The twenty-third of the thirty-three Kwan-non, the 'Ruri', holds a round object in her hand. According to an ancient Chinese (Taoist) legend, there was once a fairy queen called Hsi-wang-mu who held her court in the K'unlun mountains; she had a garden of miraculous peach-trees which conferred the gift of immortality, but only bore fruit every three thousand years.

[3] Other versions say that she was 'carried over the water on a lotus' (Eitel). In the *Butsuzo Zui* the twelfth Kwan-non is represented standing on a lotus-petal on the sea, the seventh is seated on a lotus-flower on the sea.

[4] The tenth of the thirty-three Kwan-non is called *gyo* (fish), *ran* (basket).

PLATE XXVIII

Shō Kwan-non (Padmapāṇi)

HĀRITĪ

(C.) *Sung-tsë Kwan-yin*, or *Kouei-tseu-mon-chen*. (J.) *Koyasu-Kwannon*, or *Ki-shi-mo-jin*.

The Hindu goddess Hāritī, protectress of children, worshipped in Northern India by bereaved parents, and believed, in Nepal, to prevent small-pox, was originally a Yakshiṇī, an ogress, a cannibal demon, who had made a vow to devour all the children in Rājagṛiha.

According to Buddhist accounts, of which there are many variations, she had 500 children, of whom she devoured 499 ; and the last one, Piṇḍola, was taken away from her by Gautama Buddha, who hid him under his begging-bowl. Hāritī forthwith repented of her evil ways and, becoming a Bhikshuṇī (Buddhist nun), was assured of her daily food by Buddhist priests.

This latter fact may possibly account for the presence of the statues of Hāritī in the refectories of the monasteries of Northern India, where, according to Yi-tsing (the Chinese pilgrim who visited India in the seventh century), she was adored as 'Giver of Children'. When the worship of Hāritī reached China and she became confounded with the goddess Kwan-yin, she was called 'Giver of Sons' (Sung-tsë).

Yi-tsing mentions the fact that her statues were always found either in the porches or refectories of the Buddhist monasteries, opposite the god of Wealth, Kuvera. In Java Hāritī was likewise placed opposite the god of Wealth. Herr von Le Coq also found the fresco-paintings of Hāritī opposite those of Kuvera in the temples that he discovered at Turfan, in Chinese Turkestan ; but in neither China nor Japan was the custom followed. Waddell,[1] in speaking of the persistence with which the Buddhist artists and sculptors coupled Hāritī and Kuvera, comes to the conclusion that Hāritī is none other than a form of Vasudhārā, goddess of Abundance, and consort of Kuvera, god of Wealth.[2]

Hiuen-tsang, who also visited India in the seventh century, mentions her worship in North-western India, where the Gandhārā school represented Hāritī in flowing garments, holding a child and with several children climbing about her. She was also sometimes represented holding a pomegranate, for Gautama Buddha is believed to have cured her of cannibalism by giving her a diet of pomegranates, the red fruit being supposed to resemble human flesh. The symbol is still used in Japan but was never adopted in China.

Hāritī was always represented with flowing garments, which varied slightly according to the country. In the Gandhārā representations she has no head-covering.

[1] 'Evolution of the Buddhist cult ; its gods, images, and art,' *The Imperial and Asiatic Quarterly Review*, Jan. 1912.

[2] Sir Aurel Stein in his *Annual Report of the Archaeological Society of India.—Frontier Circle*, for 1911–12, gives, opposite page 8, the illustration of a relievo-frieze from a *stūpa* at Tahkt-i-Bahi representing Kuvera seated beside Hāritī, who holds a *cornucopia* filled with flowers and fruit.

In Java, on the contrary, she was given an ornate mitre-shaped head-dress. In the frescoes discovered by Sir Aurel Stein at Domoko, in Central Asia, she has a string of pearls wound in her elaborately dressed hair.

A small painting of Hārītī [1] was found by Herr von Le Coq in a temple at Turfan, which resembles the representations in China of the form of the feminine Kwan-yin, called 'Sung-tsë'.

She is seated, offering her breast to the child in her arms. A drapery falls over her shoulders from the high head-dress and her garments are flowing.[2]

This form in China holds the child but does not offer the breast. In Japan it does not always hold the child, but corresponds, nevertheless, with the Chinese goddess Kwan-yin, feminine form of Avalokiteśvara.

The goddess Hārītī, as such, does not exist in China, while in Japan she has both the form of saint and ogress, holding the child, and is worshipped under the name of Koyasu Kwan-non as saint, and Kishi-mo-jin as ogress.[3]

[1] Now in the Völkerkunde Museum, Berlin.

[2] v. illustration, A. Foucher, *La Madone bouddhique*, Monuments et Mémoires publiés par l'Académie des Inscriptions et Belles-Lettres, tome 17 a.

[3] She is believed in Japan to have had 10,000 children; v. *Koyasu Kwan-non.*

FORMS OF KWAN-NON

TABLE VIII

Kwan-non. One head.	I. Two arms.	I. Lotus and vase, rosary or 'charity' *mudrā* .	Shō.
		II. Crown of eleven heads	Ju-ichi-men.
		III. I. Non-Tantra . . . / II. Six arms . . .	Nyo-i-rin.
	II. Six or more arms.	I. Horse's head, *mudrā* renge-no-in, Tantra symbols	Ba-to.
		II. Sword and banner, *mudrā* renge-no-in, Tantra symbols . .	Juntei (feminine).
		III. Jizō's staff (*shakujo*), rosary and lasso, lotus and *mudrā* . .	Fukū-kenjaku.
	III. 1,000 arms.	I. Tantra and non-Tantra symbols	Sen-ju.
Forms not authorized in the Japanese Buddhist Scriptures.	I. Holding a child		Koyasu Kwan-non.
	II. Holding a pomegranate and sometimes a child		Kishi-mo-jin.
	III. Group of thirty-three feminine Kwan-non.		

KWAN-NON

God of Mercy.

(S.) *Avalokiteśvara.* (C.) *Kwan-yin.*

Kwan-non holding a child.

(C.) *Sung-tsë Kwan yin.* (J.) *Koyasu Kwan-non.*

KWAN-NON, god (or goddess) of Mercy, is the Japanese form of the Chinese divinity Kwan-yin, manifestation of Avalokiteśvara. His worship is said to have been introduced into Japan during the reign of the Empress Suiko (593–628), forty years after the introduction of Buddhism,[1] and has lasted up to the present time.

There are three different non-Tantra manifestations of Kwan-non found in the temples and museums of Japan. The first, and probably the most ancient, is modelled after the Indian representation of Avalokiteśvara in his non-Tantra form of Padmapāṇi: a slight, youthful figure, with long-lobed ears, dressed like an Indian prince, and with often a moustache slightly outlining the upper lip.

The second form, which was brought into Japan from India and Central Asia via China, is a female figure, seated or standing, with graceful, flowing garments, and a crown or head-drapery.

The third form is Japanese in aspect, but the long-lobed ears are Indian and the folds of the drapery indicate the influence of the Gandhāra School. The figure is seated with the head leaning on the right hand.

The evident confusion in art in regard to the sex of Kwan-non has also existed among the worshippers even to the present day. The common people pray to the divinity as 'goddess of Mercy', while the priests and the more educated classes worship the god as a masculine deity, for he is believed to dwell on the right hand of Amitābha in the Western Paradise of Sukhāvatī,[2] where no woman without attaining masculinity, through merit, can enter. Some of the sects, however, worship Kwan-non as sexless, for it is claimed that as objects of worship, all male or female beings should be looked upon as of no fixed sex.

Professor Lloyd says in his *Creed of Half Japan* that the Bodhisattva might be considered as non-sexual, or bi-sexual, while in his *Shinran* he writes: 'It is a mistake to speak of Kwan-non as a female deity. Kwan-non is the son of Amitābha, capable of appearing in many forms, male or female, human or animal, according to circumstances. But he is never manifested except as a means of practically demonstrating the divine compassion for a suffering creation.'

[1] According to some, 100 years after the introduction of Buddhism into Japan, A.D. 552. Others claim 150 years later.

[2] v. Glossary.

It is very difficult to determine when the different forms of Kwan-non appeared in Japan. Chiso, a Chinese priest, is said to have brought Buddhist images into Japan A. D. 564 (or 571). In the *Nihongi* there is the following reference to a statue of Avalokiteśvara: 'In the seventh month, after the Empress Suiko's reign (A. D. 593–628), the king of Shiraki (a portion of the present Korea) sent an ambassador to the Japanese court to make homage to the empress and to present her with a gold-copper statue of Avalokiteśvara. Prince Shōtoku, who was regent to the empress, accepting it, ordered Hata-no-Ka-wakatsu to put up a sanctuary for the image.' It is also recorded elsewhere that Shōtoku put up statues and shrines to Kwan-non, and that whenever he was troubled by any serious state affairs, he shut himself up in one of the shrines and offered prayers to Avalokita.

At the end of the seventh century, Dōshō, a Japanese priest, went to China to study Buddhism with Hiuen-tsang,[1] the famous Buddhist pilgrim and scholar, and brought back with him many Buddhist images. Hiuen-tsang was a fervent admirer of Avalokiteśvara,[2] although he was not worshipped by the Hossō sect. It is therefore not improbable that among the images that Dōshō brought back, there were representations of Avalokiteśvara, possibly in both the masculine and feminine forms.

The foreign gods, however, were not popular until the ninth century, when the Japanese Buddhist priest Kukai (Kōbō Daishi) returned from China, where he had been studying the dogmas of the Yogācārya, or Tantra school, under Hiu-kio (Keï-kwa), the celebrated Buddhist scholar.

After founding the Shin-gon [3] sect, he proceeded to popularize the divinities of the Mahāyāna by the same tactics that his master, Hiu-kio, had employed, with success, in China. Hiu-kio, in his turn, had adopted the method of Asaṅga in India several centuries before, and the method was a very simple one. It consisted in accepting the gods of a people one intended to convert, at the same time proclaiming that these gods were manifestations of the divinities one was about to impose.

Kukai went to the holy Shinto shrine of Isé and prostrated himself before the altar of the god [4] of Abundant Food, Toyuki-Bimé no Kami. After days of fasting he succeeded in getting a revelation. The god appeared to him, expressed his belief in the power of the gods of the Mahāyāna, and informed him that the Shinto gods were *avatārs* and incarnations of the Buddhist divinities. And so, with the approbation of this most popular and powerful deity, he began the work of revealing the names of the Buddhist gods, of which the Shinto divinities were but manifestations, and of popularizing them.

As Kōbō Daishi brought the Tantra doctrine into Japan, it is not improbable that he also introduced the Tantra form of Avalokiteśvara, the Sen-ju, or thousand-armed Kwan-non, for it is recorded that, like Dōshō, he brought back images with him when he returned from China.

[1] Founder of the Hossō sect in China (Yogācārya school).

[2] v. Beal, *Buddhist Records of the Western World*, translated from the Chinese of Hiuan-tsang, vol. ii, pp. 60 and 127.

[3] The Shin-gon sect belongs to the Yogācārya or Tantra school.

[4] In the Shinto religion the gods are not 'imaged'.

There are seven forms of Kwan-non in Japan, which show the influence of the Tibetan Mahāyāna school :

1. Shō Kwan-non.
2. Ju-ichi-men.
3. Sen-ju.
4. Jun-tei.
5. Fukū-Kenjaku.
6. Ba-to.
7. Nyo-i-rin.

These seven forms are in two groups of six, for the Tendai sect does not include the Jun-tei Kwan-non, and the Shin-gon omits the Fukū-Kenjaku. There is also a group of thirty-three (sometimes thirty-four) Kwan-non made up from these seven forms, which was established by the Emperor Kwazan, who abdicated the throne in the tenth century, and himself made a pilgrimage to the thirty-three shrines in the Yamato.

The Japanese Buddhists look upon these seven forms as manifestations of Avalokiteśvara, but only three of them, the Shō, Sen-ju, and Ju-ichi-men (with possibly the Fukū-Kenjaku), resemble the Tibetan forms of the god of Mercy. The Ba-to is modelled after the Tibetan god, Hayagrīva, while the Jun-tei resembles the Tibetan goddess, Cundā or Cuntī.

The Japanese do not absolutely follow tradition in their representations of the Bodhisattva. The crown, when without the heads,[1] is not usually five-leaved like the Tibetan, but high, complicated, and most ornate, with ornaments hanging on either side of the head to the shoulders. The breast and shoulders of the Japanese Bodhisattva are bare, but he wears a necklace and the traditional scarf, which crosses his breast from the left shoulder and is wound around the body several times, falling in graceful loops like garlands with the ends hanging over the arms.

The lower limbs are covered by a full, gracefully draped skirt-like garment which falls to the ankles, and the folds often show the influence of the Gandhāra school. The lobes of the ears are always long, indicating the Indian school, but the eyes may be Japanese in shape. There is usually the *ūrṇā* and, behind the crown, the *ushṇīsha*. The Japanese Bodhisattva is sometimes represented dressed like a Buddha, with only his high, complicated head-dress, indicating his rank as a Bodhisattva.

I. *The Shō Kwan-non* (the All-wise One). In Japan the Shō Kwan-non is called 'Āryāvalokiteśvara', while in Tibet the term is used for the most complicated form of Avalokiteśvara, which in Japan is called 'Sen-ju'.

The Shō Kwan-non is the simplest form of Avalokita, and therefore corresponds with his manifestation called 'Padmapāṇi'. In fact, like Padmapāṇi, he is represented as a graceful youth, standing with the right hand in *vitarka* (teaching) *mudrā*, and the left denoting 'charity'. His symbol, the lotus, which is generally a bud, may be held in the right hand, or, if in the left, is sometimes in a vase. The eyes, half closed, may be Indian in form, and the lobes of the ears are always long. The hair is drawn up in a mitre-shaped *ushṇīsha* behind the complicated crown. The

[1] The crown of heads is only found in Chinese Turkestan, China, and Japan.

PLATE XXIX

a. Ratnapāni

b. Kwan-yin (Sung-tsĕ)

c. Kwan-yin (Sung-tsĕ)

d. Kwan-yin

ūrṇā is on the forehead, and the upper lip is often outlined by a moustache, which one never sees on the Indian form. On the other hand, the antelope skin, which is sometimes worn by the Indian Padmapāṇi, is never seen on the Shō Kwan-non. His shoulders and breast are bare and he may wear many jewels, which do not, however, correspond to the thirteen traditional Bodhisattva ornaments, nor is his dress exactly the same. He may also be without jewels. The Shō Kwan-non, however, resembles more closely the Tibetan type than any of the other Japanese forms (Pl. XXVIII).

II. *Ju-ichi-men Kwan-non* (Eleven-headed). The Ju-ichi-men Kwan-non, having but two arms, resembles the Shō Kwan-non, with the exception of the head-dress, which is a crown of eleven heads disposed in two rows of three and a row between of five (the author has never seen them disposed in three tiers like the Ārya-Pāla). The head of Amitābha rises out of the *ushṇīsha*. The Ju-ichi-men may, however, also have four arms. In his left hand he holds a vase, in which is generally a lotus-flower, and his right hand, in 'charity' *mudrā*, either holds a rosary or a *shakujo* (alarm staff). He is sometimes surrounded by a glory, in which, on each side, are five suns and a *cintāmaṇi* (magic jewel).

One often sees the central head of the first or second row replaced by a small figure, standing or sitting like a Buddha, closely draped, and with the hands always covered. The little figure might represent Kikuta Sanzo, an Indian prince belonging to the Ritsu sect who came to Japan from India between the seventh and eighth centuries. He was much venerated, and was always represented *with the hands covered.*

III. *Sen-ju Kwan-non* (Thousand-armed). The Sen-ju Kwan-non resembles the 'Ārya-Pāla' or Tantra form of Avalokiteśvara. He either wears the crown of eleven heads of the Ju-ichi-men Kwan-non, or a high crown without heads. He may also have a low crown with a standing figure in the centre (Pl. XLI, fig. *d*).

His many arms are outstretched, with the exception of two pairs which are held in front and against him, the upper hands holding the *pātra* or begging-bowl, or in 'prayer' *mudrā*, while the lower ones hold the ambrosia vase. All the other hands hold Tantra and non-Tantra symbols. The two upper hands at the back may be raised above the crown of heads forming *añjali* (salutation) *mudrā*, sometimes holding a *sanko* (*vajra*), or (but rarely) a small image of Amitābha,[1] like the Indian 'Ārya-Pāla'.

IV. *The Jun-tei Kwan-non* (San. Cuntī). The only feminine form among the seven Kwan-non is Jun-tei, who is believed to have performed the three meditations, after which she was directed in her actions by the Buddha himself.

She is called Kotī-śrī, or Sapta-koṭī-Buddha-mātrī-Cuntī-devī, or the goddess Cuntī, mother of 70,000 Buddhas. It is believed by the Japanese that the goddess is taken from Indian mythology and is Durga devī, wife of Śiva, but the legend vaguely resembles that of the ogress Hāritī.[2]

[1] v. *Butsuzo Zui*, Japanese manual of the Buddhist Pantheon.

[2] Hāritī is believed, in Japan, to have had 100,000 children.

Jun-tei is sometimes represented as an angry goddess, but is usually pacific. She has the third eye and eighteen arms, all the hands holding different symbols. The two original ones are against the breast, the hands forming the *mudrā* 'renge-no-in',[1] but it differs somewhat from the *mudrā* of the Ba-to in that only the ring and little fingers are locked. The second fingers are upright and touching at the tips. The index fingers touch the first joints of the second fingers, thus forming a kind of 'triangular' pose. The hands of the two upper arms hold a sword and banner (Pl. XII, fig. *c*).

According to the *Butsuzo Zui* the god is represented seated in the form of a woman. The *ushṇīsha* is covered by a stiff, highly decorated, cone-shaped turban, and she is clothed in flowing draperies.

V. *Fukū-Kenjaku* (San. Amoghapāśa). Fukū-Kenjaku made his appearance in Japan much later than the others, and was not adopted by the Shin-gon sect, but is a popular deity with the Tendai sect.

He may be seated or standing with eight (or only six) arms, and wears a high crown. The original arms are held in front and against him, the hands forming *namaḥkāra* (prayer) *mudrā*. The upper arms hold Jizō's staff (*shakujo*) and a lotus-flower. Two of the lower ones hold a rosary and lasso, and the other two form *vara* (charity) *mudrā*, but the symbols may be disposed differently.

There is a form of Fukū-Kenjaku which wears the 'Ju-ichi-men' crown; but he is usually represented with a complicated crown without heads and may be without the *ūrṇā*. He carries the vase, in which is the lotus-flower, in the left hand, and in the right is his usual symbol, the *shakujo*, or alarm staff.

VI. *Ba-to Kwan-non* (San. Hayagrīva). Ba-to, the horse-headed Kwan-non, takes the form of the Tibetan masculine divinity Hayagrīva, and nevertheless remains for the common people the 'goddess of Mercy'.

In Tibet Hayagrīva is the protector of horses, and is supposed to frighten away the demons by neighing like a horse. There may also be some such idea in Japan, for he is worshipped chiefly in the north, where many horses are raised, and effigies of the god may be seen along the roadside. He is, in fact, the patron god of the horse-dealers.

The horse's head in the hair of the Ba-to Kwan-non is a Northern Buddhist symbol, and in the legends of the *Mahāyāna*, the horse, especially if white, played an important rôle. In the *Mahāyāna sūtra*, Śākyamuni tells of the miraculous horse [2] that saved Siṃhala (in reality himself, Buddha) [3] from the wiles of the Rākshasa.[4] It was on the white horse, Kaṇṭhaka, that the Buddha left his palace to become an ascetic. Legend says that the horse died of grief at being separated from his master and was reborn in the Trayastriṃśa heaven as the *deva* Kathagata.[5]

The white horse played an important part in Chinese Buddhism in the following manner:

[1] v. Glossary.

[2] The horse was white, according to the *Abhinishkramaṇa sūtra*.

[3] Burnouf, *Introduction*.

[4] Cannibal demons.

[5] Fa-hian.

PLATE XXX

Kwan-non

'In the year A. D. 63, the Chinese emperor, Mingti, had a vision. A man holding a bow and arrow[1] in his hands announced to him the appearance in the world of a "Perfect Man". He was impressed by the vision and sent a commission of eighteen men to go to the west and find him.

As the commissioners were on their way they met two men holding a white horse laden with books, images, and relics. The commissioners recognized the men as those they were seeking, and, turning back with them, brought them to Loyang, the residence of the Han emperor, where they were installed in the "White Horse Monastery", which is the earliest Buddhist sanctuary in China.'[2]

The tradition of the white horse also reached Japan, for the horse's head in Ba-to's hair must be white to be efficacious.

It is curious that a white horse (albino, if possible) is always attached to important Shinto shrines, and that the Restoration in abolishing all Buddhist symbols from the Shinto temples should have allowed the horse to remain.

Ba-to Kwan-non is represented seated, either with the legs locked, or the right knee raised in the attitude called 'royal ease'. Unlike the other types of Kwan-non, his expression is always angry and in his forehead is a third eye. The hair stands upright, and protruding from it is a horse's head, the characteristic mark of this god (Pl. XXXII, fig. *c*).

Sometimes there are three heads, one on either side of the central head, each face having a different but angry expression, and above the central head is that of a horse (Pl. XXXII, fig. *d*). This form closely resembles one of the manifestations of Hayagrīva.

There are generally eight outstretched arms, of which five hands hold the same symbols as Hayagrīva: wheel, sword, lasso, &c., and the sixth can be making the *vara mudrā*, or holding a symbol. The two normal arms are against the breast, the hands forming the Japanese *mudrā* called 'renge-no-in',[3] which is emblematical of the lotus-flower all fingers locked except the indexes that point upwards and touch at the tips.

VII. *Nyo-i-rin Kwan-non* (San. Cintāmaṇī-cakra). The Nyo-i-rin Kwan-non, called 'The Omnipotent One', is a manifestation of Avalokiteśvara, seldom found outside of Japan. In Tibet, however, there are a few rare examples of this non-Tantra form, and, with a slight variation, it is also found in China.

The non-Tantra form of Avalokiteśvara, in his manifestation of Nyo-i-rin, is seated European fashion, with the right foot supported by the left knee. The right elbow rests on the right knee, while the head leans on the index, or both the index and second finger of the right hand. The left hand rests on the right ankle with the palm underneath, and the left foot is supported by a small lotus *āsana*.

This attitude of the god signifies 'meditating on the best way to save mankind'.

In China the divinity, which is found mostly in the Honan, differs from the usual Nyo-i-rin in that the head does not usually rest on the right hand, which,

[1] Hayagrīva sometimes carries a bow and arrow.

[2] Lloyd, *Development of Japanese Buddhism.*

[3] It resembles the *mudrā* of k'Lu-dban-rgyd-po or 'Buddha Liberator of the Nāgas'. v. Glossary.

in that case, holds a lotus-bud. Both shoulders are covered, but the breast is bare, and he is generally accompanied by two acolytes, who are without symbols, or definite *mudrā* unless in prayer attitude. The group may be under a 'bodhi-tree'.

In Japan, the Nyo-i-rin Kwan-non is either represented with a crown, or with the hair drawn up mitre-shaped, or in different complicated forms, which may be ornamented on the top by a moon-crescent, in the centre of which is the flame symbol. The upper part of the body is bare, with the exception of ornaments on the breast and arms. The lower limbs are covered by a skirt-shaped drapery which falls from the waist to the feet, and shows the influence of the Gandhāra school in its graceful folds. The Hōryūji temple owns a bronze in the traditional pose, as well as a Nyo-i-rin Kwan-non where the head is not supported by the right hand, which is in *vitarka mudrā*. In Japan the non-Tantra form never holds a symbol.

In his Tantra form the Nyo-i-rin Kwan-non is seated in the attitude called 'royal ease' with the right knee raised, while the left is bent in the usual position of a Buddha. In this form he has six arms. His head rests on his normal right hand, and the elbow may rest on the right knee, but does not always do so. The normal left arm is extended in 'charity' *mudrā*. Of the two arms underneath, the right holds the *cintāmaṇi* against his breast, while the left, in 'teaching' *mudrā*, holds a lotus-bud. The third right arm is pendent, holding a rosary, and the third left arm is raised, balancing a wheel on the index finger.

This form is called by the Japanese *Cintāmaṇi-cakra*, probably on account of the two symbols, the magic jewel (*cintāmaṇi*) and the wheel (*cakra*) which he carries. The Tantra form of the Nyo-i-rin does not exist outside of Japan ; but although Tantra, his expression is never ferocious, nor has he the third eye. The *ūrṇā* is often missing, and although the lobes of the ears are always long, the features are more Japanese than Indian, and express great calm and intense introspection.

KOYASU KWAN-NON

(Holding a child).

(S.) *Hāritī.* Ogress form : *Kishi-mo-jin* (holding a pomegranate).
(C.) *Sung-tsë Kwan-yin.*

The form of Kwan-non with flowing garments and a head-drapery, holding the child, was unquestionably brought to Japan from India via Central Asia and China ; but at what epoch it is most difficult to determine.

If the form was introduced into China by Fa-hian, Hiuen-tsang, or Yi-tsing, it might easily have made its appearance in Japan by the middle of the eighth century. In fact, it seems possible that the form was already known there by that time, for, according to certain accounts, the Empress Kōmyō, in the year A. D. 718, had a vision of Kwan-non holding a child.

The empress, so the legend runs, was with child, and prayers were being said in the holy shrine of Isé for an easy deliverance. The empress slept, and in a dream she saw Kwan-non at her bedside. She awoke, and the image, holding a child, remained and was later enshrined in a three-storied pagoda called Koyasu-tō (child-ease), and worshipped as 'Giver and Protector of Children'.

According to tradition handed down by Japanese artists, the Empress Kōmyō caused a statue of the Koyasu Kwan-non, holding a child, to be modelled after her own image; and a statue of Kishi-jo-ten (owned by the Jōruriji temple, Yamashiro) is also claimed to have been modelled after the Empress Kōmyō, who was celebrated for her beauty, both mental and physical.

The Japanese Buddhist priests place little credence in these accounts; but even if legendary, the fact remains that tradition has been handed down associating the form of Kwan-non holding the child with the eighth century, and in all probability with reason.

It is also claimed by the Japanese Buddhist priests that the forms of Kwan-non which seem feminine in aspect are, in reality, masculine, but are given a female appearance to symbolize the qualities of love, compassion, and benevolence, which are conceded to be rather feminine than masculine. The student of the iconography of these gods, however, must look upon the images of the deities which are *unquestionably female in appearance* as feminine, although, according to the tenets of Japanese Buddhism, the female form is only symbolical.

The Koyasu Kwan-non, 'Giver and Protector of Children', resembles too closely the Chinese 'Giver of Sons' as well as the Indian 'Giver of Children' for any doubt to exist as to its origin; and not only was the pacific form of the Indian goddess Hārītī adopted by the Japanese (Pl. XXXII, fig. *b*), but also her demoniacal form [1] as ogress, with the Indian symbol, the pomegranate. These two forms are also found in Japan, merged in one, that is, the Kwan-non holding the child *and the pomegranate*,[2] but the pomegranate may be missing (Pl. XXXII, fig. *a*).

The *kichi-jo-kwa*, or pomegranate, is the special symbol of Kishi-mo-jin, the demoniacal form of Koyasu Kwan-non. When she is represented holding the child and the pomegranate, or her special symbol alone, she may be either in pacific or demoniacal form. If the former, she wears a flowing garment, a crown, and many jewels. If the latter, her hair is dishevelled and she is portrayed as a terrifying demon.

The Koyasu Kwan-non never holds the pomegranate. The mild form of Kishi-mo-jin holding the *kichi-jo-kwa* and the child is represented in the Exterior Diamond section (Vajrānubhāva-vṛitti) in the Maṇḍala of the Garbhadhātu of the Shin-gon sect, while in the temple paintings of the Ritsu sect, she is placed in the Eating Hells. She is especially worshipped in her ogress form by the Nichiren sect, who look upon her as Protector of the Saddharma-puṇḍarīka.

[1] In China the demoniacal form was never adopted, nor, judging from the excavations in Chinese Turkestan, was it ever popular in Central Asia.

[2] In Japan, however, the ogress form, Kishi-mo-jin, is not looked upon as a demoniacal form of Koyasu Kwan-non, and nei her form is authorized in the Japanese Buddhist scriptures.

Among the Japanese Imperial treasures there is a small bronze statue which, according to the inscription on its base, was cast in the beginning of the seventh century A. D. The bronze is catalogued as a 'Shō Kwan-non' because of the round object in its hands which, according to the *mantra* of Avalokita, 'Om, *maṇi* padme, hūṃ!' might be a magic jewel!

The compiler of the catalogue of the Imperial treasures admits that there is no traditional example of a Shō Kwan-non holding a magic jewel, when he bases his hypothesis as to the name of this idol on the fact that the Hōryūji temple owns a somewhat similar statue with the *cintāmaṇi* on the lotus-throne instead of in the hands. He also admits that there are 'peculiarities' which may be of 'Korean art or due to Indian influence'.

As the bronze in question,[1] although more archaic, resembles in every important detail the gilt bronze statue illustrated on Pl. xxx, it will easily be seen that the 'peculiarities' are indeed striking if one compares it with the traditional representation of a Shō Kwan-non.

The symbol of the Shō Kwan-non is a lotus-bud (or flower), sometimes held in a vase. The hands are in 'charity' and 'teaching' *mudrā*; the breast and shoulders, aside from the ornaments and scarf, are bare, and the lower limbs are covered by a full, skirt-shaped garment which falls from the waist *to the ankles.*

The bronze figure, on the contrary, is completely covered by a long, complicated garment, which falls *below the feet* almost to the second row of petals of the lotus-throne. (In the archaic statue the garment is longer than in the larger one illustrated in the same plate.)

It is therefore evident that if the statue were standing on a flat surface the garment would fall on the ground like the long trailing robes which the Japanese court ladies have worn, in the interior, from time immemorial. The fact of the long garment alone indicates a feminine rather than a masculine divinity.

The statue in the Imperial treasures wears a crown, in which, however, there is no small image of Amitābha which would indicate the Shō Kwan-non.

The round object which is held in the left hand might be a magic jewel were it not covered by the right hand. The *cintāmaṇi*, both in the Tibetan form as well as in pearl shape, is represented *flaming*.[2] Even if it is not so portrayed, it is *understood*, and it would be against all tradition to represent the magic jewel held in this way. If it is not a *cintāmaṇi*, is it a pomegranate? There is no other Northern Buddhist symbol that is round. If, then, the divinity is feminine and holds a pomegranate, it is Hāritī, which fact would prove that the worship of the goddess Hāritī was introduced into Japan as early as the seventh century.

It is believed by some that the form of the goddess holding the child did not appear in Japan until the Tokugawa Shogunate (beginning of the seventeenth century), when the Roman Catholics were repressed and persecuted. It is claimed that the Catholics caused this form to be made in porcelain, or bronze, in which was

[1] v. small image, Pl. xxx.

[2] On a Japanese temple banner, belonging to M. Goloubew, smoke arises from the flaming pearl held in the right hand of Jizō.

PLATE XXXI

KWAN-NON (GYO-RAN OR 'FISH BASKET')

inserted a cross, and that they worshipped the Koyasu Kwan-non as the Virgin Mary. There are examples of these images in the Imperial Museum at Tokyo; but this does not prove that the form of Koyasu Kwan-non did not exist long before that epoch.

One of the most popular forms of the female Kwan-non is the Byakuye, or the white-robed Kwan-non, which was first brought to Japan from China in the Ming dynasty in the fifteenth century, when Chinese painters, sculptors, and casters came to Japan, and enriched the country by more than one masterpiece.

According to the *Butsuzo Zui* (the Japanese manual of the Buddhist divinities) the Byakuye Kwan-non belongs to the group of thirty-three female Kwan-non, which are all represented with the flowing garments and either a crown or the head drapery of the Indian goddess. Several of the thirty-three Kwan-non indicate, either by their names or by their representations, events in the legends of Miao-chen (v. legend), while others refer to the Chinese goddess Kwan-yin.

The Byakuye Kwan-non (sixth) (white-robed).	When, at the command of the Buddha, Miao-chen retired to the island of P'u-to to meditate, she clothed herself in white. 'White-robed' is also one of the titles of the Chinese Kwan-yin.
The Yen-Kwo Kwan-non (fourth) (sitting in bright rays).	When the father of Miao-Chen ordered her to be decapitated, 'a light breaking forth, surrounded Miao-Chen.'
The Gyo-ran Kwan-non (tenth) (fish-basket), Pl. XXXI. The Ryūzu Kwan-non (second) (Dragon-head). The Anoku Kwan-non (twentieth) (protects against aquatic demons).	When Miao-Chen saw that the son of the Dragon King of the Sea (who had taken the form of a fish) had been caught by a fisherman and was to be sold, she sent her acolyte, Chen-Tsai, to buy the fish and set it at liberty.
The seventh, twelfth and thirteenth Kwan-non are represented on a lotus-flower, a lotus-petal, and a lotus-leaf on the sea.	Miao-Chen was miraculously carried across the sea to the island of P'u-to on a lotus-flower.
The Ruri Kwan-non (twenty-third) holds a round object.	The Dragon King of the Sea sent Miao-Chen a luminous pearl. The Buddha gave her a peach to secure her immortality.
The Yōryū Kwan-non (first) (willow). The eleventh Kwan-non holds a willow branch and the fourteenth has a vase at her side in which is a willow branch.	The willow is the special symbol of the Chinese goddess Kwan-yin, with which she is believed to sprinkle about her the Nectar of Life.
The Haye Kwan-non (twenty-second) (clothed in leaves).	The images of Kwan-yin sent to the temples and monasteries of P'u-to by the Emperor K'ang-hsi were clothed in leaves.

In fact, all the forms of the thirty-three female Kwan-non show Chinese influence, and were possibly introduced into Japan at the same time as the Byakuye Kwan-non by the Chinese artists, in the fifteenth century. Some of these forms, however, are not authorized by the Japanese Buddhist scriptures.

The Japanese Buddhist priests do not look upon the *Butsuzo Zui* as an absolute authority on Japanese Buddhism; but until another manual is compiled, the Western student must continue to refer to this Japanese manual of Buddhist divinities, especially as, in so many respects, it has been found to be perfectly reliable.

No satisfactory conclusion, however, has yet been arrived at in regard to the Koyasu Kwan-non, nor the Chinese Kwan-yin, Sung-tsë. The dominant questions still remain unanswered: When did these forms first make their appearance in their respective countries? Is the Chinese princess and saint, Miao-Chen, their legendary ancestress?

Until these two questions have been satisfactorily answered, every hypothesis is of value in that it may contain the germ of enlightenment in regard to one of the most interesting Buddhist manifestations, the goddess Kwan-shï-yin.

VIŚVAPĀṆI (Dhyāni-Bodhisattva)

Viśva (*vajra*) pāṇi.

(Double-thunderbolt holder).

Symbol: *viśva-vajra* (double thunderbolt).
Fifth Dhyāni-Buddha: Amoghasiddha.
Dhyāni-Bodhisattva: Viśvapāṇi.
Mānushi-Buddha: Maitreya.

The Dhyāni-Bodhisattva Viśvapāṇi is very obscure. One seldom finds representations of the god either in bronzes or paintings. He is seated, dressed in all the Bodhisattva ornaments, his left hand lying on his lap, palm turned upward; and the right hand, in charity *mudrā*, holds his symbol, the double thunderbolt.[1]

Viśvapāṇi is believed to be in contemplation before the Ādi-Buddha, while waiting for the fifth cycle, when he will create the fifth world, to which Maitreya will come as Mānushi-Buddha.

[1] v. Pander, *Das Pantheon des Tschangtscha Hutuktu*, iii. 81.

PLATE XXXII

a. KI-SHI-MO-JIN

b. KOYASU KWAN-NON

c. BA-TO KWAN-NON

d. BA-TO KWAN-NON

ĀKĀŚAGARBHA (Dhyāni-Bodhisattva)

(Essence of the Void Space above).[1]

(T.) *nam-mk'ahi sñiṅ-po* (the matrix of the sky).
(M.) *oqtarghui-in jirüqen* (the essence of the heaven).
(C.) *Hü-k'ung-tsang* (虛空藏).
(J.) *Kukuzo.*

Mudrā : *vitarka* (argument).
vara (charity).
Symbol : *sūrya* (sun).

Ākāśagarbha, whose essence is ether, is one of the group of eight Bodhisattva. He is usually standing, with his hands in *vitarkā* and *vara mudrā*, in which case his special symbol, the sun, is supported by a lotus at his right shoulder, while at his left is a lotus-flower supporting a book, the symbol carried by four Bodhisattva of this group.

According to Pander's *Pantheon*, he is seated, his legs loosely locked. His right hand holds the stem of a flower which is not a lotus, nor is there a disc rising from it as indicated by the text.[2] The left hand forms *abhaya* (protection) *mudrā*. But in the work of Oldenburg,[3] Ākāśagarbha is represented with a white lotus supporting the sun in his right hand; the left hand forms 'charity' *mudrā*.

In the reproduction in the *Five hundred Gods of sNar-t'an* he is represented seated, holding in his left hand the stem of a lotus, from which springs a sword.[4] Both hands seem to be in *vitarka mudrā*. In this form he resembles Mañjuśrī.

In both China and Japan he is represented practically in the same way. He is standing, a graceful drapery falls from his waist, and a long narrow scarf is wound loosely around the body from the left shoulder to the right hip. The breast and the right shoulder are bare, and the hair is drawn up in a *stūpa*-shaped *ushṇīsha* like Maitreya. If there is a crown, a *stūpa*-shaped ornament is in the central leaf of the five-leaved crown. There are no symbols, but the left hand forms the 'triangular pose' (all fingers extended with the tips of the thumb and index touching, forming a triangle—see *vitarka*), and the right is in *vara* (charity) *mudrā*. The features are Indian, with long-lobed ears, and he has the *ūrṇā*.

[1] E. Denison Ross, *Sanskrit-Tibetan-English Vocabulary*, Memoirs of the Asiatic Society of Bengal.

[2] p. 76, illust. 150.

[3] No. 1, *Selection of Images of the three hundred Buddhist divinities, &c.*

[4] Grünwedel, *Mythologie du Bouddhisme*, p. 143.

KSHITIGARBHA (Dhyāni-Bodhisattva)

(Matrix of the Earth).

(T.) *sa̱hi-sñiṅ-po* (the matrix of the earth).
(M.) *ghaǰar-un ǰirügen* (the essence of the earth).
(C.) *Ti-tsang p'u-sa* (地藏菩薩).
(J.) *Jizō.*

Mudrā: *vitarka* (argument).
vara (charity).
Symbols: *cintāmaṇi* (magic jewel).
khakkhara (alarm staff).

Kshitigarbha belongs to the group of eight Bodhisattva, and is, according to Beal, the great 'Earth Bodhisattva', invoked by Buddha to bear witness that he resisted the temptation of Māra, god of Evil.[1]

The name of Kshitigarbha often appears in the ceremonies of initiation to the Northern Buddhist priesthood, and he is believed to be the Bodhisattva of the Mysteries of the Earth.

Kshitigarbha, unlike Ti-tsang in China, or Jizō in Japan, seems in no way connected with the infernal regions, although he is considered in both countries to be their Indian manifestation. In Tibet the 'Over-Lord of Hell' is Yama, while in China Yama holds a subordinate position under Ti-tsang, who is 'Over-Lord of Hell'. In Japan Jizō, while looked upon as incarnation of Ti-tsang (and Kshitigarbha), holds a subordinate position, and Emma-Ō is 'Over-Lord of Hell'.

But although Kshitigarbha, Ti-tsang, and Jizō hold different posts in their respective countries, the three manifestations have this in common, that they are believed to have made a vow to do the work of saving all creatures from hell during the interim of the death of Śākya-muni and the advent of Maitreya.

In Tibet statues of Kshitigarbha are rare and are seldom found outside of the group of 'eight Bodhisattva', where he is represented, like all the other Dhyāni-Bodhisattva, with the thirteen ornaments, and is standing with his right hand in 'argument', while his left hand his in 'charity' *mudrā*. His symbol, the magic jewel, generally in shape of a flaming pearl,[2] is supported by a lotus-flower on a level with his right shoulder. There is sometimes a book supported by a lotus-flower at his left shoulder.

Kshitigarbha may also be represented seated, holding an alarm staff in his two hands. On his head is a five-leaved crown, in each leaf of which is the representation of a Dhyāni-Buddha (Pl. XXXIII, fig. *c*). The *chodpan* crown is only worn by the Northern Buddhist priests and never by the gods; but this bronze is undoubtedly the representation of a god, for the personage is seated on the lotus-flower, and the alarm staff has six loose rings, which number indicates a Bodhisattva. As Kshitigarbha is

[1] According to the usual Buddhist legend, Buddha invoked the earth goddess Prithivī or Sthāvarā.

[2] v. group of eight Bodhisattva in the Museum für Völkerkunde, Berlin, and illustration, Oldenburg, *Izviestia, &c.* (Bull. Musée Pierre-le-Grand), St. Petersburg, 1909.

especially worshipped by those entering the Northern Buddhist priesthood, it may be that he is adored by them in this special form.

Among the temple banners discovered by Sir Aurel Stein in Chinese Turkestan, and now in the British Museum, are some very beautiful paintings of Kshitigarbha. He is either represented seated, holding the alarm staff in his right hand and the flaming pearl in his left, or standing, with one foot on a yellow and the other on a white lotus, holding the flaming pearl in his right hand. In almost all the temple banners from the Khotan his head is enveloped in a turban-shaped head-dress with the ends falling over the shoulders.

Kshitigarbha is also represented as Master of the Six Worlds of Desire, which is a very popular form of representing the god in Japan in temple pictures. He is surrounded by :

1. A Bodhisattva, symbolizing the heaven of the gods.
2. A man, symbolizing the world of men.
3. A horse and an ox, symbolizing the world of animals.
4. A demon armed with a pitchfork, symbolizing the hells.
5. An asura, representing the world of asuras.
6. A preta, representing the world of spectres.

A temple picture representing this subject was found by Sir Aurel Stein in Chinese Turkestan, proving that the form of Kshitigarbha with his alarm staff and as 'Master of the Six Worlds of Desire' was brought into Japan from Central Asia.

In Japan he may wear a crown, and be represented carrying a lotus-flower in his left hand. The right either holds the magic jewel, or is in mystic *mudrā* : the fingers are all extended upwards, and the thumb bent inwards touching the palm, a *mudrā* which the Japanese call 'semui'. It seems to be a corruption of the *vitarka mudrā*. His usual form, however, in Japan, is his manifestation, Jizō.

TI-TSANG (Dhyāni-Bodhisattva)

(Over-Lord of Hell).

Chinese manifestation of Kshitigarbha.

Symbols: *khakkhara* (alarm staff).[1] *cintāmaṇi* (magic jewel).

Before the god Ti-tsang became a Dhyāni-Bodhisattva and 'Deliverer from Hell',[2] he was, according to the *Ti-tsang sūtra*, a Brahman maiden, and his legend runs as follows: There was once a Brahman maiden whose mother died slandering the 'Three Treasures' (Buddha, Dharma, Saṅgha), and to save her parent from the torments of the damned, she made daily offerings before the image of an ancient Buddha, imploring his help. One day she heard a voice telling her to return home and meditate on the name of Buddha. She did so, and while in deep meditation her soul visited the outposts of Hell, where she met the Demon-Dragon, who informed her that through her prayers and pious offerings her mother had already been released from Hell. Her heart was so touched by all the suffering souls she saw still in Hell, that she vowed through innumerable *kalpas* to perform acts of merit to release them.

In this same *sūtra* Buddha announces to Mañjuśrī that the Brahman maiden has become a Bodhisattva through her acts of merit and that her name, as such, is 'Ti-tsang'. Thus the Brahman maiden became a masculine divinity and 'Over Lord of Hell'.

Although Ti-tsang is the Regent of Hell, he does not judge the souls but, according to Edkins, 'opens a path for self-reformation and pardon of sins'. He seeks to save mankind from the punishments inflicted on them by the ten Judges or Kings of Hell.

Ti-tsang is sometimes represented surrounded by the ten Kings of Hell, of which the fifth, Yen-lo-wang, is the Chinese manifestation of the Indian god of Death, Yama. The ten kings are always represented standing when in his presence.

Ti-tsang may be represented standing or sitting, and always as a round-faced, benevolent person, carrying his special symbol, the alarm staff, topped by loose rings, in his right hand, and the magic jewel in his left.

Women who have ugly faces pray to him and believe that, if they are devout enough, they will be born for a million *kalpas* with beautiful countenances.

His place of pilgrimage is at Chin-hua-shan, on a mountain crater, where a pagoda, ornamented with images of Ti-tsang and dedicated to him, soars above the monasteries and temples that cluster about it, and forms a pious landmark from the plains below.

[1] Carried by mendicant Buddhist monks to 'warn off small animals lest they be trod upon and killed' (Waddell). v. *Khakkhara*.

[2] *Ti-tsang-wang p'u-sa*.

JIZŌ (Dhyāni-Bodhisattva)

Japanese Manifestation of Kshitigarbha.

Symbol : *shakujo*[1] (staff topped with loose metal rings).

Jizō is the 'Compassionate Buddhist Helper' of those who are in trouble and of women desiring maternity, in which latter case he is called Koyasu Jizō. He is also the patron god of travellers, and, as such, his image is often seen used as a signpost on the highways. Stones are sometimes heaped about his statues by bereaved parents, who believe that Jizō will 'relieve the labours of the young, set by the hag Sho-zuko-no-baba, to perform the endless task of piling up stones on the banks of the Sai-no-Kawara, the Buddhist styx' (Satow).

The position of Jizō in Hell does not seem to be so closely defined in Japanese Buddhism as his manifestation in China. During the Kamakura period Jizō was believed to be an incarnation of Yama-rāja, king of Hell, the idea probably coming from China ; but he has never been confounded, however, with Emma-Ō, 'Over-Lord of Hell'.

Jizō is worshipped as Master of the Six Worlds of Desire. In this form he is only represented in paintings, and is surrounded by a Boddhisattva, a man, a horse and an ox, a demon, an asura, and *preta,* thus symbolizing the Six Worlds of Desire.

The Tendai sect worship a group of six Jizōs, or 'Compassionate Helpers', which may correspond to the 'Six Muni', presidents of the six worlds of rebirth of Northern Buddhism. Three of these Jizōs have the title of 'King of Hell'.

Legend recounts that a certain holy monk went to visit Emma-Ō, King of Hell, and saw Jizō sitting among the damned, in the lowest of the hells, undergoing torments for the sins of mankind (Satow). This, however, would not be incompatible with his being king of Hell, for Yama, the Tibetan king of Hell, undergoes the same torments as his subjects.

Jizō is usually represented as a shaven priest with a benevolent countenance, sitting or standing.[2] He wears the monastic robe, and, although a Bodhisattva, has no ornaments, but may wear a crown. In his right hand he carries his distinctive symbol, the *shakujo,* an alarm staff topped by six metal rings, which represent his vow to save all who follow the Six-Fold Path. In his right hand he may carry the magic jewel, a rosary, or a Kongo flag. He is sometimes represented without the *shakujo,* but rarely.

[1] San. *Khakkhara* ; v. Glossary.

[2] v. Pl. XXXIII, figs. *a*, *b*, and *d*.

SARVANĪVARAṆA-VISHKAMBHIN (Dhyāni-Bodhisattva)

(The Effacer of all Stains).[1]

(T.) *sgrib-pa rnam-sel* (he who makes the realms of darkness).
(M.) *tüitger-tejin arilghaqči* (the cleaner of moral spots).
(C.) *Ch'u-chu-chang* (除諸障).

(J.) *Jo-gai-shō* (removing-covering-obstacle).
Mudrā: *vitarka* (argument).
vara (charity).
Symbol: *candra* (moon).
Colour: white.

In the Lotus of the Good Law the Bodhisattva Sarvanīvaraṇa-vishkambhin is mentioned as holding conversation with Gautama Buddha, during which he expresses the desire to see the wonderful form of Avalokiteśvara. Thereupon Śākya-muni sends him to Benares, where Avalokita miraculously appears to the sage Vishkambhin, who ever after 'enumerates the qualities of this divine being'.[2]

Vishkambhin belongs to the group of eight Bodhisattva found in the Northern Buddhist temples, and according to Oldenburg[3] is standing with hands in *vitarka* and *vara mudrā*. His special symbol, the full moon, and a symbol which is also carried by several of the Bodhisattva of the group, the *pustaka* (book), are supported by lotus-flowers at either shoulder.

According to Pander,[4] he may hold the sun, but the disc is more probably meant to represent the *full* moon,[5] for the sun is the special symbol of Ākāśagarbha of this group. The Bodhisattva is seated with legs closely locked. The right hand, in *vitarka mudrā*, holds the stem of a lotus on which is a disc, and the left is in *vara mudrā*.

If in company with the Buddha, as Liberator of the Serpents, and Maitreya, Avalokita, and Mañjuśrī, he may hold a *cintāmaṇi* and an ambrosia cup.

In his Yi-dam form he stands with legs apart, on a prostrate personage lying face downward. He wears a tiger-skin hung around his waist, and a garland of heads. On the top of his *ushṇīsha* is a half-thunderbolt; he has the third eye; his right hand holds a *kapāla* (skull-cup) and his left a *grigug* (chopper).

[1] E. Denison Ross, *Sanskrit-Tibetan-English Vocabulary*, Memoirs of the Asiatic Society of Bengal.

[2] Burnouf, *Introduction*, p. 201.

[3] Oldenburg, III. (Materially: 5, note on several images and Bodhisattva.)

[4] *Das Pantheon des Tschangtscha Hutuktu*, p. 76, illus. 149.

[5] Sarva-nīvaraṇa never carries the moon-crescent, but the full moon, and as his Sanskrit name signifies 'effacer of spots', and his Japanese name 'removing-covering-obstacle', may there not be here a reference to the eclipse?

PLATE XXXIII

a. Jizō (Kshitigarbha)

b. Jizō

c. Kshitigarbha

d. Jizō

FORMS OF MAÑJUŚRĪ

Table IX

I. Human form.	I. With sword and book.	I. White (symbols on lotus supports); *vitarka mudrā*.	I. Mañjugosha.
		II. Yellow (symbols on lotus supports); *dharmacakra mudrā*; seated on a lion.	II. Siṃhanāda-Mañjugosha.
		III. Yellow (sword held in the hand); may be *siṃhanāda*.	III. Mañjuśrī.
	II. With blue lotus.	I. Yellow (attitude 'royal ease'); on lion throne.	IV. Mahārājalīla-Mañjuśrī.
		II. Yellow (*dharmacakra mudrā*); leg pendent; on lion or lion throne.	V. Mañjuśrī.
		III. Yellow (*dharmacakra mudrā*); legs locked; seated on a lion.	VI. Siṃhanāda-Mañjuśrī.
		IV. White (*dhyāna mudrā*); from *sādhana*.	VII. Dharmaśanka-samādhi-Mañjuśrī.
		V. White (*vara mudrā*); legs locked; from *sādhana*.	VIII. Siddhai-kavīra-Mañjuśrī.
	III. With sword and *utpal*.	I. Black or dark blue (kneeling, third eye).	X. Mañjuśrī.
II. Tantra forms.		I. Yellow (one head, four arms); symbols: lotus, book, bow and arrow.	XI. Mañjuśrī Jañānasattva.
		II. Yellow (one head, four to six arms) from *sādhana*.	XII. Vajranāga.
	III. Three or four heads.	*a.* Three heads, six arms.	XIII. Mañjuvajra.
		b. Three or four heads, six or eight arms.	XIV. Dharmadhātu-vagiśvara.
		IV. Dharmapāla form.	XV. Yamāntaka.
		V. Archaic form with *śakti*.	

MAÑJUŚRĪ[1] (Dhyāni-Bodhisattva)

(God of Transcendent Wisdom).

(T.) *ḥdjam-dpal*[2] (pleasing splendour).
(M.) *manǰusri*.
(C.) *Wên-shu-shi-li* (文殊師利).
(J.) *Monju*.
Mudrā: *dharmacakra* (turning the Wheel of the Law).

Symbols: *khaḍga* (sword).
pustaka (book—the Prajñāpāramitā).
utpala (blue lotus).
Colour: saffron or white, red or black.
Vāhana (support): lion.
Śakti: Sarasvatī.
Different names: Mañjugosha, Kumāra, Vajiśvara, &c.

Mañjuśrī, personification of Transcendent Wisdom, is the first Bodhisattva mentioned in the Buddhist scriptures, and as such his name frequently occurs in the 'Lotus of the Good Law' in connexion with Śākya-muni. In the *Nāmasaṅgīti* he is called 'Ādi-Buddha', while in some of the *sūtras* he is referred to as an historical character.

According to Chinese Buddhism, the Bodhisattva Mañjuśrī was informed by Gautama Buddha that it was his duty to turn the Wheel of the Law for the salvation of the Chinese, and the place chosen for the manifestation was Pañcaśīrsha (mountain of five peaks) in the Shan-si province. Legend relates that the five peaks of five different colours were once upon a time of diamonds, sapphires, emeralds, rubies, and *lapis lazuli*, that a flower grew on each peak of its especial colour, and that a different shaped pagoda was on the summit of each peak.

When the time came for the manifestation of Mañjuśrī, Gautama Buddha caused a golden ray to burst from his forehead. It pierced a *jambu*-tree which grew from the foundation of the mountain Pañcaśīrsha. A lotus sprang from the tree, and 'from the interior of the flower was born the prince of sages, Ārya Mañjuśrī. His colour was yellow; he had one face and two arms; in the right hand he brandished the sword of Wisdom; in his left he carried a book on a lotus of Utpala; he was endowed with the superior and inferior marks of beauty; he was covered with many ornaments, and he was resplendent.'[3] Thus he was born without father and mother, and 'free from the pollution of the common world'.

But he is also referred to as being mortal. It is recorded in the Chinese Buddhist books that the activity of Mañjuśrī, in the first century, at Wu-t'ai-shan (mountain of five peaks), was brought to the attention of the Emperor Ming-ti, while, according to the Buddhist writer Yi-tsing, it was popularly believed in India in the seventh century that Mañjuśrī was at that time teaching the doctrine in China.[4]

[1] Mañju-śrī. *Monju*, according to certain authorities, may possibly be a Tokharian word corresponding to the Sanskrit word *kumāra* (hereditary prince).

[2] According to Hodgson, *Jam-yang*.

[3] Grünwedel, *Mythologie*, p. 138.

[4] Foucher, *Iconographie bouddhique*, p. 114.

PLATE XXXIV

a. PU-H'IEN (SAMANTABHADRA)

b. WEN-SHU (MAÑJUŚRĪ)

c. MONJU (MAÑJUŚRĪ)

d. KWAN-YIN

In the *Svayambhū-purāṇa*[1] it is related that Mañjuśrī left Mount Pañcaśīrsha to visit the shrine of Svayambhū (Ādi-Buddha), which was on a mountain near the Lake Kālihrada.[2] He found the lake filled with aquatic monsters and the temple inaccessible. He therefore 'opened, with his sword, many valleys on the southern side of the lake . . . the waters of the lake rushed through the opening, leaving dry land at the bottom', and this was Nepal.

He is believed by some to have been the founder of civilization in Nepal. By others, to have been a 'Wanderer' (mendicant Buddhist priest) who carried Buddhism into Nepal. He is also supposed either to have been, or to have manifested himself as the prime minister[3] of the Tibetan king, Srong-tsan-Gampo, who was sent to India in the seventh century to study the Buddhist scriptures. It is also believed that Mañjuśrī may have been originally the deified hero of one of the Northern Chinese tribes. Mitra claims that he wrote the *Svayambhū-purāṇa* in the tenth century. Both Padmasambhava and Tson-ka-pa are said to have been his incarnations.

The first day of the year is dedicated to Mañjuśrī. He is looked upon by certain sects as the god of Agriculture, by others as the Celestial Architect, and is believed to have inspired, with his divine intelligence, those who have been active in the propagation of the Buddhist doctrine. He is the god of Science, and swings his sword of Wisdom with its flaming point to dissipate the darkness among men, to cleave the clouds of Ignorance. The Chinese say that when he preaches the Law every demon is subjugated, and every error that might deceive man is dissipated. He is an extremely popular deity in all the Northern Buddhist countries, and one often sees his image in magic paintings, charms, and *maṇḍala*.

Mañjuśrī belongs to the group of eight Dhyāni-Bodhisattva, and is therefore represented like a prince with all the Bodhisattva ornaments. He may have a small image of Akshobhya in his crown, and his *ushṇīsha* is sometimes ornamented at the top by a flaming pearl. The *ūrṇā* is generally on his forehead, and, if painted, his colour is usually yellow, but may also be white, red, or black.

Mañjuśrī or Mañjugosha, as he is frequently called in the *sādhana*, has two distinct types: one with the sword and book, which is his more usual form, and the other with the *utpala* or blue lotus.

The sword symbolizes the cleaving asunder (dissipating) of the clouds of Ignorance; the book[4] is the *Prajñāpāramitā*, Treatise on Transcendent Wisdom. It is represented in the usual form of the Nepalese book, which is made of palm-leaves, cut long and narrow, the manuscripts being placed between two pieces of flat wood, the whole bound together by a string. The book may be held in the hand of Mañjuśrī, but is more generally supported by an *utpala*, and surmounting it is sometimes a flaming pearl.[5]

The representation of Mañjuśrī with the sword and book has several variations.

[1] Mitra, *Nepalese Buddhist Literature*, p. 249. v. also Hodgson, *The Languages, Literature, and Religion of Nepal and Tibet*, p. 116.

[2] v. Nepalese temple painting, Bibliothèque de l'Institut de France, No. V.

[3] *Thu-mi-Sam-bhota.*

[4] *Pustaka*; v. Glossary.

[5] *Cintāmaṇi*; v. Glossary.

1. He is seated with the legs locked; the right arm is lifted brandishing the sword; the left hand holds the book on his lap.[1]

2. Like the above, except that the book is supported by a lotus-flower at his left shoulder. The stem of the lotus is held in the left hand in *vitarka mudrā*. This form may be on a lion.

3. Both the sword and book are supported by lotus-flowers; the stems are held by the hands; the right hand is in *vara mudrā*, the left in *vitarka*. He is white and is usually called *Mañjughosha*. When this form is standing, it belongs to the group of eight Bodhisattva.

4. Like the above, except that the hands are in *dharmacakra mudrā*; the left leg is pendent; the deity is usually seated on a lion or lion throne.

The above forms of Mañjuśrī are more commonly found in bronzes, while the forms with the blue lotus are oftenest seen in paintings and sculpture.

The representation of the blue lotus differs from the pink in that the petals are closed, elongated in form, and presented in profile. Sometimes the first row of outside petals is turned back, but the centre of the *utpala* is always hidden by the petals.

There are various forms of Mañjuśrī holding the blue lotus, which symbolizes the teachings of Buddha:

1. *Mahārājalīla-Mañjuśrī.* He is seated, as his name indicates, in the attitude called 'royal ease', with the right knee lifted, over which hangs the right arm; the left leg is bent; the left hand, holding the stem of the *utpala* (which is on a level with the left shoulder), leans on the lion throne or on the back of the lion support. If painted, he is yellow. Several very fine examples of this form were found in the Magadha, and one of them, seated on a lion, reverses the above attitude, the left knee being lifted.[2] Mahārājalīla-Mañjuśrī, when seated on a lion, closely resembles the Siṃhanāda-Lokeśvara, but the latter may be identified either by the antelope skin over his left shoulder (Pl. XXXV, fig. *d*) or by a trident,[3] while the Mañjuśrī has no distinguishing mark besides the blue lotus, not even the sword, which, in the representations of the Siṃhanāda-Lokeśvara, usually rises from the lotus-flower. If painted, they are easily identified, for the Mahārājalīla-Mañjuśrī is yellow on a blue lion, while the Lokeśvara is white on a white lion.

2. He is seated with legs closely locked, or, if on a lion or a lion throne, with the right leg pendent. The hands are in *dharmacakra* (teaching) *mudrā*, with the stem of the *utpala*, which is on a level with his left shoulder, wound around the left arm above the elbow. If painted, he is yellow.

3. Mañjuśrī may be seated on the lion throne with the left leg pendent; the hands are in *dharmacakra mudrā* and the *utpala* is at the left shoulder. His colour is yellow.

4. Like the above, except that the legs are locked and he is seated on a lion.

[1] In Java the book is sometimes held at the breast.

[2] A. Foucher, *Iconographie bouddhique*, illus., p. 115.

[3] v. Foucher, *Iconographie bouddhique*, Partie ii, p. 33.

PLATE XXXV

a. Mañjuśrī

b. Mañjuśrī

c. Mañjuśrī

d. Siṃhanāda-Lokeśvara

5. He is seated with the legs locked ; the hands are in *dhyāna mudrā*. This form is white, and is called *Dharmaśanka-samādhi-Mañjuśrī*.

6. Like the above, except that the right hand is in *vara mudrā*, and the left holds the stem of the lotus. He is also white and is called *Siddhai-Kavīra*.

Mañjuśrī may have only the sword and *utpala*, and be sitting, standing, or kneeling on one knee.[1] The right arm, which is lifted, holds the sword, and around the left arm is wound the stem of the lotus. If painted, in this form, he is black, and has the third eye.

There are various other forms of Mañjuśrī :

Mañjuvajra is a form of Mañjuśrī represented with his *śakti*. Both have three heads (the centre head is red ; the one to the right, blue ; to the left, white). Symbols : two *vajras*, a sword and lotus, bow and arrow. The *yab* is red and the *yum* is pink.

Vajranāga Mañjuśrī is standing and may have four or six arms. Symbols : sword, *utpala* (or book), bow, arrow ; if six arms, with a mirror and branch of *aśoka* as well. If painted, he is yellow.

Dharmadhātu Mañjuśrī is seated. He has four heads : centre, white ; to right, saffron : to left, reddish yellow ; behind, rose. He has eight arms ; the normal arms are in 'teaching' *mudrā* ; the six others hold sword, book, bow and arrow, &c.

Mañjuśrī, archaic form (see illustration, Pl. XXXV, fig. *b*). He is with his *śakti*, whom he holds on his knee in the archaic fashion, instead of in the attitude *yab-yum*. He has five heads, the fifth being above the central one, and eight arms, with four holding swords and the others books. He may also hold the sword and lotus with various other symbols (Pl. XIX, fig. *c*).

Mañjuśrī is one of the 'eight Terrible Ones' in his Dharmapāla form of Yamāntaka. His head, yellow in colour and with a slightly irritated expression, is usually above the head between the horns of the Bhairava form of Yamāntaka (Pl. LII, figs. *c* and *d*).

In China as 'Wenshu', and in Japan as 'Monju', Mañjuśrī is seldom worshipped, except in a triad with Amitābha and Samantabhadra. He is represented in both countries seated on a lion and holding a sword (Pl. XII, fig. *b*, and Pl. XXXIV, fig. *c*).

The monastery of Wu-t'ai in the Shan-si province is one of the most holy places of pilgrimages in China, and Mañjuśrī is worshipped there by the Mongols as well as by the Chinese.

[1] v. Pl. LXIII, fig. *g*.

MAHĀSTHĀNAPRĀPTA (Dhyāni-Bodhisattva)

(He that has obtained great strength).

(C.) *Ta-shih-chih* (大 勢 至).
(J.) *Sei-shi*, or *Dai-sei-shi*.

Mudrā: *vitarka* (argument).
vara (charity).

Mahāsthānaprāpta is believed to be the deification of Maudgalyāyana, 'the right-hand disciple of Gautama',[1] and although he is a Dhyāni-Bodhisattva, he does not belong to either the group of five or of eight Dhyāni-Bodhisattva. He is mentioned with Avalokiteśvara in the Lotus of the Good Law as well as in the *Sukhāvatī-vyūha*, which dated from the first century A. D., but Mahāsthāna does not seem to have been represented in either paintings or bronzes in Nepal or Tibet.

In China, however, one frequently finds him in a triad at the right of Om-i-to Fo (Amitābha), with Kwan-yin (Avalokiteśvara) at the left, which is the place of honour in China.

In Japan he is looked upon as the manifestation of the wisdom of Amida.[2] One finds him in a triad with Amida and Kwan-non, or worshipped alone. There is a statue of Mahāsthānaprāpta at the Zen-ko-ji temple, said to have been made by Śākya-muni from gold found at the foot of a Beiruri-tree on the south side of Mount Meru (Satow).

TRAILOKYA-VIJAYA[3]

(Subduer of the Three Worlds).

(C.) *Kiang-san-kie* (降 三 界).
(J.) *Gō-san-ze*.
Mudrā: *vajra-hūṃ-kāra*.

Symbols: *vajra* (thunderbolt).
ghaṇṭā (bell).
Colour: blue.

In the *Trailokya-vijaya sādhana*, translated into French by M. A. Foucher,[4] there is the following description of this divinity about whom very little is as yet known: On a sun (red platform) from the blue syllable 'Hūṃ!' was born the lord Trailokya-vijaya; he is blue, with four faces and eight arms: his first face expresses amorous fury; that at the right, anger; that at the left, disgust; the face at the back,

[1] Grünwedel, *Buddhist Art*, p. 205.
[2] v. *Amida*.
[3] *Trai* (*tri*, three), *loka* (*loka*, world), *vijaya* (conqueror). v. *Loka*.
[4] *Iconographie bouddhique*, Partie ii, p. 58, illus., p. 59.

heroism ; in his two (original) hands are the bell and thunderbolt ; he makes on his breast the gesture called *vajra-hūṃ-kāra* ; his three hands at the right hold (beginning at the top) a sword, elephant-goad, and an arrow ; the hands at the left carry (beginning from below) the bow, lasso, and a disc ; he is upright, stepping to the right on the breast of Pārvatī ; among other ornaments, he wears a garland made of little images of Buddha.[1]

In the court-yard of the Brahman convent at Bodh'-Gayā there is the statue of a divinity which corresponds with this description in every particular, except the minor detail of the bow and arrow being held in different hands in the statue from the description in the *sādhana*.

Trailokya-vijaya (Gō-san-ze) is worshipped in Japan as one of the five Devas who are called *myō-ō* (*mahā deva*). He is believed to wage war against and conquer the evil spirits who pretend to have created the Universe, and to be Protectors of the Three Worlds, and who seek to upset the laws of Karma. He is represented making the *mudrā* of anger (*djō Fudō*) with both hands, and the wrists are crossed to indicate intensity of anger.

In the Vajradhātu there is a magic circle of nine assemblies. The eighth assembly is called Trailokya-vijaya-karma, or the 'three-world-subduing-action-assembly'. Nanjio writes[2] that 'it shows the state of Mahā-krodha-kāya (great-anger-body) manifested by *Vajrasattva*[3] to destroy the enemies of the three worlds'. Again, in the ninth assembly, there is reference to Vajrasattva. 'It shows the state of the form of Samaya or argument[4] of Vajrasattva *who holds the bow and arrow.*'[5] We see from this that in Japan Vajrasattva is the *Subduer of the Three Worlds* ; first, to destroy the enemies of Buddhism in the three worlds, and, secondly, when holding the bow and arrow, to warn living beings. It might be inferred from this that Trailokya-vijaya is a special manifestation of Vajrasattva when conquering the celestial and terrestrial worlds, as well as the 'under' world.

[1] In Java several statues have been found which correspond with this description. A. Foucher, 'Notes d'archéologie bouddhique,' *Bulletin de l'École française de l'Extrême-Orient*, 1909, p. 48.

[2] *A Short History of the Twelve Japanese Buddhist Sects*, p. 95.

[3] v. *Vajrasattva*.

[4] Is not 'agreement' here meant ? Samaya means : convention, contract, engagement, and also 'identification with the Buddha'.

[5] v. *Kongō-satta*.

FEMININE DIVINITIES[1]

Table X

- I. One head.
  - I. Two arms.
    - I. Attributes.
      - I. Green; right foot pendent on lotus support . . . . . Green Tārā.
      - II. White; legs locked . White Tārā.
      - III. Yellow; right foot may be pendent . . . Yellow Tārā.
    - II. Lute . . . . Sarasvatī.
    - III. Lute and white snake . . . . . Āryajangulī.
    - IV. Chopper and skull-cup . . . . Ekajaṭā.
  - II. Four to sixteen arms . . . . Cundā.
  - III. Eight arms, sword, wheel, arrow, lotus . . . Ekajaṭā with Tārā.
- II. Several heads.
  - I. One or three heads.
    - I. Two to six arms.
      - I. Draws the bow, dancing . . . . . . Kurukullā.
      - II.
        - I. Angry, red . . Bhṛikuṭī (angry).
        - II. Calm, white . . Bhrikuṭī (calm).
      - III. Vase, spike of grain . Vasudhārā.
      - IV. Book . . . . . . Prajñāpāramitā.
    - II. Six to ten arms
      - I. One head, two arms . Mārīcī.
      - II. Three heads, of which one is that of a sow Mārīcī.
  - II. Three heads.
    - I. Six arms . . . . Bhṛikuṭī (angry).
    - II. Six or eight arms, apron of leaves . Parṇaśavarī.
    - III.
      - I. Double thunderbolt . . . . Ushṇīshavijayā.
      - II. Two parasols, third eye, sometimes four heads . . . . Sitātapatra.

Ḍākinī
- Vajra-varāhī.
- Na ro-mk'ẖa-spyod-ma.
- Vajra-ḍākinī.
- Siṃhavaktrā.

The Pañca Dhyāni-Buddha Śakti
- Vajradhātvīśvarī.
- Locanā.
- Māmakī.
- Pāṇḍarā.
- Tārā.

[1] Table of J. Deniker.

FEMININE DIVINITIES.

UNTIL the female principle was glorified by Kṛishṇa, the Aryans had exclusively worshipped Agni, the male principle in the universe, their only feminine divinity being the virgin goddess of the Dawn, Ushas.

The Aryans did not admit the feminine principle in their worship until civilization in India had become more refined, but, at the same time, weakened. Brahmā was given a feminine counterpart—Sarasvatī, goddess of Speech and Learning and patroness of the Arts and Sciences; Vishṇu received as consort the goddess of Love and Beauty, Lakshmī; while the Mahā-Devī, Pārvatī, whose ferocious forms are Durgā and Kālī, goddess of Death, became the *śakti* of Śiva.

The Mahāyāna school had also its period of the exclusive adoration of the male principle, from the first to the middle of the sixth century A. D., at which epoch the Yoga system was grafted on to the Northern Buddhist school by Asaṅga, and the adoration of the feminine principle was introduced in the form of the goddess Tārā. In the seventh century she took on two distinct forms, and in the succeeding centuries her forms multiplied, forming a group of twenty-one Tārās. Other goddesses, also having the rank of Bodhisattva, made their appearance, but none of them gained the popularity of Tārā.

By the seventh century the corrupt influence of the Tantra system had begun to weaken the austerity of the Northern Buddhist school, and not only did Tantra, or ferocious forms of the goddesses, appear, but the adoration of the *śakti*, or female energy of a god, was introduced, and the 'green' Tārā was declared the *śakti* of Avalokiteśvara.

Gradually the popular belief throughout Tibet and Mongolia developed in favour of the view that a god was more disposed to listen to and grant their requests when worshipped in company with his *śakti*. As a result, nearly every god was given a female energy, who was represented with him in the *yab-yum* [1] attitude, which was the final sign of degradation of the Mahāyāna school.

In China the only feminine divinity whose popularity equalled the masculine deities was the goddess Kwan-yin. She was, however, not worshipped as the consort of Avalokiteśvara, but as a feminine manifestation of the god himself, for a specific purpose—as was also the goddess Kwan-non in Japan.

The worship of the *śakti* was never adopted in China or Japan. The only representations of a god in *yab-yum* attitude are found in the few Lama temples still existing in China.

In Japan several goddesses of the Mahāyāna pantheon are worshipped; but

[1] v. Glossary.

in both China and Japan the male principle alone is considered of primal importance, since no woman, without gaining masculinity through re-incarnation, can enter Sukhāvatī, the paradise of Amida.

There are three forms of feminine divinities: goddesses with rank of Bodhisattva, *śakti*, and *ḍākinī*.

The goddesses are divided into two classes: the pacific and the angry.

The *pacific goddesses* are generally represented seated, and wear the thirteen Bodhisattva ornaments, including the five-leaved crown. They are of smiling expression, and usually have the *ūrṇā* on the forehead. The hair is long and wavy.

The *angry goddesses*, with dishevelled hair, the third eye, and Tantra ornaments and attributes, resemble the Dharmapāla form of the gods.

The *śakti* are rarely represented alone, but in the embrace of the gods, and are of pacific or angry form according to the god with whom they are represented. They are generally covered at the hips by a tiger or lion skin, and have either Bodhisattva or Tantra ornaments and attributes.

The *ḍākinī* are divinities of lesser rank, and are generally represented standing in a dancing attitude. Although they may have either pacific or angry forms, they are always represented with Tantra ornaments and attributes, and generally carry the *khaṭvāṅga*, or magic stick claimed to have been invented by Padmasambhava. The *ḍākinī* are believed to have given to the *guru* Padmasambhava the books in an unknown language, on which he is said to have founded the doctrines he preached in Tibet.

There is a group of five *ḍākinī* that seems to correspond with the five Dhyāni-Buddhas and Bodhisattva:

Buddha *ḍākinī* holding a wheel.
Vajra ,, ,, thunderbolt.
Ratna ,, ,, jewel.
Padma ,, ,, lotus.
Viśva ,, ,, double (thunderbolt).

Pander[1] gives still another *ḍākinī* called 'Karma', holding a sword.

[1] *Das Pantheon des Tschangtscha Hutuktu*, p. 91, No. 226.

PLATE XXXVI

WHITE TĀRĀ 'OF THE SEVEN EYES'

TĀRĀ (rank of Bodhisattva)

(The Saviouress).

(T.) *sgrol-ma* (döl-ma), or *röl-ma* (the Saviouress).
(M.) *dara eke* (Tārā, the mother).
(C.) *T'o-lo* (陁 羅).
(J.) *Ro-tara-ni-bi.*
Mudrā: *vitarka* (argument).
vara (charity).
Symbol: *padma* (lotus).

Colour: white or green.
Tantra forms: blue, yellow, or red.
Consort of Avalokiteśvara: white.
Śakti of Avalokiteśvara: green.
Different names: Jaṅgulī, Ekajaṭā, Bhṛikuṭī, Kurukullā, Sitatārā, &c.

The goddess Tārā was enrolled among the Northern Buddhist gods in the sixth century; by the seventh, according to Hiuen-tsang, there were many statues of her in Northern India, and between the eighth and twelfth centuries her popularity equalled that of any god in the Mahāyāna pantheon. Many temples and colleges were dedicated to her, and there was hardly a household altar without a statue of Tārā. Her worship extended to Java, but neither Tārā nor any other goddess was worshipped in Ceylon,[1] Burma, and Siam. The Southern Buddhist school never adopted the feminine divinities.

'Tārā', the Sanskrit name of the goddess, according to M. de Blonay, is derived from the root 'tar' (to cross). In other words, Tārā helps to cross the Ocean of Existence. The Tibetan translation of 'Tārā' is *sgrol-ma* (pro. döl-ma), which means 'saviouress' or 'deliveress'. Her Mongolian name 'Dara eke' means 'Tārā mother', and she is called the 'mother of all the Buddhas and Bodhisattvas'. The faithful may appeal to her directly without the intermediary of a lama, which is not the case with the other deities of first rank, and possibly accounts for her great popularity.

Her titles are to the mystic number of 108, and the manual of worship of Tārā is commonly found throughout Tibet. It is called the 'Praises and Spells (*dhāraṇī*) of the pure, original Tārā', and is believed to have been written by the Dhyāni-Buddha Vairocana;[2] but the author was more probably the monk Vairocana, who lived in the eighth century.

There are infinite legends in regard to the origin of Tārā, one of them being that she was born from a blue ray that shone from the eye of Amitābha. The generally accepted legend, however, is that a tear fell from the eye of the god of Misericordia, Avalokiteśvara, and, falling in the valley beneath, formed a lake. From the waters of the lake arose a lotus-flower, which, opening its petals, disclosed the pure goddess Tārā.

The lamas believed that Tārā was incarnate in all good women, and in the seventh

[1] A plaque, considered to be of the ninth century, however, has been found in Ceylon, on which is inscribed a prayer to the goddess Tārā.

[2] Also alleged to have been composed by the first of the seven mythical Dhyāni-Buddhas, Vipaśyi.

century they declared the two pious wives of the Tibetan Buddhist king, Srong-tsan-gampo, incarnations of Tārā. She was then given two distinct forms: the 'white', believed to be incarnate in the Chinese princess Wen-ch'eng, daughter of the emperor of China;[1] and the 'green', incarnate in the Nepalese princess Bribsun, daughter of the Newar king Aṃśu Varman. The white and green Tārās thus became distinct deities. The former was given as symbol the full-blown white lotus, while the latter carried the *utpala*, or blue lotus with the petals closed.

As the lotus opens by day and closes by night, the white Tārā with the full-blown lotus, and the dark Tārā with the *utpala* having its petals closed, may symbolize 'day' and 'night'[2]. Or in other words, since they were born from the tears shed by Avalokiteśvara, they may represent his never-ceasing grief at the miseries of mankind. Or they might also symbolize the willingness of Tārā to soothe human suffering by day as well as by night, for it is believed that Avalokiteśvara imposed on her that duty.

In support of the above hypothesis, M. de Blonay mentions a representation of Tārā found in a Jain temple in the fort of Dambal.[3] She is seated, holding a full-blown lotus in her hand. To the right is a sun, to the left a moon under which is a standing figure holding a lotus with its hand in *namaḥkāra* (prayer) *mudrā*. In the library of the Institut de France there is a temple-painting of Padmapāṇi, with the sun emanating from the right eye and the moon from the left (see Padmapāṇi with twelve emanations). The white Tārā was born from a tear which fell from the right eye, and the green Tārā from a tear from the left eye of Avalokiteśvara. It is also interesting to note that the second Tārā in the group of twenty-one Tārās is called 'of white moon brightness', and that the seventeenth Tārā carries a sun and a moon.

The Tantra forms of Tārā made their appearance when the Northern Buddhist school became weakened by the pernicious influence of the Tantra system. These ferocious forms of the goddess were represented in the three colours: red, yellow, and blue, which, with the white and green pacific forms, completed the five colours of the five Dhyāni-Buddhas of whom they were believed to be the *śakti*.

In the collection of Tibetan temple pictures belonging to M. Bacot, there is a painting of Tārā with 'one thousand heads and arms'. The heads are arranged in two rows on either side of the central row, superposed one above the other *ad infinitum*, and the five rows are painted green, red, white, yellow, and blue. She is represented standing, which is very unusual in Tibetan representations of the goddess (Pl. XXXVIII).

The Tārās are almost always seated, but if they accompany Avalokiteśvara, or any other important god, they are usually standing. Tārā may be surrounded by her own manifestations as well as by other gods.

The non-Tantra forms of Tārā wear all the Bodhisattva ornaments, and are

[1] Wen-ch'eng is believed to have brought with her from China the sandal-wood statue of the Buddha, which is now at Lhassa; it is said to be gilded.

[2] In the *Vibasha Shaster* the question is asked, What is it determines the period of day and night in Heaven? The reply is that it is determined 'by the closing of the Padma flower and the opening of the Utpala flower: in the former case, it is night; in the latter, day'. Beal, *Catena*, p. 78.

[3] Godefroy de Blonay, *Matériaux pour servir à l'histoire de la déesse bouddhique Tārā*, p. 9.

PLATE XXXVII

a. TĀRĀ

b. TĀRĀ (SIṂHANĀDA)

c. TĀRĀ

d. TĀRĀ

smiling and graceful. Their hair is abundant and wavy. The Tantra forms have the ornaments and symbols of the Dharmapāla, with the hair dishevelled and the third eye.

In Japan Tārā is found more often in temple banners than in statues, and is little worshipped.

The Japanese believe that Tārā made two vows: to conquer evil (as green Tārā) and to save human beings (as white Tārā). There is, however, in Japan but one form of the goddess. She holds the lotus, and may be making 'charity' and 'argument' *mudra*, or have the hands folded. Her colour is a whitish green, and she never has eyes on the palms of her hands or the soles of her feet like the Tibetan white Tārā. She holds the blue lotus or the *kichi-jis-kwa* (pomegranate), which is believed, as in India, to drive away evil.

In China her worship is practically unknown, although Hiuen-tsang mentions a statue of the goddess Tārā, 'of great height and endowed with divine penetration', and says that on the first day of each year, kings, ministers, and powerful men of the neighbouring countries brought flower offerings of exquisite perfume, and that the religious ceremonies lasted for eleven days with great pomp.

WHITE TĀRĀ

(S.) Sitatārā.

(T.) *sgrol-dkar* (pro. *dö-kar*) (the white saviouress).
(M.) *Jaghan dara eke* (the white mother Tārā).
Mudrā: *vitarka* (argument).
vara (charity).

Symbol: *padma* (full-blown white lotus).
Consort of Avalokiteśvara.

The white Tārā symbolizes perfect purity, and is believed to represent Transcendent Wisdom, which secures everlasting bliss to its possessor. She is the consort of Avalokiteśvara, and is represented at his right hand, generally standing.

In Tibet she is considered a form of the green Tārā, but in Mongolia, where the goddess is extremely popular, she is looked upon as equal, if not superior, to the green Tārā.

This form of Tārā is white, as she is believed to have been incarnate in the Chinese wife of the Buddhist king Srong-tsan-gampo, who was of white complexion according to Buddhist accounts, but was probably painted, following the Chinese custom.

When alone or surrounded by acolytes, Sitatārā is represented seated, with the legs locked, the soles of the feet turned upward (Pl. XXXVII, fig. *d*). She wears the same garments and ornaments as a Bodhisattva, and her hair is abundant and wavy. Her right hand is in 'charity' *mudrā*, and her left, holding the stem of the full-blown lotus, is in 'argument' *mudrā*. She generally has the third eye of fore-knowledge, and if there are eyes on the palms of her hands and the soles of her feet, she is called 'Tārā of the Seven Eyes' (Pl. XXXVI). This form is most popular in Mongolia, and may be found (but rarely) in China. As the *śakti* of Amoghasiddha (according to the system of the five Dhyāni-Buddhas) she is represented seated with legs closely locked, her hands in 'argument' and 'charity' *mudrā*, holding the stems of lotus-flowers which support the *viśvavajra* or double thunderbolt, symbol of the fifth Dhyāni-Buddha.[1]

Jāṅgulī-Tārā is a Tantra form of Sita-Tārā, and is invoked to cure serpent stings. She is represented with four arms; with the normal ones she plays on a lute, with the second right hand she makes the *mudrā* of protection, and with the second left hand she holds a snake. If painted, she is white,[2] as well as her clothes, ornaments, and the *snake* she holds.

It is interesting to note that, in Japan, Sarasvatī is worshipped in the form of a *white snake*. The lute which the Jāṅgulī-Tārā carries is the special symbol of Sarasvatī, while the white snake, which is the special symbol of the Jāṅgulī-Tārā, symbolizes Sarasvatī!

GREEN TĀRĀ

(S.) Śyāmatārā.

(T.) *sgrol-ljaṅ* (pro. *dö-ngon*) (the green saviouress).
(M.) *noghoghan dara eke* (the green mother Tārā).
Mudrā: *vitarka* (argument).
vara (charity).

Symbol: *utpala* (blue lotus, closed).
Śakti of Avalokiteśvara.

The green Tārā is considered by the Tibetans to be the original Tārā. In fact, the Tibetan name for the goddess is *dö-ngon*, which means 'the original Tārā'; but *ngon* (original) has been confused by the ignorant lamas with *sngo*, meaning 'green' (or blue), and the epithet 'green' has become inseparable from this form of Tārā, which symbolizes the Divine Energy.

She is represented seated on a lotus-throne, the right leg pendent, with the foot[3] supported by a small lotus, the stem of which is attached to the lotus-throne. She is slender and graceful in her pose, which is somewhat more animated than that of the white Tārā. She is dressed like a Bodhisattva and wears the thirteen ornaments, and usually the five-leaved crown (Pl. XXXVII, figs. *a* and *c*).

Her hair is abundant and wavy. Her right hand is in 'charity' *mudrā*, and her left, which is in 'argument' *mudrā*, holds the blue lotus presented in profile.

[1] Represented on the walls of the Vihar of Yama Guti in Cathmandu.

[2] There is a green form of Jāṅgulī with four arms, and a yellow form with six arms and three heads.

[3] In one of the miniatures in the MS. Add. 1643 in the University Library, Cambridge, she has both legs pendent.

The *utpala* is represented either with all the petals closed or the central petals closed, while the outside rows are turned back. The artists, however, do not always follow tradition and sometimes erroneously give the green Tārā the full-blown lotus of the white Tārā (Pl. XXXVIII). She may be represented 'Siṃhanada', that is to say, that her lotus-throne is supported by a roaring lion (Pl. XXXVII, fig. *b*). The goddess may also be represented with a small image of Amoghasiddha in her head-dress, both when alone or as a *śakti*, and she usually has the *ūrṇā* on her forehead.

If represented in company with several gods, she is usually at the left of the principal god, but in miniatures is sometimes at the right of Avalokiteśvara. She may be accompanied by eight green Tārās or only by her manifestation, Ekajaṭā, and the goddess Mārīcī, or by Jāṅgulī and the goddess Mahāmayurī.

In the latter case she is called *Dhanada*, 'giver of treasures', and has four arms. The upper normal ones make the usual *mudrā*, while the other two hold a lasso and elephant goad.

The green form of the Jaṅgulī-Tārā has four arms and holds Tantra symbols.

The 'Tārās of the four Dreads' is a group of four ferocious Tārās, of which, unfortunately, the author has been unable to find either examples or description.

The titles of the twenty-one Tārās,[1] according to Mr. Waddell, are the following:

1. Tārā the supremely valiant.
2. ,, of white-moon brightness.
3. ,, the golden coloured.
4. ,, the victorious hair-crowned.
5. ,, the 'Hun' shouter.
6. ,, the three world best worker.
7. ,, suppressor of strife.
8. ,, bestower of supreme power.
9. ,, the best providence.
10. ,, dispeller of grief.
11. ,, cherisher of the poor.
12. ,, brightly glorious.
13. ,, universal nature worker.
14. ,, with frowning brows.
15. ,, giver of prosperity.
16. ,, subduer of passions.
17. ,, supplier of happiness.
18. ,, excessively vast.
19. ,, dispeller of distress.
20. Realization of spiritual power.
21. Completely perfect.

[1] For description of the twenty-one Tārās, see Waddell, 'The Indian Buddhist cult of Avalokita and his consort Tārā', *The Journal of the Royal Asiatic Society*, Jan. 1894.

YELLOW TĀRĀS

Bhṛikuṭī.

(The goddess that frowns.)

(T.) *k'ro-gñyer-can-ma* (she whose face is wrinkled with anger [or frowning]).
(M.) *kilingtü eke* (the angry mother).
Mudrā: *vara* (charity).

Symbols: *triśūla* (trident).
mālā (rosary).
padma (lotus).
kalaśa (vase).

Bhṛikuṭī [1] is an angry form of Tārā, and has one head and four arms. The lower right hand is in 'charity' *mudrā*, sometimes holding a lotus; the upper one holds a rosary. In the left hands are a trident and a vase. She is generally standing, especially if she accompanies Amoghapāśa, a form of Avalokiteśvara, but, according to a *sādhana* translated by M. Foucher, she may be reclining. She has the third eye and her brows are frowning.

Bhṛikuṭī may also have three heads and six arms, but in this form she is blue (v. *Blue Tārā*).

Khadiravaṇi-Tārā is a form of the yellow Tārā. She is represented seated, with the right leg pendent, but the foot is not supported by a small lotus *āsana* like the green Tārā. The right hand is in 'charity' *mudrā* and holds the stem of a full-blown lotus-flower. The left hand is in 'argument' *mudrā* and holds the stem of an *utpala*. She may be accompanied by the goddesses Mārīcī and Ekajaṭā.

Vajra-Tārā is represented with four heads, eight arms, and the third eye. She is often found in Maṇḍala, where the four doors of the magic circle are guarded by the Yoginī (fairies) Vajrāṅkuśī, Vajrasphoṭī, and Vajraghaṇṭā. The four corners are guarded by four Tārās, 'of the flowers', 'of the incense', 'of the lamp', and 'of the perfume'. The right hands hold a thunderbolt, arrow, and conch-shell, and form the *mudrā* 'charity'. The left hands hold the blue lotus, bow, elephant goad, and lasso. If painted, she is yellow.

Jāṅguli-Tārā is represented with three heads and six arms. The yellow form does not carry the lute as does the white Jāṅgulī, but holds all Tantra symbols.

[1] Pl. LXI, fig. *a*.

PLATE XXXVIII

Tārā

BLUE TĀRĀ

Ekajaṭā (or Ekajaṭī)

(She who has but one chignon)

or Ugra-Tārā (the ferocious Tārā).

(T.) *ral-gcig-ma* (lit. 'she who has one knot of hair').

Ekajaṭā is a ferocious form of Tārā, and, with Lhamo (see), is one of the most terrifying manifestations in the Mahāyāna pantheon. In her simplest form she is the assistant of the green Tārā, and is represented seated, holding in her two hands the chopper and skull-cup.

When not the assistant of Tārā, she has from four to twenty-four arms, and is generally standing and stepping to the right on corpses. She has the third eye, is laughing horribly, her teeth are prominent, and her protruding tongue, according to the *sādhana*, is forked. Her eyes are red and round. Her hips are covered by a tiger-skin, and she wears a long garland of heads. If painted, her colour is blue, and her chignon is red. She is dwarfed and corpulent. Her ornaments are snakes. If she has but four arms her symbols are: sword, knife, blue lotus, and a skull-cup, or she may carry the bow and arrow instead of the last two symbols. If she has twenty-four arms, she carries several non-Tantra symbols and the rest are all Tantra. They are the following:

1. Sword.
2. Thunderbolt.
3. Disc.
4. Jewels.
5. Elephant goad.
6. Arrow.
7. Lance.
8. Hammer.
9. Bludgeon.
10. Knife.
11. Tambourine.
12. Rosary.
13. Bow.
14. Lasso.
15. Index raised.
16. Flag.
17. Hammer.
18. Trident.
19. Cup.
20. Blue Lotus.
21. Bell.
22. Chopper.
23. Brahmā head.
24. Skull-cup.

RED TĀRĀ

Kurukullā.

(Goddess of Wealth.)

(T.) *ku-ru-ku-le* (goddess of wealth).
Mudrā : *abhaya* (blessing of Fearlessness).

Symbols : *cāpa* (bow).
śara (arrow).

The goddess Kurukullā is called by M. Foucher 'the heart of Tārā'. She is worshipped by unhappy lovers, but can only be invoked when no woman is near. Red is the colour of love in India, and, according to the *sādhana* translated by M. Fouchier :[1] The Happy One is red of colour ; red is the lotus on which she is seated ; red is her clothing ; red her crown ; she has four arms ; at the right, she makes the *abhaya mudrā*, and with the other hand holds the arrow ; at the left, with one hand she holds the precious bow, and with the other the red lotus. Amitābha is seated in her tiara ; she lives in a grotto in the Kurukullā mountain ; she beams with the emotion of love in all the freshness of youth ; it is thus that one must imagine Kurukullā.

She is usually represented in dancing attitude, sometimes on the demon Rāhu, but she may be seated. If standing, the right leg is raised and she stands on the left, which is also bent. She either wears a crown of skulls or a band surmounted by five ornaments, the central one of which is a wheel surmounted by a skull. A small image of Amitābha may be in her head-dress. Her expression is ferocious and she has the third eye. She wears a long garland of heads and a scarf, the stiff folds of which rise above her shoulders at the back of her head. Her breast and hips are covered with ornaments. With her normal arms she draws the bow and arrow. With the other two hands she may make the *abhaya mudrā* and hold a *vajra* or lasso. Her colour is red, her hair is yellow (Pl. XLIII, figs. *a* and *b*).

She is the goddess of Wealth and follows in the suite of the god of Wealth, Kuvera, but is not his consort or *śakti*.

There are other still more ferocious manifestations of Kurukullā, with six and eight arms, represented dancing on corpses.

[1] *Iconographie bouddhique*, p. 73.

PLATE XXXIX

a. Aizen-myō-ō

b. Marīci

c. Buddha, ascetic

d. Juntei Kwan-non

SARASVATĪ

(Goddess of Music and Poetry).

(T.) *dbyaṅs-can-ma* (having a melodious voice), or *ṅag-gi-lha-mo* (goddess of speech).
(M.) *kele-jin ükin tegri* (goddess of speech).
(C.) *Ta-pien-ts'ai-t'ien ngiu* (大辯才天女) (goddess of great eloquence), or *Miao-yin-fo-mu* (妙音佛母).

(J.) *Ben-zai-ten* (or *Benten*).
Symbol: *vinā* (lute).
Colour: white.
Vāhana: peacock.
Śakti of Mañjuśrī.

Sarasvatī is the *śakti* of both Brahmā and Mañjuśrī. As goddess of music and poetry, she is revered alike by Brahmans and Buddhists, and her worship has penetrated as far as China and Japan.

In India and Tibet she is generally represented seated, holding with her two hands the *vīṇa*, or Indian lute; but in Tibet she may hold a thunderbolt, in which case she is called Vajra-sarasvatī. If painted, her colour is white and her mount a peacock.[1]

The Āryajāṅgulī, a form of the white Tārā, also holds a lute in two of her four hands, but the special attribute of this goddess is a white snake. In Japan the white snake is believed to be a manifestation of Sarasvatī, from which we must infer that the Japanese have confounded the two goddesses, Sarasvatī and Jāṅgulī.

According to the *sādhana*,[2] she has a Tantra form in Tibet which is red, with three faces, six arms, a warlike pose, and Tantra attributes.

In Japan the goddess Benten is looked upon as a manifestation of Sarasvatī. Her full name is *Dai-ben-zai-ten*, or 'Great Divinity of the Reasoning Faculty', and she is believed to confer power, happiness, riches, long life, fame, and reasoning powers. She is also one of the Seven Gods of Good Luck—the only feminine divinity of the group.

In regard to the goddess Benten, there is the following ancient Japanese legend: Once upon a time there was a monstrous dragon that devoured all the children who lived in the neighbourhood of the cave where he dwelt. A violent earthquake took place and the goddess Benten appeared on a cloud. From the waters suddenly emerged the island Enoshima, and the goddess Benten, descending to the island, 'married the dragon,[3] and put an end to his ravages'. It is probably in reference to

[1] v. Pl. XLII.

[2] A. Foucher, *Iconographie bouddhique*, vol. ii, p. 89.

[3] It is not impossible that this Japanese legend originated in China, for, according to Yu-kie, who recounted his travels to the Chinese emperor and his court in the beginning of the sixth century A.D., there existed to the north-west, 'about 1,000 li from China, a kingdom of women who took serpents for husbands. These serpents were inoffensive. They remained in holes while the women, their wives, lived in houses and palaces.' Marquis d'Hervey de St. Denis, *Mémoire sur le pays connu des anciens Chinois sous le nom de Fou-sang*.

this legend that the goddess is generally represented either sitting or standing on a dragon or huge snake. She has only two arms, and holds a *biwa* or Japanese lute.

Hayashi Razan, a sixteenth-century writer, states in his *Jinshakō* (studies on shrines) that Tairo-no-Tokimasa once repaired to the shrines of Enoshima to pray to the goddess for the prosperity of his descendants. She appeared to him in the form of a beautiful woman, prophesied as to the future of his descendants, and then, turning into a huge snake, wriggled away into the sea.

It is probably on account of the belief that Benten is closely connected with snakes and dragons that her shrines are always in caverns, on islands, or near the sea. In one of the temples of Kamakura there is the representation of a coiled snake [1] with a man's head having a scraggy beard, which the common people worship as the goddess Benten. Yanagiwara Motomochi, a writer of the eighteenth century, states in his *Kansōjigo* that a painting of Benten with three heads and a serpentine body had been handed down in his family for generations, and was believed to have come originally from a temple in Kyoto.

Tse Teijō, another eighteenth-century writer, says, in his *Anzaizuihitsu,* that the form of Benten which has a woman's head and a serpentine body came from Roman Catholicism, where 'Deus was so represented'. He further states that when Catholicism was repressed and the followers were persecuted by the government, at the end of the sixteenth century, they worshipped this form of God, calling it Benten.

But, although there are many legends of Benten connecting her with the snake, there is nothing which explains the meaning of the snake, or whether Benten and the snake are one and the same or only 'mistress and servant'.

The goddess Benten also has, in Japan, a Tantra form with eight arms. Her attributes are: a sword, spear, axe, box, arrow, lasso, thunderbolt, and a 'Wheel of the Law'.

According to Satow, Benten is believed, by certain sects, to be a sister of Vishṇu, and by others a feminine manifestation of Vairocana; but in her form with the lute she is unquestionably a manifestation of Sarasvatī.

[1] v. illustration, Pl. LVIII.

Marīci (?)

CUNDĀ

(T.) *tsunda.*
(C.) *Chun-ti* (準提).
Mudrā: *dhyāna* (meditation).

Symbols: *kalaśa* (vase).
mālā (rosary).
pustaka (book).
Colour: red (or white).

The goddess Cundā has two representations—one with four arms and another with sixteen. She may even have eighteen, for there is a statue of Cundā in the courtyard of the house of the Mahant of Bodh-Gayā with eighteen arms.

According to the *sādhana*, the form with four arms is red, and the upper hands hold the rosary and book, while the lower are in 'meditation' *mudrā* and hold the vase. She has a sweet expression.

Cundā with sixteen arms is warlike in appearance, but besides the sword, hatchet, bow, arrow, and thunderbolt, she carries a rosary, lotus, vase, &c., and one of her hands may be in 'charity' *mudrā*, while the original pair of hands are in 'teaching' *mudrā*.

VASUDHĀRĀ (or Vasundharā)

(Goddess of Abundance).

Mudrā: charity.
Symbols: *kalaśa* (vase).
spike of grain.

Colour: yellow.
Śakti of Kuvera.

Vasudhārā, goddess of Abundance, is the *śakti* of Kuvera, god of Wealth. She is always represented with one head, but may have from two to six arms, and wears all the Bodhisattva ornaments. When she has but two arms, the left hand holds a spike of grain, while the right holds a vase, out of which pour a quantity of jewels.

Vasudhārā, represented with six arms, holds in the lower left hand her characteristic symbol, the vase: the hand above holds another distinguishing attribute, the spike of grain. The third hand holds a book, the *Prajñāpāramitā*. The lower right hand, lying on the knee, is in 'charity' *mudrā*, and may hold a lotus-bud; the one above holds a jewel, while the upper hand makes a *mudrā* of salutation. The right leg is usually pendent, and the foot is unsupported or rests upon a vase which is supported by a lotus *āsana*, like her consort Kuvera. In the Nepalese miniatures, however, she is sometimes white instead of yellow, and holds the bow and arrow, a spike of grain and three peacock feathers.

She may have a small image of Ratnasambhava in her head-dress, and be accompanied by four minor goddesses or eight Yakshiṇī. According to Waddell Vasudhārā is a form of the Indian goddess Hāritī.[1]

[1] v. *Hāritī.*

PRAJÑĀPĀRAMITĀ[1]

(Goddess of Transcendent Wisdom).

(T.) *śes-rab-pha-rol-tu* (lit. 'she who has arrived on the other side of superior wisdom').
(M.) *bilig-un činadu kijaghar-a kürüksen* (being possessed of more than superior wisdom).

Mudrā: *dharmacakra* (turning the Wheel of the Law).
Symbols: *pustaka* (book).
mālā (rosary).
Colour: yellow.

Prajñāpāramitā is a personification of the attribute she carries, the sacred book, which Gautama Buddha is believed to have given the Nāgas to guard until mankind should become sufficiently enlightened to understand its Transcendent Wisdom. The goddess is, in fact, an incarnation of the Divine Word.

In Nepal, according to Bhagvanlal Indraji, she is worshipped by those who desire to know the true doctrine, and in Java she is also popular, but in Tibet she is almost unknown.

Prajñāpāramitā is represented with all the Bodhisattva ornaments, and may have two or four arms. If there are but two arms the book is supported by a blue lotus at her left shoulder, and the hands are in 'teaching' *mudrā*.[2]

If she has four arms the upper hands carry the book and rosary, or the upper left hand may hold the stem of a blue lotus which supports the book, and the upper right make the *abhaya mudrā*, while the lower hands in both cases are in *dharmacakra mudrā*.

A small image of Akshobhya may be in her head-dress, and there is usually the *ūrṇā* on her forehead.

By certain sects she was looked upon as the *śakti* of Vajradhara.

[1] *Prajñā* (wisdom), *pāra* (farther side), *mitā* (arrived at). The *Prajñāpāramitā* is the name of one of the divisions of the sacred books, the *Kanjur*.

[2] See illustration, Havell, *Indian Sculpture and Painting*, Pl. XIV.

MARICĪ (rank of Bodhisattva)

(lit. Ray of Light)

(Goddess of the Dawn).

(T.) *hod-zer-can-ma* (she of the brilliant rays).
(J.) *Marishi-ten.*
Symbols: *aśoka* (branch).
vajra (thunderbolt).

Colours: yellow or red.
Vāhana: seven pigs.
Consort of Hayagrīva.
Different names: Vajravarāhī and Aśokakāntā.

The goddess Mārīcī is called in China 'Queen of the Heavens' and 'Mother of the Dipper'. In Tibet her title is 'Goddess of the Dawn', and, according to M. Foucher, is invoked by the lamas every morning at sunrise. Among the common people she is not so popular as Tārā, but there are several shrines dedicated to her in Tibet, and in her Vajravarāhī form she is believed to be incarnate in every successive abbess of the monastery of Semding.

Vajravarāhī means the 'Adamantine sow', and there is a legend [1] to the effect that one of these abbesses had an excrescence behind her ear which resembled a sow's head. A Mongol warrior, Yun-gar, when attacking the monastery, called out insulting challenges for the abbess to come forth and show her sow's head. When the walls were destroyed and the army invaded the place, they found it inhabited by sows and pigs, led by a sow bigger than the rest. Yun-gar was so amazed at the sight that he stopped the pillage, at which the sows and pigs became transformed into monks and nuns, and the largest sow into the abbess herself. Yun-gar became converted at the miracle and enriched the monastery.

This legend does not, however, explain the origin of the name 'Vajravarāhī', which is more ancient than Mārīcī, nor why, when the goddess is represented with three heads, the one at the left is that of a boar; nor the reason for her chariot being drawn by seven pigs.

In Japan Mārīcī is believed to reside in one of the seven stars forming the constellation of the Great Bear. In India the Āryans may also have identified her with that constellation which they called *ṛiksha*, Sanskrit word for either 'bear' or 'star'. If that was the case, it is not impossible that the first representations of Mārīcī were made with a bear-support (instead of a boar). As the bear was little known in India the artists may have represented an animal which somewhat resembled a wild boar. The Great Bear itself is not true to nature, having a long tail. In the statues of Mārīcī from the Magadha, especially the one in the Calcutta Museum, the head which, according to tradition, should resemble a sow, resembles

[1] v. Waddell, *Lhassa*.

no animal in particular. If we accept the hypothesis that the original animal associated with Mārīcī was a bear, the representations of which, with time, changed into a boar and sow, the seven pigs that draw her chariot might represent the seven stars of the constellation of the Great Bear.

Mārīcī is evidently the goddess Aurora of the Āryans, for the *sādhana* refer to her as riding in her chariot surrounded by a glory of flame-shaped rays. Her seven pigs were possibly inspired from the seven horses that draw the chariot of Sūrya, the Sun God.

When Mārīcī accompanies the green Tārā she is always at her right and is called *Aśokakāntā*. She is seated on a lotus-throne, which may be supported by a pig, yellow in colour, and her legs are either locked or with the right leg pendent. She has the third eye. In her left hand she carries a branch of the *aśoka*-tree, and her right is generally in 'charity' *mudrā*, but may be in 'argument' *mudrā* or holding the *vajra*. She may, however, be seated on the pig with the right hand in *vara* and the left in *vitarka mudrā* (Pl. XLI, fig. *a*).

She has a yellow form with three heads and eight or sixteen arms. The face at the right is red and the one at the left, a boar's head, is blue; on each face is the third eye. Her attributes are: the thunderbolt, hook, arrow, needle, branch of *aśoka*, bow, thread, and a hand in *mudrā* with the index raised. Vairocana is in her head-dress. She steps to the right on a chariot drawn by seven pigs, or may be seated on a lotus supported by seven pigs. According to the *sādhana*, she is surrounded by the four goddesses: Vattalī (red), Vadālī (yellow), Varālī (white), Varāhamukhī (red). It is this form that is called 'Vajra-varāhī', and is represented more often in sculpture than in paintings.

A red form of Mārīcī has three heads and ten arms, and is her most hideous representation. She is corpulent, and brandishes in her ten arms only warlike attributes. In her dishevelled hair is a horse's head, and as she is the consort of Hayagrīva it is probably in this form that she is considered his *śakti*.

According to the *sādhana*,[1] there is a white Mārīcī with ten arms and four legs, treading on Brahmā, Vishṇu, and Śiva, as well as a red Mārīcī with six heads and twelve arms. In this latter form the first head is red; the second, blue; the third, green; the fourth, yellow; the fifth—on top of the heads—white; and, above this, the sixth, which is a sow's head. She carries practically the same attributes as the other forms, and has for covering a tiger-skin and wears a long garland of skulls. She is seated on a sow, and is most hideous and terrifying.

The Vajravarāhī form of Mārīcī may be a *ḍākinī* with a sow's head and woman's body, nude, and stepping to the left on a prostrate body. She has a skull crown, the third eye, and wears a long garland of heads and many ornaments. In her left hand is a skull-cup and in her right a chopper. She is usually accompanied by two acolytes.

In Japan Mārīcī is generally represented seated on a lotus-throne supported

[1] A. Foucher, *Iconographie bouddhique*, vol. ii, p. 96.

PLATE XLI

a. Mārīcī

b. Ushṇīshavijaya

c. Ushṇīshavijaya

d. Kwan-non

by seven pigs (Pl. XXXIX, fig. *b*). She has three heads, of which the one at the right is a sow's head (while in India it is always placed at the left), and has usually six arms, the original ones holding the thread and needle. Behind her head, instead of a nimbus, is sometimes the eight-spoked Buddhist wheel.

There is a curious Japanese example of Mārīcī (Pl. XL) holding a *caitya*. Behind her head are three faces, of which one is a sow's head.

PARṆAŚAVARĪ

(T.) *Lo-ma-gyon-ma* (dressed with leaves). Colour: yellow.
Distinctive mark: apron of leaves.

Parṇaśavarī is a follower of Tārā, and is specially interesting on account of the apron of leaves that she wears, which, according to Mr. Grünwedel, shows that she was worshipped by the aboriginal tribes of India. One of her names is 'Sarvasavarāṇām bhagāvatī', or goddess of all the Savaras (Savar or Saora),[1] and there is still a tribe in Eastern India known by that name.

She is represented turning to the left, but kneeling on her right knee. She is yellow, and has three heads—white, yellow, and red, and although her expression is irritated, she is smiling. In her six hands she holds a thunderbolt, hatchet, arrow, bow, lasso, and a branch of flowers.[2]

In the miniature (Pl. LXI, fig. *b*) she is not represented according to the text. Her colour should be yellow instead of green, and the three heads are white, green, and blue. The apron of leaves is missing, and, instead of the *vajra*, she holds a sword. Otherwise, the symbols are the same as the above representations.

[1] *Savar* means a 'mountaineer' or 'savage'.

[2] Pander, *Das Pantheon des Tschangtscha Hutuktu*, p. 80, No. 165.

USHṆĪSHAVIJAYĀ

(lit. Victorious Goddess of the Ushṇīsha).[1]

(T.) *gtsug-tor-rnam-par rgyai-ma* (victorious mother with a complete ushṇīsha).
(M.) *rasiian usnir-tu* (she who has a nectar (anointed [2]) head-dress).
Mudrā: *dharmacakra* (turning the Wheel of the Law), or *vara* (charity).

Symbols: *viśva-vajra* (double thunderbolt). ambrosia cup. small image of Buddha.
Colour: white.

Ushṇīshavijayā, 'having the intelligence of the most splendid Perfect One', is a very popular goddess in Tibet as well as in Mongolia, and is one of the earliest feminine divinities.

She is always represented seated, her legs closely locked, and with the soles of both feet apparent. She has three heads, of which the one at the right is yellow, the central head is white, and the face to the left is black. They are all, as a rule, sweet in expression, and have the third eye. She has eight arms. The two normal ones either hold a double thunderbolt at her breast, or are in *dharmacakra mudrā.* The ones underneath are either in 'meditation' *mudrā*, holding an ambrosia vase, or the right is in 'charity' *mudrā*, while the left holds the vase. Of the two upper arms, the hand at the right holds a small figure of Buddha, which may be supported by a lotus-flower, while the left is in *abhaya mudrā.* The other symbols vary, but may be the bow and arrow, lasso, *vajra*, or one of the hands in *abhaya mudrā*, or with the index raised (Pl. XLI, figs. *b* and *c*).

Her hair is drawn up in a high chignon (*ushṇīsha*) behind the crown, in which may be a small image of Vairocana. Ushṇīshavijayā is sometimes accompanied by Avalokiteśvara at her right and Vajrapāṇī at her left.

In the bronze statues the vase she carries somewhat resembles the ambrosia vase of Amitāyus. There are the four ornaments falling from under the cover of the vase, and from the cover itself rises an *aśoka* branch. The vase, however, is sometimes perfectly plain, and, according to a *sādhana* translated by Mr. Grünwedel, may be 'crowned by Vairocana's crown'. M. Foucher, in his translation of another *sādhana*, calls it the 'vase de fortune'.

In Japan her form resembles the Tibetan representation of the goddess, but she is little known.

[1] *Ushṇīsha*; v. Glossary.

[2] In the MS. Add. 864 in the University Library, Cambridge, there are several representations of ambrosia being poured over the *ushṇīsha* of the gods.

PLATE XLII

SARASVATĪ

SITĀTAPATRA

(Invincible goddess of the White Parasol).

(T.) *gdugs-dkar-can-ma* (goddess of the white parasol).
(M.) *caghan sigürtei* (having a white parasol).

Symbol: *ātapatra* (parasol).
Colour: white.

Sitātapatra (lit. white parasol) is one of the titles of Avalokiteśvara, according to the *sādhana*,[1] but there is also a goddess, Sitātapatra, who is looked upon as a form of Tārā, and has the rank of Bodhisattva. She may possibly be a feminine manifestation of the god of Misericordia, or the *śakti* of a special form of the Avalokiteśvara.

The goddess Sitātapatra is white in colour and may have three heads (blue, white, and red), or four heads with one at the back. With either form she has eight arms, and the two normal hands hold her special symbol, the parasol, under which she is believed to protect all true believers. (With the right she holds a parasol at her breast, with the left another on her knee.) The other hands hold the wheel, bow, arrow, book, and lasso. She may have the third eye, but her expression is sweet.

NA-RO-MK'ẖA-SPYOD-MA (*ḍākinī*)

(Na-ro residing in the heavens).

(S.) *Sarva buddhaḍākinī.*
Symbols: *kapāla* (skull-cup).
grigug (chopper).
khaṭvānga (magic stick).
Colour: red.

The *ḍākinī* Na-ro-mk'ẖa-spyod-ma is patroness of the Saskya sect and an acolyte of the *ḍākinī* Vajra-varāhī.[2]

She is represented stepping to the left on two personages and drinking blood from the skull-cup in her left hand, while the left holds the chopper. She has the third eye, and wears a crown of skulls, a long garland of heads, and many ornaments. She balances the magic stick, the *khaṭvānga,* on her left arm. If painted, she is red, and the two personages under her feet are red and blue (Pl. LV).

[1] A. Foucher, *Iconographie bouddhique*, vol. i, p. 110.

[2] v. *Mārīcī*

SIṂHAVAKTRĀ (*ḍākinī*)

The lion-headed *ḍākinī* Siṃhavaktrā is in the suite of Lhamo, whom she follows, carrying a chopper and skull-cup.

When she is represented alone she dances on a personage, and holds, besides the above symbols, a *khaṭvānga*. She has a lion's head, her hair is erect, and she wears a crown of skulls. If painted, she is blue with a white head. She may be accompanied by the lion-headed witch Vyāghravaktrā and the bear-headed witch Ṛikshavaktrā.

VAJRA-ḌĀKINĪ.

She dances with one foot on a man lying on his back. In her right hand is a *vajra* and a skull-cup in her left. Under the arm is a *khaṭvānga*. She has a third eye, her hair is erect, and she wears many ornaments. The personage under her feet may be missing (Pl. XLIII, fig. *c*).

THE PAÑCA DHYĀNI-BUDDHA ŚAKTI

On the wall of the Vihār of Yama Guti in Cathmandu are, according to Hodgson, high reliefs of the five *śakti* of the Dhyāni-Buddhas. (See illustration, *Sketch of Buddhism*, Royal Asiatic Society, vol. ii, Pl. III.)

All of the five *śakti* are dressed as Bodhisattva with the five-leaved crown, and have the lower limbs in the same position, called by Hodgson the 'Lallita-āsana', but the more common term is 'royal ease' (v. *Āsana*). They all hold the right hand in *vara mudrā*, and the left in *vitarka* pose, except:

1. *Vajradhātvīśvarī*, whose hands are in *dharmacakra mudrā*, like her Dhyāni-Buddha Vairocana. A lotus-flower at each shoulder supports a flaming pearl in which is the Nepalese *yin-yang*. Her symbol may also be the triangle (v. *trikoṇā*).

2. *Locanā*, *śakti* of Akshobhya. Her hands in *vara* and *vitarka mudrā* hold the stalks of lotus-flowers, each of which supports a *vajra* standing on end.

3. *Māmakī*, *śakti* of Ratnasambhava, has the same attitude and *mudrā* as above. Both of the lotus-flowers support three peacock feathers.

4. *Pāṇḍarā*, *śakti* of Amitābha. The lotus-flowers are closed (the *utpala*) and do not support a symbol (v. *Green Tārā*).

5. *Tārā*, *śakti* of Amoghasiddha; the lotus-flowers support double *vajras*.

PLATE XLIII

a. A Kurukullā

b. Kurukullā

c. Ḍakinī

THE YI-DAM (TUTELARY GODS)[1]

Table XI

The Yi-dam.	I. Derived from Dhyāni-Buddhas.	I. Vajra at his feet			I. Vajrasattva.
		II. With *śakti*, holds bell and	*cakra*.		II. Vairocana.
			vajra.		III. Akshobhya.
			cintāmaṇi.		IV. Ratnasambhava.
			pātra.		V. Amitābha.
			viśva-vajra.		VI. Amoghasiddha.
	II. Derived from the Bodhisattva Mañjuśrī.				VII. Mañjuvajra.[2]
	III. Derived from Dharmapāla.	Vajrapāṇi.			VIII. Mahācakra.[3]
		Mañjuśrī.			IX. Yamāntaka.
		Kuvera.			X. Jambala[4]
	IV. Forms purely Yi-dam.	I. Seven heads, sixteen arms, four legs			XI. Hevajra.
		II. Less than seven heads.	I. Three heads, six arms		XII. Sang-dui.
			II. Four heads.	I. Four arms.	XIII. Mahāmāyā.
				II. Twelve arms.	XIV. Saṃvara.
					XV. Kālacakra.

[1] Table of J. Deniker.

[2] v. *Mañjuśrī*.

[3] v. *Vajrapāṇi*.

[4] v. *Kuvera*.

THE YI-DAM (GOD-PROTECTORS)

EVERY lama puts himself under the protection of a special Yi-dam. He prepares himself for the event by solitude, meditation, and asceticism, after which, if the divinity accepts the guardianship, he will reveal himself when the lama is in a proper meditative state. The Yi-dam may be chosen for a lifetime, or for a given enterprise. A lama may even choose several at a time, but his choice must be kept secret to be efficacious.

It is possible for a layman to be put under the protection of a Yi-dam through the intercession of a lama; but he cannot appeal directly to his tutelary god, he can only do so through a lama. Tārā is the only divinity of first rank to whom a layman may appeal directly.

The Yi-dam are almost invariably represented with their *śakti*. In fact, the *yab-yum* attitude is the Yi-dam form of the five Dhyāni-Buddhas. It is considered that a tutelary god is more efficacious if worshipped in company with his consort.

The god-protectors have the rank of Buddha and are divided into two classes: the 'mild' and the 'angry' types.

The 'mild' Yi-dam are 'crowned' Buddhas represented with the thirteen ornaments of the Bodhisattva. They hold the usual symbols: wheel, rosary, lotus, jewel, &c.

The 'angry' Yi-dam are less fierce in aspect than the Dharmapāla. They wear the crown of skulls, but the skulls are smaller and are ornamented by Bodhisattva ornaments. The hair is drawn up in a high *ushṇīsha,* and they wear many ornaments besides the long garland of heads. Their symbols are Tantra: skull-cup, *vajra,* chopper, &c., and, if painted, their colour is blue.

PLATE XLIV

a. Hevajra with his Śakti

b. Hayagrīva

c. Hayagrīva with his Śakti

d. Kuvera (Nara-vahana) with his Śakti

PLATE XLV

Hevajra

HEVAJRA (Yi-dam)

(T.) *kye-ba-rdo-rje* (oh, eternal thunderbolt !).
(M.) *kevajra.*

Symbol : *kapāla.*
Colour : blue.

The tutelary god Hevajra is described, with all the rites and ceremonies used in his worship, in the *sūtra* of the *Hevajra tantra*, which figured historically in the conversion of the Mongolian emperor Khoubilaï in the thirteenth century A. D.[1]

Hevajra is represented with eight heads, sixteen arms, and four legs. There are three heads on either side of the central head, which is larger than the rest, and all have the third eye. Above the central head is another head. The heads, however, may be disposed in two tiers of three, with a head on top. In this form there are only seven heads.

All of the sixteen hands hold skull-cups. In those at the right are figures of animals : an elephant, a horse, a mule, a bull, a camel, a man, a deer, and a cat.

In the skull-cups held by the left hands are personages which, according to Grünwedel, are :

1. God of the water—Varuṇa : yellow.
2. God of air—Vāyu : green.
3. God of fire—Agni : red.
4. God of the moon—Candra : white.
5. God of the sun—Sūrya : red.
6. God of death—Yama : blue.
7. Goddess of riches—Vasudhārā : yellow.
8. A terrestrial god— (?) : yellow.

The colour of Hevajra is blue, and the three heads at the right of the central head (which is blue) are red, blue, and white. The three heads at the left are yellow, brown, and blue. The eighth head, which surmounts them, is a reddish brown.

Two of the legs step to the right on human beings, while the two legs at the back are in dancing position.

He is generally represented in *yab-yum* attitude (Pl. XLV ; and Pl. XLIV, fig. *a*), and the *śakti*, who encircles the body of the *yum* with her legs, holds a *grigug* in her outstretched right arm, while the left is around the neck of the god. Both the *yab* and the *yum* wear many ornaments, and all the heads are crowned, either with the skull or the Bodhisattva crown. Hevajra wears a long garland of heads, as well as the usual Bodhisattva scarf, and from a girdle hang many ornamented ribbons. If painted, he is blue as well as the *śakti.*

[1] v. *Mahakala.*

SANG-DUI (Yi-dam)

(S.) Guhyasamāja.

(T.) *dpal gsaṅ-ba-ḥdus-pa* (the secret assembly).
(C.) *Kuan-tsi-tsai fo.*

Symbols: *cakra* (wheel).
cintāmaṇi (magic jewel).
vajra (thunderbolt).

Sang-dui belongs to the mild type of Yi-dam and is dressed like a Bodhisattva, or rather a 'crowned' Buddha, for he has the rank of a Buddha. He is always represented seated, and has three heads. Each head has a five-leaved crown. In the central leaf of the crown, on the middle head, there is generally a wheel, and his high *ushṇīsha* is surmounted by a flaming pearl. He has six arms. The original ones are crossed behind the back of the *śakti* and hold the *vajra* and *ghaṇṭā*. The others hold the wheel, magic jewel, &c. The *śakti* also has three heads, and in the central leaf of the crown, on the middle head, is a small image of Amitābha. She has six arms and holds the same symbols as the *yab*.

MAHĀMĀYĀ (Yi-dam)

(T.) *ma-hḵa, mḵa-yaḥ,* or *tsaṅs-pa* (Brahmā).
(C.) *Ta-huan-kin-kang.*

Symbols: *kapāla* (skull-cup).
cāpa (bow).
śara (arrow).
Colour: blue.

Mahāmāyā is the Yi-dam form of Brahmā and, as a 'mild' Yi-dam, is dressed like a 'crowned' Buddha. He has four heads, on each of which is a Bodhisattva crown, and he does not have the third eye. He has four arms, the two normal ones are crossed at the back of the *śakti* and hold each a *kapāla*. The other hands hold a bow and arrow. There is sometimes a human skin over the shoulders. The *śakti* also holds a bow and arrow. Mahāmāyā is generally seated, but may be standing, in which case he rests on one foot while the other is raised, as if he were dancing. In this case he, however, holds the *śakti* in the same attitude as if he were seated.

PLATE XLVI

a. LHAMO

b. SAṂVARA ON THE MULE OF LHAMO
(LHAMO AS ŚAKTI ?)

SAMVARA (Yi-dam).

(T.) *bde-mc'og* (the best happiness).
(C.) *San pa-lo* (三跋羅).
Mudrā: *vajra-hūṃ-kāra* (arms crossed on breast).

Special symbol: four-faced head of Brahmā.
Colour: blue (*śakti*, cherry).

Saṃvara is believed to be incarnate in the Dalai-lamas of Peking, and his place of pilgrimage, in the province of Tsa-ri, is visited not only by Chinese Buddhists but by pilgrims from Nepal and Tibet.

As Yi-dam he has the rank of Buddha, and is the most complicated manifestation in the group. His four heads, if painted, are: the central one, blue; the one at the right, white; the one at left, green; the one at the back, red. On each head is a crown of five skulls, above each of which is a flaming pearl, or an ornament like that on the Bodhisattva crowns.

In the central ornament may be the small image of a Dhyāni-Buddha. The high *ushṇīsha* is surmounted by a flaming pearl, and is decorated, at the left by a half-moon, and in front by a double thunderbolt. Each face has a third eye and angry expression.

He is represented with twelve arms. The original ones are crossed in *vajra-hūṃ-kāra mudrā*, and hold the *vajra* and *ghaṇṭā* (thunderbolt and bell). The upper arms hold an elephant skin, which entirely covers his back (Pl. XLVII, figs. *c* and *d*). The others hold the head of Brahmā (four-faced), a *khaṭvāṅga* (magic wand), and other Tantra symbols. He wears a long garland of heads, and in the illustration in Pander's *Pantheon* he has a tiger-skin hanging from the waist. He steps to the left on the nude figure of a four-armed woman holding a *khaṭvāṅga*, and on the right treads on a four-armed man with a tiger-skin covering. The group is on a lotus with jagged petals.

Like all the Yi-dam, he is often represented with his *śakti*, whom he clasps to his breast, his arms crossed behind her back. The *śakti* holds a skull-cup and a chopper, and, if painted, is cherry colour, while Saṃvara is blue. There may be a glory of flames [1] surrounding the group.

There is an example of Saṃvara (Pl. XLVI, fig. *b*) which, as far as the author knows, is unique. He is seated on the mule of Lhamo with the eye in the haunch, and holds a *śakti*, which is probably Lhamo herself.

In the Museum für Völkerkunde in Berlin there is a most curious fresco of Saṃvara, brought from Turfan by Herr von Le Coq.

[1] Illus. 63, *Das Pantheon des Tschangtscha Hutuktu.*

KĀLACAKRA

(Wheel of the Time).

(T.) *dus-k'or* (wheel of time).
(M.) *čagh-un kürde* (he who turns the wheel of time).
Mudrā: *vajra-hūṃ-kāra.*

Symbols: *vajra* (thunderbolt).
khadga (sword).
Colour: dark blue, or tricolour (blue, white, red).
śakti (orange).

Although the god Kālacakra is represented in all the Tibetan paintings of the Tsok-shin, or assembly of the gods, he is but rarely mentioned in the Northern Buddhist texts. As *Kālacakra* is the title of a work in one of the divisions of the *Kanjur*, on a mystic system in Nepal (also called *Kālacakra*), it is possible that the god Kālacakra is a personification of that work, in the same way that Hevajra personifies the *Hevajra Tantra,* and the goddess Prajñāpāramitā, the *Prajñāpāramitā,* or Treatise on Transcendent Wisdom.

In the temple banners Kālacakra is represented either as a Bodhisattva or a Yi-dam. As a Bodhisattva he wears a five-leaved crown, the traditional Bodhisattva ornaments, and is yellow; but this form is very rare. He is usually represented as a Yi-dam with four heads, on each of which is a third eye. He may have twelve or twenty-four arms, but never has more than two legs. In his Yi-dam form he is dark blue, his body is covered by a tiger-skin, and he wears a belt formed of *vajras.*

Kālacakra is always represented in the *yab-yum* attitude, and may hold his *śakti,* with either two or four arms. If the former, he carries a *vajra* and *ghaṇṭā.* If the latter, he holds two *vajras,* a flaming sword, and a symbol difficult to determine. In a Tibetan drawing belonging to M. Deniker[1] he has twenty-four arms and holds many symbols, among which are, at the right: a flaming sword, a trident, a chopper, an arrow, an axe, &c. At the left his hands carry: a *khaṭvāṅga,* a *kapāla,* a bow, a lasso, &c. These symbols, however, vary in the different Tsok-shin. In the *Three hundred Burquan* of Oldenburg, Kālacakra has only twelve arms.

He is always represented stepping to the left on two prostrate personages or demons, with four arms. The personage under the right foot holds a bow and arrow; the one under the left a trident and *khaṭvāṅga.* There are sometimes two other demons who seem to be supporting the heels of the god, but may be also represented supporting the heads of the prostrate personages.

The *śakti* is represented with only one head, in the *Pantheon des Tschangtscha Hutuktu* of Pander, No. 65, but in the text she is mentioned as having four heads,

[1] I am indebted to M. Deniker for various iconographic details in this study.

PLATE XLVII

a. YAMA

b. YAMA

c. SAṂVARA

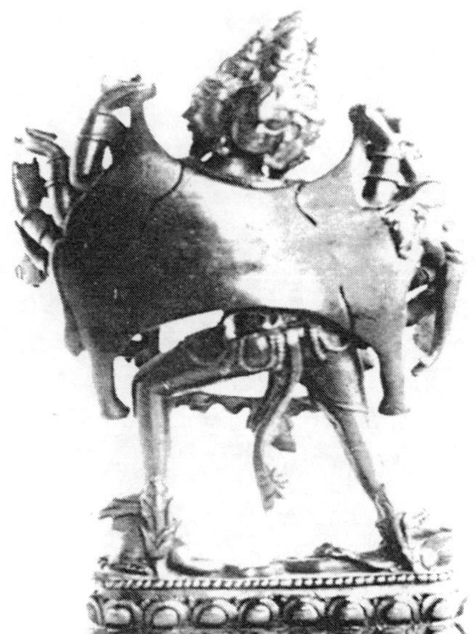

d. SAṂVARA

which is her usual number (v. Frontispiece). She may, however, have only two heads, and always has eight arms. With one of her arms, at the left, she encircles the neck of the god, while the others carry various symbols: a lasso, a flower, a *grigug*, a *vajra*, &c., and one hand may be making a *mudrā*. Her two legs are parallel with those of Kālacakra and step on the same personages; her colour is orange.

In one of the temple banners of the Tsok-shin, belonging to M. Bacot, Kālacakra is represented with the central head blue, that to the right white, while the two to the left are yellow and red. Of his twenty-four arms, eight are blue, eight are white, and the other eight are red. The right leg is white, and the left red. The *śakti* is orange in all the Tsok-shin.

THE DHARMAPĀLA

(The Eight Terrible Ones). (T.) Drag-ched.[1]

TABLE XII

I. Feminine divinity on a mule					I. Lha-mo.
II. Masculine divinities.	I. One head.	I. Two arms.	I. Warrior.	I. On a horse or dragon . . .	II. Ts'aṅgs-pa.
				II. Stands on a personage . . .	III. Beg-ts'e.
			II. Not a warrior.	I. Stands on a bull and woman . .	IV. Yama.
				II. Sometimes on a lion	V. Kuvera.
		II. Four to six arms.		I. Horse's head in head-dress . .	VI. Hayagrīva.
				II. Stands on one or two elephants .	VII. Mahākāla.
	II. More than one head . . .			Stands on animals and demons . .	VIII. Yamāntaka.

[1] Table of J. Deniker.

THE DHARMAPĀLA

(Drag-ched)

'The Eight Terrible Ones' (Defenders of the Law).

THE Dharmapāla, Defenders of Northern Buddhism, are Tantra divinities with the rank of Bodhisattva, and are supposed to wage war without mercy against the demons and all enemies of Buddhism.

The Drag-ched are worshipped singly or in a group of eight, called 'the Eight Terrible Ones', and are not malignant deities, as erroneously supposed, but are represented in ferocious form to inspire malignant spirits with fear.

Their worship was instituted in the beginning of the eighth century A. D. by Padmasaṃbhava when he went to Tibet at the request of the Buddhist Tibetan king Detsan. He waged war against and conquered all the malignant gods in Tibet, only sparing those that promised to become Defenders of the Law (Dharmapāla). Padmasaṃbhava, in his turn, promised to enroll them in the Northern Buddhist Pantheon, and to see that they were properly worshipped.

The Dharmapāla forms, which seem horrible and even disgusting to the uninitiated, are, to the devotee, however crudely expressed, the symbol of a religious thought. Even the *yab-yum* [1] attitude, which so offended the more refined taste of the Chinese and Japanese, is, according to M. Deniker, but 'an expression of divine ecstasy'. It symbolizes the Yoga system, or spiritual communion with the Most High.

The only goddess among the Dharmapāla is Lha-mo, who is also one of the most terrifying manifestations in the group. The only god who is not represented as ferocious is Kuvera, god of Wealth, and one wonders at his presence among the 'Eight Terrible Ones', since he has no ferocious form. The explanation might possibly be found in the fact that in every group of ferocious deities there must be, following tradition, at least one pacific divinity; but against this hypothesis one must admit that in almost all the temple pictures of this group of eight Drag-ched a pacific deity, Buddha or Bodhisattva, is added.

The 'Eight Terrible Ones' are:

1. Lha-mo.
2. Ts'aṅgs-pa.
3. Beg-ts'e.
4. Yama.
5. Kuvera.
6. Hayagrīva.
7. Mahākāla.
8. Yamāntaka.

[1] v. *Vairocana* and *yab-yum*; v. Glossary.

The lamas, however, sometimes make other combinations, putting one of the ferocious forms of Vajrapāṇi in the place of one of the usual group ; or some other Dharmapāla manifestation of a Dhyāni-Bodhisattva, taken for some special purpose, like Mañjuśrī, who took the ferocious form of Yamāntaka to conquer the god of Death, Yama.

In worshipping this group of eight Dharmapāla the priests wear a special five-leaved crown called *chodpan*, and special vestments.

The eight gods, with the exception of Kuvera and Ts'aṅgs-pa, are represented with a crown of five skulls, above each of which is generally a flaming pearl, and the dishevelled hair stands on end in flame shape. There is the third eye, the brows are scowling, and the expression shows great anger. Around the neck is a long garland of heads. The lower body is covered by a tiger, elephant, or human skin. They tread on human beings, or animals, and, if painted, are red, dark blue, or black.

The most ferocious gods of the group are represented on a pinkish lotus with jagged petals, and, with the exception of Yama, Kuvera, and Ts'aṅgs-pa, are almost invariably represented with their *śakti.*

(T.) LHA-MO (Dharmapāla)

'The goddess'.

(T.) *dpal-ldan-lha-mo* (the glorious goddess).
(S.) *Kāladevī, śrī-devī,* or *śrīmatīdevī.*
(M.) *ökin tegri* (lit. 'goddess-daughter').

Symbols : *khaḍga* (sword).
beng (mace).
Colour : blue.
Vāhana : horse (or mule).
Consort of Yama.

Lha-mo, the only feminine divinity among the 'Eight Terrible Ones', is one of the most terrifying manifestations in the Northern Buddhist Pantheon, and being the only goddess, Defender of the Mahāyāna school, she was armed by the gods. Hevajra gave her two dice to determine the life of men, Brahmā gave her a fan of peacock's feathers, and from Vishṇu she received two luminous objects, of which she wears one in her head-dress, while the other hangs over her navel. Kuvera, the god of Wealth, gave her a lion, which she wears in her right ear ; and Nanda, the serpent-god, gave her a serpent which hangs from her left ear. From Vajrapāṇi she received a hammer. Other gods gave her a mule, whose covering is the skin of a Yaksha or demon, and the reins are of venomous serpents.

Lha-mo is represented seated sideways on her mule. She wears all the Dharmapāla ornaments, and behind the skull crown her hair, in which there is a serpent and half-*vajra*, rises in flame shape, sometimes surmounted by a moon. She has the third eye, her expression is ferocious, and on either side of her head rise the stiff folds of a scarf like that worn by several of the Dharmapāla. She wears a long garland of heads, and over her navel hangs a wheel-shaped ornament. Her covering is a tiger-skin. In her right upraised hand she brandishes the *beng*, or sceptre, sometimes surmounted by a skull, while the left holds the skull-cup at the breast. The back of the mule is covered by the skin of a demon, with the head hanging downwards. According to the legend given by Schlagintweit,[1] the skin is that of her son whom she killed, having made a vow that if she were unable to convert her people to Buddhism, she would kill her own son (Pl. XLVI, fig. *a*).

The mule, if painted, is white, and has a disc between its ears; above the forelegs hang the dice given by Hevajra, and on its haunch is an eye, the legend of which is the following: In one of her incarnations, Lha-mo is believed to have been the wife of the king of the Yakshas in Ceylon. The goddess had made a vow to convert her husband to Buddhism, or failing, to extirpate the royal race; and finding it not in her power to influence her husband, she 'flayed her son alive, drank his blood, and even ate his flesh'. The king was so incensed, that he seized his bow and shot off an arrow after his fleeing wife. It pierced the haunch of her mule, and she pulled it out, pronouncing the following sentence: 'May the wound of my mule become an eye large enough to overlook the twenty-four regions, and may I myself extirpate the race of these malignant kings of Ceylon!'

The goddess then continued her journey northward through India to Tibet, Mongolia, and China, and is supposed to have settled in Eastern Siberia.

Lha-mo is accompanied by two acolytes: the *ḍākinī* Makaravaktrā (blue), who is either elephant- or dolphin-headed and holds the bridle of the mule; and the *ḍākinī* Siṃhavatra (red), with a lion's head, who follows her, holding a chopper and a skull-cup. The group walks on a lake of blood, in which float skulls and human bones.

Although she is the consort of Yama, there is an example of Lha-mo in the embrace of Saṃvara with the elephant-skin over his shoulder, who is seated sideways on the mule (Pl. XLVI, fig. *b*).

Lha-mo is sometimes surrounded by four ferocious goddesses, who are, according to Grünwedel:

1. Goddess of Spring (blue), seated on a yellow mule, holding a sword and a skull-cup.
2. Goddess of Summer (red), on a blue yak, and holds a hatchet and skull.
3. Goddess of Autumn (yellow), on a deer, and holds a knife and skull-cup, and around her neck are peacock plumes.
4. Goddess of Winter (blue), on a camel. She carries a hammer and a skull-cup.

In Tibet, Lha-mo is looked upon as the Protectress of the Dalaï-lama of Lha-sa and Tachi-Lumpo.

[1] *Buddhism in Tibet*, p. 112.

(T.) TS'AṄGS-PA DKAR-PO (Dharmapāla)

'White Brahmā'.

(M.) *esrua* (proper name).
(S.) *Brahmā.*
(C.) *Fan-wāng.*

Symbol: *khaḍga* (sword).
Vāhana: white horse (or dragon).

Although Ts'aṅgs-pa is one of the 'Eight Terrible Ones', but very little is known about him. He may be represented seated on a white horse, brandishing a sword, and sometimes carrying a banner. Like Beg-ts'e, he is a warrior god, but not so ferocious in aspect. Behind his crown is a turban, in which there may be a conch-shell, and he wears flowing garments and long sleeves. He sometimes accompanies one of the Five Great Kings, in which case he rides on a ram.

According to Pander,[1] Ts'aṅgs-pa may be represented with four heads, like the Hindu form of Brahmā, in which case he holds the Buddhist wheel at his breast with the right hand. The left seems to be in *abhaya mudrā.*

(T.) BEG-TS'E[2] (Dharmapāla)

(lit. 'hidden sheet of mail').

God of War and Protector of Horses.

(T.) *lcam-sriṅ* (brother and sister), or *Beg-ts'e* (hidden shirt of mail).
(M.) *egeči degüü* (sister-brother).

Symbol: *khaḍga* (sword, with a shrimp-shaped handle).
Colour: red.

Little is known of the ferocious warrior-god, Beg-ts'e, who seems to be confounded by the Northern Buddhists with Hayagrīva, whom some of the sects also call 'Protector of Horses'.

We hear of Beg-ts'e in a Mongolian legend[3] as appearing before the Dalaï-lama, mKasgrub bDod-nams, at the head of an army of demons in the guise of different animals—horses, camels, rats, &c. The Dalaï-lama had been summoned from Tibet by the powerful king, Altan Khan, to convert the Mongols to Buddhism, and when he found himself thus confronted he took, by his magic power, the form of the four-armed Avalokiteśvara, with the two original arms at his breast in 'prayer' *mudrā.* The

[1] *Das Pantheon des Tschangtscha Hutuktu,* No. 278.

[2] Lit. 'breastplate-covered'.

[3] Grünwedel, *Mythologie du Bouddhisme,* p. 82.

PLATE XLVIII

a. Kuvera

b. Kuvera

c. Kuvera

d. Kuvera

footsteps of his horse left the marks of Avalokiteśvara's mantra, '*Ōm, maṇi padme hūṃ !*' and Beg-ts'e, becoming convinced of his superior power and wisdom, was converted to Buddhism.

Beg-ts'e belongs to the group of the 'Eight Terrible Ones', and, as a warrior, wears a breastplate, while on his feet are Mongolian boots. His hair stands upright like flames of fire, he wears the skull crown, and has the third eye. His expression is ferocious. The right arm brandishes the sword—with a curious shrimp-shaped handle; the left hand holds a heart with the thumb and index, as if he were about to put it in his mouth—but this symbol may be missing. His left arm holds, against his body, a sword, bow, and flag. His lower limbs are covered by a tiger-skin, and he wears a long garland of heads. The god steps to the right on a prostrate horse, and his left foot treads on a human being. He may be accompanied by two small acolytes, a warrior seated on a wolf, and a nude figure of a woman seated on a lion. As *lcam-srin* means 'brother and sister', Grünwedel believes he may be so named on account of these two little figures.

YAMA (Dharmapāla)

or Dharmarāja.

God of Death.

(T.) *cos-rgyal* (king of the religion), or *gśin-rje* (lord of the dead).
(M.) *erlik qan* (king Erlik).
(C.) *Yen-lo-wang* (閻羅王).
(J.) *Emma-Ō.*
Colour: dark blue, red or white (or yellow).
Symbols: *dbyng-pa* (sceptre).
pāśa (lasso).
grigug (chopper).

Distinctive mark: wheel ornament on the breast.
Consort: Lhamo.
Attendant: his sister Yamī.
Different forms: Phyi-sgrub.
Snag-sgrub.
Gsang-sgrub.
Yama is a Dharmapāla (Drag-ched) with rank of Bodhisattva.

Yama, the Indian Pluto, was originally a king of Vaiśālī, who, when engaged in a bloody war, wished he were master of hell, and was accordingly reborn as Yama in hell,[1] together with his generals and army. His palace, made of copper and iron, was, according to the *purāṇas*, 'at the extremity of the earth, southward, and floating on the waters'. The wicked had 688,000 miles to travel, through terrifying ordeals, to reach it and receive their final punishment.

Yama, king and judge of the dead, is believed to sit in the centre of the regions of hell, which comprise eight hot and eight cold hells, as well as innumerable other

[1] Eitel, *Handbook of Chinese Buddhism.*

places of punishment. The wicked are brought before him to be questioned and judged, and are then conducted to their punishment by demons.

Yama is generally accompanied by his sister Yamī, whose duty is to look after the female culprits. Although he is supreme ruler of hell, Yama nevertheless undergoes the same torments as the rest, in order to expiate his own sins, when he will be reborn as Samantarāja.

Pander, in his *Pantheon des Tschangtscha Hutuktu*, gives the following legend in regard to Yama : There was once a holy man who lived in a cave in deep meditation for fifty years, after which he was to enter into Nirvāṇa. On the night of the forty-ninth year, eleventh month, and twenty-ninth day, two robbers entered the cave with a stolen bull, which they proceeded to kill by cutting off its head. When they discovered the presence of the ascetic, they decided to do away with him as witness of their theft. He begged them to spare his life, explaining that in a few moments he would be entering into Nirvāṇa, and that if they killed him before the time he would lose all the benefit of his fifty years' penance. But they refused to believe him, and cut off his head, whereupon his body assumed the ferocious form of Yama, King of Hell, and taking up the bull's head, he set it on his own headless shoulders. He then killed the two robbers and drank their blood from cups made of their skulls. In his fury and insatiable thirst for victims he threatened to depopulate the whole of Tibet. The Tibetans appealed to their tutelary deity, Mañjuśrī, to protect them from this formidable enemy, whereupon he assumed the ferocious form of Yamāntaka and waged war against Yama. A fearful struggle ensued, in which Yamāntaka (lit. 'he who conquers death') was victorious.

Yama has three forms, of which there are many variations : Phyi-sgrub, Snag-sgrub, and Gsang-sgrub. It is under this last form, Gsang-sgrub, that Yama was conquered by Yamāntaka.

Gsang-sgrub. In this form he has a bull's head, third eye, and crown of skulls, behind which his hair rises in flame shape. He steps to the right on a bull, and holds a *grigug* (chopper) in his right hand and *kapāla* (skull-cup) in his left. He may, however, hold a *cintāmaṇi* (magic jewel) in his right hand instead of the *grigug*, in which case he is looked upon as a 'God of Wealth'. He may also hold a mace and lasso (Pl. XLVII, fig. *a*). If painted, he is red. He is often accompanied by the Citipati or two skeletons dancing the Tsam dance (Pl. LII, fig. *b*).

Phyi-sgrub, or minister of the exterior. He is represented with a bull's head, third eye, crown of skulls, hair rising in flame shape, and is naked, but has a belt of heads and many jewels. On his breast is an ornament representing the Buddhist wheel, his distinctive mark, for Tsoṅ-ka-pa, before his death, appointed Yama protector of the Yellow Bonnets (Ge-lug-pa sect) with great ceremony. He steps to the right on a bull, under which is a woman, and his attitude and expression show great excitement and fury. He is never represented with a *śakti*, but may be accompanied by his sister Yamī, in which case, if painted, Yama is dark blue and Yamī pale blue. Yamī stands at his left holding a skull-cup. If Yama is without his sister he is painted white or yellow.

PLATE XLIX

Dharmapāla undetermined

Snag-sgrub, minister of the interior. In this form he is Judge of Hell. He is like the preceding, except that he steps to the left on a man and his symbols are *grigug* and *kapāla*. He is sometimes accompanied by two acolytes, each treading on a bull. If painted, his colour is dark blue.

Yama may be represented with a human face and with two of his six arms raised above his head in prayer *mudrā*. On his breast is his distinctive mark, the wheel, and he may step directly on the lotus-throne (Pl. XLVII, fig. *b*).

In China Yen-lo-wang (Yama) is not regent of the Buddhist hells, he is a subordinate under Ti-tsang (see) and the fifth of the ten Kings of Hell, who reign over ten courts of judgement. They are represented in Chinese temples, standing when in the presence of Ti-tsang, and surrounded by representations of the torments of the different hells.

Yen-lo-wang is believed to be assisted by his sister who judges the women, while he judges the men. They are called the Gam-ma-rāja (閻羅王與其妹) or the *Royal Pair*. He is referred to in the *Ti-tsang sūtra* as 'coming from the Iron Mountain, where the Buddhist hells are situated, to the Tau-li heaven (*Trayastrimśa*) to hear Śākya-muni Buddha deliver a *sūtra* there'.

In Japan Emma-Ō (Yama) is regent and holds the same position as Yama in India. In both China and Japan the representations of Yama are practically alike, a middle-aged man with a fierce expression and a beard. On his head is a judge's cap, and he is dressed in flowing garments with the feet always covered. He is seated with the legs locked and in his right hand is the mace of office.

FORMS OF KUVERA

Table XIII

Yi-dam.	Jambala.	Special emblem: Jambhara (lemon). Symbols: *nakula* (mongoose). *lai-bumpa* (flat vessel).
Dharmapāla.	I. Kuvera.	Regent of the North. Special emblem: *dhvaja* (flag). Symbol: *nakula*. Dressed like a warrior.
	II. Vaiśravaṇa.	Symbols: mongoose. trident. *lai-bumpa* or sword, &c.
Tantra (?) form.		Five heads, three legs, eight teeth. Mudrā: *vajra-hūṃ-kāra*. Symbols: *vajra* (thunderbolt). *ghaṇṭā* (bell). *grigug* (chopper). *kapāla* (skull-cup).

PLATE L

a. MAHĀKĀLA

b. MAHĀKĀLA

c. MAHĀKĀLA

d. MAHĀKĀLA

KUVERA (or Kubera) or VAIŚRAVAṆA (his patronymic)

God of Wealth.

Guardian of the North.

(T.) *rnam-t'os-sras* (*Nam-toi-sre*) (son of *rnam-t'os*).
(M.) *bisman tegri* (the god Bisman).
(C.) *Ts'ai-shên* (財 神), or *To-wen*.
(J.) *Bishamon.*
Special symbol: *nakula*[1] (mongoose vomiting jewels).
Symbols: trident.
dhvaja (banner).
lai-bumpa (flat vessel, &c.).

Colour: yellow.
Vāhana: *pushpaka* (self-moving chariot) elephant or lion.
Śakti: Vasudhārā.
As Dharmapāla (Drag-ched): Kuvera or Vaiśravaṇa.
As Yi-dam: Jambala (Dsambhala).
Special symbol: *jambhara* (lemon).
Symbol: *nakula* (mongoose).

According to Hindu mythology Kuvera was the son of a sage called 'Viśravas', hence his patronymic, Viśravaṇa or Vaiśravaṇa. He is said to have performed austerities for a thousand years, in reward for which Brahmā gave him immortality and made him god of Wealth, guardian of all the treasures of the earth, which he was to give out to whom they were destined.

Kuvera also became one of the Lokapāla, or Regents of the Four Cardinal Points, who were likewise guardians of Mount Sumeru, the centre of the universe. His city was Alaka in the Himālayas, abounding in wealth and magnificence, where he was attended by the Yakshas[2] and the horse-headed men called 'Kinnaras'. According to some accounts, Kuvera's abode was on Mount Kailās,[3] while others state that when Brahmā appointed him god of Riches, he gave him Laṅka (Ceylon) as his capital, and, according to the *Mahābhārata*, presented him with the car, *pushpaka*, which was of immense size, and 'moved at the owner's will at marvellous speed'.[4]

It is believed that the name 'Kuvera' may be a corruption of the word *kutana* (vile body), in reference to his ugliness, for, according to Hindu mythology, he had three heads, *three legs*, eight teeth, green eyes, and a white leprous body. He wore a crown and carried a mace, and was covered with jewels.

[1] Nakula (Chin. *No-ku-lo*) is also the name of the fifth of the eighteen Lohans or Sthaviras, disciples of Buddha, and his sphere of action was Jambudvīpa (India). His name is found enrolled in the list of gods in the Chinese, Japanese, and Korean temples, and he is represented in Tibetan temple pictures with a mongoose under his arm, or in his hand, or holding a three-legged frog. T. Watters, *Eighteen Lohans of Chinese Buddhist Temples*, Shanghai, 1899.

[2] Cannibal demons.

[3] Presumably the synonym of Mount Sumeru.

[4] Wilkins, *Hindu Mythology*.

The representations, however, of Kuvera do not follow the tradition of three legs, either in Nepal or India. In fact, a statue of Kuvera found at Gandhāra[1] might be taken for a Roman emperor, were it not for the kneeling youth at his feet pouring out money from a long narrow bag under his arm, which is in the shape of the traditional mongoose of Northern Buddhism; but the images from the Magadha follow more closely the corpulent, self-complacent god of the Mahāyāna Pantheon.

Kuvera has no worship in India. He is mentioned in very ancient texts, but, unfortunately, without reference to his symbols. Statues of him in Nepal date back to the eleventh century, while in India, in the Magadha, they are much earlier, and it is believed that the most ancient statues of Mahākāla (the Great Black One) were in reality but statues of Kuvera, for in Nepal they held the mongoose, and in India the long narrow bag of gold.

The Lamas claim that the mongoose symbolizes Kuvera's victory over the Nāgas, guardians of the treasures. The *nakula*, however, is merely a bag made of the skin of a mongoose, replacing the long narrow sack of the earlier images. In Java, according to Oldenburg, the long narrow sack is rarely finished by the head of a mongoose as it is in the Magadha, but the neck is left open resembling a mouth.[2]

Kuvera has both Yi-dam and Dharmapāla forms. As Yi-dam he is called Jambala, probably from the *jambhara* (lemon) this form always carries in his right hand. Under his left arm is the usual mongoose, vomiting jewels.[3] With but very few exceptions, of which one is in the British Museum, only the Jambala form of Kuvera carries the large mongoose under the arm, while all the other forms hold on the palm of the left hand a small mongoose with a single jewel in its mouth.

There is an example of Kuvera in a crouching position holding a *kapāla* in the right hand, while the left rests on the neck of a mongoose which hangs over the left knee. He wears serpent ornaments, and in his head-dress is the small image of a Dhyāni-Buddha.

Kuvera is always represented corpulent and covered with jewels. His right foot is generally pendent and supported by a lotus-flower on which is a conch-shell, or a *lai-bumpa*, a low, flat vessel used in the Lamaist ceremonies as an object of contemplation, to procure perfection in abstract thought. The vessel is usually represented overturned, with jewels sometimes issuing from it and falling over the lotus-throne. The conch-shell may also be supported by a vase. He may also carry a vase somewhat in the shape of an ambrosia vase under his right arm.

[1] v. Grünwedel, *Mythologie du Bouddhisme*, illust., p. 24, fig. 14.

[2] Oldenburg, *A propos de l'histoire du type des images de Kuvera avec Nakula.* Publications du Musée d'Anthropologie et d'Ethnologie, St-Pétersbourg, 1903, vol. iv. In the Musée Guimet, however, there are five examples of the Javanese Kuvera, where the mongoose is represented in the usual manner. In the British Museum there is a bronze with the *nakula* holding a purse in its mouth.

[3] Pl. XLVIII, fig. *d*.

According to Oldenburg, his foot may rest on a bag of precious things supported by a lotus-flower.

His Dharmapāla form is called 'Kuvera', and he is either represented sitting on a lion[1] (white, with green mane), or on several cushions called *kholbok*,[2] the number of cushions indicating the rank given him. He may also be seated on a horse[3] (Pl. XLVIII, fig. *a*), and Grünwedel mentions a form sitting or standing on a demon.[4] He carries the *dhvaja*, or victorious banner, or a trident, in his right hand, and a small mongoose, with a jewel in its mouth, in the palm of his left hand. According to Schlagintweit, he is accompanied by eight Vaiśravaṇas, each with his own special symbol in his right hand: a jewel, a sword, a *lai-bumpa*, a small shrine several stories high, called *khangtsig*, &c. They all carry, in the left, a small mongoose with a jewel in its mouth.

Kuvera may have a third eye, and is often represented with a closely cut beard under the chin, reaching from ear to ear. He is found in a triad with the Dīpaṅkara Buddha and Manla, Buddha of Medicine.

There is a special ceremony in Tibet for imploring Kuvera for riches, which is called Yanyung, and he plays an important part in the Tantras, in sorcery and exorcism.

The illustration on Pl. XLIX is a bronze which, as far as the author knows, is unique, and might possibly be a representation of the Tantra form of Kuvera. Its three legs agree with the description of Kuvera in Hindu mythology, but there are five heads instead of three, one on either side of the central head, and one above the central one (all of which have the third eye and an angry expression). The second head above the central one (which would be Ratnasaṃbhava if the god is Kuvera) has a sweet expression. The hair stands upright from the heads, in flame shape, forming a nimbus for the two upper heads. He has eight arms. The two normal arms are in *vajra-hūṃ-kara mudrā* (crossed on the breast), and the hands hold *kapāla* (skull-cups) which are supported by the arms from underneath. The other hands hold the *ghaṇṭā* (bell), *vajra* (thunderbolt), and *grigug* (chopper). The hips are covered by a human skin and the feet of the three legs rest on skulls. The necklets, bracelets, and anklets are snakes.

Kuvera is also one of the four Lokapāla which are supposed to inhabit the lowest compartments of the heavens, guarding the regions assigned them from the wicked spirits called Asuras. Each has an immortal elephant, eight generals, and an army of demons, and all are worshipped with fervour by the common people as well as by the priests.

For his Chinese and Japanese forms v. *Lokapāla*.

[1] Pl. XLVIII, fig. *b*.

[2] Pl. XLVIII, fig. *c*.

[3] In one of the miniatures in the Nepalese MS. Add. 1643, in the University Library, Cambridge, there is a personage seated on a horse at the foot of Avalokiteśvara, and holds an object, which may be a mongoose, in his hand.

[4] Called *nara-vāhana*, Pl. XLIV, fig. *d*.

HAYAGRĪVA (Dharmapāla).

(T.) *rta-mgrin* (pro. *tam-din*) (lit. 'with the voice of a horse').
(M.) *morin qogholai-tu* (with the voice of a horse).
(C.) *Pi-mih-ma-t'en-kin-kang*.
(J.) *Ba-to Kwan-non*.

Symbols: *vajra* (thunderbolt).
beng (mace).
Colour: red or dark brown.
Śakti: Mārīcī (light blue).
Distinctive mark: horse's head in head-dress.

Hayagrīva, as a Dharmapāla, has the rank of Bodhisattva, but, according to Grünwedel,[1] may also take a Yi-dam form, in which case he would have the rank of a Buddha.

He is worshipped in Tibet principally by the horse-dealers, for, although he is not the god, Protector of Horses, he is believed to frighten away the demons by neighing like a horse. When invoked, he is said to announce his coming by neighing, which may account for the presence of a horse's head, his distinctive mark, in his head-dress.

The horse is one of the Sapta Ratna (the Seven Precious Things), and Lungta, the 'airy horse', is extremely popular among the nomadic tribes of Tibet, as he may be invoked without the intervention of a lama. Schlagintweit says, 'The efficacy of any *dhāraṇī*, or mystical sentence, for happiness in this existence is supposed to become more certain by the presence of Lungta; and from this belief it has become customary to add to the *dhāraṇī* a horse supporting the precious stone Norbu, or a figure, allegorical of the horse, or at least an address directed to Lungta.'[2] Hayagrīva's popularity may therefore possibly be attributed to the usual presence of the horse's head in his dishevelled hair, but it is sometimes missing.

In his most simple form he is normal, and swings a sword in his right hand and holds a lasso in the other. His hair is dishevelled, and protruding from it is a horse's head. He wears a crown of skulls, and under a belt of heads hangs a tiger-skin. He may have one head and four arms, in which case his upper hands hold the mace (on the top of which may be a skull) and a flower. The lower left hand holds a wheel (or lasso) against the breast. The right hand makes a mystic *mudrā* and he steps to the right on a lotus-throne.

There is a form with three heads, four arms, and four legs, which is believed to be his manifestation when invoked by the Indian Paṇḍit Atīśa, who was invited by the Tibetan king in the tenth century A. D. to reform the Northern Buddhist faith in Tibet. He is represented like the above with dishevelled hair, crown of skulls, belt of heads, and a tiger-skin covering. The upper hands hold a thunderbolt and a flower, the lower hands draw the bow. He steps to the right on demons.

He may have still another form with three heads, six arms, and eight legs. His

[1] *Mythologie du Bouddhisme*, p. 166.

[2] *Buddhism in Tibet*, p. 254.

symbols are the thunderbolt, trident, lasso, &c., and from his dishevelled hair may protrude three horses' heads (Pl. XLIV, fig. *d*).

Hayagrīva may have *garuḍa* wings. In this form he has three heads, a third eye, a necklace of heads, wears a lion's and elephant's skin, and steps to the right on demons. He has six arms, the upper hands holding the double thunderbolt and sword, the next the mace and *khaṭvāṅga* (magic stick). The lower arms encircle the *śakti* if he is in *yab-yum* attitude, and hold the *kapāla* (skull-cup) in the left, while the right is in mystic *mudrā*. The *śakti* has a crown of heads, a third eye, and holds a skull-cup and a flower. She encircles the *yab* with her legs, and her mouth almost touches the tongue of the god. If painted, she is light blue (Pl. XLIV, fig. *c*).

In the miniatures Hayagrīva is never represented otherwise than as an assistant. According to M. Foucher, a form of the god found in the *sādhana* has three heads: the first blue, showing the tongue; the second, red and smiling; the third, white, biting its lips. They are placed one on either side of the central head, which is red. He has eight arms, and carries a thunderbolt, mace, flower, lotus, bow, and arrow, and two hands make a mystic gesture. In his hair is a small image of Akshobhya.

The *phur-bu*,[1] magic dagger, is believed to be a form of Hayagrīva.

Hayagrīva with Tārā, Sudhanakumāra, and Bhrikuṭī often accompany Avalokiteśvara, in which case Hayagrīva is always at his left.

His manifestation in Japan is apparently Ba-to Kwan-non,[2] for the resemblance is too close to admit of any doubt. In China he seems to have been little known.

MAHĀKĀLA (Dharmapāla)

The Great Black One.

(T.) *mgon-po* (the protector), or *nag-po c'en-po* (the Great Black One).
(M.) *jeke qara* (the Great Black One).
(C.) *Ta-shên-wang* (大神王).
(J.) *Dai-ko-ku*.

Special symbol: *triśūla* (trident).
Colour: black (or dark blue) or white.
Distinctive mark: treads on one or two elephants.
One of the 'Eight Terrible Ones' (Drag-ched).

It is claimed that Mahākāla, holding the trident, is no other than a form of the Greek god Poseidon[3] copied from Indo-Scythian coins; but it seems also possible that he is merely the result of a misnomer; in other words, that Mahākāla and Kuvera are one and the same divinity. Yi-tsing, the Chinese author and pilgrim, relates that at the doors of the Indian monasteries there was usually the statue of a deity, seated, with one leg pendent, holding a bag of gold. He further says that this god was called 'Mahākāla' (the Great Black One), because he was blackened by the oil constantly

[1] v. *Phur-bu*. [2] v. *Ba-to Kwan-non*. [3] Grünwedel, *Mythologie*, p. 24.

poured over him by the faithful in performing *puja*.[1] This description of the god assuredly indicates Kuvera ;[2] and the Nepalese Mahākāla, holding a mongoose under his arm, resembles Kuvera even more closely. The Tibetan form of Mahākāla, however, is definite and in no way resembles Kuvera, although one of his manifestations is called 'god of wealth'.

The tutelary god of Mongolia is Mahākāla, but he was not popular until the sixteenth century, when the Dalaï-lama, mK'asgrub of Lhasa, was summoned to the court of Altan Khan, and so influenced the king that all non-Buddhist idols were burned, and the six-armed Mahākāla was proclaimed Protector of the Mongolian Buddhists.

Mahākāla may be both Yi-dam and Dharmapāla, and has innumerable forms; but they may all be classed under four heads, or five, if we include the special manifestation of mGon-po Bramzei.

Mahākāla Son-dkar, god of Wealth, is the special protector of the Mongolian Buddhists. He has one head, which is sometimes deformed to resemble a bull, his hair stands upright behind the crown, flame-shaped, he has the third eye, and his expression is angry. He has six arms. The *cintāmaṇi* (magic jewel) is in the hand of his right (original) arm and is held against his breast. In the left is a *kapāla* (skull-cup) held underneath the magic jewel. The other four hands hold chopper, small drum, trident, and elephant goad. He has an elephant-skin covering, and a scarf rises stiffly from his shoulders, almost forming a nimbus around his head. He stands on two elephants, and, if painted, he is white (Pl. L, figs. *c* and *d*).

Mahākāla mSon-po resembles the white Mahākāla with the exception of two symbols. Instead of the *cintāmaṇi*, he holds a *grigug* in his original right hand. The other four symbols are: a rosary of skulls, a trident, a lasso, and a disc. His two upper arms hold an elephant-skin over his shoulders. He wears a belt of heads, and steps to the right on a prostrate elephant-headed god, the demon Vinataka (Brahman god Gaṇesa), who holds a flower in one hand and either a skull-cup or rat in the other. If painted, he is dark blue. This form is also popular in Mongolia (Pl. LI).

There is an unusual example of this form with only two arms. The right holds a sword and the left is in a mystic *mudrā*. He stands on an elephant-headed personage. In his hair is a small image of a Dhyāni-Buddha (Pl. L, fig. *a*).

Mahākāla, Protector of Science, is seated on a personage and has one leg pendent. He has four arms. His symbols are: trident, sword, skull-cup, and a fruit. He is dark blue.

Mahākāla, Protector of the Tent, holds a *grigug* (chopper) and lasso, and horizontally on his arms he balances a stick. He treads on a personage and is dark blue.

mGonpo Bramzei is a special form taken by Mahākāla to manifest himself to the great lama Pago-pa in the thirteenth century, when he was called to the Imperial court to convert the Emperor Koubilaï, who was already conversant with the *sūtra* of the *Hevajra-tantra*. Pago-pa, on the contrary, had never seen this *sūtra*, and finding it impossible to reply to the questions of the emperor, begged that the discussion be

[1] A. Foucher, *Iconographie bouddhique*, p. 126. [2] v. *Kuvera*.

put off until the next day. That night, while in utter despair at being unable to get hold of the *Hevajra-tantra*, there appeared, to his astonishment, an old white-haired Brāhmaṇa, who told him to arrange his lamp and then put before him the coveted *sūtra*. He was thus able to confer with the emperor on the following day and convert him. The old Brāhmaṇa was none other than Mahākāla under the form of—

mGonpo Bramzei (Mahākāla Brāhmaṇarūpa). In this form he has one head and wears a long white beard. He may have a third eye. In his right hand is a trumpet made of a human thigh-bone, and in the left is a *kapāla* full of blood. Around his left arm is a rosary of skulls. He may step to the right on a personage or be kneeling on him, in which case he holds the trumpet to his mouth.

In Japan, Dai-ko-ku, god of Wealth, has a form which in no way resembles the Tibetan Mahākāla, for he is represented as a very fat, jolly-faced man, always seated, and with a huge bag of grain at his side. He is the Japanese form of the Mahākāla Son-dkar.

YAMĀNTAKA (Dharmapāla)

Conqueror of Death (Yama).

(T.) *gsin-rje-gśed* (exterminator of the Lord of Death), or *ḥjegs-byed* (he who causes fear).
(M.) *erlig-jin jarghaqči* (exterminator of Erlik).
(C.) *Yen-man-tê-kia* (閻曼德迦).
Symbols: *grigug* (chopper).
kapāla (skull-cup).
Colour: red (when alone), black or dark blue.

Distinctive mark: bull's head.
Different names: Śrivajrabhairava, Vajrabhayaṅkara, Vajrabhairava, Bhairava, and Yamāri.
One of the 'Eight Terrible Ones' (Dharmapāla or Drag-ched).
Yi-dam of the Ge-lug-pa (Yellow Bonnet) sect.[1]

Yamāntaka, the ferocious emanation of Mañjuśrī, is the most complicated and terrible of all the Northern Buddhist divinities. Under this form he conquered the demon king of Death, Yama, who was depopulating Tibet in his insatiable thirst for victims.

Both Yama and Yamāntaka are represented with bulls' heads, but Yama always has an ornament, shaped like a wheel, on his breast, which is his distinctive mark.

Yamāntaka as Vajrabhairava may be represented with a human head. According to Vidyābhūṣaṇa,[2] in his description of certain Tibetan scrolls found in a monastery near Gyantse, Vajrabhairava 'possesses a disproportionately large head, scowling brows, three cruel eyes, and a gaping mouth, showing canine fangs and rolling tongue'. Nor does he figure with a bull's head in the two *sādhana* mentioned by M. Foucher,[3] for in the first he has six faces, and in the second one face.

[1] Grünwedel, *Mythologie*, p. 100.
[2] *Memoirs of the Asiatic Society of Bengal.*
[3] *Iconographie bouddhique*, vol. ii, p. 56.

The simplest form of Yamāntaka has one head (a bull's) and two arms. He has a crown of skulls and the third eye. In his right hand is a chopper and in his left a skull-cup (*kapāla*). He has a belt of heads and steps to the right (Pl. LII, fig. *a*).

In the *Śrīmahāvajrabhairava tantra* there is a detailed account of the way Yamāntaka should be represented if painted.[1] He is to have sixteen feet, thirty-four arms, nine heads, is naked and black ; he steps to the right, and his aspect is more than terrible. The first head is that of a bull. Next to the right horn, he must have three heads : blue, grey, and black (description of three heads on left side omitted). Between the horns must be painted a head, red and terrible, above which must be the head of Mañjuśrī with a slightly irritated expression. The hands hold all the Tantra symbols (list given in the *tantra*). The right feet tread on animals and the left on birds. In the bronzes Yamāntaka may be treading on demons, under which are animals and birds, or the reverse, or the demons may be supporting the throne as in the accompanying illustration (Pl. LII, fig. *d*).

Yamāntaka has a skull diadem, a belt of heads, a third eye, and steps to the right. He may have five heads, and hold the skin of a human being over his shoulders. He is usually represented with his *śakti* (Pl. LII, fig. *c*).

As Yamāri, however, he is not represented with a *śakti*. In this form Yamāntaka holds a sceptre topped by a skull in his right hand and a *kapāla* in his left, and steps to the right on a corpse, under which is a bull.

[1] Grünwedel, *Mythologie*, p. 104.

PLATE LII

a. Yamāntaka

b Citipati

c. Yamāntaka

d. Yamāntaka

a BISHAMON

b. LOKAPĀLA

c. BISHAMON

d. FUDŌ

MINOR GODS

TABLE XIV

I. Lokapāla.
II. The Five Kings.
III. The Ni-ō (Ni-wō).
IV. The Citipati.
V. Nāgas and Garuḍas.

HISTORICAL PERSONAGES DEIFIED

TABLE XV

I. Arhat (Lohan, Rakhan).
II. Nāgārjuna.
III. Padmasambhava.
IV. Tson-k'a-pa.
V. Mil-ras-pa.

THE FOUR LOKAPĀLA

(S.) *catur mahārāja.*
(T.) *rgyal-c'en-bshi* (the four kings).
(M.) *mahārāja.*
(C.) *Hu-shih-chê* (護世者).

THE Lokapāla, or guardians of the Four Cardinal Points, are believed to dwell on Mount Sumeru (Kailāsa) at the gates of the paradise of Śakra (Indra), who is looked upon as a protector of Buddhism.

The four Guardian Kings are mentioned in the earliest Buddhist writings as visiting Gautama while he was in the Tushita heaven waiting for the time to come for him to manifest himself on earth as Mānushi-Buddha. They are alluded to in the *Nidāna-Kathā* as having been present when Māyā's couch was carried to the place of incarnation of the Buddha. They assisted at his birth, and received the Buddha 'on the skin of a spotted tiger'. They held up the hoofs of the horse Kaṇṭhaka when Gautama secretly left his palace to go into the wilderness. After his fasting and meditation under the Bodhi-tree, they offered the Buddha four bowls of food, which he miraculously merged into one (*pātra*, v. Glossary). In fact, they assisted at every important event in the life of the Buddha, and were present at his *parinirvāṇa.*

Images of the Lokapāla were placed at the four sides of the Indian topes (*stūpa*) to guard the sacred relics. The earliest known statues are on the Sanchi Tope, which dates from between the second and first centuries B. C. The Buddhist Guardians were generally represented in full armour standing on Nāga demons,[1] while the mounts of the Brahman Lokapāla were elephants.[2] They became very popular deities in Tibet, China, and Japan, and were also taken up by the Southern Buddhists of the Hīnayāna school.

The four Indian Lokapāla are :

North : *Kuvera* (Vaiśravaṇa), King of the Yakshas (supernatural beings that bring disease). Symbols : *dhvaja* (banner) in right hand and mongoose in the left. Colour : yellow.

South : *Virūḍhaka,* King of the Khumbhaṇḍa (giant demons). Symbol : sword. Colour : blue or green. Instead of the usual helmet, he wears the skin of an elephant's head.

East : *Dhṛitarāshṭra,* King of the Gandharvas (demons feeding on incense). Symbol :

[1] L. A. Waddell, 'Evolution of the Buddhist cult ; its gods, images, and art', *The Imperial Asiatic Quarterly Review*, January, 1912.

[2] In Japan the Lokapāla are usually represented treading on demons, but on Pl. IV, fig. *a*, they are supported by elephants.

PLATE LIV

To-wen (Bishamon)

PLATE LV

Ḍākinī

stringed instrument. Colour : white. He wears a high helmet, on the top of which is a plume and from which hang ribbons and bows.

West : *Virūpāksha,* King of the Nāgas (serpent-gods). Symbol : *chorten* (a small shrine), or a jewel and a serpent. Colour : red.

Of these four guardian kings, Vaiśravaṇa is the only god whose worship, singly, became popular. As the Northern regions were believed to produce endless treasures, the guardian of the North was looked upon as god of Wealth.

In Japan he is worshipped under the name of *Bishamon,* and is represented in armour ornamented with the seven precious jewels, and is generally standing on one or two demons. In his left hand he holds either a small shrine or the flaming pearl, while in his right is a jewelled lance (Pl. LIII, fig. *a*).

The *maṇi,* or jewel, on the top of his staff, is believed to signify 'completeness of fortune and virtue'. The small *caitya,*[1] or shrine, represents the Iron Tower in India where Nāgārjuna found the Buddhist scriptures. He is represented looking at the shrine, for, as one of the guardians of Buddhism, he must keep watch over its greatest treasures (Pl. LIV).

A bronze example of Bishamon (Chinese) belonging to Mr. Goloubew is, as far as the author knows, unique. It somewhat resembles the illustration on Pl. LIV, with the exception that instead of holding the hands in the traditional pose, they are in prayer *mudrā,* and the treasure, balanced on the fore-arms, is not a *stūpa* but an object resembling a temple banner when rolled.

Bishamon is believed to have revealed himself to Shōtoku Taishi in battle, and it is said that in the helmet of Shōtoku Taishi were four small images of the Lokapāla. The Japanese Vaiśravaṇa is not, however, god of War, but the god of Good Fortune, and belongs to the group of Seven Gods of Good Fortune (Shi-chi-fu-ku-jin). With the exception of Benten he is the only god of the group worshipped to any extent singly.

Amoghavajra introduced the worship of the Celestial Guardians of the Four Quarters of the Heavens into China in the eighth century of our era, and one often sees them at the temple gates. The Chinese look upon them as symbolizing the four seasons.

North : *To-wen* (多聞) (Kuvera) or *Wei-p'o*—yellow (autumn : a black warrior). Symbols : right hand, a banner or lance, left hand, a pearl, or *stūpa* or mongoose, out of the mouth of which pour jewels.

South : *Tseng-chang* (增長)—blue (spring : red bird) ; may stand on a monkey and a demon. Symbol : sword.

East : *Ch'i-kwo* (持國)—white (summer : blue dragon). Symbols : stringed instrument.

West : *Kwang-mu* (廣目)—red (winter : white tiger) ; may also be green with red beard. Symbols : right hand, a *caitya,* left hand, a serpent.

In Chinese paintings the colours of the Four Guardians often vary and they are sometimes all represented flesh colour. They may also have no symbols, with the exception of To-wen, who always holds the treasure.

[1] v. Glossary.

The Shi-tennō or Japanese Celestial Guardians of the Four Cardinal Points are :
North : *Bishamon* (Kuvera).[1] Symbols : *caitya* (small shrine) and lance or flag.
South : *Komoku.*
East : *Jikoku.*
West : *Zōchō.*

They are also represented as warriors, and are generally standing on demons. In the illustrations in the *Butzuzo Zui*, with the exception of Bishamon, they hold no symbols.

In Chinese Turkestan representations of the Four Guardian Kings were found by Sir Aurel Stein at Tun-huang, on temple banners, and by Herr von Le Coq at Turfan, in frescoes, which are now at the Museum für Völkerkunde in Berlin. Vaiśravaṇa was also represented alone in frescoes at the entrance to the temples opposite Hāritī (v. *Hāritī*). According to Waddell she is a form of his consort, Vasudhārā (v. *Kuvera*). In all the representations of the Lokapāla found in Chinese Turkestan they are elaborately dressed, usually in armour, holding their respective symbols, and also standing, as a rule, on crouching demons.

THE FIVE GREAT KINGS

(T.) *sku-lnga* (or *Dam-can*) (five persons or bodies), or *Naï-chin chon jon* (the guardians of [the oracle] Nauchin).

(M.) *tabun qaghan* (five emperors).

The Five Great Kings are objects of very active worship in Tibet as they are believed to 'protect man efficaciously against evil spirits and enable him to attain the accomplishment of every wish' (Schlagintweit).

According to Waddell, these king-fiends, or spirits of demonified heroes, are supposed to have been originally five brothers who came from Northern Mongolia. They are said to have been 'kings'; of the East, mystically called 'the Body'; of the West, 'Speech'; of the North, 'Deeds'; of the South, 'Learning'; and of the centre—difficult to determine. They were necromancers and astrologers, and became oracles of different monasteries.

The oracle of Na-ch'un[2] was brought to Tibet by Padmasambhava, and after being admitted to the Lamaist order was made state-oracle. He is believed to incarnate himself in every successive religious guardian of the monasteries, who is called after him, Choi-chong (C'os-rje).

The names of the Five Great Kings are the following :[3]

Bi-har, the special protector of monasteries, who rides on a red tiger.

Choi-chung, incarnate in the state-oracles, who rides on a yellow lion (Pl. LVI, fig. *c*).

[1] Pl. LIII, fig. *c*.

[2] Waddell, *Lamaism*, p. 478.

[3] Schlagintweit, *Buddhism in Tibet*, p. 157.

PLATE LVI

a. VARUṆA

b. VARUṆA

c. UNDETERMINED

d. DAM-CAN

PLATE LVII

AMIDA WITH THE NI-Ō

Dahla is the tutelary god of warriors, and rides on a yellow horse.

Luvang, the god of the Nāgas, rides on a blue crocodile.

Tokchoi, rides on a yellow deer.

In this form they accompany the thirty-five Buddhas of Confession.

According to Schlagintweit, when one of these gods is represented alone, he is accompanied by :

Damchan dorje legpa, on a camel.
Ts'aṅgs-pa, on a ram.
Chebu damchan, on a goat.

According to Grünwedel, it is Dam-can rdor-legs who is on the goat and not on the camel (Pl. LVI, fig. *d*).

All of the Five Kings wear a broad-brimmed hat and long, flowing garments which, if painted, are red with a green border.

It is claimed that when Padmasambhava wished to build the convent of bSam-yas he forced the Five Kings to make a vow to protect it. For that reason they are called Dam-can, or 'he who has made a vow'.

According to certain accounts, the chief of the Kings is Pe-har or Pe-dkar, who is probably the 'Bi-har' quoted above. He has six arms and is white, seated on a white lion. He brandishes a sword, knife, and bow and arrow. The president of the Five Kings is said to be identical with the fourth guardian of the world, Dhṛitarāshtra, and is also claimed by others to be the president of the Four Lokapāla.

The second King is blue, on a white elephant. He has two arms, and holds a knife and lasso.

The third King is blue, on a blue lion. He holds a *vajra* and a *khakkhara* (alarm staff).

The fourth King is red on a blue mule, and holds an elephant goad and a bludgeon.

The fifth King is green on a black horse, and holds an axe.

In the paintings of the Five Kings, Padmasambhava is usually represented above Pe-har, the chief of the Kings.

NI-Ō (Ni-wō)

The Japanese god, Ni-ō, guardian of the Buddhist scriptures, is believed to reside on the four peaks of Mount Sumeru, the centre of the universe, but will manifest himself whenever enshrined and worshipped with proper ceremonies.

Although his name *Ni-ō* literally means 'two kings', he is, in reality, one deity, but may be represented by any number of gods, even, according to the *Surāṅgamasamādhi sūtra*, as many as 'ten times the grains of sand of the river Ganges'. The Shōbōnenkyō call the deity Misshakukongō.

Ni-ō, however, is best known in his dual form of Missaku and Kongō,[1] or the two guardians enshrined on either side of the gateway of Buddhist temples (Pl. LVII).

These 'two kings' probably find their origin in a Japanese legend, which runs to the effect that there was once a king whose first wife bore him a thousand sons, whom he wished to acquire perfect enlightenment. His second queen bore him two sons, one of whom desired to turn the Wheel of the Law for his thousand brothers, while the other vowed to protect the Law which his brother preached. The former was called Missaku, and the latter Kongō.

The king Kongō is the Japanese Vajrapāṇi. He is represented at the right of the gateway of a Buddhist temple and holds a *vajra* (thunderbolt). The name 'Kongō' means *vajra*, or thunderbolt, with which the god is believed to destroy all evil.

The king Missaku is enshrined at the left of the gateway, and is believed to propagate goodness.

The 'two Kings' are sometimes termed the Vīdyārāja, and, as such, are called Rāga (Aizen) and Acala (Fudō), and are represented by the Maṇḍala of the Two Parts.[2]

Rāga belongs to the Garbhadhātu (matrix section), or the material world of the five elements: earth, water, fire, air, and ether. He is represented by the sound 'a' and his statues have the mouth open.

Acala belongs to the Vajradhātu (diamond section), or spiritual world of one element: the mind. He is represented by the sound 'hūṃ', and his statues have the mouth closed.

The deity Ni-ō is thus the union of the Spiritual with the Material, or the 'two Kings' in one. In other words, he is the dual form of Vairocana (Dai-nichi Nyorai).

THE CITIPATI

(T.) *dur-k'rod bdag-po* (the lord or master of the cemetery).

The Citipati are two skeletons, one of a man and the other of a woman, who are represented with arms and legs interlaced, dancing the Tsam dance on two corpses. Each brandishes a sceptre topped by a skull, and one holds a skull-cup and the other a vase, or else they both carry the same symbol (Pl. LII, fig. *b*). They are usually represented in the suite of Yama, but may also accompany the *ḍākinī*, Naro-mk'ha-spyod-ma.

[1] From the Myōkyōjōchinshō.

Name	Misshaku	Kongō
Manifestation	Rāga (Aizen)	Acala (Fudō)
Mouth	open	closed
Heaven	Garbha	Vajra
Germ	*a*	*hūṃ*

[2] v. *Vairocana*.

PLATE LVIII

Nāga god. Printed mamori or charm from the Enkakuji temple, Kamakura, Japan

PLATE LIX

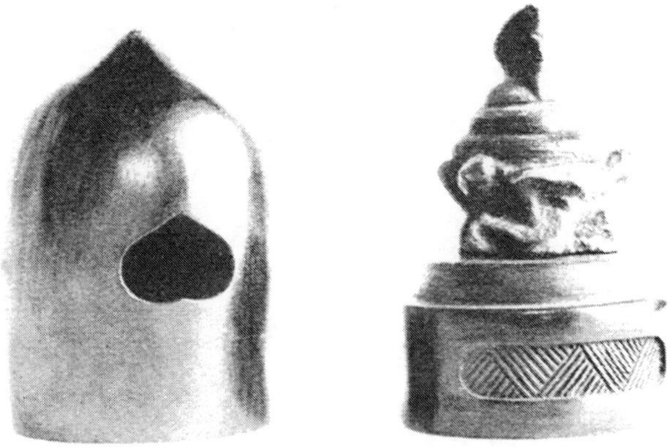

a Nāga

b. Garuḍa

c. Nājarāja

In Pander's *Pantheon* (No. 253) they are represented each on a separate lotus-flower and not following the text.

According to a Northern Buddhist legend, the Citipati were, in a former existence, two ascetics who were once lost in such deep meditation that they did not notice that a thief had cut off their heads and thrown them in the dust. Since that time they have been ferocious enemies of the thief and have vowed eternal vengeance. It somewhat resembles the legend of Yama.

NĀGAS AND GARUḌAS.

The Nāgas, or serpent-gods, are minor deities, but superior to man, and believed to be the protectors of the Law of Buddha. In fact, Buddhist legend claims that the sacred book, the *Prajñāpāramitā*, was put under the protection of the Nāgas by Gautama Buddha himself until such a time as the human race should have acquired sufficient knowledge to understand it. In the first century of our era, the sage Nāgārjuna claimed to have received from the Nāgas the *Prajñāpāramitā*, on which he founded the Mahāyāna School.

The seat of Nāga worship was in Kashmir and spread south into India along the Indus. When Hiuen-tsang entered the valley in the beginning of the seventh century A. D. he found, in almost every place he visited, a shrine dedicated to a local Nāga. He relates that it was even believed that a member of the Śākya family (that of Gautama Buddha) had married the daughter of a serpent-king, and he also tells of a Buddhist priest who was reborn as a serpent because he 'killed' the Elāpatra-tree.[1] In a Tibetan scroll[2] it is related, in regard to the Elāpatra Nāga, that he assumed the guise of a monarch in order to hear the Blessed One preach. The All-Knowing Buddha, perceiving him among his hearers, addressed him as follows: 'O King of Snakes, during the ministry of Buddha Kāśyapa you violated the rules of moral conduct, for which you were condemned to be born a snake. Have you now come here, assuming a false appearance, like a hypocrite, while I am preaching? Assume your own shape and listen to my sermons, if your nature permits you to do so!' Next day there appeared in the audience a huge serpent on whose head was grown an Elāpatra-tree. His body measured many miles, for while his head came to hear Buddha's sermon in Rajāgriha, his tail lay in Taxila.

In Japan there is a legend in regard to a priest who was reborn as a fish, out of whose head grew a huge tree.[3] It is probably a version of the Elāpatra Nāga legend.

The Nāgas play an important rôle in the legend of Gautama Buddha. They

[1] For legend v. *Journal and Text of the Buddhist Text Society of India*, vol. ii, Part I, 1894, p. 3.

[2] Translated by Satis Chandra Vidyabhusana, *Memoirs of the Asiatic Society of Bengal.*

[3] For legend see the *Open Court* for June, 1911.

assisted at his birth and gave him his first bath (Pl. VII). They came to hear him preach and became his disciples. It is recounted that once when Buddha remained in a state of *samādhi* (form of deepest meditation) for seven days, under a tree near a pond, the blind Nāga that lay in the pool was restored to vision by the light that shone from the Buddha's body and became his disciple. When Māra, god of Evil, unchained the fury of the elements to disturb Buddha's meditation, Mucalinda, a serpent-king, wound his coils about him and spread his hood over the Tathāgata's head to protect him during his *samādhi* (Pl. VI, fig. *a*).

The serpent, from the annual renewal of its skin, is a symbol of immortality, and when represented with its tail in its mouth forming a circle symbolizes the Yoga principle of Union, or the Circle of Regeneration. The Nāgarāja Mucalinda, who wound his coils around the body of the Buddha to protect him from the temptations of the god of Evil, typifies the impenetrable armour which the Tathāgata fashions for himself by the observance of the ten Pāramitās. The Nāga god protecting Śākyamuni may be represented with five, seven, or many heads, the last form being purely Indian (Pl. XI, figs. *a* and *b*). The nimbus of Amoghasiddha in Nepal is represented surrounded by Nāgas, and that of Nāgārjuna has seven overhanging serpents.

In Kashmir serpent-worship existed as early as the fifth century B. C. In Ceylon the serpent-worshippers were converted to Buddhism in the third century B. C., but the worship has now practically disappeared, while in India the Nāga god is still reverenced, especially in the South.

The Indian representations of the Nāga gods from the third century B. C. to the twelfth A. D. were of human form, with, behind the head, a spread cobra's hood having three, five, or seven heads. After the twelfth century, the Nāgas were represented with the body ending in a serpent's tail. When the cobra-hood had only three or five heads, the tail was spotted ; if seven or nine heads, the serpent was represented covered with scales. The more modern representations are merely that of a cobra capella with the hood spread.

The Chinese used the snake symbol much less than that of the dragon, although the Nāga god was worshipped in China from the earliest times. Fergusson [1] mentions that 'two heaven-sent serpents watched over the first washing of Confucius'.

In Japan the serpent has been worshipped from prehistoric times, and many Nāga shrines may still be found throughout Japan. At Kamakura there is a temple dedicated to a local Nāga, who is represented coiled in spiral shape with the head of a bearded man [2] (Pl. LVIII). It is worshipped as the goddess Benten by the common people, but is probably a relic of serpent (or phallic) worship. The goddess Benten (Benzai-ten), one of the seven gods of Good Luck, is usually represented riding on a snake (or a dragon). As she is a very popular divinity, it may be that the serpent has become identified with her as an object of adoration. Her shrines as related above

[1] *Tree and Serpent Worship.*

[2] On the tip of its tail is balanced a *cintāmaṇi*, in the form of a flaming pearl. In the Nepalese MS. Add. 864, in the University Library, Cambridge, the four-headed Nāga, on the coils of which the Buddha is seated, has also the *cintāmaṇi* on the tip of its tail.

PLATE LX

a. Mi-la ras-pa

b. Ts'oṅ-k'a-pa (?)

c. Man-la

d. Undetermined

PLATE LXI

a. Vasudhārā

b. Bhṛkuṭī

Two leaves from a Nepalese book

are generally on islands, and always near a river, lake, or the sea. When the snake is white, it is believed to be a special manifestation of the Indian goddess Sarasvatī.

On Pl. LIX, fig. *a*, there is a small household shrine of a Nāga god in bronze with a human head, resembling the example on Pl. LVIII, which is in wood, and claimed at the temple to have been carved by Kōbō Daishi.

According to Hindu mythology, the Nāgas were in constant terror of the Garuḍas, or fabulous golden-winged birds, and especially of their king. This gigantic bird would fly up into a huge tree called Kūṭaśālmali, which is at the north of the Great Ocean, and flapping his wings to divide the waters, swoop down upon the serpent-gods, pick them up with his beak, and eat them. In their distress the Nāgas that had been converted to Buddhism appealed to the Buddha to protect them against their mortal enemies, and he appointed the god Vajrapāṇi[1] their special protector. The Tathāgata then gave them his monastic garment, which was divided into infinitesimal pieces and distributed among them. No Nāga, with this inviolable talisman, could be harmed by a Garuḍa. Vajrapāṇi, as related above, in order to combat these formidable birds, assumed the shape of a Garuḍa.

One of the Garuḍa's most formidable enemies is Nanda, the Nāgarāja, king of the serpents. He is represented in human form as far as the waist, and the rest of the body as a serpent. He may have one head, with a serpent crown, and two hands holding a serpent; or have four heads and six arms, two of the hands of which are drawing a bow (Pl. LIX, fig. *c*).

The Nāgas were not considered malignant gods, but, on the contrary, were kindly disposed towards mankind. They were believed to control the rain-clouds, and, when properly propitiated, would protect from lightning, bring beneficial showers, or stop too abundant rains.

The king of the Nāgas is Virūpaksha, one of the four Lokapāla, or Celestial Guardians of the Four Cardinal Points. His kingdom is the continent west of Mount Meru, which was supposed to be the centre of the universe; but the chief residence of the Nāgas is Bhogavatī, 3,000 *yoganas* under the sea.

ARHAT[2] (or Arhān, or Sthavira).

(T.) *gnas-brtan* (pro. *netan*), or *netan cudug* (the sixteen sthavira).
(M.) *dain-i darughsan* (the vanquisher of enemies), or *batu-aqči* (steady, constant, or firm).
(C.) *Lo-han.*
(J.) *Rakhan.*

An Arhat is one who has reached the end of the Eight-Fold Path, and is not only perfect himself, but can give perfection to others. Gautama Buddha, before making the Great Vow of the Bodhisattva, was, in one of his incarnations, the Arhat Sumedha.

[1] v. *Vajrapāṇi.*

[2] *Arhat,* lit. 'fit', 'worthy'.

In the Buddhist temples of Tibet, China, Japan, and Corea, along the east and west walls of the principal hall, are rows of figures usually seated. These are the Arhats, disciples of the Buddha, patrons and guardians of Buddhism, and may be either five hundred in number or in a group of sixteen. In China, however, as well as often in Tibet, one finds a group of eighteen Arhats. The reason for the addition of two Arhats to the traditional group of sixteen is not clear, for, according to Watters,[1] in the ancient Chinese literature, there is only question of sixteen Lo-han.

Besides these two groups of Arhats there are the four 'great Bhikshu' to whom the Buddha entrusted the propagation of Buddhism after his death. They are Mahākāśyapa, Piṇḍola (Manla), Kuntēs-pan-t'an, and Rāhula. These men were to 'remain in existence and not experience Nirvāṇa until the advent of Maitreya as Buddha'. Two of these, Piṇḍola and Rāhula, are among the eighteen Lo-han.

The fifth Arhat is called Nakula in China, and is represented like Jambala with a mongoose under his arm (v. *Kuvera*). Some of the names of the Arhats vary in the different countries.

NĀGĀRJUNA

(T.) *klu-sgrub* (the serpent saint).
(M.) *naganjuna bakśi* (*Nāgārjuna*, the teacher).

Mudrā : *dharmacakra* (teaching).

Nāgārjuna is usually called the 'founder' of the Mahāyāna system; but it is claimed by some that he was only its principal expounder. The Japanese look upon Aśvaghosha, the probable master of Nāgārjuna, as the founder of the doctrine of the Great Vehicle. Others, still, believe that Nāgārjuna founded the Mādhyamika school and was the first to teach the Amitābha doctrine. It is thought that he lived in the beginning of the second century A. D., but the exact dates of his birth and death are still unknown.

He was born in Southern India, and his parents were of the Brahman caste. At his birth, according to an old Tibetan legend, it was predicted that he would only live seven days. In consideration of the acts of merit performed by his parents, the gods delayed his death until seven weeks, and then to seven months, and finally to seven years. Before the seven years were up, he was sent to the convent of Nalanda, where he learned to adore Amitāyus, god of Long Life, and succeeded in so propitiating the god that he is said to have lived three hundred years on earth, ending his life only by cutting off his own head.

Nāgārjuna was the greatest Buddhist philosopher and mastered all the sciences, and especially magic art. He is said to have acquired Siddhi, by which magic power he obtained the 'rainbow' body (*jahlus*), and was thus able to become invisible at will and transport himself from one place to another by supernatural power.

[1] *The Eighteen Lohan of the Chinese Buddhist Temples.*

PLATE LXII

a. Citipati

b. Dharmapāla

c. Skull-cup

d. Dai-nichi Nyorai (Vairocana)

PLATE LXIII

b. Padmapāṇi

a. Vairocana

c Amitābha

d. Gautama Buddha

e. Tārā

g. Mañjuśrī

f. Mahākāla

The Tibetan Buddhists claim that Nāgārjuna was the fourteenth of the twenty-seven Patriarchs that propagated the Buddhist faith, beginning with the senior disciple of the Buddha, Kāśyapa, and ending with Bodhidharma, who carried Buddhism into China in the sixth century A. D.

According to the Chinese and Japanese Buddhists, he was the third of the eight Patriarchs of the Yogācārya school, beginning with Vairocana and ending with the Japanese sage Kukai (Kōbō Daishi). According to the Buddhist texts, Śākya-muni predicted the rebirth of his disciple Ananda under the name of 'Nāgārjuna', founder of the Mahāyāna system. Nāgārjuna is believed by the Shin-gon sect to have received the secret Yoga doctrine directly from the second Patriarch, Vajrasattva, whom he visited in his Iron Tower in Southern India.

Other Mahāyāna Buddhists (the Amitābha sects), however, claim that he received the treatise on which he expounded and developed the Mahāyāna school from the serpent-gods, the Nāgas; and that the Nāga king himself revealed to Nāgārjuna the holy texts in the Dragon palace under the sea. They further claim that Gautama Buddha had given this treatise, the *Prajñāpāramitā*, to the Nāgas to guard until such a time as the world should become sufficiently enlightened to understand its transcendent wisdom; and that the Nāgas, after converting Nāgārjuna to Buddhism, handed over to him their precious treasure.

In the representations of Nāgārjuna, who was deified and enrolled among the Northern Buddhist divinities, he has an aureole on which are seven snakes. If painted, the middle one is yellow and the others grey. He is represented like a Buddha with the *ushṇīsha*, *ūrṇā*, and long-lobed ears, and wears the monastic garments. He has no symbols, and his hands are in *dharmacakra mudrā*. If painted, he is white.

PADMASAMBHAVA

(Lotus-born).

(T.) *pad-ma hbjuṅ-gnas* (lotus-born), or *u-rgyan-pa* (the crowned one).
(M.) *padmasambhava*.

Symbols: *khaṭvāṅga* (magic stick).
vajra (thunderbolt).
pātra (begging-bowl).

In the middle of the eighth century A. D. the Tibetan king Thi-Sron Detsan sent to India inviting the learned *guru* Padmasambhava to come to Tibet. Padmasambhava was renowned for his knowledge of *dhāraṇī* (mystical sentences) and of their efficacious application, and was warmly welcomed. He remained fifty years in the country, founding monasteries and teaching the Tantra-Yogācārya doctrine. He is said to have subdued all the malignant gods in Tibet, sparing only those that became converted to Buddhism and that promised to be defenders (Dharmapāla) of the doctrine. Padmasambhava, in his turn, promised to enroll them in the Mahāyāna Pantheon and to see that they were properly worshipped. He claimed to have received from the ḍākinī the books from which he acquired his miraculous powers.

At the end of fifty years Padmasambhava disappeared miraculously, and is said to have entered the body of a Yaksha king, Me-wal, where he has reigned supreme 'over all the Yakshas up till the present day and in perpetual youth, is preaching the doctrine of Lamaism in a paradise which rivals that of Amitābha's western heaven of Sukhāvatī' (Waddell, *Lamaism*).

Padmasambhava was deified and is still worshipped by the Northern Buddhists of Tibet. He is represented seated on a lotus *āsana* with the legs locked, the right hand holding the *vajra*, and the left, lying in his lap, the *pātra*. He holds his special symbol, the *khaṭvāṅga* (which he is believed to have invented), pressed against his breast with the left arm. The *vajra* was also made popular in Tibet by Padmasambhava, who used it in casting spells and exorcising devils.

His garment is flowing, and, if painted, is red, as well as his peaked cap, which sometimes ends in a half *vajra*. The lappets over the ears are divided and turned back, thus resembling a lotus-flower, for Padmasambhava is believed to have been born from a red lotus-flower.

Besides the bronzes, one often finds Padmasambhava represented in the temple paintings of the Dharmapāla. He is probably put in their company because he subdued them, and also because, according to the Mahāyāna traditions, there must always be one pacific deity among the ferocious gods. He is always placed at the top of the picture above them, and is sometimes accompanied by two disciples.

In China and Japan his worship is practically unknown.

TS'OṄ-K'A-PA

(lit. 'Man from Ts'oṅ-k'a').

(S.) *Sumatikīrti.*
(T.) *blo-bzan grags-pa* (pro. *lobsan dagha*).
(M.) *ǰonqaba.*

Mudrā: *dharmacakra.*
Symbols: *khaḍga* (sword).
pustaka (book).

Ts'oṅ-k'a-pa was born in Tibet, in the valley of Ts'oṅ-k'a, in the middle of the fourteenth century, and it is said that the tree which overshadowed the house in which he was born has the imprint of a Buddha on its leaves.

Ts'oṅ-k'a-pa, the Northern Buddhist reformer, founded the Ge-lug-pa sect, which he called the 'virtuous'. In spite of the severity of its rules and the practice of celibacy which it enforced, the Ge-lug-pa sect became very popular, quickly spreading over Tibet, and has remained the most important sect up to the present day.

They were called 'yellow bonnets' from the pointed yellow caps which

PLATE LXIV

KWAN-YIN

they wore in opposition to the 'red bonnets' (Kar-gyu-pa), a sect founded over three centuries before, which allowed the priests marriage, besides many other liberties, and permitted the practice of sorcery.

Ts'oṅ-k'a-pa, at his death, put the church under the protection of the god of Death, Yama (some say under Yamāntaka), and repaired to the Tushita heaven, where he is believed to be sitting beside the future Buddha, Maitreya. He was canonized as an incarnation of Mañjuśrī, and enrolled in the Northern Buddhist Pantheon.

Ts'oṅ-k'a-pa is represented seated on either a *kholbok* or a lotus. He wears the yellow pointed cap with the long ear-lappets, and his hands are in *dharmacakra mudrā*, holding the stems of lotus-flowers, which support, at each shoulder, the sword and book (Mañjuśrī's symbols). His garment, if painted, is red.

He is generally represented in temple pictures with two of his disciples, while below is sometimes Yamāntaka.

MI-LA-RAS-PA

(T.) *grub-pai dbaṅ-p'yug Mi-la* (the mighty saint, Mi-la).

Mi-la-ras-pa, mendicant monk and poet, lived in the beginning of the twelfth century A.D., and spent his life wandering through Tibet performing miracles, converting the nomadic people to Buddhism, and writing his 100,000 songs, which have never, as yet, been translated into English.[1]

He was deified and enrolled in the Northern Buddhist Pantheon, but does not figure in the Pantheon of the Tschantscha Hutuktu.

Mi-la-ras-pa is represented in the bronzes seated on a gazelle-skin on a lotus *āsana*. He has short, curly hair, the *ūrṇā*, is dressed in monastic garments, and always holds his right hand with the fingers extended and the palm turned outwards behind his right ear, as if he were listening to the 'echoes of nature', to use his own words. His left hand holds a begging-bowl (Pl. LX, fig. *a*).

[1] There is a fragment translated into French, Grünwedel, *Mythologie du Bouddhisme*, p. 62.

TS'OGS-ŚING (TSOK-SHIN)

NEPALESE PAINTING OFFERED TO A TEMPLE IN 1809.[1]

A. Left medallion: two Bodhisattva and 42 lamas or saints.
B. Central medallion: two Divinities and 22 lamas or saints.
C. Right medallion: two Bodhisattva (Mañjuśrī and ?) with 42 lamas or saints.
D. The summit of the Pyramid.
  1. Śākya-muni.
  2. Śariputra.
  3. Maudgalyāyana.
  4. Atiśa.
  5. Ts'oṅ-k'a-pa.
  6. Nāgārjuna.
  7–17. Saints and lamas.
E–F. Space on the right and left of the Pyramid: flying deities, praying monks, &c.
G. The Pyramid.
  1. Vajravarāhī (T. Rdo-rje-p'ag-mo), incarnation of an abbess of Central Tibet (see No. 7) (red).
  2. Hevajra.
  3. Yamāntaka (P. 61).
  4. Sangdui (T. Gsaṅ-ba ḫdus-pa) (P. 62).
  5. Saṃvara.
  6. Combination of Mahāmaya (P. 67) and Buddha Kapāla (P. 69) (blue).
  7. Vajravarāhī ? (see No. 1) (red).
  8. Kurukullā (T. Rig-byed-mo) (red).
  9. Simhavaktrā (T. Seṅ-gdoṅ-ma Ḍākiṇī) (G. p. 174).
  10. Mahāśakra Vajrapāṇi (G. p. 161) (black).
  11. The red Yamari (T. Gśed-dmar) (G. p. 123).
  12. Kālacakra (T. Dus-ḫk'or) (P. 65) (blue).
  13. The black Yamari (dark blue).
  14. Hayagrīva with three heads (T. Rta-mgrin).
  15. First Tathāgata or Buddha (?) with a jewel (yellow).
  16. Second Tathāgata or Buddha (?), the hands turned in the same direction.
  17. Uśnīśasita (P. 162).
  18. A Bodhisattva (?).
  19. Vajrapāṇi.
  20. Mañjughośa (?) (G. p. 99).
  21. Vajrapāṇi.
  22. A Bodhisattva (?).
  23. Sarasvatī (P. 157).
  24. Third Tathāgata (black).
  25. Fourth Tathāgata (T. Rgyal-ba Gyul-las) (P. 127) (black).
  26. Parnaśavari, Śakti de Mañjughośa (P. 165) (red).
  27. Acala (black).
  28. A Bodhisattva with four arms (undeterminable, being erased).
  29. The white Mañjughośa (erased).
  30. Kun-rig (P. 76).
  31. Acala (black).
  32. The white Tārā.
  33. Fifth Tathāgata (colour of cinnamon).
  34. Sixth Tathāgata (T. Rgyal-ba Dpaṅ-poḫi (?)) (black).
  35. Seventh Tathāgata (red).
  36. The green Tārā.
  37. Vajrapāṇi (simple form) (black).
  38. Bodhisattva or White Tārā ?
  39. A Bodhisattva (colour of cinnamon).
  40. Mila-ras-pa ?
  41. Jambhala nag-po (P. 267 ?) (black).
  42. Eighth Tathāgata (T. Rgyal-ba mts'on-dpal) (P. 124).
  43. Ninth Tathāgata (T. Rgyal-ba Śin-tu-rnam-par) (P. 126).
  44. Tenth Tathāgata (yellow).
  45. Uśnīśavijaya (T. Rnam-par) (P. 164) (white).

[1] The indications in parentheses signify the corresponding figures in Pander's *Pantheon*, e. g. (P. 61), or the pages of Grünwedel's *Buddhism in Tibet*, where the figures are to be found, e. g. (G. p. 166). The images of this book are indicated by the roman numbers of plates, e. g. XII.

46. Amytāyus (T. Tse-dpag-med) (P. 85).
47. Akshobhya (without Śakti) (dark green).
48. Ratnasambhava (colour of cinnamon).
49. Avalokiteśvara.
50. Samantabhadra [after the explicative list of the lama] (P. 152) (dark blue).
51. Sman-bla (P. 142) (dark).
52. Viśvapāṇi (Dhyani-Bodhisattva of Amoghasidi ?).
53–61. Eleventh to nineteenth Tathāgata.
62. Twentieth Tathāgata (T. Klu-dbaṅ-gi) (P. 100) (white).
63–68. Twenty-first to twenty-sixth Tathāgata.
69. First Bodhisattva: Sarvanīvaraṇaviśkambhī ? (green).
70. Second Bodhisattva: Kśitigarbha (yellow).
71. Third Bodhisattva: Mañjuśrī ? (yellow).
72. Fourth Bodhisattva: Vajrapāṇi? (yellow).
73. Fifth Bodhisattva: Ākāśagarbha (yellow-brown).
74. Sixth Bodhisattva: Avalokiteśvara (white).
75. Seventh Bodhisattva: Samantabhadra ? (yellow).
76. Eighth Bodhisattva: Maitreya (yellow).
77–82. Twenty-seventh to thirty-second Tathāgata.
83–90. The eight acolytes of Sman-bla (P. 136–441, 142, 143).
91–95. Thirty-third to thirty-seventh Tathāgata.
96. First Sthavira: Rdo-rje mo-ẖi (P. 197).
97. Second Sthavira: Nags-na (P. 195).
98. Third Sthavira: Dus-ldan (P. 196).
99. Fourth Sthavira: Ma-p'am-pa (P. 194).
100. Fifth Sthavira: Yan-lag-ẖbyuṅ (P. 193).
101. Śākya Muni or Sman-bla ?
102. Sixth Sthavira: Bakula (P. 201).
103. Seventh Sthavira: Sgra-gcan-ẖdsin (P. 202).
104. Eighth Sthavira: Bhara-dvadsa (P. 204).
105. Ninth Sthavira: Lam-p'ran-bstan (P. 203).
106. Tenth Sthavira: Sbed-byed (P. 207).
107. (?)
108. (?)
109. Eleventh Sthavira: Hva-śang (Chin. Hwa-chang) (P. 210).
110. Twelfth Sthavira: Bha-ra-dva-dsa gser-can (P. 200).
111. Thirteenth Sthavira: Gser-behu (P. 199).
112. Fourteenth Sthavira: Bsaṅ-po ? (without his book) (P. 198).
113. Vajraḍākinī (P. 224 ?).
114. Padmaḍākinī (P. 227).
115. Ḍākinī ?
116. Buddhaḍākinī ? (P. 223).
117. Ratnaḍākinī (P. 225).
118. Karmaḍākinī (P. 226).
119. Viśvaḍākinī (P. 228).
120. Fifteenth Sthavira: Lam-bstan (P. 205).
121. Sixteenth Sthavira: Klu-ẖi-sde (P. 206).
122. Seventeenth Sthavira: Mi-pyed (P. 208).
123. Eighteenth Sthavira: Dharma-tala (P. 209).
124. First Dharmapāla: Vajrapāṇi with Garuḍa wings (P. 184–186) (blue).
125. Second Dharmapāla: Acala (T. Mi-gyo-ba) (typical form dark blue).
126. Third Dharmapāla: Mgyon-po p'yag-bji (P. 243) or Ye-ces (G. p. 177) (black).
127. Fourth Dharmapāla: Kubera (P. 263) (brownish-yellow).
128. Fifth Dharmapāla: Yama gsaṅ (P. 240) (red).
129. Sixth Dharmapāla: Yama snaṉ (blue).
130. Seventh Dharmapāla: Yama Pyi (without his sister) (P. 239) (blue).
131. Eighth Dharmapāla: Blue Mahākāla (T. Mgon-po) (P. 230).
132. Ninth Dharmapāla: White Mahākāla (T. Mgon-dkar) (P. 229).
133. Tenth Dharmapāla: Gur-gyi mgon-po ? (protector of the tent) (P. 242).
134. Eleventh Dharmapāla: Brag-ca (P. 260).
135. Twelfth Dharmapāla: Lha-mo sol-ma (P. 245).
136. Thirteenth Dharmapāla: Beg-tse (P. 254).
137. Fourteenth Dharmapāla: Lha-mo tsandika (P. 244).
138. Fifteenth Dharmapāla: Lha-mo skyoṅs-ma (P. 246) or Ma-cig-pal (P. 256).

H. Zone of the Guardians of the temple (Lokapāla), &c.

- I. The guardian of the North (P. 280).
- II. The guardian of the East (P. 284).
- III. Brahmā offering a cakra (P. 278?).
- IV. Dbaṅ-po-śi offering a jewel (P. 156).
- V. The guardian of the West (P. 282).
- VI. The guardian of the South (P. 281).

J. The lowest space.

1. The 'seven jewels': *a.* the wheel, *b.* the jewel, *c.* the horse, *d.* the elephant, *e.* a military chief, *f.* a civil dignitary, *g.* a wife.
2. The five senses: *a.* sight (mirror), *b.* hearing (conch), *c.* smell (vase for perfume), *d.* touch (silk), *e.* taste (fruits).
3. A Stūpa.
4. A rock or tree-stock; at its base a flaming pearl on two balls, and under which there are playing musicians; on every side of the rock, a Nāga.
5. The 'eight emblems': *a.* conch, *b.* bumba, *c.* umbrella, *d.* standard, *e.* fishes, *f.* wheel, *g.* diagram, *h.* flowers.
6. A monk offering a sort of pyramidal cake; before him, the musicians.

K. Inscription (Langsha characters).

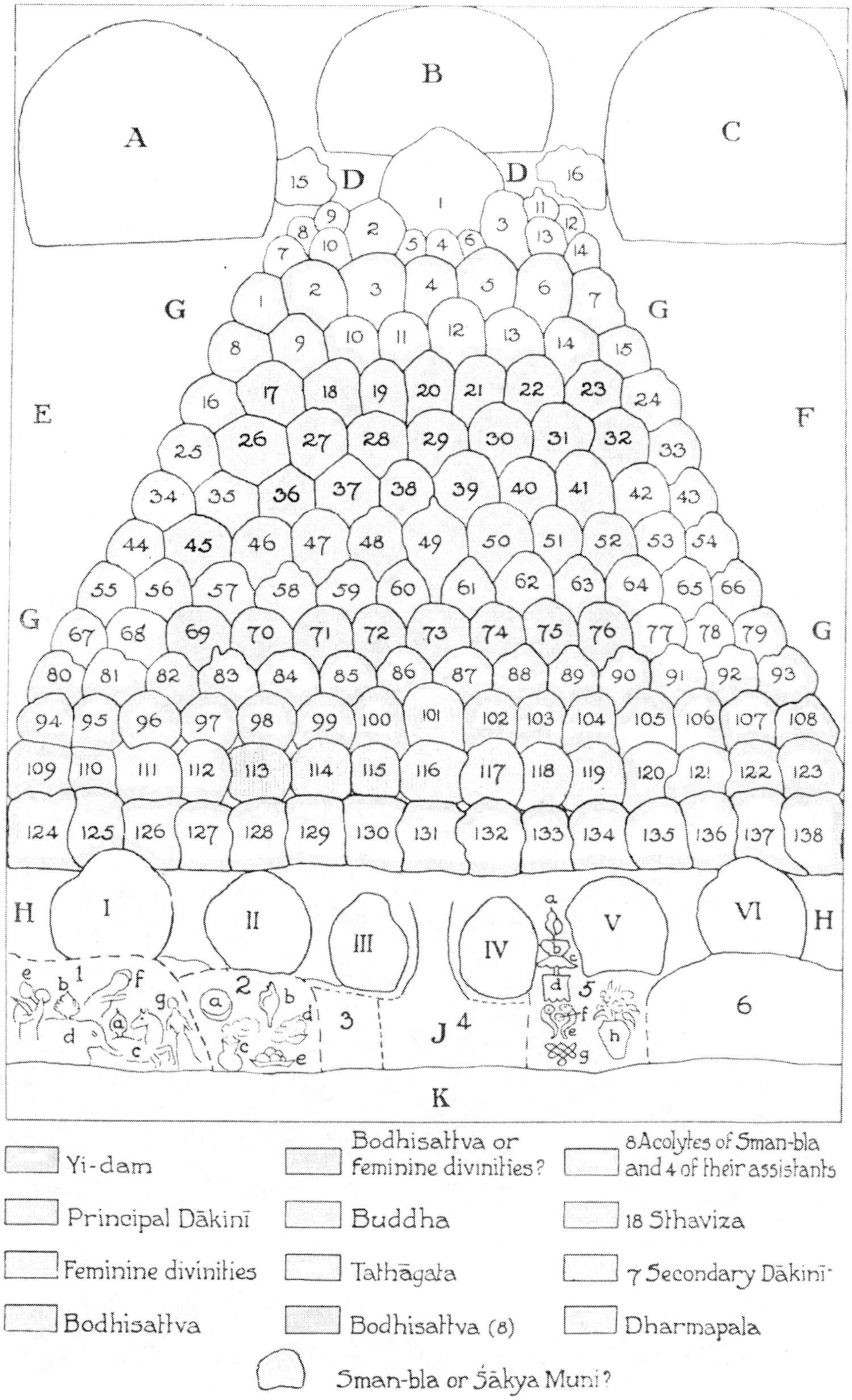
Yi-dam
Bodhisattva or feminine divinities?
8 Acolytes of Sman-bla and 4 of their assistants
Principal Dākinī
Buddha
18 Sthaviza
Feminine divinities
Tathāgata
7 Secondary Dākinī
Bodhisattva
Bodhisattva (8)
Dharmapala
Sman-bla or Śākya Muni?

Face p. 162.

CHRONOLOGICAL TABLE

B.C.	
6th century.	Gautama Buddha—his birth, 557; assumed Buddhahood, 528; his Parinirvāṇa, 447 (v. *Śākya-muni*).
	Confucius, 551–478.
	Date of the birth of the Buddha according to the Singalese, 623; Siamese and Burmese, 653; Chinese, 1027.
4th century.	Alexander of Macedonia invaded India, 326.
3rd century.	First Buddhist Missionaries in China, 217.
A.D.	
1st century.	Beginning of the Gandhāra school, about 30.
	Emperor Mingti's mission returned to China from India, 65.
	Aśvagosha wrote the *Mahāyāna-śraddhotanda-śastra.*
2nd century.	Worship of Avalokiteśvara introduced into China.
	Patañjali founded the Yoga school in India.
	Nāgārjuna founded the Madhyamika system and expounded the Mahāyāna doctrine 150-200.
3rd century.	*Amitāba Vyūha sūtra* translated in China, 222–280.
4th century.	Buddhism carried into Nepal, 350.
	Buddhism entered Corea, 372.
5th century.	Fa-Hian made a pilgrimage to India, 399–414.
6th century.	Yoga school grafted on the Mahāyāna by Asaṅga, about 550.
	Buddhism spread to Japan, 552.
	Tantrism made its appearance.
7th century.	Shōtoku Taishi, 593–621.
	Worship of Avalokiteśvara introduced into Japan.
	Hiuen-Tsang made a pilgrimage to India, 629–645.
	Buddhism introduced into Siam, 639.
	Worship of Avalokiteśvara and Tārā introduced into Tibet.
	Death of the Tibetan king, Srong-tsan-gampo, 650.
	Yi-tsing travelled in India, 671–695.
8th century.	The Yoga system was introduced into China, 720.
	Padmasambhava carried the Mahāyāna doctrine into Tibet, 747.
9th century.	Kōbō Daishi, 774–834.
	Tendai sect founded, 805.
	Shin-gon sect founded, 806.
11th century.	Buddhist Reformer, Atisa.
12th century.	Ts'oṅ-ka-pa.

EXPLANATIONS OF THE SANSKRIT (S.), TIBETAN (T.), CHINESE (C.), MONGOLIAN (M.), AND JAPANESE (J.) WORDS USED IN THE TEXT

Abhaya (S.) *Mudrā* of Protection ('Blessing of Fearlessness')—the gesture of the right hand of the Buddha in the episode of the mad elephant. The arm is elevated and slightly bent. The hand is lifted, with the palm turned outward, and all the fingers are extended upward. *Mudrā* of the Dīpaṅkara Buddha and of Amoghasiddha. (Pl. VI, fig. *c*.)

Ākāśa (S.) Ether or void. According to Hodgson, *ākāśa* is 'established, governed, perfected by its own nature. All things are absorbed into it; it is uncreated or eternal; it is revealed by its own force; it is the essence of creation, preservation, and destruction; it is the essence of the five elements; it is intellectual essence . . . for infinite things are absorbed into it. The five colours are proper to it as well as the five Dhyāni-Buddhas. From Vairocana proceeded *ākāśa*.'

Ālīḍha (S.) Attitude of drawing the bow. Attitude of Kurukullā.

Amṛita (S.) Nectar of Life, called by the Chinese 'sweet dew'. v. *Vajrapāṇi* and *kalaśa*.

Añjali (S.) *Mudrā* of Salutation. The arms are stretched upward, and both of the palms are turned upward with all the fingers extended. Attitude of Avalokiteśvara (Tantra form) when holding a small image of Amitābha.

Aṅkuśa (S.) Elephant goad.

Āsana (S.) 1. Support of a god, or group of gods.

All of the Northern Buddhist divinities are represented either seated or standing on lotus supports, with but few exceptions. In Tibet and Nepal the lotus support is usually represented with two rows of petals, of which the outer row is turned down, while the inner row stands upright, thus representing an *utpala* (blue lotus); but there may be more than two rows, and there are also examples, in Tibet, where all the petals stand upright, which is the usual form in Japan. In the temple paintings and frescoes from Central Asia, Kshitigarbha is sometimes represented (as well as the Dīpaṅkara Buddha) standing with a small lotus-flower under each foot.

According to the Buddhist tradition, the Buddhas, when 'turning the Wheel of the Law', should be represented seated on a lion support (*siṃhāsana*). Mañjuśrī may be seated on a throne supported by lions, instead of on a roaring lion. In the Chinese cave-temples of Yun-Kang and Long-men, Maitreya is seated on a lion-throne, European fashion, with the feet crossed. Yamāntaka's throne may be supported by demons. Kuvera is sometimes seated on a *kolbok*, or *āsana* made of cushions.

The *vajrāsana* is the diamond throne on which the Buddha sat when meditating under the *bodhi*-tree, and the fact is indicated by a *vajra* lying before him on the lotus-throne. Instead of the *vajra*, there may be a *svastika*, marked on the throne, which probably refers to the esoteric doctrine of Buddha, for the *svastika* was adopted as a special symbol of the doctrine by several Buddhist sects.

2. A small support for the foot or feet of a god is also called *āsana*, and is generally in the form of a small lotus-flower, with the stem attached to the lotus-throne. Maitreya, as Buddha, has usually no support for his two pendent feet, but as Bodhisattva each foot is supported by a small lotus-flower. The left foot of the green Tārā has also a similar support, as well as the left foot of the Nio-i-rin Kwan-non in Japan. The left foot of Jambala may rest on a conch-shell, or a *lai-bumpa* which is supported by a lotus *āsana*.

Some of the gods do not touch, directly, the lotus support.

Mahākāla treads on one or two prostrate elephants. Yama may stand on a man or a bull, or on a bull on top of a woman.

Yamāntaka (eight legs) treads on eight birds under which are different animals.

Hevajra stands on animals and genii.

Saṃvara stands on a man and a woman.

Ts'aṅgs-pa treads on a man and a prostrate horse.

3. An *āsana* is also the position of the lower limbs of a god. In the 'adamantine' pose the legs are closely locked with the soles of both feet apparent, while in the *sattva* attitude the legs are loosely locked and the soles of the feet scarcely visible. According to Waddell, this pose indicates the 'first emergence from meditation'. The attitude called *rājalīlā* or 'royal ease' (by Hodgson, *Lalita-āsana* pose) is with the right knee raised, the left remaining bent in the usual position of a Buddha. In the 'enchanter's pose' the left remains bent, while the right is pendent. Maitreya is seated with both of the legs pendent. The Nio-i-rin Kwan-non has the right foot supported by the left knee. The masculine Kwan-yin may also have this position in China when meditating upon the best means of saving mankind.

Aśoka-flower. Attribute of the yellow Mārīcī and of Kurukullā. The *aśoka*-tree is called the tree of Consolation, and it was between the *bodhi*-tree and the *aśoka*-tree that the Buddha was born. The *aśoka*-flower is red, and should be represented somewhat like a rose in shape, with small jagged leaves.

Asura (S.) Lit. 'those who are not *devas*'. The *asura* are the mortal enemies of the *devas.*

Ātapatra (S.) Parasol—symbol of the goddess Sītātapatrā.

Aum! v. *Ōm!*

Beng (T.) Mace.

Bhagavat (S.) or *Bhagavān.* Epithet of a Buddha; lit. 'The Happy One'.

Bhikshu (S.) Buddhist monk. One who assumes the alarm staff (*khakkhara*) and begging-bowl (*pātra*), and gives himself up to contemplation.

Bhūmisparśa (S.) *Mudrā* called 'witness' (lit. 'earth-touching'). The right arm is pendent over the right knee. The hand, with the palm turned inward, has all the fingers extended downward. The left hand lies on the lap, palm upward. This mystic gesture was used by Buddha to invoke the Earth-goddess as witness of his having resisted the temptation of Māra, god of Evil. It is also the *mudrā* of Akshobhya. (Pl. VIII.)

Bija (S.) v. *vija.*

Bodhi (S.) Enlightenment.

Bodhi-druma (S.) Lit. 'Tree of Enlightenment'. Each Buddha has a special tree called his 'bo-tree' (or *bodhi*-tree), under which he is supposed to have been born, do penance, preach, and die. The 'bo-tree' under which Gautama Buddha is believed to have received *bodhi* is the fig-tree (*Ficus religiosa*), or, according to others, the banyan-tree (*Pippala*).

The Buddha is said to have seated himself in meditation under four different trees symbolizing the four stages of *dhyāna*: under the fig-tree, the banyan-tree, the Mucalinda-tree (protected by the serpent), and the Rājāyatana-tree.

Buddhasmaraṇa (S.) *Mudrā* of Salutation. The right hand is raised to a level with the head, with all the fingers extended upward, the palm outward.

Bum-pa (T.) v. *kalaśa.*

Caitya (S.) or *Stūpa* (T. *Chorten*). A Buddhist sanctuary.

In the open square of every *vihāra* (Buddhist monastery) there is a *caitya* dedicated to Ādi-Buddha and the five Dhyāni-Buddhas. In Nepal, around the base (which may be square or quadrangular), are four niches, in which are placed the statues of the four Dhyāni-Buddhas: Akshobhya, Ratnasambhava, Amitābha, and Amoghasiddha. Vairocana is believed to occupy the interior, and in Java. according to Hodgson, his image is immured. Vajrasattva, the sixth Dhyāni-Buddha, is never represented; but as Ādi-Buddha he is symbolized by the flame-shaped spike at the top of the *caitya*, in the centre of a moon-crescent (v. *Vajrasattva*). In China, on the four sides of a pagoda, are placed stone images of the four great Bodhisattva: Ti-tsang (Kshitigarbha) on the south; Kwan-yin on the east; Wen-shu (Mañjuśrī) on the west; P'u-hien (Samantabhadra) on the north.

The 'elemental' *caitya* of Tibet and Japan is made up of five parts superposed, representing the five elements. The lower structure which holds the relic is the first element, *earth* (*garbha*), and may be either bell-shaped or quadrangular. Above it is either a dome (if the lower structure is quadrangular) or a square capital (if the lower part is bell-shaped), which represents the second element, *water*. This part is surmounted by a tapering pinnacle, sometimes divided into thirteen step-like segments representing the thirteen Bodhisattva heavens, and is the third element, *fire* (v. Pl. XIX, fig. *d*). In the 'elemental' *caitya* the pinnacle is surmounted by a moon-crescent, representing the fourth element, *air*. In the centre of the moon-crescent is a *liṅga*-shaped spike which represents the fifth element, *ether*.

There are, however, many variations of the *caitya*, especially in the upper part. The quadrangular cone often terminates, in Nepal, in a *liṅga*-shaped pinnacle which represents the Akanishṭha Bhuvana of Ādi-Buddha. This part is surmounted by a five-spoked umbrella, the spokes representing the five Dhyāni-Buddhas; or there may be five umbrellas, one above the other. In Tibet the dome is usually inverted, being larger at the top than at the base (v. illus. in Waddell, *Lamaism*, p. 263).

Miniature *caitya* are often found in Tibet and Japan (Pl. XIII), and the *cintāmaṇi* is frequently replaced in Japan by a small *caitya* representing the Iron Tower in which were hidden the Buddhist Scriptures (v. Nāgārjuna). As a symbol, it is held by Bishamon (the Japanese form of Kuvera) as well as by his Chinese form To-wen (v. Pl. LIV), and by Ratnapāṇi (Pl. XXIX, fig. *a*), and Mārīcī (v. Pl. XL).

In the caves of Ellora, three circles placed side by side with the third on the top, thus forming a triangle, symbolize a *caitya* as well as the *Tri-ratna* (v. *Ratnapāṇi*).

Cakra (S.) Wheel, symbol of absolute completeness. In the Vedic times the wheel was symbolical of occult powers, but in Buddhism it symbolizes the Wheel of the Law, which turns twelve times, or three revolutions for each of the Four Noble Truths. It is represented with eight spokes (or multiples of eight), indicating the Eight-Fold Path of Self-Conquest.

The wheel is one of the sixty-five marks on the footprints of the Buddha, which, at Amaravātī, are represented on the footstool below the vacant throne of the Buddha, behind which is also the Thousand-spoked Wheel of Victory. Buddhist legend relates that the Buddha, at his birth, took seven steps toward each of the four cardinal points, and thus indicated the conquering of the 'circle' or universe (v. temple painting in the Musée Guimet, Bacot Collection). The mystic *mudrā* called *dharmacakra* represents the 'turning of the Wheel of the Law'.

In pre-Buddhist times a great ruler was called a 'Wheel King' (*cakra-vartin*), and at his investiture a golden wheel was believed to fall from heaven. The Pāli term *chakkavatti* (*chakka*, wheel; *vatti*, ruler) was applied to the Buddha as the spiritual ruler of the world. In the earliest sculptures and frescoes the Master is symbolized by the Wheel, which is sometimes flanked by two gazelles. A trident may rise from the wheel (v. *Triśūla*).

The wheel symbol was first represented as a sun-disc which developed into a full-blown lotus with the centre surrounded by eight petals, and from that it developed into a wheel with eight spokes.

The origin of the thousand-spoked wheel is also probably the sun and its rays. According to Hiuen-tsang, the 'diamond' throne (*vajrāsana*) of the Buddha reposed on the *circumference* of a thousand-spoked wheel. (See illus. in Simpson, *Buddhist Prayer Wheel*, p. 48, fig. 12, and

Havell, *Indian Sculpture and Painting*, Pl. IV.) At the Buddha's Parinirvāṇa, the thousand-spoked wheel appeared outside of his coffin.

In Nepal the wheel of Vairocana is represented by the seed-vessel of the lotus, in the centre of which is the Nepalese *Yin-yang*.

The *cakra* is believed to symbolize Karma, 'a wheel of Fate that revolves relentlessly and ceaselessly'. It is the symbol of Maitreya, Vairocana, and Sitātapatra (when holding the parasol). Yama as well as Gon-po Bramzai wear it on the breast, and Sangdui has it in his head-dress. Ts'aṅgs-pa may also hold the *cakra*.

Cāmara (S.) Tail of the *yak* used as a fly-whisk. Tantra symbol.

Campa (T). White flower with yellow centre, emblem of Maitreya, whose two symbols are supported by two *campa* flowers, of which he holds a stem in each hand. *Campa* is also the Tibetan name of Maitreya.

Candra (S.) Moon. The full moon is the special symbol of Sarva-nivaraṇa-vishkambhin. Saṃvara has the crescent-moon in his head-dress, as does also Avalokiteśvara when Siṃhanāda. v. *sūrya*.

Cāpa (S.) Bow (of Mercy), attribute of Kurukullā, Cundā (sixteen arms), Hālāhāla-Avalokiteśvara, and the red Mārīcī.

Caraṇa (S.) Footprint. The footprints of Mañjuśrī have an eye in the centre of the *charan*. The Buddha has the eight glorious emblems and the thousand-spoked wheel figured in his footprints. v. *cakra*.

Chodpan (T.) Five-leaved crown worn by the Northern Buddhist priests when worshipping the 'Eight Terrible Ones'.

Chorten (T.) Buddhist sanctuary. v. *caitya*.

Churī (S.) Knife. Tantra symbol.

Cintāmaṇi (S.) Lit. 'magic gem', which satisfies all desires (v. *Maṇi*). It is the special symbol of Kshitigarbha, Samantabhadra, Ratnapāṇi, Ratnasambhava, and Mahākāla, as well as of Jizō and the six-armed Nyo-i-rin Kwan-non. Avalokiteśvara may also carry it, but rarely, and it is the accessory symbol of several other gods.

The *cintāmaṇi* is represented in several different ways. The *maṇi*, or jewels, may be nine in number, in which case they represent the *nava ratna*, or the nine jewels borrowed from Brahmanism. Or they may represent the *sapta ratna*, or seven precious jewels, much considered in Tibet and China (v. *ratna*). The *maṇi* may also be six, or only three in number (more frequent in Japan), representing the *tri-ratna*, Buddha, Dharma, Saṅgha.

In the usual Tibetan representation of the *cintāmaṇi*, the *maṇi* are bunched together and are surrounded by a flame-shaped glory. They are represented like the profile of an elongated eyeball, and in Japan the three *maṇi* are often enclosed in a flaming pearl.

In China as well as in Japan the *cintāmaṇi* may take the form of a flaming pearl without the *maṇi*, the origin of which is possibly the luminous pearl sent to Miao Chen by the Dragon King of Sea (v. legend Miao Chen). In Japan, in the paintings, the flame around the pearl has three points, vaguely indicating a *triśūla*. In the statues it may be without the flame, or represented with three lines of flames which meet at the top, dividing the pearl into three equal divisions (v. Pl. XII, fig. *b*).

The flaming pearl may also take the place of the traditional form of the *cintāmaṇi* in Tibet (v. illustration of Mahākāla, Pl. L, fig. *c*).

In the frescoes discovered at Turfan by Herr von Le Coq, the Bodhisattva have the *ūrṇā* on the forehead and sometimes on the breast, outlined by a red flame, thus resembling the flaming pearl. Kshitigarbha is also represented in the frescoes from Chinese Turkestan holding a flaming pearl. In China Ratnapāṇi may hold a pearl with a three-forked flame issuing from it.

In Tibet the *cintāmaṇi* is represented in charms, supported by the airy horse, Lungta.

The *cintāmaṇi* also takes the form of the *stūpa* or *caitya* (v. Glossary).

According to the esoteric doctrine, the *cintāmaṇi*, in pearl shape, is the symbol of the *manas*, the sixth sense. It is the 'glorious vesture of the soul', the radiant vehicle of the divine essence which, united with matter, forms man. v. *Vajradhātu*.

Dagoba (S.) Precious tower. v. *caitya*.

Ḍamaru (S. and T.) Hand-drum. Tantra symbol supposed to be made of two half-skulls.

Daṇḍa (S.) Magic wand.

Dhāraṇī (S.) A magical prayer, or merely a suite of mystic syllables for the purpose of casting spells. At the beginning and in the middle of a *dhāraṇī* is a *mantra* (see), and at the end is the *māhātmya*, or the purpose of the *dhāraṇī*; that is to say, for what particular thing the *dhāraṇī* is supposed to be efficacious—in bringing rain, or getting advantage over an enemy, or obtaining children, &c. (Illustration of *dhāraṇī* with miniature of the god to be evoked, Pl. LXI.)

Dharma (S.) Buddhist Law. One of the Tri-ratna.

Dharmacakra (S.) *Mudrā* of teaching. Lit. 'Law (*dharma*), wheel (*cakra*)', usually interpreted 'turning the Wheel of the Law'. In Tibetan it is called *Thabdong-shesrab*, lit. 'Wisdom-matter', or the union of the Spiritual with the Material.

The *dharmacakra mudrā* varies somewhat according to the different schools and countries. The Indian mystic gesture is: the right hand at the breast, with the united tips of the index and thumb touching one of the fingers of the left hand, the palm being turned inward (for illustration see A. Foucher, *Iconographie bouddhique*, partie I, p. 88). In Tibet both hands are held against the breast with the left hand covering the right, but it may be below the right, which is upright, while the left is on a line with the fore-arm. (Pl. XIV.) The Gandhāra school differs considerably. The fingers of the right hand are closed, the palm turned inward. The index of the left hand is loosely held by the closed fingers of the right, while the thumb touches the closed fingers at the tip, and the other fingers of the left hand are loosely closed (Grünwedel, *Buddhist Art in India*, p. 173, and A. Foucher, *L'Art gréco-bouddhique du Gandhāra*, p. 192). This gesture, in Japan, became the *mudrā* of the Six Elements (v. *Vairocana*, and illustration, Pl. II, fig. *a*).

Dhyāna (S.) Also called *Samādhi*. *Mudrā* of meditation. The hands lie in the lap, the right on the left with all fingers extended, and the palms turned upward. In Japan the fingers are locked, with the exception of the thumbs and indexes, which touch at the tips and form the 'triangular' pose (v. *Vitarka*). The indexes touch each other between the first and second joints, the palms being turned upward. (Pl. XVIII.)

Dhvaja (S.) Banner of Victory. Symbol of Vaiśravaṇa.

Dīpa (S.) Lamp.

Dvīpa (S.) Island.

Fuh-shou-kan (C.) A horned lemon, called by the common people in China 'Buddha fingers', from the finger-like tendrils of its base. It is sometimes in the hand of the Medicine Buddha.

Gaja (S.) Elephant, symbolizing 'care, caution, and a mighty dignity'. It is the support of Samantabhadra, and is represented in Tibet with one head, while in Japan, as support of Fugen, it has usually six tusks. The white elephant with six tusks symbolizes the reincarnation of the Buddha. The elephant support of Kongōsatta has three or four heads. Mahākāla treads on one or two elephants, and Saṃvara may have an elephant-skin over his shoulders. The elephant as a Northern Buddhist god is the demon Vinataku.

Garbhadhātu (S.) Matrix element. v. *Vajradhātu*.

Ghaṇṭā (S.) Bell with *vajra* handle carried by Vajradhara, Vajrasattva, and Trailokya-vijaya.

Grigug (T.) Chopper. Tantra symbol.

Hīnayāna (S.) Lit. *hīna* = small, *yāna* = conveyance. In other words, the simplest vehicle of salvation, doctrine of Śākya-muni. v. *Tri-yāna*.

Īśvara (S.) Lit. 'Lord'. In Nepal Ādi-Buddha was called *Īśvara* by the Aiśvarika sect.

Jambhara (S.) Lemon, symbol of Jambala, a form of Kuvera.

Jambu. A tree with triangular leaves, considered sacred by Northern Buddhists. v. *Mañjuśrī.*

Jñāna (S.) Wisdom.

Kalaśa (S.) (T. *tsé-bum.*) Vase believed to hold the *amrita*, or Water of Life. The special symbol of Padmapāṇi is the vase which he usually holds by the neck, but it may also be supported by a lotus-flower, of which he holds the stem in his right hand. In the former case the vase is round, or oval if Indian, and pointed if of the Gandhāra school, and without a base. If, however, the *kalaśa* is supported, it has a base and generally a spout.

The feminine Kwan-yin may hold the vase, or have it at her side, and in it (or held in her hand) may be a willow-branch, with which she is believed to sprinkle around her the Nectar of Life which in China the *kalaśa* is also supposed to contain.

The masculine form of Kwan-yin, both in China and Japan, often has a lotus-bud in the vase. The vase and the willow-branch, or lotus-flower (or bud) symbolize the *mandala* of the Two Parts. v. *Vajradhātu.*

Maitreya has the *kalaśa* as an accessory symbol with the wheel. He rarely carries it, but it is supported by a lotus-flower at his left shoulder.

The goddess Vasudhārā has the vase symbol, from which pour jewels.

Amitāyus holds the ambrosia vase, which differs from the usual *kalaśa*. It is low and has a cover, out of which issues an *aśoka*-branch. From under the cover, falling in garlands around the vase, are strings of beads, representing sacred pills used in the ceremony of praying for long life.

Ushṇīshavijaya also carries a similar covered vase which is, however, much less ornamented.

Kuvera may have one under his arm, and his right foot is sometimes supported by an *overturned kalaśa.*

Kalpa (S.) Period of time transcending calculation.

Kapāla (S.) Skull-cup. A Tantra symbol carried by the Dharmapāla, Yi-dam, and their *śakti*, and by the Ḍākinī. The origin of the skull-cup is probably found in the legend of Yamāntaka (see), who, before waging war on Yama, killed the three robbers, and, making cups of their skulls, drank their blood. The *kapāla* is represented filled with blood when in the hands of the gods, but in temple pictures it is sometimes filled with eyes, ears, and tongues of demons—offerings to the gods. In the skull-cups held by the various hands of Hevajra are animals and *devas*. In the Tantra ceremonies a skull-cup is filled with wine to represent the blood, and offered to the god. In the temples it is usually on a bronze stand with a bronze cover. (Pl. LXII, fig. *c*.)

Khaḍga (S.) Sword, symbol of the enlightenment of the world, for 'as the sword cuts knots, so does the intellect pierce the deepest recesses of Buddhist thought'. The *khaḍga* is the special symbol of Mañjuśrī, either carried in his hand or rising out of a lotus-flower. Fudō, in Japan, also carries the sword, and it is held as accessory symbol by Cundā (sixteen arms).

Khakkhara (S.) (T. *Khar-gil*, J. *Shakujo.*) Sounding staff. The *khakkhara* was believed to be a purely Japanese symbol until temple banners and frescoes dating from the fifth century were found, in Chinese Turkestan, by Sir Aurel Stein at Tun-huang, and by Herr von Le Coq at Turfan, representing Kshitigarbha with the sounding staff. As Buddhism did not enter Japan until A.D. 552, this fact proves that the use of the *khakkhara* as a symbol came into Japan from Central Asia. It was practically never used as such in Nepal or Tibet.

Although the *khakkhara* is nowhere mentioned in the teachings of the Southern school of Buddhism, reference to it is found several times in the Mahāyāna Scriptures, and it is looked upon by the Northern Buddhists as one of the eighteen indispensable articles that a Bhikshu must possess.

According to the command of Gautama Buddha, the Bhikshu (mendicant Buddhist priest), when on a pilgrimage, must carry the *khakkhara.*

If the Bhikshu wishes to enter a dwelling he may not speak, but after knocking, if it is asked who is there, the sounding staff is to be shaken.

Again, according to the Buddha, no life must be taken, and a Bhikshu, by shaking the *khakkhara*, warns all crawling life of his approach and thus avoids treading on them. It is also believed that if the Bhikshu shakes his sounding staff while walking through a thicket or grassy ground, all wild beasts and poisonous insects will be frightened and do him no harm.

The *khakkhara* is a long, hexagonal wooden staff, capped with a metal capital, which has a pagoda-shaped head with two, three, or four crotchets, into which four, six, or twelve loose metal rings are inserted.

The different numbers of metal rings have each a special meaning, according to the different teachings of Buddhism.

The staff carried by the Bhikshu should only have four metal rings, which represent the Four Noble Truths: suffering, the cause of suffering, the cessation of suffering, and the path leading to the cessation of suffering.

The staff with three crotchets and six rings was invented by Kāśyapa Buddha, and is carried by the Bodhisattva, who, as a preliminary condition of their attainment of Buddhahood, must exercise the six Pāramitā, or Perfections.

The *khakkhara* with four crotchets and twelve metal rings was invented by Gautama Buddha, and can only be carried by Pratyēka Buddhas. The twelve rings represent the Twelve-Fold Chain of Causation.

It is claimed by certain Buddhist sects that the whole *khakkhara* signifies Mount Sumeru, and that each part of the staff has its special meaning, but the explanation, although extremely complicated, resolves itself into this, that the metal part represents the Garbhadhātu and Vajradhātu, or the Maṇḍala of the Two Parts. v. *Vairocana.*

The *khakkhara* is practically never used as a symbol in Tibet, but is carried by Ti-tsang in China and by Jizō and Fukū kenjaku in Japan.

Khantsig (T.) Small shrine several stories high. v. *stūpa.*

Khar-gil (T.) v. *khakkhara.*

Khaṭvāṅga (S.) Magic stick which is believed to have been invented by Padmasambhava and is carried by him, as well as by the Ḍākinī. The top of the *khaṭvāṅga* is composed of an ambrosia vase, on which reposes a *vajra*, or double *vajra*, above which are two Buddha heads and a skull superposed. The skull may be surmounted either by a *vajra* placed upright, or a *triśūla*, which latter form is usually carried by Padmasambhava. According to Grünwedel, *khaṭvāṅga* have been found in Tibetan temple paintings which have *rings hanging from the lower vajra like the khakkhara.*

Kichi-jo-kwa (J.) Pomegranate, symbol of the goddess Hāritī, and may also be carried by the Japanese Tārā.

Kin-kang (C.) Diamond; v. *vajra.*

Kolbok (M.) Cushions piled one on top of the other forming a seat, in general use in Mongolia for Buddhist priests, the number indicating the rank. Vaiśravaṇa may be represented seated on a *kolbok.*

Kongō (J.) Diamond; v. *vajra.*

Lai-bumpa (T.) Tibetan low flat vessel, symbol of perfection in abstract thought, object of contemplation used by the Lama priests when meditating.

Lakshana (S.) The thirty-two superior marks (*mahāpurusha lakshana*) of a Buddha are: 1, a protuberance on the skull (*ushṇīsha*); 2, the hair, glossy black, arranged in short curls, each curl turning from left to right; 3, the brow is broad and smooth; 4, between the eyebrows is a little ball (*ūrṇā*) or tuft of hair, shining like silver or snow; 5, the eyelashes are like those of a bull; 6, the eyes brilliant black; 7, he has forty teeth of perfectly equal size; 8, they lie close to one another; 9, and are dazzling white; 10, his voice resembles Brahmā's; 11, he has an exquisite sense of taste; 12, the tongue is large and long; 13, the jaws are those of a lion; 14, the shoulders and arms are perfectly rounded and full; 16, the space between the shoulders is filled out; 17, the skin has a tinge of gold colour; 18, the arms are long, and when he stands upright the hands reach to the knees; 19, the upper part of the body is like that of a lion; 20, his figure is like that of a banyan-tree (*Ficus religiosa*); 21, only one hair grows from each pore; 22, these little hairs curl from above towards the right; 23, nature has concealed the marks of sex; 24, the thighs are well rounded; 25, the legs are like those of a gazelle; 26, the fingers and nails are long; 27, the heel is elongated; 28, the instep is high; 29, the feet and hands are delicate and slender; 30, the fingers and toes have a web between; 31, under the soles of the feet appear two shining wheels with a thousand spokes; 32, the feet are flat and stand firm.

For the eighty inferior marks (*anuvyañjana-lakshana*) see Grünwedel, *Buddhist Art in India* (English translation), p. 161.

Lungta (S.) Airy horse which supports the *cintāmaṇi*—considered indispensable on charms, especially by the nomadic Tibetan tribes.

Madhyamayāna (S.) Lit. (*Madhyama*) middling, (*yāna*) conveyance, doctrine founded by Nāgārjuna. v. *Tri-yāṇa*.

Mahāyāna (S.) Lit. (*mahā*) great, (*yāna*) conveyance. The real founder of the Mahāyāna system is unknown. In the first century A.D. the *Mahāyāna-śraddhotanda-śastra* was written by Aśvaghosha. In the second century the Mahāyāna system was developed by Nāgārjuna and took a definite form. v. *Tri-yāṇa*.

Mālā (S.) Generally translated as *rosary*, but is possibly symbolical of the necklace of pearls referred to in the 'Lotus of the Good Law', when the Akshayamati Bodhisattva, addressing the Buddha, says: 'World Honoured One, let me now present an offering to the Bodhisattva Kwan-shai-yin' (Avalokiteśvara). Then, loosening from his neck an entire pearl necklace of the value of 100,000 pieces, he presented it to the Bodhisattva as a religious offering, but Kwan-shai-yin refused it until the Buddha begged him to accept it. He then 'accepted the necklace and, dividing it into two parts, presented one part to Śākya-muni and the other part to the *stūpa* of the Buddha Prabhūtaratna' (Beal, *Catena*, p. 389).

The *mālā* is the special symbol of Avalokiteśvara as well as that of his Chinese manifestation Kwan-shi-yin. It may also be carried by Prajñāpāramitā (four-armed), Cundā, and Vasudhārā.

Maṇḍala (S.) Magic circle geometrically subdivided into circles or squares, in which are painted Buddhist symbols and divinities. v. *Vairocana* and *vajradhātu* (illus., Pl. XVI).

Maṇi (S.) A jewel. According to Eitel, it is 'a fabulous pearl which is ever bright and luminous, therefore a symbol of Buddha and of his doctrine'. v. *cintāmaṇi* and the Legend of Miao Chen. In the *Kāma-Śāstras* the name *maṇi* is applied to the male principle. v. *Ōm*.

Mantra (S.) Short mystic formula, often meaningless. It figures at the beginning and in the middle of a *dhāraṇī*, and is believed, when recited, to be most efficacious. v. *Ōm*.

Meru (Mount) v. *Sumeru*.

Mudrā (S.) Mystic pose of the hand or hands. According to Eitel, 'a system of magic gesticulation consisting in distorting the fingers so as to imitate ancient Sanskrit characters of supposed magic effect'. The use of the *mudrā*, as well as the *mantra*, was introduced into Japan by Kōbō Daishi, and is only used by the Shin-gon sect.

Muni (S.) Saint or sage, one who is inspired.

Nāga (S.) Mythical serpent-god. v. *Nāgas*.

Nāga pushpa (S.) v. *campa*.

Nāga-taru (T.) *Nāga*-tree (eight-branched coral), seen usually in the Tibetan temple pictures. In the Museum für Völkerkunde in Berlin there is a large *nāga*-tree in wood, painted to represent coral, and on each branch there is a small Buddha.

Nakula (S.) Mongoose—attribute of Kuvera (v. s.).

Namaḥkāra (S.) *Mudrā* of Prayer. The hands are at the breast in the devotional attitude, with the palms and fingers touching. It is the special *mudrā* of Avalokiteśvara when with more than two arms.

Nirvāṇa (S.) Nirvāṇa, according to the Northern Buddhist, is not annihilation after death, but the extinction of all worldly desires, 'the blowing out of the flame of selfish longing'. To arrive at Nirvāṇa is to reach the highest stage of bliss, since it is an escape from the ever-turning wheel of transmigration.

Norbu (T.) Jewel. v. *ratna*.

Nyorai (J.) Lit. 'Lord'.

Ōm! Ōm, the mystic syllable of *A-u-m*, is venerated by the Brahmans as well as by the Buddhists. The most devout esteem it to be too sacred to be uttered aloud, the word being only formed by the lips.

In the *Svayambhū-Purāṇa* it is written that when all was void 'the triliteral syllable *Aum* became manifest, the first created, the ineffably splendid, surrounded by all the radical letters (Vīja-Ākshara) as by a necklace'.

From *Aum* the alphabet was produced, called *Mahā Varṇa*, the letters of which are the 'seed of the universe'. v. *vīja*.

Ādi-Buddha, at his will, proceeded from *Ōm*. 'In that *Aum*, he (Ādi-Buddha), who is present in all things, formless and passionless, who possesses the Tri-ratna, was produced by his own will' (*Svayambhū-Purāṇa*). According to the Nāmasangīti, the Ādi-Buddha became manifest in the greatest Śūnyatā (void) as the letter *A*. In the *Pujā-Khaṇḍa* it is written that when all was Śūnyatā, Prajñā Devī (Ādi-Dharma) was revealed out of Ākāśa (ether) with the letter *u*. According to the *Svayambhū-Purāṇa*, the *vīja mantra* of Sangha is *m*. Thus the letters A-u-m are the *vīja mantra* of Buddha, Dharma, and Saṅgha. v. *Tri-ratna*.

The *mantra* generally begin with *Ōm* and end with *hūṃ*. The most widely known *mantra* is the six-syllable one of Avalokiteśvara, 'Ōm, maṇi padme, hūṃ!' (v. *Avalokiteśvara* and *Vajradhātu*). The Tibetans claim that it fell from the heaven in the fourth century A.D. In China and Japan there is a six-syllable *mantra* A-ba-ra-ka-ki-un. *A* corresponds with *Ōm* and *un* with *hūṃ*. The Ni-ō (v. s.) symbolize these two syllables.

Pada (S.) Absorption. *Nirvāṇa pada*, absorption into Ādi-Buddha.

Padma (S.) (J. *Ren-ge*.) The *padma* is a symbol of self-creation. Every Buddha and Bodhisattva being *svayambhū*, or self-existent, is supported by a lotus-flower to indicate his divine birth. The *padma*, as symbol of self-generation, was also adopted by the most important Buddhist sect in China, the Svābhāvika, as their special emblem, with the *triśūla*, indicating the Tri-ratna issuing from its centre (v. p. 5).

The lotus-flower is in itself a prodigy, being productive of itself, and, to use the words of Mr. Payne Knight, 'vegetating from its own matrix without being fostered in the earth. It was naturally adopted as a symbol of the productive power of the Waters upon which the active spirit of the Creator (Ādi-Buddha) acted in giving life and vegetation to matter.'

At the beginning of the world Ādi-Buddha manifested himself in the form of a flame rising from a lotus-flower. In the Nepalese paintings (see No. V in the library of the Institut de France) the stalk of the *padma* may rise from a triangle (v. *tri-koṇa*) lying on the seed-vessel of an eight-leaved lotus-flower; but the usual representation is rising from water.

According to the Nepalese legend, when the ancient Buddha Vipaśyi went to Nepal, accompanied by his disciples, to worship the Svayambhū (Ādi-Buddha), he thrice made the round of the lake, Nāga Vasa. He then said several *mantra* over the root of a lotus, and, throwing it into the water, exclaimed: 'With time, this root shall produce a flower, then, from out of the flower, Svayambhū, the Lord of the Agnishṭha Bhuvana, shall be revealed in the form of a flame; and then shall the lake become a cultivated and populous country. (For legend see Hodgson, *The Languages, Literature, and Religion of Nepal*, p. 115.) v. *Mañjuśrī*.

The lotus-flower symbolizes the female principle. In the *Śatapatha Brahmāṇa* it is written, 'the lotus leaf is the womb', and in the *mantra*, 'Ōm! maṇi padme, hūṃ!' the *padma* represents the Material and the *maṇi* the Spiritual elements. v. *Ōm*.

The *padma* in the hand of Padmapāṇi denotes creative power. In Nepal and Tibet it is generally a full-blown lotus-flower; while in China and Japan the Kwan-yin and Kwan-non often hold a lotus-bud. If the *padma* is in the vase it represents the union of the Spiritual and the Material. The lotus-flower in the hand of Mañjuśrī represents the teachings of Buddha, replacing the usual book (*Prajñāpāramitā*); while in the hands of the Tārās it symbolizes perfect purity, for although the *padma* may rise out of impure water, it remains undefiled.

The pink lotus-flower is represented full-blown, with the centre apparent. It is the special symbol of Padmapāṇi and of the white Tārā.

The blue lotus may either be represented with all the petals upright, or with several of the outside rows turned back. The centre is always hidden and the *utpala* is almost invariably presented in profile. It is the special symbol of Mañjuśrī and the green Tārā. The lotus-bud is a more frequent form in China or Japan than in Tibet.

When the symbols are not held in the hands of the gods they are supported by lotus-flowers, of which the stems are held by the gods, and in that case the hands generally make a mystic gesture (*mudrā*) as well.

The teachings of the Buddha were symbolized by a full-blown lotus-flower with eight petals, indicating the Eight-Fold Path of Self-Conquest. The lotus was also used to represent the Buddhist wheel, the eight petals being the eight spokes. In the paintings of the *maṇḍala* (magic circles) there is usually an eight-petalled lotus-flower, in the centre of which is an important god, and on each petal an assistant. v. Pl. XVI, and *maṇḍala*.

The lotus support of a Buddha, or Bodhisattva, if painted, is red; of a Dharmapāla, pink. The fiercest forms of the Dharmapāla are supported by a pink lotus with jagged petals. v. *āsana*.

The god, however, may not be on a lotus-throne, but have his divine birth indicated by a lotus-flower under each foot. In the paintings discovered at Tun-huang by Sir Aurel Stein the first steps of the Buddha are represented by lotus-flowers which sprang up under each foot as he walked; and Jizō (Kshitigarbha) is represented with a small yellow *padma* under one foot and a white one under the other.

In the frescoes found at Turfan, by Herr von Le Coq, the Dīpaṅkara Buddha is represented with a lotus-flower under each foot, while all the Bodhisattva stand on lotus-thrones.

The Northern Buddhists believe that in Sukhāvatī, the western paradise of Amitābha, there is a lotus-pond, and that whenever a Buddhist is born a lotus-bud rises to the surface of the water, and is believed to bloom or fade according to the life the Buddhist leads. v. *Sukhāvatī*.

The *mantra* of Avalokiteśvara is 'Ōm, maṇi padme, hūṃ!' 'Oh, the jewel (of creation) is in the lotus.' v. *Ōm*.

Paraśu (S.) Axe. Tantra symbol.

Parinirvāṇa (S.) Death of the Buddha.

Pāśa (S.) Lasso, sometimes with a small thunderbolt at each end—symbol of Amoghapāśa, Mārīcī, Yamāntaka, and Acala and Fudō.

Pātra (S.) Begging-bowl carried by wandering Buddhist priests. The *pātra* is often represented in the Buddha's left hand, possibly in reference to a Buddhist legend, which is the following: On the seventh day of the third month the spirit of a tree under which Buddha had for seven weeks been in a state of *samādhi* (deep meditation) took notice of Buddha's long absence from food. Some travelling merchants passed at that moment, and their way being blocked by insurmountable objects, they asked the spirit of the tree to help them. He called their attention to the presence of the Buddha, and told them that they should offer him food. The four Kings of the Devas (Lokapāla) had four sweet-smelling bowls, which they filled with the barley mixed with honey that the merchants offered. Buddha took all the four bowls through fear of offending one of the kings, and, placing one on top of the other on his left hand, formed them into one (Edkins, *Chinese Buddhism*, p. 24). It is believed that when Maitreya comes upon earth as a Manushi Buddha the *pātra* will again become four bowls.

The *pātra* may also be carried by Amitābha, Avalokiteśvara, and Manla.

Phurbu (J.) Lit. 'peg' or 'nail'. Tantra symbol supposed to prevent evil spirits from inflicting mischief. It is a dagger in form of an elongated triangle, and often has a very complicated handle, in which there is usually a head, believed to represent Hayagrīva (Tamdin), who is looked upon as a special protector against malignant spirits.

Prajñika (S.) Atheistic triad: Buddha, Dharma, Saṅgha.

Pratyēka (S.) A Buddha without master or disciples.

Prēta (S.) (M. *Birit.*) Lit. 'hungry demon'. They have large stomachs, narrow mouths, and exhale fire, but cannot drink. The Prētas are believed to be visible only at night.

Pustaka (S.), or book, made originally of palm-leaves cut long and narrow, and held together between two pieces of flat wood of the same size and shape, the whole bound by a string.

The *pustaka* as a symbol represents the *Prajñāpāramitā*, a treatise on Transcendent Wisdom, supposed to have been given to the Nāgas by the Buddha to guard until mankind had become wise enough to grasp its profound truths.

Nāgārjuna claimed to have received the book from the Nāgas and to have founded the Mahāyāna school on its teachings. v. *Nāgārjuna*.

The *pustaka* is the symbol of Mañjuśrī, Avalokiteśvara, and of the goddesses Prajñāpāramitā, Cundā, and Vasudhārā, and may be carried as an accessory symbol by other gods.

Rākshasa (S.) or *Rākshas*, demons that devour men. Invoked by sorcerers.

Ratna (S.) Jewel. The Sapta Ratna (M. *dologa erdeni*), or the seven Buddhist jewels, are: 1, the golden wheel believed to fall from heaven on the investiture of a 'Wheel King', symbol of Perfection of the Law; 2, a precious stone (*maṇi*), symbol of the accomplishment of wishes; 3, a royal consort (a noble woman) symbolizes the 'calming caress'; 4, the best horse (a white horse), symbol of prompt success in the acquisition of the qualities of the Buddha; 5, the best elephant, as bearer of 84,000 sacred books, symbolizes the infinite propagation of the religion; 6, the best treasurer (civil officer), who by his generosity removes poverty, and by his justice assures the well-being of people; 7, the best leader (military chief), who with his sword of wisdom repels the enemies. (These last two are sometimes interpreted: 6, guardian spirits; 7, soldiers and servants.) v. also *Tri-ratna*.

Ren-ge (J.) Lotus-flower. v. *padma*.

Renge-no-in (J.) *Padma mudrā* or gesture of the lotus. v. *Uttara-Bodhi*.

Sādhana (S.) Formula for the invocation of a god, which must be carried out in the following manner: On a certain day the Buddhist magician priest makes his proper toilet and goes out to a solitary spot, which, according to his humour, is either gay like a wood, or the confluence of two rivers, or to a place of cremation. He then seats himself on a spot already purified for the occasion, where he proceeds to invoke the Buddhas and Bodhisattvas, offering imaginary or real flowers or perfumes. He begins by a confession of sins, pronounces his act of faith in the three jewels (Buddha, Dharma, Saṅgha), and, after deep meditation, succeeds in abolishing his own personality and identifying himself with the divinity which he wishes to invoke, proceeding according to the Sādhana.

As an example, the Siṃhanāda Sādhana proceeds as follows: He (the Buddhist priest) must see, developed from the white syllable 'Ōm!', a moon disc;[1] above this, from the white syllable 'Aḥ!', a white lion; and above this, from the white syllable 'Am!', a white lotus, on the heart of which he is to see the syllable 'Hriḥ!', white and shining. Having developed all this, he must see himself in form of Siṃhanāda, a body all white with two arms, one face, and three eyes; his hair in form of a tiara, his head-dress ornamented with a small image of Amitābha; crouched in Indian fashion, with one knee raised, seated on a lion covered with a tiger-skin, the five Dhyāni-Buddhas emanating from his person. Having thus meditated on all this, tired of meditation, let the conjurer pronounce the formula of conjuration (A. Foucher, *Iconographie bouddhique*, partie II, p. 8).

The priest is then believed to be visited by the god, whereupon he presents the petition of his client.

Śakti (S.) (T. *uns-ma*), or the more popular expression *yum* (v. *yab-yum*). Female energy of a god.

Samādhi (S.) (Sam-ā-dhi), lit. 'self-possessed'. The deepest form of abstract meditation.

Saṅgha (S.) The Buddhist community, or church. Esoteric sense, *union*. v. *Tri-ratna*.

Śankha (S.) Conch-shell, symbol of the preaching of the Buddha as well as of the feminine principle.

Śara (S.) Arrow (of confession). v. *Capa*.

Śarīra (S.) (M. and J. *shari*.) Lit. particles of bones, relics, or ashes of a Buddha preserved in *stūpas* and worshipped. They are sometimes called *Dharmaśarīra*. v. *tsa-tsa* and *shari-to*.

Shakujo (J.) v. *khakkhara*.

Shari-tō (J.) Japanese shrine containing a *śari* or Buddha bone. In the ninth century cremation was introduced into Japan, and in the ashes of Buddhist saints were found small cartilaginous balls which were looked upon as holy gems and kept as relics in crystal shrines.

Siṃha (S.) Lion—symbolizes 'boldness, bravery, and a fresh, eager, and advancing spirit'—emblem of Vairocana. v. *lakshana*, 13 and 19.

Siṃhanāda (S.) Lit. 'with the voice of a lion'. According to legend, the roarings are believed to awaken stillborn babes. A god seated on a roaring lion is believed to cure leprosy. Avalokiteśvara (Kwan-yin), Mañjuśrī, and Jambala may be Siṃhanāda, as well as the female Kwan-yin and the green Tārā. (v. Pls. XXXV and XXXVII.)

Siṃhāsana (S.) Lion throne. v. *āsana*.

Skugsum (T.) v. *Tri-kāya*.

Stotra (S.) Buddhist hymn.

Stūpa (S.) (J. *sotoba*.) Lit. 'precious tower'—a tower to hold relics. v. *caitya*.

Sukhāvatī. The Western Paradise of Amitābha. The common people look upon Sukhāvatī as equivalent to Nirvāṇa, but, according to the Mahāyāna teachings, it is the last stage before Nirvāṇa. M. de la Vallée Poussin calls it a 'Buddha field' to prepare the souls for Nirvāṇa. It is here that the Bodhisattva, who have not elected to acquire merit by becoming Mānushi-Buddhas, sit on lotus-flowers and accumulate merit until they are eligible to Nirvāṇa. v. *Amitābha*.

Sumeru (Mount) or Mount Meru—supposed highest peak of the Himālayas, and believed to be the centre of the universe. In the *Bhadra Kalpāvadāna* it is written: First air, then fire, then earth, and in the centre of the earth, Sumeru, the sides of which are the residence of the thirty-three millions of gods (*Devatas*). Sakra lives in his paradise which is on its summit, and its four sides are guarded by the four Lokapāla.

Śūnyatā (S.) Emptiness, unreality, nothingness.

Sūrya. Sun, special symbol of Ākāśagarbha. The sun-disc and the moon are held by one of the twenty-one Tārās as well as by Āryāvalokiteśvara, especially in China and Japan.

[1] Platform on which the god is seated.

The sun-disc, surmounted by a trident, is called the *sūrya-maṇi* or sun-jewel (v. *cintāmaṇi*). In the *Sūryanāma Sūtra* it is said that Buddha 'caused to issue from the summit of his head a flood of glory composed of a hundred precious rays' (Beal, *Catena*, p. 424). The Nepalese Buddhas are sometimes represented with the *sūrya-maṇi* above the *ushṇīsha*. The symbol is also used in Nepal, issuing from a lotus-flower, to represent the Svayambhū or Ādi-Buddha at the creation of the world. v. *Triśūla*.

Sūtra (S.) From the Sanskrit root *siv*, 'to sew', meaning to thread or string. In other words, a *sūtra* is a body of doctrine. It must be composed of words coming from the Buddha's own lips—words 'strung together' in form of a sermon.

Svabhāva (S.) Lit. *sva* (own); *bhava* (nature), 'self-existent'. Ādi-Buddha is called Svabhāva by the Svābhāvika sect.

Svastika (S.) The svastika is one of the sixty-five marks of Buddhahood found in the imprint of the Buddha's foot. On some of the images of the Buddha it is on his breast, and may also be represented before him on the lotus-throne. It is called by the Chinese *sin-yin* (heart-seal). As a Buddhist symbol it represents the esoteric doctrine of Buddha, and was adopted by several sects. The *svastika*, however, is found in many other countries, and is the subject of much controversy. (Pl. II, fig. *c*, and Pl. XVIII, fig. *a*.)

Svayambhū (S.) Lit. 'spontaneity', or that which is self-existent. The Ādi-Buddha is called Svayambhū.

Tantra (S.) Lit. 'treatise'. The *Tantra*, or mystic treatises, comprise twenty-two volumes. The *Anuttara Tantra* treats of the worship of the Active Producing Principle on which the Tantra-Yoga system is based.

The Mahā-Tantra system is a debased form of the Yogā-cārya school, and made its appearance toward the end of the sixth century. The worship of the *śakti*, or female energy of the gods, began to influence the Mahāyāna system in the seventh century, and became very popular in Tibet and Mongolia, but was never adopted by the Chinese or Japanese in the *yab-yum* form.

The Tantra forms of the gods often have several heads, and always more than two arms. They may be peaceful, but are usually ferocious in aspect, in which case their symbols are warlike, and their ornaments are skulls and serpents. The most popular Tantra symbol, which is held by both the god and his *śakti*, is the *kapāla* or skull-cup filled with blood, or with the eyes, ears, and tongues of demons.

Tarjanī mudrā (S.) Menacing with the index.

Tathāgata (S.) Tathāgata is the highest epithet of a Buddha, and is generally used for the seven principal Buddhas. It sometimes designates the Tri-kāya (v.s.). There is a divergence of opinion as to the correct translation of the word. Hodgson gives: 'Tathā, *thus*; gata, *gone*, or he who does not come again.' In other words, he who will have no more rebirths. The Buddhist scriptures say, 'it does not come again'. Rémusat translates it as the 'avenu'. Eitel gives: 'like—to come', or 'one who (in coming into the world) is like the coming (of his predecessors)'. According to Waddell, 'similarly gone'; while Mead interprets Tathāgata as 'He-who-has-reached-the-That-stage, meaning the state of Perfection'. Hodgson says that the term should only be applied to Ādi-Buddha, and alludes to his 'voluntary secession from the versatile world into that of abstraction'.

Thabdong-shesrab (T.) or union of Spirit and Matter. v. *Dharmacakra*.

Tri-kāya (S.) (T. *Shugsum*.) Three (*Tri*), bodies (*kāya*), a threefold embodiment. It is believed by some of the Northern Buddhist sects that a Buddha may live in three separate spheres at the same time.

According to Eitel (*Handbook of Chinese Buddhism*) there are three representations of Buddha:

1. Statues, Teachings, Stūpas.
2. The historical Buddha unites in himself three bodily qualities:
   I. Nirmāṇa-kāya—human, mortal, and ascetic;
   II. Sambhoga-kāya—body of Supreme Happiness;
   III. Dharma-kāya—abstract body.
3. Buddha having passed through and existing in three forms:

I. Śākya-muni on earth.	Earthly Buddha endowed with Nirmāṇa-kāya, having passed through innumerable transformations on earth.
II. Locana in Dhyāna Saṅgha.	Heavenly Dhyāni-Bodhisattva endowed with Sambhoga-kāya of absolute completeness.
III. Vairocana in Nirvāṇa.	Dhyāni-Buddha endowed with Dharma-kāya of absolute purity in Nirvāṇa.

Tri-koṇa (S.) Triangle. The *tri-koṇa* is the symbol of the Tri-ratna, and, according to the secret doctrine of certain sects, represents the *yoni*, 'from which the world was manifest', the source of all things. The triangle is often found in Nepalese temples dedicated to the Buddha-*śaktis* and figures in the *Garbhadhātu maṇḍala* immediately above the five-leaved lotus enclosure (v. *Vajra-dhātu*, *Tri-ratna*, and Pl. xvi). The Japanese look upon the triangle as a flame-symbol—'body of fire' (third element)—which destroys all that is impure.

The Buddha, according to Beal, once 'discoursed on the symbol "I" with three dots ∴ arranged as a triangle resting on its base', and 'used the triangle as a symbol of the embodied form of the Tathāgata'.

When seated in *dhyāna-mudrā* the Buddha forms a perfect triangle resting on its base, and it is believed by Buddhists to have been his attitude in the womb of his mother. In the *Garbha-dhātu maṇḍala* the triangle rests on its base, and, according to the esoteric doctrine, is the form which is symbolical of material essence. The triangle with the point below is the symbol of the highest form of spirituality—the spiritual essence of Ādi-Buddha.

Triloka (S.) The celestial, terrestrial, and infernal divisions of the versatile universe created by Brahmā.

Trimūrti (S.) Buddhist triad: Mañjuśrī, Avalokiteśvara, and Vajrapāṇi.

Tri-ratna (S.) The three jewels—Buddha, Dharma, Saṅgha (Buddha, the Law, the Community). The three jewels are symbolized by the *triśūla*, by the triliteral syllable *a-u-m* (v. *Ōm !*), and by the *trikoṇa*.

In the Buddhist scriptures it is written that Ādi-Dharma revealed herself from a point in the centre of the triangle. From one side of the triangle she 'produced Buddha; from another side, Dharma; and from the third side, Saṅgha'. Ādi-Dharma is therefore the mother of the Buddha that issued from the first side (right side of the triangle. *All the Buddhas are born from the right side* of their mothers). The Dharma that issued from the second side is the 'wife of the Buddha of the first side and the mother of the other Buddhas'. (v. Hodgson, *The Languages, History, and Religion of Nepal and Tibet*, p. 87.)

According to the esoteric doctrine, Buddha represents the spiritual essence, 'the efficient cause of all'. Dharma is the material essence, the 'plastic cause'—'a co-equal bi-unity with Buddha'. Saṅgha is the compound of Buddha and Dharma, 'the immediate operative cause of creation'.

Certain Northern Buddhist sects interlink the doctrine of the Tri-ratna with that of the Tri-kāya, and look upon Dharma as the *Dhyāni-Buddha*, and Saṅgha as the *Dhyāni-Bodhisattva*.

Triśūla (S.) Lit. *tri* (three), *śūla* (points), a three-forked flame which Burnouf believes to be the invocation of the 'highest'. The *triśūla*, which is an emblem of Buddhism, is represented in the form of a trident, and may surmount a round object, which Beal believes to symbolize the sun with a flame or '*Empyrean* above it'.

There is much diversity of opinion in regard to the *triśūla*. According to d'Alviella, 'some have seen therein the monogram of Buddha; others, the symbol of Dharma, the Law, which sums up the doctrine of Buddhism; others, again, a representation of the *tri-ratna*, the threefold jewel formed by Buddha, his Law, and his Church'. Sir George Birdwood claims that the *triśūla* stands for the Tree of Life, and by some it is looked upon as a symbol of lightning. According to Burnouf, it is merely one of the sixty-five signs of Buddhahood which adorn the impression of the Master's feet.

The Singalese Buddhas have a three-forked flame issuing from the *ushṇīsha*. The Svābhāvika sect, a generally accepted school of Buddhism in China, took for its emblem a *triśūla* rising out of a lotus-flower (v. p. 5). The *ūrṇā* on the forehead of some of the Buddhas in the Turfan frescoes discovered by Herr von Le Coq have a red flame-glory forming three points. Among these Buddhist frescoes[1] is one of a trident surmounting an eight-spoked wheel, on either side of which is a gazelle, thus symbolizing the sermon of the Buddha in the deer-park at Benares.

Tri-yāṇa (S.) Lit. 'three vehicles'—the Mahāyāna (great vehicle), the Madhyama-yāna (middling vehicle), Hīnayāna (lesser vehicle), the three Buddhist means of attaining Nirvāṇa.

Tsa-tsa (M.) Moulds of Buddhist gods made of ashes of saints mixed with mud and corn. v. *Śarīra.*

Tse-bum (T.) v. *Kalaśa.*

Upāyikā (J.) Theistic triad—Dharma, Buddha, and Saṅgha.

Ūrṇā (S.) The *ūrṇā* is the fourth of the thirty-two superior marks of a Buddha, and is represented by a small, round protuberance above the bridge of the nose.

The Sanskrit word *ūrṇā* means 'tuft of hair', which, according to tradition, should be white and 'shine like silver'. It indicates a predestination to Bodhi.

In the Buddhist scriptures the *ūrṇā* is referred to as follows: 'The countenance of Buddha was transfigured, while the tuft of hair on his forehead radiated forth a brilliant light.' And again, 'Gautama was seated on a white lotus supported by a white elephant. From a white spot on his forehead shone a brilliant light which illuminated the universe.' The Japanese believe that five colours radiated from the *ūrṇā*.

The *ūrṇā* is the divine eye—a sign of spiritual insight. According to Havell, it is the 'spiritual consciousness of soul-sight as distinguished from eyesight and intellectual perception' (*Ideals of Indian Art*, p. 50).

Both the Buddhas and Bodhisattva have the *ūrṇā* on the forehead as well as, sometimes, on the palms of the hands and soles of the feet. The Bodhisattva on the frescoes brought from Turfan by Herr von Le Coq have the *ūrṇā* on the forehead and breast outlined by a red flame, thus resembling the flaming pearl (v. *cintāmaṇi*).

It is difficult to make out the origin of the *ūrṇā* unless it came from the superstition of the people of Northern India, who believed that if the eyebrows met over the bridge of the nose it was a sign of great mental superiority.

Ushṇīsha (S.) (T. *Tsugtor.*) The protuberance on the skull of the Buddhas.

The *ushṇīsha* is the seat of the intellectual faculties—the receptacle of the divine *manas* of Buddha. The Platonists believed that the soul was centred in the head, which notion, according to Mead, was 'presumably the influence of the old Oriental mystic doctrine of Asia Minor or higher Asia'. They further believed that the soul had a radiant vesture (Augoeides) which manifested itself 'spark-like'. If we accept the hypothesis that the *ushṇīsha* is the receptacle of the *manas* of the Buddha, might not the flame, which is sometimes represented issuing from the protuberance, indicate the 'spark-like' radiance of the 'vesture of the soul'?

The *ushṇīsha* is the first and most important of the thirty-two superior signs of a Buddha, and probably the last acquired. In the Indian scriptures the Buddha at his birth, or in the different

[1] In the Museum für Völkerkunde, Berlin.

episodes of his life before his supreme Enlightenment, is not represented with the protuberance of the skull. It is not until he achieves Buddhahood under the Bodhi-tree that he is represented with the full-sized *ushṇisha*. (v. the Buddhas.)

Ushṇīsha means 'turban' or 'dressed hair'. The Gandhāra school never represented the Buddha with the protuberance on the skull, but with the long wavy hair drawn up on the top of the head in a cluster of curls, or a knot which concealed, or took the place of, the protuberance. They thus seem to have followed the Brahmanical representations of the Buddha, for the ninth *avatār* of Vishṇu was represented with long hair arranged in a knot on the top of his head.

According to Buddhist tradition, which was followed by the Indian artists, the hair of the Buddha should be short, the curls falling from left to right, and the protuberance should also be covered with short curls.

The shape of the *ushṇīsha* varied somewhat in different countries.

In Nepal the protuberance was round on the top and placed nearer the forehead than in North-Eastern India, where it was represented more pointed in shape. The *ushṇīsha* of the Nepalese Buddhas was sometimes surmounted by a ball from which issued a flame. In the *Sūryanāma sūtra* it is written, 'Buddha caused to issue from his head a flood of glory composed of a hundred precious rays'.[1]

In Tibet the protuberance was higher than in India, and often surmounted by a flaming pearl. There are examples of a small protuberance above the usual *ushṇīsha*, the whole surmounted by a pearl.

In China and Japan the *ushṇīsha* was generally low and large at the base, sometimes with a tonsure on the top of the protuberance. The Tibetan type, however, was often followed. In Japan the *ushṇīsha* is called *Fou-ken-tcho-so*, or the 'invisible form of the skull'. It was believed that only the initiated were able to see the protuberance on the skull of a Buddha.

In Burma and Siam there was either a high, pointed flame issuing from a low *ushṇīsha*, or a spike-shaped head-piece, often elaborately ornamented, entirely covering the protuberance. In Cambodia the *ushṇīsha* was very pointed.

In Java the protuberance was either low and small at the base, or high and large at the base.

In Ceylon the *ushṇīsha* is usually very low, and the Buddha almost always has a three or five-forked flame rising from the top of the protuberance. It is one of the characteristics of the Singalese Buddhas.

The protuberance of the skull, according to Grünwedel, was regarded as a sign of supernatural wisdom of a Buddha. According to Eitel the *ushṇīsha* was first a coil of hair, which later took the form of a protuberance on the skull. Schlagintweit claims that the Buddhist sculptors adopted the style of representing the Buddha with a coil of hair on the top of his head because it was the Brahmanical way of dressing the hair. They thus 'conferred on their sublime Master this prerogative of the highest Indian caste'.

Utpala (S.) Blue lotus. v. *padma*.

Uttara-bodhi (S.) *Mudrā* of best perfection. (J. *Renge-no-in*.) All the fingers are locked (the palms turned underneath), with the exception of the thumbs and indexes, which touch at the tips, the fingers being extended upward. In Japan the second fingers are also often upright, while the other fingers are in the above pose. The attitude is emblematic of the lotus-flower, and is the *mudrā* of Buddha, Liberator of Serpents, Avalokiteśvara (p. 63 and Pl. XX), Kwan-yin (Pl. LXIV), and of Bato Kwan-non (Pl. XXXII, figs. *c* and *d*).

Vāhana (S.) The mount of a god. The mount of Amitābha and Sarasvatī is a peacock; that of Akshobhya, Samantabhadra (Fugen) and Kangō-satta is an elephant. The mount of Vairocana is a lion; Ts'aṅs-pa, is a horse or dragon; Lhamo, is a mule.

[1] Beal, *Catena*, p. 289. v. *sūrya*.

Avalokiteśvara, Mañjuśrī, Tārā, and the female form of Kwan-yin, as well as Jambala, may be on a roaring lion. v. *Siṃhanāda*.

Vajra (S.) (T. *rdo-rje*, M. *vačir* or *očir*, C. *kin-kang*, J. *kongō*.) Lit. 'diamond', or that which is indestructible. Generally translated 'thunderbolt', or that which destroys but is itself indestructible. It is likened to the Mystic Truth which cannot be destroyed, or to Wisdom that destroys all passions.

The *vajra* is claimed by some to be of Western origin and an adaptation of the thunderbolt symbol held by Jupiter. The Assyro-Chaldean gods were represented holding a trident (v. *tri-śūla*) with the points zigzag-shaped, representing lightning. In Mesopotamia the gods hold a double trident, which is also found in the caves of Ellora, as well as other parts of India, in the hand of Śiva. The Northern Buddhists believe that Buddha wrested the *vajra* (double trident) from the Hindu god Indra, and adopted it as a Buddhist symbol with the slight change of closing the points of the darts. The Indian *vajra* with three darts is flat and the points do not touch. The Tibetan 'thunderbolt' with four darts is round, and as the points are closed the two ends resemble lotus-buds in form. A fifth dart runs through the centre of the *vajra*, from end to end, making five darts, which represent the five bodies of the Dhyāni-Buddhas.

In Japan the *vajra* (*kongō*), called *doko*, has only one dart, which is four-sided. There is also a three-darted *vajra*, the *san-kō*, which resembles the Indian form in that it is flat and that the points are not closed. The five-darted *kongō*, the *go-kō*, differs from the Tibetan *vajra* in that all the five darts are outside. It is looked upon as representing the five elements as well as the five bodies of the celestial Buddhas.

Padmasambhava introduced the *vajra* into Tibet, and through his influence it became most popular. The priests adopted its use to exorcise devils, and it was also introduced into the ceremonies for worshipping Amitāyus (v. s.).

In the esoteric doctrine the *vajra* is the mystic symbol of the *liṅga*, and the expression, 'in *vajra* attitude', is the attitude of *yab-yum*.

The *vajra* is the special symbol of Akshobhya and of Vajrapāṇi. Vajradhara holds it in his right and the *vajra*-handled bell in his left hand, as does also Trailokyavijaya, Kongōsatta, and Aizen-myō-ō; Vajrasattva holds it balanced on his right hand, while the left hand holds the *vajra*-handled bell on his hip. The *vajra* is carried as an accessory symbol by all the Yi-dam, but not by the Dharmapāla.

Vajra-dhātu (S.) The *maṇḍala* of the Two Parts (*Vajra-dhātu* and *Garbha-dhātu*) occupies a most important position in the teachings of the Yoga doctrine. v. *maṇḍala*.

According to Kōbō Daishi, who founded the Yoga school (Shin-gon) in Japan, the teachings of the mystic doctrine were too profound to be expressed by words, and could only be taught to the ignorant by means of illustrations. The 'Two Parts' are therefore represented by two diagrams, for details of which see Bunyiu Nanjio, *A Short History of the Twelve Japanese Sects*, p. 88.

The *Vajra-dhātu* is the 'diamond' element. *Vajra* is here translated 'diamond' rather than 'thunderbolt', and represents the Spiritual world, or complete Enlightenment—the esoteric teachings of the Dharma-kāya as against the exoteric teachings of the Nirmāṇa-kāya. It is the sixth element, the *manas* (mind), and is symbolized by the triangle with the point below (v. *tri-koṇa*), as well as by the full moon. It is located in the West, and is symbolized by the setting of the sun.

The *Garbha-dhātu* is the 'matrix' or 'embryo' element—the Material World. It is likened to the womb in which all of the child is conceived—its body, mind, &c. It is the *vīja mantra A*, which contains all the universe—protects and nourishes it. It is *reason*, form, and the five elements—earth, water, fire, air, and ether. It is symbolized by the triangle resting on its base, which is found in the diagram of the *Garbha-dhātu* above the five-leaved lotus enclosure in the Sarvajña section (Pl. xvi). The full-blown lotus (in reality, the sun) is also its symbol.

The location of the Matrix-element is in the East, and is symbolized by the rising of the sun.

The *Vajra-dhātu* and *Garbha-dhātu* are one, for Wisdom cannot exist without Reason, nor Reason without Wisdom, and this is expressed by the *Maṇḍala* of the Two Parts, as well as by the *mudrā* of the Six Elements (v. *Vairocana*). The Union of the Spiritual and the Material is symbolized in Nepal by the flame rising from the lotus-flower or moon-crescent (v. *Vajrasattva*) and by the flame rising from the *kalaśa* as seen in the paintings on the inside of the covers of the MS. Add. 1643 in the University Library, Cambridge; in Tibet, by the *aśoka* branch in the ambrosia vase; in China, by the willow in the *kalaśa*; in Japan, by the *vajra* issuing from the ambrosia vase (Pl. XVI), and in both the Chinese and Nepalese *yin-yang*. (The Japanese *yin-yang* contains three segments.) The *mantra*, 'Ōm, maṇi padme, hūṃ!' is an expression of the Mystic Union (v. *Ōm*), as is also the *mudrā* of the dogmatic form of Avalokiteśvara; and the Ni-ō signify the Two Parts. In fact, the Yoga school of Mahāyāna Buddhism is founded on the *One-ness* of the *Vajradhātu* and *Garbhadhātu*.

Vajra-hūṃ-kāra (S.) *Mudrā* of Buddha Supreme and Eternal. The wrists are crossed at the breast which indicates intensity, and the hands hold symbols, usually the *vajra* and *ghaṇṭā*. Special *mudrā* of Vajradhara, Saṃvara, Trailokyavijaya, and of most of the gods when holding their *śaktis*.

Vajrāsana (S.) v. *Āsana*.

Vara (S.) or *Varada*. *Mudrā* of Charity. The arm is pendent, with all the fingers extended downward, and the palm turned outward. *Mudrā* of the Tārās and of many gods.

Vihāra (S.) Buddhist monastery.

Vīja (S.) (J. *Shu-ji*.) Root, radix, seed. The germ of a *mantra* (v.s.)—a mantra-seed. A *vija mantra* is a letter or syllable used in casting spells and in the invocations of the gods (v. *dhāraṇī* and *sādhana*). The elements came from the *vījas*. In the *Pujā Kāṇḍa* it is written: 'from the *vija* of the letter *Y*, air; from that of the letter *R*, fire; from that of letter *V* (or *B*), water; from that of the letter *L*, earth, and from the letter *A* proceeded Ākāśa, or ether (v. *Vajradhātu* and *Ōm*). The most commonly known *vija mantra* is that of Avalokiteśvara, 'Hri!' which is a contraction for *Hridaya* or '(Sacred) Heart'.

Viśvavajra (S.) Lit. 'double-*vajra*', or thunderbolt, is the special symbol of Ushṇīshavijayā and Amoghasiddha and his *śakti*, Tārā. Saṃvara has it in his head-dress. v. *Vajra*.

Vitarka (S.) *Mudrā* of argument. The dogmatic attitude is represented with the arm bent and all the fingers extended upward, except either the index or the ring finger, which touches the tip of the thumb, forming the 'triangular pose'. The palm of the hand is turned outward. Mystic gesture of the Tārās and of the eight Bodhisattva. In Japan the *mudrā* called *semmui* corresponds with the *vitarka*, the only difference being that the index and thumb do not touch at the tips. The thumb is pressed against the palm of the hand.

Yab-yum (T.) Lit. 'Father-Mother'. Attitude of a god (*yab*) when embracing his *śakti* (*yum*), also called 'in *vajra* attitude'.

Yaksa (S.) Demons in the suite of Kuvera.

Yāna (S.) Vehicle. v. *Tri-yāna*.

Yin-yang (C.) Lit. 'female-male', or the two first causes. The primal causation is represented by a circle divided into two equal parts. In China the two equal segments are in tadpole shape. In Nepal they are divided by a wavy line (v. Hodgson, *The Journal of the Asiatic Society*, vol. xviii, Pl. III). In Japan the corresponding symbol is a circle divided into three equal tadpole-shaped segments.

Yoga (S.) From the Sanskrit root *Yuj* or 'union'. It signifies the union of the Spiritual with the Material, or communion with the Universal Spirit, and is represented by the *Maṇḍala* of the Two Parts. v. *Vairocana*.

The Yoga is the practice of ecstatic meditation, and was introduced into Hinduism by Patañjali in the second century B.C. It was grafted on the Mahāyāna System by Asañga, in the middle of the sixth century A.D., introduced into China A.D. 720, and into Japan by Kōbō Daishi in the ninth century.

Yogacārya (S.) Lit. 'school of Yoga'.

Zuchi (J.) Small Japanese travelling shrine in which is enshrined the image of a god.

BIBLIOGRAPHY

ALVIELLA (GOBLET D').—*La Migration des symboles.* Bruxelles, 1897.

BEAL (S).—1. *The Buddhist Tripitaka.* Printed for the India Office, Devonport, 1876.

—— 2. *Buddhist Records of the Western World,* translated from the Chinese of Hsiuen Tsiang. London, 1906.

—— 3. *Catena of Buddhist Sculptures.* London, 1871.

—— 4. *Life of Hsiuen Tsiang.* London, 1911.

—— 5. *The Romantic Legend of Sakya-Buddha,* from the Chinese-Sanskrit. London, 1875.

—— 6. *Travels of Fah-Hian and Sung Yun from China to India* (A.D. 400 and A.D. 518). London, 1869.

BLONAY (G. DE).—*Matériaux pour servir à l'histoire de la déesse bouddhique Tara.* Paris, 1895.

BURGESS (J).—1. *The Report of the Ellura Caves.* London, 1883.

—— 2. *The Buddhist stūpas of Amarāvatī and Juggayyapeta.* London, 1887.

BURNOUF (E.).—1. *La Science des Religions.* Paris, 1885.

—— 2. *Introduction à l'histoire du Bouddhisme indien.* Paris, 1876.

CARUS (P.).—'The Mythology of Buddhism.' *The Monist,* vol. vii, No. 3, 1897.

CHURCHWARD (A.).—*Signs and Symbols of Primordial Man.* London, 1910.

CLARKE (J. F.).—*The Ten Great Religions.* Boston, 1890.

CHAVANNES (E.).—*Mission archéologique dans la Chine septentrionale.* 2 vol. of plates published by l'École française de l'Extrême-Orient, Paris, 1909.

COOMARASWAMY (A. K.).—'Mahāyāna Buddhist Images from Ceylon and Java' (with three plates). *The Journal of the Royal Asiatic Society of Great Britain and Ireland,* April, 1909.

CSOMA DE K'ORÖS (A.).—*Dictionary, Tibetan and English.* Calcutta, 1834.

CUNNINGHAM (Brev. Major A.). *The Bhilsa Topes or Buddhist Monuments of Central India.*—London, 1854.

DAS (SARAT CHANDRA).—1. *Journey to Lhasa and Central Tibet.* London, 1904.

—— 2. 'Progress of Buddhism in Tibet.' *Journal of the Asiatic Society of Bengal,* Nov. 1, 1882.

DAVIDS (W. RHYS).—1. *Buddhist Birth Stories,* translated from the Pali. London, 1880.

—— 2. *Early Buddhism.* London, 1908.

DAWSON (J.).—*Classical Dictionary of Hindu Mythology.* London, 1903.

DHALKE (P.).—Buddhist essays translated from the German by Bhikku Silacara. London, 1904.

EDKINS (J.).—*Chinese Buddhism.* London, 1893.

EITEL (E.).—1. *Handbook of Chinese Buddhism.* London, 1888.

—— 2. *Three Lectures on Buddhism.* Hong-Kong, 1884.

FA-HIAN.—*Foe Koue Ki ou Relations des royaumes bouddhiques: Voyages dans la Tartarie, dans l'Afghanistan et dans l'Inde, exécutés à la fin du IVe siècle par Chy Fa-Hien.* Traduit du chinois par Abel Rémusat (Ouvrage posthume); revu, complété et augmenté d'éclaircissements nouveaux, par MM. Klaproth et Landress. Paris, 1836.

FERGUSSON (J.).—*Tree and Serpent Worship.* Second edition, London, 1873.

—— 2. *The Cave Temples of India.* London, 1880.

FOUCAUX (PH. ED.).—*Histoire de Buddha Sakya-Mouni.* Traduite du tibétain. Paris, 1868.

FOUCHER (A.).—1. *Étude sur l'iconographie bouddhique de l'Inde.* 1re partie, Paris, 1900. 2e partie, 1905.

—— 2. *L'Art gréco-bouddhique du Gandhāra.* Paris, 1905. Vol. i.

FOUCHER (A.).—3. *La Madone bouddhique. Monuments et mémoires publiés par l'Académie des Inscriptions et Belles-Lettres.* t. xvii, Paris, 1909.

—— 4. *Catalogue des peintures népalaises et tibétaines de la Collection B.-H. Hodgson, à la Bibliothèque de l'Institut de France.* Paris, 1897.

—— 5. *Les Débuts de l'art bouddhique.* Paris, 1911.

—— 6. *Notes d'archéologie bouddhique. Bulletin de l'École française de l'Extrême-Orient.* 1909.

FUJISHIMA (R.).—*Le Bouddhisme japonais.* Paris, 1889.

GARRETT (J.).—*Classical Dictionary of India.* Madras, 1871.

GEMMEL (W.).—*The Diamond Sutra* (*Chin-kang-ching*) *or the Prajnaparamita*, translated from the Chinese. London, 1912.

GRIFFIS (W. E.).—*The Religions of Japan.* New York, 1907.

GROOT (J. DE).—'Fête de Kouan Yin, Déesse de la Grâce Divine.' *Annales du Musée Guimet*, t. ii, Paris, 1886.

GRÜNWEDEL (A.).—1. *Buddhistische Kunst in Indien.* 2nd ed. Berlin, 1900.

—— 2. *Buddhist Art*, translated from the German by Agnes Gibson, revised and enlarged by J. Burgess. London, 1901.

—— 3. *Mythologie du Bouddhisme au Tibet et en Mongolie, basée sur la Collection lamaïque du Prince Oukhtomsky.* Leipzig, 1900.

—— 4. 'Padmasambhava und Verwandtes.' *Baesler-Archiv.* Berlin, 1912.

—— 5. *Altbuddhistische Kultstätten in Chinesisch-Turkestan.* Berlin, 1912.

HARDY (S.). *A Manual of Buddhism.* London, 1860.

HIDENOBU (T.).—*Butsuzo Zui.* Japanese Manual of the Buddhist Divinities, in five volumes. Compiled by Tosa Hidenobu in 1690. Printed in Kyoto in 1796.

HUTH (G.). *Geschichte des Buddhismus in der Mongolei.* Strassburg, 1896.

KAEMPFER (E.).—*Histoire naturelle, civile et ecclésiastique de l'Empire du Japon;* composée en allemand et traduite en français sur la version anglaise de J. G. Scheuchzer, en trois volumes. La Haye, 1732.

KIRCHER (A.). *China monumentis qua sacris qua profanis . . . illustrata.* Amstelodami, 1667.

KOEPPEN (K. F.).—*Die Religion des Buddha und ihre Entstehung.* Berlin, 1857.

KURODA (S.). *Outlines of the Mahāyāna as taught by Buddha.* Tokyo, 1893.

LAMAIRESSE (E.).—*Le Bouddhisme en Chine et au Thibet.* Paris, 1894.

LAUFER (B.).—1. *A Chinese Madonna.* Chicago, 1912.

—— 2. *Chinese Grave Sculptures of the Han Period.* Paris, 1911.

LE COQ (A. VON).—*Chotscho. Koeniglich Preussische Turfan-Expedition.* Berlin, 1913.

LEGGE (J.). *A Record of Buddhistic Kingdoms, being an Account by the Chinese Monk Fā-Hien of his Travels in India* (A. D. 399–414). Oxford, 1886.

LILLIE (A.).—*Buddhism in Christendom.* London, 1887.

LLOYD (A.).—1. *The Development of Japanese Buddhism.* Asiatic Society of Japan. Tokyo, 1908.

—— 2. *Shin-ran and his Work.* Tokyo, 1910.

—— 3. *The Creed of Half Japan.* London, 1911.

—— 4. *The Praises of Amida.* Tokyo, 1908.

—— 5. *Formative Elements of Japanese Buddhism.* Asiatic Society of Japan, 1908.

MASSON-OURSEL (M. P.).—*Les Trois Corps du Bouddha. Journal Asiatique* (Mai–Juin 1913). Paris.

MAYERS (W. F.).—'Illustrations of the Lamaist System in Tibet drawn from Chinese Sources.' *Journal of the Royal Asiatic Society*, vol. iv, No. 1, 1869.

MITRA (R.).—*The Sanscrit Buddhist Literature of Nepal.* Calcutta, 1882.

MINAYEFF.—*Recherches sur le bouddhisme*, translated from the Russian. Paris, 1894.

MÜLLER (MAX).—*Buddhism and Buddhist Pilgrims.* A review of M. Stanislas Jullien's *Voyages des Pèlerins bouddhistes.* London, 1857.

NANJIO (B.).—*A Short History of the Twelve Buddhist Sects.* Tokyo, 1886.

OLDENBERG (H.).—*Buddha; his Life, his Doctrine, his Order.* London, 1882.

OLDENBURG (S. F.).—1. *Sbornik izobrajeniy 300 Burhanov, etc.* (Recueil des images des 300 divinités bouddhistes d'après l'Album du Musée Asiatique, édité avec des observations par S. Oldenburg, 1re partie (seule parue); Dessins, préface (en russe) et index (en tibétain). St-Pétersbourg, 1903, in-8° (forme le 5e vol. de *Bibliotheca buddhica.*) [2 ii + 6 pages, plus 100 planches représentant exactement, par le procédé photo-mécanique, les 300 images originales de l'édition du *Panthéon bouddhiste de Canca-Qutuqtu* (Chancha-khutuktu), dont Pander (voy. *Das Pantheon des Tschangtscha Hutuktu*) n'a donné que des copies imparfaites en omettant certaines images.]

—— 2. *Materialy po buddiyskoy ikonografii, &c.* (Matériaux pour l'iconographie bouddhiste: 1. Quelques images de Maitreya; 2. Quelques représentations de Maitreya au Tibet; 3. Une statuette japonaise d'Avalokiteśvara; *Publications du Musée d'Anthropologie et d'Ethnographie de l'Académie Impériale des Sciences de St-Pétersbourg* (en russe), No. 3, 1901, 10 pp. avec 6 pl.)

—— 3. *Materialy, etc.* (Matériaux, etc.): 4. Album des images bouddhistes conservées à l'Académie ecclésiastique de Kasan; 5. Sur quelques images des Bodhisattva; 6. Sur un bas-relief de Gandhāra, représentant le Dieu de l'Enfer, Yama; 7. Contribution à l'étude des images de Kuvera avec la mangouste (nakula). *Même recueil*, No. 4, 1903, 15 pp. et 6 pl.

OLDHAM (C. F.).—*The Sun and the Serpent.* London, 1905.

PANDER (E.).—*Das Pantheon des Tschangtscha Hutuktu.* Berlin, 1890.

POUSSIN (L. DE LA VALLÉE).—1. *Bouddhisme, Études et Matériaux.* Londres, 1898.

—— 2. 'The Bodhisattva.' *Hastings's Encyclopaedia of Religions and Ethics*, vol. ii. London, 1909.

—— 3. 'The Three Bodies of a Buddha.' *Journal of the Royal Asiatic Society of Great Britain and Ireland*, October, 1906.

POZDNIEEV (A.).—*Ocherki byta buddiyskih monastyrei, etc.* (Esquisse de la vie des couvents et du clergé bouddhiste en Mongolie.) Zapiski, etc. (*Mémoires de la Société Impériale de Géographie*, section d'ethnographie, T. xvi, St-Pétersbourg, 1887, in-8°, 192 pp., avec plusieurs planches.)

REED (E. A.).—*Primitive Buddhism.* Chicago, 1896.

RIJNHART (S. C.).—*With Tibetans in Tent and Temples.* Chicago, 1901.

ROCKHILL (W. W.).—1. *Notes on the Ethnology of Tibet.* Washington, 1895.

—— 2. *The Life of the Buddha.* London, 1907.

ROSS (E. D.).—Sanskrit-Tibetan-English Vocabulary. A translation of the *Mahātpatti* of A. Csoma de Körös. *Memoirs of the Asiatic Society of Bengal*, vol. iv, No. 1, 1910.

RUDNEV (A. D.).—*Zamietki o tehnikié, &c.* (Notes sur la technique de l'iconographie bouddhiste chez les *zurachin* (artistes) actuels d'Ourga, de Transbaïkalie et de la province d'Astrakan.) *Publications du Musée d'Anthropologie et d'Ethnographie de l'Académie Impériale des Sciences de St-Pétersbourg* (en russe), n°. 5, 1905, 15 pp. avec 1 pl.

SCHLAGINTWEIT (E.).—*Buddhism in Tibet*, with a folio atlas of 20 plates. Leipzig, 1863.

SMITH (V.). *A History of Fine Art in India and Ceylon.* Oxford, 1911.

STEIN (SIR A.).—1. *Ruins of Desert Cathay.* London, 1912.

—— 2. *Annual Report of the Archaeological Survey of India, Frontier Circle, for* 1911–12. London, 1912.

—— 3. *Ancient Khotan.* Oxford, 1907.

SUZUKI (D. T.).—1. *The Outlines of the Mahāyāna Buddhism.* London, 1907.

—— 2. *Açvagosha's Discourse on the Awakening of Faith in the Mahāyāna.* Translated from the Chinese. Chicago. 1900.

TOKI (H.).—'Shi-do-in-dzou. Gestes d'Officiant dans les cérémonies mystiques des sectes Ten-dai et Shin-gon (Bouddhisme japonais).' *Annales du Musée Guimet*, tome viii. Paris, 1899.

VASSILIEFF (M. V.).—*Le Bouddhisme, ses dogmes, son histoire et sa littérature*, traduit du russe par G. A. Comme. Paris, 1863.

VIDYABHUSANA (S. C.).—'On certain Tibetan Scrolls and Images.' *Memoirs of the Asiatic Society of Bengal*, vol. i, No. 1, Calcutta, 1905

WADDELL (L. A.).—1. 'The Indian Buddhist Cult of Avalokita and his consort Tara, the "Saviouress"; illustrated from the remains of Magadha.' *The Journal of the Royal Asiatic Society*, 1894.

—— 2. *The Buddhism of Tibet or Lamaism.* London, 1895.

—— 3. 'Evolution of the Buddhist Cult; its Gods, Images and Art.' *The Imperial and Asiatic Quarterly Review*, January, 1912.

—— 4. 'The "Dharani" cult in Buddhism; its Origin, deified Literature and Images.' *Ostasiatische Zeitschrift.* Heft II, Juli, 1912.

—— 5. *Lhassa and its Mysteries.* London, 1905.

WATTERS (T.).—*The Eighteen Lohan of the Chinese Buddhist Temples.* Shanghai, 1899.

WILLIAMS (SIR M.).—*Buddhism.* London, 1890.

WILSON (I.).—*The Svastika.* Washington, D. C., 1896.

WOROBIEV (N. I.).—*Opis sobraniia, etc.* (Inventaire d'une collection de statuettes acquises au Siam, en 1906, par N. I. Worobiev.) *Publications du Musée d'Anthropologie et d'Ethnographie de l'Académie Impériale des Sciences de St-Pétersbourg* (en russe), No. 12, 1911, 29 pp. avec 4 pl.

INDEX

Oxford: Horace Hart M.A. Printer to the University